i

The New York Institute for Gestalt Therapy in the 21st Century

The New York Institute for Gestalt Therapy in the 21st Century

An Anthology of Published Writings Since 2000

Edited by Dan Bloom and Brian O'Neill

R a v e n w o o d   P r e s s

Developed and Published by the
Ravenwood Press a subsidiary of the
Illawarra Gestalt Centre.
Po Box 141 Peregian Beach
Queensland 4573
AUSTRALIA.

Cover illustration, text design and art work: B O'Neill

ISBN applied for.

For more information on Ravenwood Press
Email: boneill@uow.edu.au
Website: www.illawarragestalt.org

 Or write to

Brian O'Neill
Illawarra Gestalt @peregian
Po Box 141 Peregian Beach
Queensland 4573
Australia

I   D e d i c a t i o n   I

To Fritz and Laura Perls whose genius lit the fires of the institute;
to Paul Goodman whose restless intellect still inspires us;
and to our members who maintain the institute
in so many different ways-- by their embodiment of
gestalt therapy, theory and practice.

The New York Institute for Gestalt Therapy in the 21st Century

An Anthology of Published Writings Since 2000

Edited by Dan Bloom and Brian O'Neill

Table of Contents

Introduction: A New York Institute, a World Institute

The future is bright for an institute almost as old as gestalt therapy itself.

This is a collection of writings by members of the New York Institute for Gestalt Therapy previously published from 2000 to 2012. Here you will find essays with much in common and with important differences. These papers reflect the authors' relationship to the institute and offer what they believe is representative of their work. This collection exemplifies the institute: our membership, our mission our sense of history—and marks our place in contemporary gestalt therapy.

Our members aren't linked by residence in New York. This book's senior editor is from New York City and its co-editor from Wollongong, Australia. Citizens of separate nations, we nevertheless are at home together at the New York Institute for Gestalt Therapy (hereinafter, NYIGT). The institute's current members are from 4 continents, 10 nations, and both hemispheres. Something other than their region brings our members together.

The NYIGT wasn't actually intended to be local membership institute. The group informally organized in 1951 around a common interest —to be taught and trained in gestalt therapy by Fritz and Laura Perls and Paul Goodman. Those they trained soon trained others and so it continues. We soon called ourselves the NYIGT. (Stohr, 1994, Bloom, 2009)

From the outset the institute's mission was clear and was formally articulated in our Certificate of Incorporation. Our purpose is " to formulate, develop, and popularize procedures and techniques in the theory, practice and programming of Gestalt therapy through research, meetings, programs, writings, lectures, and similar means." (*Certificate of Incorporation of the New York Institute for Gestalt Therapy Inc*. filed with the New York State Education Department, June 25, 1970)

It is this mission which guided the institute for decades and gathers us members from all parts of the world.

We hold seminars, study groups, workshops, training, practicum, and discussions on our online discussion group in which we continue "to formulate, develop, and popularize" the core theory/practice of gestalt therapy. The classic model of the founding text, *Gestalt Therapy, Excitement and Growth in the Human Personality* by Fritz Perls, Ralph Hefferline, and Paul Goodman (1951) is the starting place for our developing gestalt therapy. While we respect the classic model, we continue to challenge and reformulate it to reflect our ongoing understanding of gestalt therapy theory/practice.

This will be clear in the chapters that follow. Over the years, we developed a model of a teaching/learning community where teacher learns from student and student teaches the teacher. The teaching/learning process, then, is a field event, an emergent function of the contact-boundary (Bloom 2009).

The institute doesn't have an office. Our mail comes to a post office box. Our telephone is voice mail only. Members take turns responding to messages. We have a website (www.newyorkgestalt.org) and an email address (info@newyorkgestalt.org). For 60 years, we've met in brick and mortar rooms rented on an ad hoc basis. We now have a members online discussion group. Our monthly membership meetings in New York City are open to anyone interested in exploring or simply curious about gestalt therapy.

Importantly, our "meetings" are wherever we meet one another to further the institute's mission.

We meet at the contact-boundary, which is not a physical location crisscrossed by longitude and latitude. It is the experienced "here" of our meetings, seminars, study groups, workshops and presentations; it the "here" where we meet one another at conferences; and it is the "here" of our online discussion groups. It is at this contact-boundary where the institute is ever-emerging, our creativity ever-refreshing, and our history ever-renewing. It is fundamentally — and contactfully — the ground of our teaching/learning community.

In this sense as you read this book, as you think along with and question our authors, you are making contact with us — the institute alive and growing in the words/ideas of our members. Being with us at this boundary of contact you have joined us at a "meeting" of the NYIGT.

Read on; engage with our members' words and ideas. Whatever understanding co-emerges from your contacting us here is at the very contact-boundary that is the thriving of the NYIGT. It is how this institute that continues to draw inspiration from its own history gathers new excitement in the present.

History is our "DNA." Our history shows itself in each chapter. It appears in the influence of our founders and teachers; it appears within the serious scholarship with which we continue to develop gestalt therapy. History as a present experience is intrinsic in our commitment to developing gestalt therapy theory/practice from the starting point of the classic or basic model; this commitment brings us together as members of this institute, an institute as old as gestalt therapy itself.

In the following chapters you will find historical names in the references. We single out three whose imprint continues to shape the institute and how its members continue to further the institute's mission.

Laura Perls (b. 1905 – d. 1990) was the president for life of the NYIGT. She trained therapists around the world from 1951 through the 1980's. Her focus on the supports for contacting was especially influential. There is hardly a gestalt therapist at the institute who hasn't been influenced by her directly or indirectly.

Isadore From (b. 1919 – d. 1994) has been called the dean of gestalt therapy trainers. Fritz was one of the first members of the NYIGT to take gestalt therapy across the country. Isadore carried it next. (Stohr, 1994) Isadore taught the basic model of gestalt therapy and time and again made sure its crucial importance wasn't missed.

Richard Kitzler (b. 1928 – d. 2009) was a central presence at the institute. He also taught the basic model of gestalt therapy —but from his own changing perspectives. He supported risk-taking and innovation within the institute — and supported many of us to come forward with our own ideas

We honor these mentors who remain central to the identity and history of the NYIGT by dedicating this book to them.

Dan Bloom and Brian O'Neill

References

Bloom, D. (2009). "The emergence of foundational gestalt therapy *focus* (pp. 73-86).Wollongong, AUS: Ravenswood Press.
Stohr T. (1994) *Here now next.* Jossey–Bass: San Francisco.
Perls F., Hefferline R., Goodman, P. *(1952) Gestalt therapy excitement and growth in the human personality.* New York: Julian Press.

Editors' Note

Since this is an anthology of previously published writings, for the most the original style choices by the authors and their publishers own editorial conventions were maintained. For example, you will a find our modality variously called "Gestalt therapy," "gestalt therapy," "Gestalt Therapy," or simply as "gestalt" or "Gestalt." You will find "contact boundary" as well as "contact-boundary." These and other variations in our terminology are the function of our differences.

We left intact the reference styles submitted to us by our authors since they were accepted by the original publishers. Double and single quotation marks and other personal conventions of punctuation, for example, were generally respected.

We edited the text with a light touch. Any changes we wade were mostly to this book's aesthetic — its layout and appearance.

The journals and publishers responsible for the original publication of the writings collected in this book deserve thanks for encouraging scholarship at the highest level in gestalt therapy. We thank them for their role in allowing us to publish this collection: *The Gestalt Journal, The Gestalt Review, The British Gestalt Journal, The International Gestalt Journal, Aw@re.com, Haworth Press, Journal of Somatic, Studies in Gestalt Therapy: Dialogical Bridges*, Routledge Publishing, BrunoAngeli, and Cambridge Scholars Publishing, and the Ravenswood Press.

We editors could not have organized our efforts to bring this collection before you were it not for the New York Institute community, which has been a gentle presence inspiring and supporting us in this task.

Selected Papers of the 21ˢᵗ Century

Chapter 1.

The Ambiguities of Origins: Pragmatism, the University of Chicago, and Paul Goodman's Self

Richard Kitzler (1927 —2008)

Chapter Introduction
Zelda Freedman[1]

I began attending meetings of the New York Institute for Gestalt Therapy in the early 1990s. I discovered myself in an atmosphere rich in vitality where everyone was welcomed and encouraged to participate in the ongoing study of gestalt theory. The experience was intensely scholarly and intensely communal. I felt that no matter when one entered the circle one could contribute to the quest for a deepening knowledge of reality within this self-identified teaching/learning community.

By then, Richard Kitzler was the only member remaining from the original founding group that had assembled in mid-twentieth century New York. Despite his historical relevance Richard was largely a silent magnet at the center of my experience, attending and assessing the group's process and intervening only now and then like a charge of lightening to warn that active awareness in the learning process was becoming clouded or rigidified. The trick was to keep the pursuit of knowing as open and exciting as gestalt theory's offering of such a path to living itself. Scholarship and living were held in a balance not to be parted one from the other.

As a scholarly child Richard's preferred interest and pleasure was the activity of reading with books stacked on the table before him. He once told me that his father, wanting him to join the sporting life outside in the street, shoved his pile of reading onto the floor. In his telling I could sense Richard's early reaction to this forceful blow to his head and his heart.

As you read the article to come you will find Richard examining difficulties within the theory of self in *Gestalt Therapy: Excitement and Growth in the Human Personality* by Perls, Hefferline and Goodman and you will see how Richard traces Goodman's academic history in regard to the competing views of his mentors in accounting for these difficulties. Richard's thorough exploration with references to Pragmatism, and most notably William James' "stream of consciousness" in contrast to Kant's "synthetic unity of apperception," underscores Richard's search over time to find in Pragmatism a kindred root of

---

[1] We are grateful to Zelda Friedman, a beloved friend and colleague of Richards, for writing this chapter introduction. — Eds.

Gestalt Therapy. The emergent self at the contact boundary is the how of our knowing.

Elsewhere, in a chapter entitled "The Ontology of Contact" in *Eccentric Genius*, the book of his collected writings published in Richard specifically experiments with contact at the boundary through stages of step-by-step embodied experiencing. In this writing, Richard, by example, invites us to move through even our most beloved texts with critical presence to test their contents on our pulses, individually and communally, in order to guard against unaware acceptance of dogma and rigidity. This is the bulwark against dualism that we need to carry from the foundational theory into the new century.

The Ambiguities of Origins: Pragmatism, the University of Chicago, and Paul Goodman's Self"2

Abstract: Gestalt therapy's theory of self principally is derived from the works of Paul Goodman and Frederick Perls. In this paper, Richard Kitzler examines the contribution of Paul Goodman and shows how unaware conflicts in Goodman's loyalties during his education at the University of Chicago are responsible for the inconsistent treatment of self in gestalt therapy theory. When Goodman presents self as an emergent function of experience, he is showing the influence of American pragmatism, and specifically, of William James. On the other hand, when he describes self as a synthetic unifier of experience, his Creator Spirit, he is showing the influence of his mentor at the University of Chicago, the Neo-Thomist Richard McKeon. This paper begins with a brief interview of Richard Kitzler by the editor.

Key words: Paul Goodman, self, American pragmatism, William James, Neo-Thomism, University of Chicago, George Herbert Mead. John Dewey, Frederick Perls, The New York Institute for Gestalt Therapy, Creator Spirit, synthetic unity of apperception.

Introduction: An interview with the author

Editor (Bloom): Richard, you taught gestalt therapy at The New York Institute for Gestalt Therapy for more than 30 years by leading your students through a close line by line reading of *Gestalt Therapy: Excitement and Growth in the Human Personality*, by Perls, Hefferline, and Goodman (1951). In the past you often said that this book was perfect in all respects. You challenged us to find a single error and were adamant in your defense of every line. Today you no longer believe this to be the case. Tell us why.

Richard Kitzler: It became clear to me that in the face of complaints about Perls et al.'s impenetrability, the impossibility of paraphrase, the only way to proceed was to create our own book in group, through group learning, which as a welcome by-product took the onus off the "bible." Over time, what I thought to be Goodman's flawless argument began to seem increasingly opaque — refusing to be clarified by our critical reading, almost as if it were pushing back and defying us. We were not to get near Goodman, despite his apparent democratic openness. With the support and encouragement of my theory group, we began to sniff around the evident foundations. By a strange paradox, we discovered that our futile attempts to understand led to an opening up of the text. Other possibilities came to hand. We could also say that through an eidetic reduction we could bracket the question "what is contact," for example, and then discover openings

---

2 Originally published *Studies in Gestalt Therapy: Dialogical Bridges*, 1(1) pp. 41 -163

within the vast forest of taken-for-granted meanings, which then exposed the cracks in the foundation itself. These cracks became opportunities. At last, the oppressive authority of an opaque text became the opportunity for us to explore other, broader, deeper, meanings within gestalt therapy.

One day, by accident, pure accident, I stumbled across the word contact in a simple lexicon of philosophy. I was doing some research about the basis of gestalt therapy, specifically then about Aristotle, and I was looking up the meaning of meaning and saw a reference to G.H. Mead's use of contact in his own philosophy of the act. Mead was on the same page as meaning. I pursued this reference and in no time at all discovered a universe of cogency around contact, which had only been hinted at through Goodman's text. From Mead, I went to on to William James and from him to Alfred North Whitehead. I have not rested since.

Editor: So this paper, "The Ambiguities of Origin," represents part of your restatement of gestalt therapy?

Richard Kitzler: Yes. This paper more or less focuses on the theory of self. I try to show that the inconsistencies in Good-man's theory had their origin in conflicts within his personal life and conflicting educational allegiances.

My original paper was directed to the occasion of the *New York Institute for Gestalt Therapy's 50th Anniversary Conference* and was three times as long as my article in this journal. In it, I called for us to reestablish our foundations as gestalt therapists and to look to the future by securely standing on this ground. I further appealed to gestalt therapists to experiment within community to develop further the radical heart of our method, turn it aside from the desert of gestalt psychology and other unsupportable ideas and for gestalt therapy to take its place as the clearest expression of human process within psychotherapy. As an example, I say that we can abandon the tyranny of the figure.

Editor: Would you explain this?

Richard Kitzler: The patient says X, etc., and we pay attention to those things as if they meant something. Where is the therapy when we attend to that figure?

Editor: What do you mean?

Richard Kitzler: Understand — I am not denying the emerging figure; I am encouraging it. The tyranny is the fixity. That is, sometimes we become absorbed by apparent meaning while missing what may be struggling to emerge.

Editor: Would an example of such a fixity be the opacity of Perls et al., which we all once thought could become clear through our persistent critical reading of the text?

Richard Kitzler: Yes. We had to go beyond the text, beyond Perls, et al. and go to the authorities they told us were their basses. Only then could we achieve clarity. A good theory of action must be perspicuous, must itself be the instrument for fluid contacting, and it cannot lose the connection with the aesthetic, the arts. Goodman was very influential in this respect—and of course, so too was James, the philosopher, psychologist, and artist.

Editor: Is there anything you hope non-gestalt therapists will take from reading your essay?

Richard Kitzler: I hope that they will be heartened to see things in a new way and that my opening up of our foundation is seen as an invitation to attempt a similar analysis of other foundational authorities.

Also, I am especially pleased to be part of the general revival of American pragmatism, which is not merely the first distinctive voice of American philosophy, but an incredibly influential movement. Without it, gestalt psychology, phenomenology, logical positivism, hermeneutics, and existentialism would have been inconceivable.

Editor: And what do you want gestalt therapists to take from your essay?

Richard Kitzler: We now have conferences with thousands of attendees. Have we lost our sense of ourselves as a minority? Have we lost our commitment to aggressing at the boundary, to challenge the unchallengeable, and to risk social ostracism?

My writings are my attempt to stick my thumb in the eye of our own cherished authorities.

Paper: The Ambiguities of Origins: Pragmatism, the University of Chicago, and Paul Goodman's "Self"

This paper is an abridged version of the document I prepared for the 50th Anniversary Conference of The New York Institute for Gestalt Therapy (NYIGT), a shortened version of which was my keynote address at that conference. I will continue my re-construction of gestalt therapy that I began in "The Ontology of Action" (Kitzler, 2006). In that paper, I displaced gestalt psychology as fundamental to gestalt therapy and introduced the American pragmatism of William James and George Herbert Mead as a firm foundation on which to build. Here I will focus on how Paul Goodman's experience at the University of Chicago influenced his later works. The conflicts at this time between the socially progressive pragmatists and the politically conservative Neo-Thomists and their impact on Goodman's work are little understood. The principle works are the book we have come to know as *Gestalt Therapy: Excitement and Growth in the Human Personality* (Perls et al., 1951) and *Five Years* by Paul Goodman (1966), which is a record of Goodman's reflections During a Useless Period (its subtitle) and gives us remarkable access to his intimate thoughts. It is here that he writes more fully of what he called the Creator Spirit—a term which I hope to show reflects the conflicting allegiances from his Chicago years. I will emphasize the impact of these influences of Goodman's theory of self, as developed in his later works.

My task, then, is to shine a light on Goodman's concept of a Creator Spirit and to determine how he deployed it in his life and work. The central theoretical conflict arises immediately. As we shall see, despite his affirmation "I am a Kantian," (Goodman, 1966, p. 209) and his power to think schematically rather than abstractly is in conflict with his notion of a Creator Spirit, his God. Moreover, he early on related his Creator Spirit to the accumulation of an artist's completed writings. When incomplete and in doubt, he prayed to his God, the Creator Spirit, and inspiration flowed down around him and bathed all in a great light.

It is my thesis that Goodman's Creator Spirit was deployed reactively to his sexual and political anarchism –– they are inseparable in him. This deploying found its way into *Gestalt Therapy* (Perls et al., 1951) as ambiguities and perhaps even avoidances. Let me be clear: This in no way diminishes the powerful original contribution that Goodman made to our theory of gestalt therapy. Thus our theory, first expressed so beautifully by Goodman, contained within it apparent inconsistencies leaving the continuing development of gestalt therapy to those who came after him. The gestalt therapy community is enriched by its differences, which derive from a powerful and evocative theory. We are therefore impelled to use our best creative efforts to engage with one another so as to develop a complex, yet coherent, body of knowledge.

Many have noted that the theory presented in *Gestalt Therapy* internal inconsistencies — especially in its theory of self. In this book, self is a field-emergent function of experience and yet is a separate "synthesizer" of experience—perhaps even the "ghost in the machine." This is an example of Goodman's unresolved conflicts with his own educational background— the conflict between the holistic pragmatists and their Aristotelian, Neo-Thomistic, Kantian successors at the University of Chicago. Briefly, the routes of those historical occasions known as William James, John Dewey, and George Herbert Mead — the latter two who were to become the famous "Chicago School" of pragmatism — deeply influenced Paul Goodman, and since Goodman's work states the basis for gestalt therapy, this influence is intrinsic to our modality. I will look closely into this in the following pages as I describe the situation at the University of Chicago where the young Goodman completed his formal academic training. Additionally, I will explore the relationship of Goodman's ideas to those of William James, whose own work as a psychologist and philosopher was the basis for the Chicago school of pragmatism.

The University of Chicago before the Arrival of Goodman

William James was born in 1842, John Dewey in 1859, and George Herbert Mead in 1863. American pragmatism emerged from this trinity of intellects. James became professor at Harvard in the 1870s after postgraduate study in Germany. There was little opportunity to study psychology in universities in the United States of America apart from the departments of evangelical religion — hence the flight to Europe where the 'old' psychology was beginning to measure everything in sight, sound, smell, touch, or taste as it strove to establish itself as a natural science. Dewey and Mead followed James's trail, the same schools and perhaps the same teachers in Germany, defining themselves, their politics, and philosophy. Those same teachers had an impact on the development of phenomenology, gestalt psychology, and existentialism. James not only directly influenced Dewey and Mead, but Edmund Husserl himself also cited him as an inspiration for his earliest works in phenomenology. It would be impossible to overstress the continuing importance of William James on psychology, phenomenology, and, indeed, all "process" philosophy, the philosophy of George Herbert Mead, John Dewey, and Alfred North Whitehead.

The political convulsions in America and in Europe in the 19th century deeply affected Dewey and Mead. These social revolutions inspired their socialism and they inspired their heady plans for their future back home where labor strife, robber barons, and malefactors of great wealth coexisted uneasily. Writing from Germany to his friend Henry Castle, October 21, 1890, Mead said:

We must get into politics of course — city politics above all things because there we can begin to work at once in what-ever city we settle because city politics need men more than any other branch — and chiefly because according to my opinion the immediate application of the principles of corporate life — of socialism in America, must start from the city.(Joas, 1985, p. 219)

The settlement house movement was to emerge in Chicago through the activism of Jane Addams and the foundation of Hull House. Indeed, it would also be the city that inspired the pioneering muckraking journalist Upton Sinclair, whose book *The Jungle* (1906) would undo the corporate atrocities of the food preparation industry. This was the Chicago of Dewey and Mead, social reformers carrying forward the pragmatism of James.

George Herbert Mead was first offered a job at the University of Michigan and joined John Dewey there in 1891. In 1894 Dewey became chair of philosophy at the University of Chicago and took Mead with him. This was a very productive period for Dewey in which he solidified his pragmatism, instrumentalism, "learning by doing" and progressive theories of education. Dewey's paper on the reflex arc — in which he redefined the process as a circuit rather than as an afferent/efferent stimulus/response splitting — was from this period (Dewey, 1896). The circuit was a complete unit and could not be split unless for purposes of analysis which kept its integrity in the foreground. Dewey's philosophy of the whole process of the circuit is nearly identical to the later important work of Kurt Goldstein on the organism, yet precedes Goldstein by many years. This idea is central to gestalt therapy's holism, and I suggest that such holism is as grounded in pragmatism as in any other source.

Dewey left Chicago for Teachers College at Columbia University, New York City, in 1904, where he remained for nearly half a century. He thus escaped the later turmoil in Chicago that arguably destroyed the life of his close colleague Mead. Furthermore, as I argue here, it remained in the background of Goodman's theory of self and led to inconsistencies in his theory. In an incisive critique of George Herbert Mead subtitled "A Contemporary Re-examination of his Thought," the German sociologist Hans Joas notes:

Toward the end of the twenties, the wave of reaction men-aced even the remnants of pragmatist thought at the University of Chicago. After teaching for almost 40 years at this university, George Herbert Mead died on April 26, 1931, deeply embittered by controversial changes in the university's internal politics that threatened to alter the nature of philosophy there, making it Catholic and reactionary in character (Joas, 1985, p. 2)

Joas further explains that the ascendancy of the new president of the University of Chicago, Robert Maynard Hutchins, and the appointment of the Neo-Thomist Mortimer Adler to professorship particularly marked this reactionary transformation. In 1934, Richard McKeon, an eminent Aristotelian from Columbia University, joined this faculty and soon he would invite his promising protégé Paul Goodman to Chicago. Both Hutchins and Adler, writes Joas

> . . . became important figures for the conservative emigrants from the Third Reich, for whom the University of Chicago became a gathering place — very much in contrast to the traditions of that university's first decades (Joas, 1985, p. 221)

The distinguished American philosopher Charles Hartshorne describes this further:

> In the next academic year after I arrived in Chicago, Robert Maynard Hutchins became president of the University. Through two friends and admirers of his, Mortimer J. Adler and Richard P. McKeon, this soon brought about considerable changes in the way philosophy was taught there. Among the results was the departure of Mead, who had been chairman. . . . What was important was the argument between Hutchins, Adler, and McKeon, on the one hand, and the pragmatists and most of the remaining faculty on the other. The dispute seemed at first, far more than it really was, between partisans of neo-scholasticism or Thomism and the then dominant American philosophy, pragmatism.(Harsthorne, 1991, p. 30.)

Paul Goodman and the University of Chicago

The historian of gestalt therapy, Taylor Stoehr writes, "It was into this conflict that Goodman, in 1936, was invited by McKeon to come and teach in the 'great books' program at Chicago. While teaching he could also take a few courses and write a dissertation for his doctorate." (Stoehr, 1994, p. 28)

Young Goodman reported for work (at the invitation of a medievalist specialist) at a school that has been "rationalized" from a bulwark of pragmatism to a reactionary institution with an increasingly religious bent. Young Goodman, the sexual anarchist, if not libertine, was here free to write his dissertation, but not to act his "ideals" of sexual liberation. The University of Chicago had the Divinity School and three theological seminaries associated with it and some part of the budget of the department of philosophy was funded through the Divinity side. Goodman was fired in 1939 because he refused to cease his sexual foraging. Could his behavioral eccentricities be explained by his conflicting allegiances?

That question cannot be answered. I propose, however, that precisely these conflicting allegiances made their unaware way into his and our theory of gestalt therapy.

Let us see what our twenty-five year old intellectual brought with him from New York to Chicago. He had been auditing McKeon at Columbia University and was enormously influenced by his mentor. McKeon was a distinguished medievalist. His two-volume opus on scholasticism was published in 1928 when Goodman was seventeen. He must have learned from it considerably, both in content and method. The argument from authority, analysis through dialogue, and attention to the history of philosophy as the basis for contemporary contemplation were the hallmarks of McKeon's contribution.

Therefore, Goodman bore a disciplined and well-trained mind to Chicago, a Chicago of social activism and yet a Chicago not without a religious turn. Indeed, Goodman later would proudly announce his "faith in" his "Creator Spirit," and in references to his use of the synthetic unity of apperception, affirm, "I am a Kantian." This could be a declaration of faith for a Neo-Thomist, but hardly one for a pragmatist. I will analyze this further as I address William James's impact. It is a staggering irony that James, Dewey, and Mead fled an America engrained with religion for the scientifically freer Germany, while Good-man left the political and social freedom of New York City for the spiritual fascism of the reconstructed University of Chicago.

This was a troubling existential situation for Goodman, with fateful consequences for his treatment of theory in Perls et al. some fifteen years later. His personal turmoil from such conflict can only be imagined. Or perhaps, there was no aware conflict at all: His foreground intellectual curiosity may have facilitated sufficient repression of the conflict into the background. Apparent inconsistencies, in his theory of self, a reaction formation or, using his concept, a foreground "conflict of objects," obscure the actual conflict. The consequences are embedded in key concepts of gestalt therapy. I suggest these are perhaps unaware, therefore not completely deliberate efforts by Goodman to protect his intellectual persona with a hodgepodge of concepts, with that "enlightened eclecticism" which, as Taylor Stoehr writes in *Here, Now, Next,* (1994) made varying views of the theory possible. Yet this provides a barrier between the concept and its meaning. Queries aimed at them bounce off as if from an invisible wall. It is one thing to be eclectic and quite another thing to be contradictory. Nevertheless, the diversity of gestalt therapy derived from our creative reading of Goodman's lyrical, magisterial, yet flawed expression of our foundational theory. (Bloom, 2004)

Soul? Self? Ego? The James behind the Goodman

When William James wrote to his brother Henry those famous words, that he had to "forge every word in the teeth of stubborn and irreducible fact," he was speaking of his *Principles of Psychology*. That work is an amazing tour de force from which "he laid down his pen in 1885," but was published to great acclaim in 1890. In this section of my paper, I will restate William James analysis of soul, self, and ego. I propose that this analysis establishes the foundation for gestalt therapy's field emergent self process, which is implicit in Goodman's discussion of self in Perls et al. It is also one element to the conflict within the theory of self, which will hopefully soon become clear.

In Chapter X of *Principles of Psychology*, "The Consciousness of Self," James considers the pure "Ego" as one of the four constituents of self, along with the material self, the social self and the spiritual self (James, 1890, Vol. I, p. 292). To James, the historical theories of the self are the Spiritualist, Associationist, and the Transcendentalist. These had significance in 19th century philosophy and remain of historical, perhaps more than of philosophical interest today. The Spiritualist self, the theory of the "Soul," is the theory of popular philosophy and of Scholasticism, "which is only popular philosophy made systematic," (James, 1890. Vol. I, p. 343). Hutchins and McKeon were in this tradition. James explains the classical theory of scholasticism and his analysis of it as opposed to his own idea of the "Stream of Thought." Thence he examines the Transcendentalist theory "which owes its origin to Kant." (James, 1890, Vol. I, p.360) "I am a Kantian," boasted Paul Goodman (1966, p, 209), a claim at odds with his debt to James.

In his discussion of the "Soul" in scholasticism, James gives Saint Thomas's "classical" argument:

> [The theory] declares that the principle of individuality within us must be substantial, for psychic phenomena are activities, and there can be no activity without a concrete agent. This substantial agent cannot be the brain but must be something immaterial; for its activity, thought, is both immaterial, and takes cognizance of immaterial things, and of material things in general and intelligible, as well as in particular and sensible ways — all which powers are incompatible with the nature of matter of which the brain is composed. Thought moreover is simple, whilst the activities of the brain are compounded of the elementary activities of each of its parts. Furthermore, thought is spontaneous or free, whilst all material activity is determined ab extra; and the will can turn itself against all corporeal goods and appetites, which would be impossible were it a corporeal function. (James, 1890, Vol. I, p. 343.)

And then, "For these objective reasons the principle of psychic life must be both immaterial and simple as well as substantial, must be what is called a Soul."

Additionally James offers these reasons from the subjective side of the argument: "Our consciousness of personal identity assures us of our essential simplicity. . . the hypothetical Arch-Ego . . . is a real entity of whose existence self-consciousness makes us directly aware," (James, 1890, Vol. I, p. 343).

And he thus concludes, foreshadowing gestalt therapy's rejection of Cartesian dualism some 70 years later:

> . . . The hypothetical Arch-Ego...is a real entity of whose existence self-consciousness makes us directly aware. No material agent could thus turn around and grasp itself — material activities always grasp something else than the agent. And if a brain could grasp itself and be self-conscious, it would be conscious of itself as a brain and not as something of an altogether different kind. (James, 1890, Vol. I, p. 343.)

Emergent Self or "Soul"?

The central point I am developing has two aspects. The first is that in Goodman's "Soul" — if you will, as conveyed in his theory of self — the Thomist dualism of soul and matter and the pragmatist monism of self as emergent function maintained an uneasy truce. In reading the above quotations from James, was it not clear that Goodman's Creator Spirit had its roots in the "Soul"? Is there not a clash, then, between self as creator and as emergent function? That is self as a version of "Soul," and self as a function of whole experience. Could Goodman's political and sexual anarchism have been an acting out of this conflict? This clash between Neo-Thomistic dualism (McKeon) and pragmatist monism (James, Dewey, and Mead) found its way into Perls et al. in the many-faceted aspects of its theory. And there is classical authority:

> This substantialist view of the soul was essentially the view of Plato and Aristotle. It received its completely formal elaboration in the Middle Ages. It was believed in by Hobbes, Descartes, Locke, Leibnitz, Wolf, Berkeley, and is now defended by the entire modern dualistic or spiritualistic or common sense school. Kant's successors, the absolute idealists, profess to have discarded it (James, 1890, Vol. I, p. 344). He then adds what I consider to be a core truth of gestalt therapy: "[The Soul] is at all events needless for expressing the actual subjective phenomena of consciousness as they appear. (James, 1890, Vol. I, p. 344).

What is James's candidate for expressing the "actual subjective phenomena of consciousness as they appear"? Nothing less than the stream of consciousness. Instead of starting with apparently simpler mental facts as sensations and building to higher ones, James begins the study of the mind "from within." This is as much as to deny that the simplest mental fact is a sensation and then constructing mind upwards: "We now begin the study of the mind from within. . . . No one ever had a simple sensation by itself . . . The notion that sensations, being the simplest things, are the first things to take up in psychology is [an] apparently innocent supposition that nevertheless contains a flaw." (James, 1890, Vol. I, p. 344.)

And as he seeks a term for states of consciousness as such, he hits upon "Thought . . . which would be the best word by far to use if it could be made to cover sensations" (James, 1890. Vol. I, p. 343.). And further, in this famous passage typical of his lyrical style:

> It is a patent fact of consciousness that a transmission [of the "title" of a collective self] be passed from one Thought to another. . . . Each pulse of cognitive consciousness . . . dies away and is replaced by another. The other, among the things it knows, knows its own predecessor, and finding it "warm," greets it saying; "Thou art mine, and part of the same self with me." Each later thought, knowing and including thus the Thoughts which went before is the final receptacle—and appropriating them is the final owner — of all that they contain and own. Each Thought is thus born an owner, and dies owned transmitting whatever realized as its Self to its own later proprietor. . . . Who owns the last self owns the self before the last, for what possesses the possessor possesses the possessed. (James, 1890, Vol. I, pp. 339f.)

It would be a misreading of the above text to take James's sharp use of metaphor to literally mean "Thought" behaves like a knowing entity, and not understand that everything James writes concerns a nonentitative experiential process.

Back to Goodman's University of Chicago

I now return to the University of Chicago, the milieu of Goodman's intellectual maturation. Perhaps the turmoil in the souls of the students at Chicago is best expressed by one of Dewey's students, Randolph Bourne. Bourne's argument shows his personal conflict — loyalty to Dewey's instrumentalism with creative adaptation at its core, and a priori values, independent from the contingencies of experience:

> The defect of any philosophy of "adaptation" or "adjustment," even when it means adjustment to changing, living experience, is that there is no provision for thought or experience getting beyond itself. . . . [That is, a priori] opportunist efforts usually achieve less even than what seemed obviously possible. . . . A philosophy of adjustment will not even make for adjustment. If you try merely to "meet" situations as they come, you will

not even meet them (Randolph Bourne, 1919, pp. 114–139, quoted in Joas, 1985, p. 29).

Since Bourne was one of Dewey's "most gifted students," Dewey's analysis in the *Quest for Certainty* (Dewey, 1930) is an appropriate response to Bourne's comment. It is also the basis for Goodman's analysis of the collapse to authority in Perls et al., which is the shock and confusion of unsupported freedom that leads to the false support of dogma, which is, sui generis, no support at all. Of course George Santayana's observation that when the end is lost sight of and the effort redoubled we have fanaticism, is the adequate statement of the consequences of dogma. Bourne is using Dewey's own argument against dogma against Dewey himself.

We have come a long way since James analyzed the notions of "Self" to the passing perishable thought that knows and appropriates the contents of the previous thought and so on. Thus the a priori nature of the "Self" becomes a myth. But Bourne's point must be taken seriously since it conveys some of what I suggest to be Goodman's conflicts that made their way into gestalt therapy theory. James deals with the a priori argument within his development of the stream of thought. The stream of thought contains and expresses all the phenomena otherwise known as "Soul." He adds: "But the Thought is a perishing and not an immortal or in-corruptible thing. Its successors may continuously succeed to it, resemble it, and appropriate it, but they are not it, whereas the Soul-Substance is supposed to be a fixed unchanging thing. (James, 1890, Vol. I, p. 345)

And then to the heart of the matter: "Soul is always means: something behind the present thought, another kind of substance, existing on a non-phenomenal plane" — a notion thoroughly inconsistent with James's Stream," (James, 1890, p. 345). Here are a few sentences from James, the tone of which runs through and through in all of Goodman's writing:

> But what positive meaning has the Soul, when scrutinized, but the ground of possibility of the thought? . . And what is the [thought] but the determining of the possibility to actuality?. . . And what is this after all but giving a sort of concreted form to one's belief that the coming of the thought when the brain-processes occur, has some sort of ground in the nature of things?" (James, 1890, Vol. I, p. 345).

This shuttlecock and battledore is within the working of Goodman's personal philosophy, which he never really resolved or even confessed. Are Creator Spirit and Eros synthetic a priori, the preexistence of which constitute reality, and the absence of which make "pain in my breast" and "I am bitter"?

I will now directly compare Goodman's discussion of self from Perls et al., with that of James's treatment of "The transcendentalist theory [of the Self] which owes its origin to Kant" (James, 1890, Vol. I, p. 360).

In the early '50s in the New York Institute for Gestalt Therapy's study group that we called the "professional group," there were frequent discussions in which everyone agreed that the theory of the self was the weakest point in psychoanalytic theory. It seemed to me that ego and self were used interchangeably leading to less and more confusion. Goodman achieves a masterly restatement which rests on 1. a 1-critique of a theory that makes the self "otiose" (i.e. Anna Freud's), and 2. a critique of a theory that "isolates the self in fixed boundaries" (Perls et al., p. 387). In the healthy situation of the otiose self, the ego does nothing, and it is only in the neurotic situation when the defenses are breaking down that the ego can be seen at work, doing its synthesizing activity in producing the mechanisms of defense against unconscious knowledge. Goodman writes:

> The "tendency to synthesis" is called "another" function of the available ego; . . . but this tendency is what Kant, for instance, judged to be the essence of the empirical ego, the synthetic unity of apperception, and it is what we have been considering to be the chief work of the self, gestalt-formation (Perls et al., p. 386).

Apparently for gestalt therapy, gestalt formation is the synthetic unity of apperception in spite of the gestalt psychologists' specific rejection of apperception in their scientific zeal to found their psychology from the starting point of physics (Köhler, 1945, p. 5; see Petermann, 1932, p. 59). This is an example of Goodman's attempt at being both Kantian and Jamesian — and evinces little understanding of gestalt psychology.

It is also very close to the Transcendental Self which "owes its origin to Kant" (James, 1890, p. 360), that James analyzed so well in his *Principles* discussed above, and which he rejected in favor of his famous stream of thought.

In his discussion of self in Perls et al., Goodman circles around the problem of "inside" and "outside," the "thought" and the "real." In the present state of philosophy, this kind of formulation seems perfectly reasonable. Yet how does one become aware of the distinction between the inside and the outside, the thought and the real? Is it not by awareness? Goodman concludes that in the case of the less restrictive "introspection" where one includes the field, (and also the body as field) one instantly has a unity and a heightened awareness, a "boundary-ness" — if not the boundary.

Goodman continues this analysis from the standpoint of the chronic low-grade emergency, which is the general lot of mankind. If in the emergency the body is in semi-paralysis, the breath restricted, the thinking is repetitious and obsessive, all of which must be in obedience to the reality principle, then the "objects of such an external world are such as require to be pushed about by an aggressive will (rather than interacted with in a process of growth), and cognitively they are alien, fragmented, etc., such as to be known only by an elaborate abstract ratiocination" (Perls et al., 1951 p. 394).

And then, "objects of such an external world are such as require to be pushed about by an aggressive will (rather than interacted with in a process of growth), and cognitively they are alien, fragmented etc., such as to be known only by an elaborate abstract ratiocination." (Perls et al., 1951, p. 391)

However in aware experiment,

> ... [t]he self, aware in middle mode, bursts the compartmenting of mind, body, and external world. [Therefore] [m]ust we not conclude that for the theory of the self and its relation to the "I," introspection is a poor primary method of observation, for it creates a peculiar condition? We must begin by exploring a wide range of concernful situations and behaviors. Then if we resume the introspection, the true situation is apparent: that the introspecting ego is a deliberate restrictive attitude of the psychosomatic awareness, temporarily excluding the environmental awareness and making the body-awareness a passive object (Perls et al., 1951, pp. 389f.).

This self — of which ego functioning is but a partial temporary structure — is an emergent whole process, an idea central to gestalt therapy and completely at peace with the pragmatism of James, Dewey and Goodman. Yet not at peace with self as the "synthetic unity of apperception.

In treating the exact same subject, James insists that the kernel of the self is neither an abstraction nor the body since they cannot be felt all separately within the stream of consciousness, "but always together with other things." The movement of air is a powerful factor in his consenting or negating — with his glottis as its "sensitive valve." He writes,

> If the dim portions which I cannot yet define should prove to be like unto these distinct portions in me, and I like other men, it would follow that our entire feeling of spiritual activity, or what commonly passes by that name, is really a feeling of bodily activities whose exact nature is by most men overlooked (James 1890, Vol. I, p. 302)

And James concludes from this introspective analysis of incessant adjustments and reactions: This is all there is. These motions are ultimate and objective:

[T]hat this Objective falls asunder into two contrasted parts, one realized as "Self" the other as "not-Self"; and that over and above these parts there is nothing save the fact that they are known, the fact of the stream of thought being there as the indispensable subjective condition of their being experienced at all. (James, 1890, Vol. I, p. 305.)

But far from concluding from this that there is a "Thinker" that is given as a logical postulate, he says such speculations "traverse common sense":

I mean by this, that I will continue to assume (as I have assumed all along . . . a direct awareness of the process of our thinking as such, simply insisting on the fact that it is an even more inward and subtle phenomenon than most of us suppose. (James, 1890, Vol. I, p. 305)

Goodman and James, a back and forth, continued

There are arresting parallels again in Goodman and James. Indeed, these parallels are so marked that I could persuade myself that a not small part of the reason that James is often cited as influence, yet it is a hard to track influence in Goodman's opus, is that it is so close that Goodman could be swallowed up in James. And then what? The following passage from Ralph Barton Perry, *The Thought and Character of William James* could have been written about Goodman himself:

Toward the charting of his own course he brought certain well-marked prepossessions, too general to commit him to any definite philosophical doctrine, but undoubtedly eliminating certain alternatives, and affecting the emphasis within those which remained.(Perry, 1935, p. 466).

It is striking that breath is central to gestalt therapy and, breathing primitively cognizes, or organizes, the field and sup-ports contact itself. James:

[T]he acts of attending, assenting, negating, making an effort, are felt as movements of something in the head. In many cases it is possible to describe these movements quite exactly. In attending to either an idea or a sensation belonging to a particular sense-sphere, the movement is the adjustment of the sense organ, felt as it occurs." (James, 1890, Vol. 1, p. 300).

Then in *Five Years* Goodman describes his experience from an altered state of consciousness to a more alert state traversing levels from less to more reality, as he "recalls his sleepy behavior":

Lying half-asleep, I move my glasses or pipe out of harm's way. Later, though I recall my action, I am less willing to affirm it as real, and of course remember it less well. This seems to indicate that by "reality" we mean the object of alert sensation and motor behavior. (Not that the real is "made of" sensations; rather, we affirm, believe in, alert sensations of the real. (Goodman, 1966, p. 208).

To return to James as he recalls his introspective efforts to "detect in the activity any spiritual element at all":

In attending to either an idea or a sensation belonging to a particular sense-sphere, the movement is the adjustment of the sense-organ, felt as it occurs. (James, 1890, Vol. 1, p. 300)

Many philosophers however, hold that reflective consciousness of the self is essential to the cognitive function of thought. They hold that a thought in order to know a thing at all, must expressly distinguish between the thing and its own self. [And in a footnote: Kant originated this view.] . . . It is a case of the "psychologist's fallacy." They know the object to be one thing and the thought another; and they forthwith foist their knowledge onto that of the thought of which they pre-tend to give a true account. To conclude, then, thought may, but need not, in knowing, discriminate between its object and itself. (James, 1890, Vol. I, pp. 274f.)

And in that restatement we have a masterful resolution of the perils of the *Cogito* as it supports the retreat to more subjective phenomenology.

Now I return to Goodman: having made that statement about his noticing his pipe and glasses, he characteristically moves to the next step:

But the act by which I notice my sleepy behavior, and am later aware of its perhaps-fantasy quality, gives me also another aspect of reality that is real and concrete but has a certain barrenness and vagueness. And I think that a part of what we call 'generalization' or 'abstraction' is the concrete but bare and schematic perception: the grasping of the object when we are as if half-asleep.

In language it is expressed in the syntax, the kinds of construction allowable, rather than in the terms. In behavior it is expressed in the method and habit rather than the acts. (Goodman, 1966, p. 208)

Continuing James's analysis of his introspection, another remarkable parallel emerges:

I cannot think in visual terms, for example without feeling a fluctuating play of pressures, convergences, divergences, and accommodations in my eyeballs. The direction in which the object is conceived to lie determines the character of these movements, the feeling of which becomes for my consciousness, identified with the manner in which I make myself ready to receive the visible thing. . . .

In reasoning, I find that I am apt to have a kind of vaguely localized diagram in my mind, with the various fractional objects of the thoughts disposed at particular points thereof; and the oscillations of my attention from one of them to another are most distinctly felt as alternations of direction in movements occurring inside the head. . . .

[I]n one person at least, "the Self of selves," when carefully examined, is found to consist mainly of the collection of these peculiar motions in the head or between the head and throat . . . I feel quite sure that these cephalic motions are the portions of my innermost activity of which I am most distinctly aware." (James, 1890, Vol. I, pp. 300f.)

Yet Goodman needs a Creator Spirit behind everything that he cannot get his hands on: "I myself find it hard to think in logical abstractions, but I think readily and habitually in schemata. I am a Kantian." (Goodman, 1966, p. 209)

There is a penalty for finding it easy to think schematically but not abstractly. The schema exists categorically and a priori so it must complete itself reflexively and continuously. It is not consumed in its own use since it is not accessible through experience. One cannot get behind it. If one has luck, it can be welcomed as the reward for good effort as the Creator Spirit. But one must learn to hope and, if at all possible, wait. It becomes not a function of self, emergent from the stream of experience, not a figure/ground process, but a Figure whose authority speaks with a spiritual hush.

Another quote from James, clarifies his own understanding of spiritual activity:

If the dim portions which I cannot yet define should prove to be like unto these distinct portions in me, and I like other men, it would follow that our entire feeling of spiritual activity or what commonly passes by that name is really a feeling of bodily activities whose exact nature is by most men overlooked. (James, 1890, Vol. I, p. 301)

Conclusion

Goodman writes in *Five Years* that sex holds out the hope of Paradise (Goodman, 1966, p.8); we are, then, its priests and votaries. Recall that practice of this religion banished him from the University of Chicago, from the presence of his mentor McKeon. My thesis is that his God had failed him, and he created the

Creator Spirit to fill the void. Goodman says that sex is our religion because it holds out the hope of Paradise, and we are its priests and votaries. His God failed him and he created the Creator Spirit to fill the void. This was a desperate attempt at a synthesis that buried the conflict between the sexually driven Goodman and his conservative intellectual mentor.

In Perls et al., the agency of contacting becomes the agent driving action and our theory of emergent self collides with itself. In his theory of self, Goodman writes both as an heir to James's pragmatism and as a student of McKeon by stressing the synthetic unity of apperception. He cannot have it both ways, try as he might. Self cannot be the emergent process of the pragmatists and the Creator Spirit or transcendental ego of the Neo-Thomists. This unaware attempt at having it both ways led to Goodman's oscillation between hope and disappointment in his personal life that he sought to be resolved in his "Works." But such a resolution cannot happen sans facing the primitive crushing fall. It can be written down, but it cannot be otherwise worked. It is too bitter a pill in one's only world. We are, however, invited to chew and swallow our own bitter pills, by the literature we continue to work within. It is such a literature, and it remains an expression of gestalt therapy theory on which I am proud to stand, and stand I do, with my critical eyes open, and from which I invite us all to take our next step.

References

Bloom, D. (2004). The emergence of foundational gestalt therapy with-in a teaching/learning community: The NYIGT celebrates its fiftieth anniversary. *International Gestalt Journal* 27/1, 97-109.

Dewey, J. (1896). The reflex arc. *Psychological Review* 3, 357-370.

Dewey, J (1929) *The quest for certainty: A study of the relation of knowledge and action.* New York: Minton, Balch.

Goodman, P. (1966) *Five years: thoughts during a useless period.* New York: Brussel & Brussel.

Hartshorne C. (1991) *The philosophy of Charles Hartshorne.* The Library of Living Philosophers. Vol. XX. Salle, Ill: Open Court,

James, W. (1890), *Principles of psychology – Vols. I & II.* New York: Holt

Joas, H. (1985). *G. H. Mead: A contemporary re-examination of his thought.* Cambridge: Polity Press.

Kitzler, R. (2006). The ontology of action: A place on which to stand for modern gestalt therapy theory. *International Gestalt Journal* 29/1, 43-100.

McKeon, R. P. (1929). *Selections from medieval philosophers.* New York: Scribner's Sons.

Perls, F. S., Hefferline, R. F., & Goodman, P. (1951). *Gestalt therapy: Excitement and growth in the human personality.* New York: The Julian Press.

Perry, R. B. (1935). *The thought and character of William James, as revealed in unpublished correspondence and notes, together with his published writings.* Boston: Little, Brown & Co.

Sinclair, U. (1906). *The jungle.* New York: Doubleday.

Stoehr, T. (1994). *Here now next: Paul Goodman and the origins of gestalt therapy.* San Francisco: Jossey-Bass.

,

Chapter 2.
Translating Somatic Experiencing and Gestalt Therapy for Trauma Resolution into Music Therapy Practice with Adults.
Frank Bosco

Chapter Introduction

The following piece was important to include here for a number of reasons. First off, I see it as a contribution to the field in that it provides an understanding of how seamlessly gestalt theory can support work in the field of music therapy. I have been utilizing gestalt therapy principles in music therapy practice for about 35 years now and I have often made the point that I do not practice "gestalt and..." music therapy, but more aptly put, gestalt therapy in the language of music. I support the position that all of the theoretical foundations consistent with the practice of gestalt therapy can be represented in dialogical music experiences.

A second reason for offering this chapter is that it contributes a reference to some cutting edge work in trauma recovery. Peter Levine's "Somatic Experiencing" trauma work is becoming very popular throughout the world and I had the good fortune to be in the first east coast training which occurred right around the time that I began to regularly attend NYIGT meetings in the mid-90's. I was impressed and intrigued by how much gestalt therapy had seemed to inform and support Dr. Levine's approach. In essence, his work incorporates the recent understandings of the physiological aspects of the process of becoming traumatized and recognizes it for what we would call in gestalt theory terms, "unfinished business." While the founders were clearly aware of the need to resolve issues related to a trauma in order to restore resiliency and, no doubt, could often accomplish this in their experiments with people, certain physiological cues or shifts were not yet understood and therefore would not routinely be given the focus of awareness or support needed for a physiological response to complete.

Translating Somatic Experiencing and Gestalt Therapy for Trauma Resolution into Music Therapy Practice with Adults[3]

Working Definitions of Trauma

Trauma refers to psychological and/or physiological overwhelm and its lingering effects.

Shock trauma refers to the result of a one-time event or events that occur over a relatively short term. Typical causes include accidents, physical or emotional abuse, and sudden and devastating illness or loss.

Developmental trauma refers to the result of events occurring over a period of time relative to a person's developmental stages. It evolves out of a process of interruption that builds from repeated and somehow (to the individual) related events. Causative factors would consist of the constant abusive or neglectful treatment from parents, siblings, and other children or adults with whom the child might have regular involvement. The long list of possible effects include: physical damage or distortions, physiological dysfunction, hyper- or hypo-activity, confusion, hyper-vigilance, depression, compulsive behaviors, and hyper- or hypo-sensitivities such as phobias, numbness, or anesthetic conditions (Bosco, 2002).

Trauma in musical terms, Peter Levine has equated trauma with an "...interruption to the (one's) rhythm" (Levine, personal communication, March 8, 2002).

Introduction

As a body-oriented music psychotherapist, my clinical practice has developed through a synthesis of theories and methods from various approaches to mental and physical health drawn from three fields: psychotherapy, music therapy, and body-oriented therapy (Bosco, 1997). When I became a licensed massage therapist, body-centered practice led to an interest in the connection between mind and body, and resulted in the complete invalidation (in my own mind, at least) of any premise that suggested a formal separation between the two, such as Rene Descartes' (1637/1998) *"Cogito ergo sum,"* or "I think, therefore I am."

---

[3] Bosco, F. (2010). Translating Somatic Experiencing® and Gestalt Therapy for Trauma Resolution into Music Therapy Practice with Adults. In K. Stewart (Ed.), *Music therapy & trauma: bridging theory and practice*. New York: Satchnote Press.

Ongoing studies led me to encounter gestalt therapy concepts such as "being in the here and now" and "going with the resistance," (Chuck Nance, personal communication, April 1, 1978). From these explorations into gestalt therapy, I developed the belief that the therapeutic process could be a more embodied experience for both the client and the therapist than analytic therapy seemed to be. I was excited by this potential, and as I continued to expand my studies of various forms of therapy, I remained committed to practicing what I now understand as a central feature of gestalt therapy: being in good *contact* with the client.

Gestalt therapy originated from the work of Fritz and Lore Perls in the 1940's, and its theory was clearly expressed in the book *Gestalt Therapy: Excitement and Growth in the Human Personality* (Perls, Hefferline, & Goodman, 1951). This work was inspired by and takes its name from Gestalt psychology, which was evolving in the late 1800's as a study of perception (Kohler, 1947). From this study came the now familiar notions: (1) the whole is more than a sum of its parts, and (2) what we see is a matter of what we attune to as a figure in the foreground, supported by what we otherwise see as background. A common example of this latter concept is an image illustrating two solid color profiles which face each other, with the resultant space (a different solid color) between them resembling a vase. The figure/ground relationship changes with our focus, but it can only be perceived one way at a time.

By incorporating such principles, gestalt therapy emphasizes an awareness of what is happening in the present moment; therefore attention to one's physical processes (e.g., breath, sensations, and movements) is an essential part of the therapy process. The primary focus of this work involves the elimination of interruptions to clear, flowing, and graceful contact with self, other, and/or the environment. The practice of gestalt therapy accomplishes this task as it constantly attends to the interaction between thought and sensation in the client's process.

My theoretical foundation to clinical practice was furthered when, in 1994, I was introduced to Dr. Peter Levine and began studying his approach to working with trauma, Somatic Experiencing® (SE) (Levine, 1997). As I familiarized myself with this relatively new approach and continued to deepen my theoretical and practical understanding of gestalt therapy, I began to recognize certain similarities between the short term interventions of SE and the potentially long term processes of gestalt therapy. For instance, organismic self-regulation, a concept central to gestalt theory, has been placed at the heart of the SE model, with the goal being to return the traumatized person to a state in which self-regulation can occur at higher levels of stress without the consequence of overwhelm.

While a full exposition of the concepts and theories of gestalt therapy would not be within the scope of this chapter, it will be helpful to the reader to review further correlations between gestalt therapy and Somatic Experiencing.

These parallels form the basis for understanding how these two perspectives can be woven together to provide short term processing of traumatic events within the context of on-going long term therapy.

Gestalt therapy (GT) and Somatic Experiencing (SE) complement each other in that they both:

1. Involve working directly with all aspects of experience and the necessary parsing out of the specific components of experience in order to create a re-integration of these parts. In SE, this is clearly addressed as working with the over- or under-relatedness, or *coupling*, of sensation, imagery, behavior, affect and meaning that would result from trauma.
2. Focus on what is incomplete in terms of a person's experience of a situation, whether it is traumatic or otherwise. In GT, this is commonly referred to as *unfinished business*; while in SE it is referred to as suspended energy due to overwhelm, which prevents the completion of a defensive action.
3. Attempt to bring a person into a sense of embodiment or presence in the current moment, even as an issue from the past is being addressed or remembered.
4. Involve taking a person through *experiments* (GT terminology). This process involves reviewing an aspect of, or situation in, a person's life with the addition of necessary or desired controls to alter the process or perceived outcome of that event in order to yield a more favorable end. The clinical direction would be toward restoring the client's sense of psychological and physiological balance, and promoting growth in their ability to self-regulate a return to balance when confronted with challenging events.

What is Somatic Experiencing?

Somatic Experiencing® (SE) is a short term approach designed by Dr. Peter A. Levine to eradicate symptoms that are considered to be the unresolved or lingering effects of traumatic experience. It involves techniques in a process that directly attends to the sense of one's bodily experience in an effort to provide a safe and gentle release of energy believed to be held in the nervous system as a result of such trauma. It was developed upon observing that certain animals in the wild undergo life threatening events routinely and yet are rarely traumatized.

> Animals in the wild utilize innate mechanisms to regulate and discharge the high levels of energy arousal associated with defensive survival behaviors. These mechanisms provide animals with a built-in immunity to trauma that enables them to return to normal (homeostasis) in the

aftermath of a highly charged life-threatening experience.(Poole Heller & Heller, 2001, p. xvii)

Studying this work was a revelation for me; it provided the missing link between the expressions, "like a deer in the headlights" and "playing possum." These expressions point to the physiological understanding of trauma response detailed in the polyvagal theory (Porges, 1995) (also see ch. 1 in this publication), which provides much of the physiological underpinnings of Levine's SE approach. From the work of Steven Porges, we now understand the neurophysiological processes at work when fight or flight are no longer effective options to a threat and when more primal brain functions put the organism into what is called an immobility response, or *freeze* state. In physiological terms this is a *dorsal vagal collapse*, which refers to an alteration of autonomic nervous system functions controlled by the vagus nerve in favor of a more conservative bodily state.

Using the deer and the possum as examples, we can understand this important piece of trauma physiology. The deer sees an on-coming set of headlights, becomes startled, and has an *arrest response* as it *orients* to its perception of a potential threat. It literally stops in its tracks as it fixates on the on-coming figure without knowing what to do for its next step. This fixation includes the tightening of muscles, giving the impression that the animal is frozen, but typically indicating a preparation to fight or flee. In this case, the deer is ready to run but is confused by the nature of the threat. Unable to determine the nature of the threat (beast?), the deer quickly becomes overwhelmed by its encroaching presence. Adding to this cognitive dissonance in the moment is the effect of the bright light. In its nocturnal grazing, the deer would have dilated pupils, a function of the sympathetic nervous system which is most active in fight and flight activation. The lights would consequently contract the pupils and stimulate a more relaxing parasympathetic response. If this two pronged arousal of the nervous system continues to mount and prevents a decision for a course of action/escape, the deer may move into a freeze state. In this dorsal vagal collapse, its muscles would go limp, causing it to collapse to the ground just as the possum would do if it clearly sensed a life-threatening situation with a predator.

Working with Trauma in the Therapy Process

With the advent of more detailed physiological discoveries and the concomitant advance in the understanding of human function, it has become increasingly evident that there is a vast range of symptoms which can be linked to the phenomenon of traumatic experience. Psychotherapists are learning about this new information by studying contemporary approaches to working with trauma that embrace these physiologically-based findings in a practical way.

Music therapists must now consider these advances in the treatment of trauma in relation to what we may contribute, given the unique qualities that music has to offer. It is important to begin this exploration by first learning how a particular trauma approach works and then, particularly with traditional verbal approaches, translate the verbally-based communications to the more primal and sensory-based communications experienced in an active musical exchange.

In an on-going psychotherapy process with adults, therapists routinely encounter issues that seem to arise from specific incidences that were disruptive to the client at a particular stage of his or her development. In my body-oriented music psychotherapy practice, these incidences would be understood as traumatic events of varying degrees, and the SE approach would be used as needed to *renegotiate* patterns of limiting behaviors. Renegotiation, in this sense, would involve altering the configuration of these patterns to create more favorable alternatives and, ultimately, resolving the activation of nervous energy associated with trauma (e.g., anxiety symptoms). Within this process, I explore how behavioral events emerge as interruptions within the experience of *contacting*, as defined by gestalt therapy theory (Perls, Hefferline, & Goodman, 1951).

Once an interruption is identified, it provides the basis for designing a gestalt experiment. In gestalt therapy, experiments are conducted as part of the on-going process. These experiments are constructed by the therapist and/or the client for the purpose of exploring experiences, real or imagined, in the present moment (what musician's call "doing it in real time"). This generally includes enacting new behaviors to replace what was done in a past situation or what one might imagine doing in a future event. To facilitate this exploration, I often use dynamic emphasis (volume changes and accents), creating musical nuance within a musical process, in order to support and encourage behavioral nuances. Inviting new behaviors can bring greater awareness to situations in which the client has lost some degree of contact or conscious connection. This loss of contact/connection is often described as feeling "out of touch with oneself," and may include a failure to enact common sense behaviors, replacing them with avoidant, deadening behavioral syndromes (e.g., dissociation, denial, depersonalization, etc.).

Conducting gestalt experiments as a means of cocreating opportunities to de-structure fixities of self-limiting behaviors can allow access to "real time" behavioral tendencies; as one imagines a scenario, the body adjusts to this imagined scenario dynamically, complete with sensations corresponding to the experience. Components of the SE approach can be introduced to and adjusted through these experiments as musical events, either accompanying or replacing words, to provide a sonic scenario of the emotional and physiological adjustments that comprise the process of trauma renegotiation. Musical definitions and translations for selected SE components are detailed below:

- *Pendulation*: Altering themes for any musical element, such as melody, rhythm, tempo, and dynamics.
- *Titration*: (1) Mixing musical quotes or references to a theme within the general context of another theme or quality of music. (2) Gradual dynamic building using elements such as crescendo and diminuendo.
- *Containment*: Maintaining a consistent sonic environment with musical representation and support of the client's movements (e.g., gestures, breathing, rocking) and altering music as necessary to create a larger context and sense of safety for an expression to be explored.
- *Joining*: Helping a client to express a statement of need in the music and to be met there through a musical accompaniment that echoes, harmonizes, matches, or otherwise supports the expression. (Bosco, 2002)

Recognizing the precise moment that a person displays an orienting response as they convey an experience of overwhelming circumstance can serve as an entrée into working with a pattern of behavior. This physical response offers a clue as to what type of behavior was initiated in the person's attempt to maintain a boundary, either defensively or offensively. In effect, this attempt was unable to complete due to the traumatic response evoked. In terms of clinical analysis, this response may appear as an interruption to the rhythmicity of their bodily movement and be observed as a covert defensive reaction, such as a tightening of the shoulders and neck or the holding of breath, or as an overt defensive reaction, such as raising their hands following the impulse to fight or push back.

In the SE approach, the moment a client enacts a defensive orienting response – for instance, while remembering a traumatic event – an opportunity is presented to interrupt this patterned reaction by drawing attention to what is happening in the moment. In this way, a client's sense of time can be slowed or halted to allow for a greater awareness of what is occurring around and within the client as he or she moves into the customarily subsequent state of overwhelm. This provides a change of focus for the client within which support can be introduced to help bring the activated defensive maneuver to a successful finish before the client's debilitating, more primal neurologically-based survival instinct (a collapse or freeze response) is reenacted.

There is great opportunity for the application of music in this process. Defensive responses can be utilized to identify and complete the attempted behavior indicated in the moment and allow the momentary fixation to be explored as musical elements are applied to support and variegate the experience. Success in this process involves moving through a defensive response experience that previously would have resulted in a breakdown or disruption of unifying aspects of personal experience (e.g., sensation, mental imprint, behavior, affect, and meaning). Such an incompletion can generally be recognized as a tell-tale sign or symptom of trauma, the resolution of which would involve completion of the process of self-regulation by the appropriate integration of these unifying aspects of experience.

Music as a Communicative Medium in Drum Dialoging

In the field of music therapy, there is a wide acceptance for the ways in which musical expression serves as a stand-alone form of communication. Aside from the subjective images and meanings derived from listening to music, we are well accustomed to the types of thoughts and feelings evoked by the experiences of seeing a live performance. The innate quality of connectedness between the sound and the action producing it reveals a phenomenon that is, on the one hand, both simple and direct in terms of cause and effect and yet, on the other hand, complex and enigmatic as a reflection of our human existence.

One example of this phenomenon is the striking of a single note on a piano. Aside from the action of pressing down on a key and perhaps holding it down for the desired length of time, we want the tone to vibrate. There is no other requirement to produce a sound on the piano; any person who can physically lift a finger could potentially do this. However, there is a vast range in the quality of tonal production from novice to virtuoso, as well as from one virtuoso's style to another's. As the virtuoso's skill and abilities have been honed by years of intensive practice of an instrument, these can be easily distinguished from the abilities of a student instrumentalist who has just learned to play a classical composition without any "wrong" notes. As we develop comfort and flexibility with regard to technical aspects of playing an instrument, it is expected that we also expand our freedom to express ourselves with an expanding palate of emotional colors. It is important to note that this freedom of emotional expression is generally met by social and musical conditioning, as influenced by the pedagogy and "norms" which dictate how an action is "supposed to" be executed. This phenomenon of expressive conditioning in music is referenced within the body of work by Manfred Clynes (1977), Sentics, which investigated qualitative similarities in the precise manner with which accomplished pianists would strike a single piano key when asked to contemplate the music of certain prominent composers. There was evidently a shared sense of the quality of touch each pianist associated with a specific composer's music.

Such duality of simplicity and complexity in one's connectedness to music is also apparent within a clinical context. While I work at times with various instruments, for the purposes of exploring this phenomenon it is useful to focus on the particularities and examples of my work with drums, such as bongos, congas, and djembes. Similar to the piano, there is a wide range of tonal colors that can be produced by striking the head (traditionally made of dried and stretched animal skin) of these drums. However, some notable differences bear mentioning. For instance, certain drums have a limited melodic range and are generally relegated to providing rhythms rather than melodies or harmonic structures. Additionally, a single drum head only produces one sound at a time but can be played in vastly different manners in order to produce a wide range of tonal effects. Combining these various tonalities in a series of sound events will produce a regular or irregular rhythm with a potential for either consistent repetition or infinite variety.

Tonal flexibility in drum play is not unlike our capacity for putting vocal sounds together from the huge variety of phonemes, inflections, accents, and so forth, which comprise words and languages. Humans have an uncanny ability to recognize sounds and their commonly associated meanings, despite the varying combinations and voices we encounter from one individual to the next. Likewise, differing drums or drum sounds can be organized to construct commonly recognized rhythmic patterns associated with specific music genres and various instances or nuances within a given musical expression.

As in other areas of living, time and experience help us to become familiar with the language of musical expression through a heightened sense of awareness of such subtleties of communicative nuances. In alignment with gestalt practice, it is important to listen to the whole of the expression with attention to whatever detail emerges as significant, interesting, or arousingly curious in the moment. Responding to these expressions, I might share my observations or impressions in the interest of experimenting in the moment with whatever it is that we are, or could become, aware of.

Offering musical involvement within a gestalt experiment is one way to stimulate an attunement to the energy of an expression and enhance the novelty of the moment. These experiments can be well supported by offering the client simple percussion instruments, such as congas or bongos, and by the therapist choosing a similar type of drum in readiness to participate and support the experiment. Such instruments are particularly well suited for this work as they can reflect the nature of the effort that is put into them. This type of reflection offers a degree of objectivity within which novelty can be introduced as shared sonic events, consensually validating moments in the client's therapy process.

Gestalt theory encompasses the notion that intersubjective communication is occurring at all times within the context of an active therapist-client dyad (Jacobs, Philippson, & Wheeler, 2007). This is particularly true for musical communication since, unlike verbal dialogue, it is common for multiple "voices" to be heard simultaneously. As another rhythmic voice in the room, I can represent myself in direct dialogue with the client or represent any other role that we might agree I should enact, given the particular design of the experiment.

As with any Gestalt experiment, the possibilities are seemingly infinite in terms of how drumming might be used. The general suggestions to follow represent techniques found to be particularly valuable within a body-oriented music psychotherapy approach.

It may be helpful to offer the client a limited assortment of drums, varying in size, pitch, texture, tone, and material design. The client's choice of an instrument can be distinctly personal and may have great significance in the therapeutic process. For those who are unfamiliar with drums and drumming, a brief period of exploration or instruction may be necessary. Exploring the instrument might involve touching or holding the drum, or discovering the variety of sounds that one might produce with it.

This approach presupposes that the use of the drum is acceptable to the client. Clients often present charged reactions to playing drums or, for that matter, any musical instrument. The first order of business in using such techniques might be to explore the client's general comfort level with the drum. Such exploration could reveal a professional level of expertise or a background condition that may severely limit the client's ability to approach a musical instrument. The notion of playing a musical instrument might represent something that a client thinks they are supposed to know how to do and/or may evoke feelings of inadequacy (i.e., that they will inevitably fail to play the instrument[s] the "right way").

Understanding trauma as it is linked to feelings of inadequacy or embarrassment can be useful in these circumstances. The mere idea of *hitting* a drum may evoke memories of childhood abuse and be a reminder of feeling treated as an object. I remember a rather dissociated young man who once described that, in his childhood his alcoholic father would go into a violent rage in their living room and stand by the only doorway to the room in an attempt to entrap his four children. The client recalled:

As we would see what was coming and try to make a break for it (run out of the room), he would just smack us down like his arms were ten feet long and we were like a human drum set. Then, with a sad smirk, he quipped, "Yeah, you might say we were like his *trapped* set."

Standard Experiments for Drum Dialogs

Drum dialoging involves working with a specific set of musical and interpersonal structures for combining verbal and rhythmic expression. These structures offer ground for many possible experiments. *Speaking with the drum* can take the form of a rhythmic accompaniment to words spoken by the client, with or without the therapist, as a background beat. An example illustrating this technique would be working with the relationship between a steady rhythm and the rhythm of the client's speech, perhaps asking the client to tap each word or syllable. In speaking with the drum, the client can imagine the words they might want, or not want, to say in the experiment and play the drum as a voice. This places the sound of the drum in the center of the client's focus and experience as it replaces the more cognitive trappings of speech and lends a direct connection to emotional energy. While this technique appears simple, it is not necessarily easy, as it requires combining elements of thought and feeling, and translating them into directed action. Often this experience provides an opportunity to observe indicators of trauma in the form of inaction or avoidant behavior.

The following five techniques may be used exclusively and in combination at various points in the client's process.

1. **Say it then play it:** The client first voices their feelings, and then plays them on the drum.
2. **Play it then say it:** When it is more difficult to articulate an emotion verbally, the client is asked to attune to it and express it through drum play. This drum play can then be translated into words and/or discussed. It can function as a step towards enhancing a client's ability to express their feelings verbally in therapy and can improve self-expression in a life situation that triggers the same or similar emotions.
3. **Say and play it together:** The therapist demonstrates the act of accompanying the articulation of each word or syllable with a tap on the drum. The client is then asked to replicate this activity as they continue their verbal process with the support of the therapist. This is a more challenging experiment which may require other supportive techniques, such as supplying a steady rhythmic accompaniment.
4. **Say it with a steady rhythmic accompaniment:** The client and/or therapist provide a background rhythmic structure to support and enhance verbal expression. The client is asked to verbalize issues pertaining to the therapy process while using the constant drum rhythm to emphasize expression and to spur the process forward. Elements of the third technique can be incorporated into this steady rhythm. This is an improvisational form, similar to a musical solo with accompaniment.
5. **Therapist adds emphasis to client's words:** Using a steady rhythm, as in the fourth technique, the therapist emphasizes the words of the client by using rhythmic accents and articulations. Repetition of the client's words, as well as appropriate verbal interventions, can be infused into this process as a variation that yields a more complete client-therapist exchange.

In these experiments, careful attention must be paid to the presence or absence of self-support, congruence or incongruence of vocal and instrumental expression, patterns which suggest forms of holding back (i.e., slowing down, stopping), or any form of interruption to the flow of expression. These issues may indicate the effects of trauma or *unfinished business*.

The purpose of working in the experimental fashion described would first be to establish music as a *resource*, which refers to any area of support a person may identify and recall in support of navigating through a trauma process. Therefore, it is important to minimize or eliminate any discomforts that the music might initially impose. The supportive aspects of the music involve its combination of innately comforting qualities and forward flowing activity. When this is internalized by the client, it becomes a resource which can be employed as a catalyst for completing their previously interrupted impulses and behaviors.

Case Study

The circumstances of the story presented below represent a case of developmental trauma resulting from a combination of conflicting and overwhelming senses of intimidation and obligation. The client depicts a scenario in which a fear of confrontation seems to obscure her sense of choice, leaving her to feel forced to choose between a situation that she knows is not right for her, and her moral conditioning, which argues that circumstances are as they should be.

Case History

Teresa is a 25-year-old woman who had recently moved to the United States from Central America and was seeking treatment due to anorexic/bulimic behaviors that started in her mid-teens. She states that she was much thinner in her late teens and now has learned to eat and chew well. Though she generally feels she does not overeat, she continues to induce vomiting about three or more times a week. As a body-oriented therapist, I tend to look to the obvious metaphor for this type of behavior, which suggests that she is rejecting, on more than one level, that which she is trying to take in "for her own good." What is, under "normal" circumstances, a source of nurturance (food), was too uncomfortable, unpleasant, and/or distasteful to keep inside and assimilate; she needed to rid herself of it. As her story unfolded, all signs were pointing towards her father as the object of her anger and disgust.

Teresa revealed that her father was manipulating her to send him money for his expenses, indicating a classic role reversal issue. She described him as being irresponsible regarding her upbringing, always putting his needs first and never being available for her or her mother. She said she could not confront him on this because he would become extremely angry and defensive, occasionally including displays of violence. I had the impression that he would often alter the appearance of a situation in order to make Teresa feel guilty for not appreciating something he had done or was doing, and claiming his efforts were about her best interests when, in fact, they were clearly to benefit himself. One example Teresa gave described a situation that took place after he had been divorced by her mother and was living elsewhere. Teresa told me he would come every morning to drive her to school, though this seemingly benevolent gesture included built in rewards: namely, breakfast and gas money, courtesy of his ex-wife. Another posture of his parental responsibility was his role as protector of his daughter. He was well known for being a braggart and a bully amongst the adolescents whom his daughter associated with. Typical behaviors Teresa described witnessing involved drinking, womanizing, and generally attempting to impress her friends, who were approximately half his age. He would also become intoxicated and/or instigate fights, and occasionally Teresa would have to walk home or make arrangements for someone to drive him home.

One might argue that this disappointing display of parenting might have been both a factor that instigated the development of other presenting problems for Teresa, including substance abuse (mainly cocaine) and, paradoxically, a factor that helped her to eventually become more responsible and aware of the need to create limits and stop abusing drugs. As she came to recognize her father's failing sense of responsibility, she began to adapt to the role of being responsible for not only her own welfare, but also his.

As may be extrapolated from this pattern of behavior, a few years later Teresa was happily married and gainfully employed in NYC, but apparently still tending to her father's needs. While earning a modest income working for a small business, she was receiving frequent collect calls from her father, who was requesting money for various expenses that included luxury items. Teresa dutifully sent him checks for regular expenses, but when he pushed for her to buy him an expensive underwater camera, she expressed feeling conflicted and sensing that something was wrong. Little by little, she became less interested in supplementing his part-time income as a private diving instructor at a vacation resort and became suspect of his childish fantasies (i.e., believing that if he would get funded to go deep-sea diving, he would one day discover a sunken treasure).

While Teresa was now a safe distance from her father, he appeared to maintain a strong foothold in her mind. During her development through childhood, she had gained a sense of being a good and respectful child who would consistently defer to her father's authority, and in our sessions, when a question arose that pertained to whether or not she should continue to defer to his authority, she would tell me, "He's my father." This defense, however, disintegrated under the scrutiny of a simple drum dialogue (see Case Vignette below). As her therapy progressed, it became increasingly clear to Teresa that it was not respect for her father, but rather fear for her father's volatile mood swings, that kept her constantly alert in his presence and distrusting of his behavior. It was this state of fear that left her confused in her later adolescence, often wondering what the greater threat was: that her father might show up where he was not wanted or expected, or that he might not show up when he was expected or needed.

Case Vignette

In one of our first drum dialogue sessions, Teresa admitted feeling her father's "grip" on her. I simultaneously became aware of her contracting body as she related to me how he might react if she asked him to pay for his phone calls or if she cut off his "allowance." She showed facility with drumming and was effortlessly maintaining a steady rhythm up to this point, but as she more deeply explored this question of "What would happen...?" the quality of her drumming changed from steady to a slower, more stilted and somehow less committed tapping, and she told me, "He wouldn't like that."

As I adjusted to her rhythmic changes, I asked, "What might he say to you?"

Teresa replied, "He wouldn't say anything...he would just get upset."

I kept the rhythm going and asked, "And what would that do to you?"

I noticed her jaw tightening as she said, "I couldn't say that to him."

"Why not? What would prevent you?" I probed.

" It's because he's my father and it wouldn't be right."

Recognizing this response as a frame from cultural and religious orientations she had described previously, I attempted to reference her contemporary state of mind. "Ok, but you've also told me you don't feel its right that he asks you for money."

Her eyes averted into a slightly downward gaze as her drumming fell behind the beat, and then into a simplified beat which resembled a slow gallop. Recognizing this as an alternative to her original steady rhythm and a movement toward dissociation, I asked, "Teresa, what are you feeling toward your father right now?"

As I enhanced and complimented her galloping rhythm she said, "I don't care."

"You don't care about what?"

"I don't care what he wants," she said softly. "I don't even like him." Losing her rhythm altogether she said, "He makes me feel sick."

Allowing emphasis of this moment to create a slight pause or cadence in the music, I asked her how and where she sensed this feeling in her body.

She answered, "Here and here," pointing to the area just under her ribs and her throat.

I then asked her if she could continue to play with me. As we started drumming again, now with a simple pulse, I asked her to try to stay in touch with her feeling as she hit the drum. As soon as I felt she was beating the drum with strength and volume, I questioned, "Can you tell me again what you are feeling about your father, but this time say it with the drum – like taking a solo while I keep the beat."

She managed to beat a few sharp syncopated notes which were slightly louder than my quiet steady rhythm. I incorporated these notes into my rhythm as a way of feeding back what I heard as her drum statement, and encouraged her to repeat these statements with my support on the drum. Once this pattern was well established, I asked if she had any words to go with this. She banged out in a clear staccato beat: "He – makes – me – feel – sick!"

I asked her if she wanted to say this directly to her father, as if her father was in the room, substituting the word "you" for "he." This action appeared too activating for her as her beating lost its clear edge and the volume decreased. Responding to this and the withdrawn expression on her face, I introduced the SE technique of imaging the threatening entity at a safe distance, which is intended to limit and control the fear inducing effect on the client and the resultant level of nervous system activation due to contact with that entity. By helping Teresa remain cognizant of her bodily sensations as she explored this possibility, we found that as we imagined moving her father back incrementally to the point where he was out of the building, she could finally relax enough to address him. I then asked her to say whatever she wanted to him.

She started to drum louder, saying, "I don't want to pay for your camera!" Then, "I don't want to talk to you anymore! You're disgusting. You make me sick! You're just a big baby, and I'm not going to take your calls! I don't want to talk to you!" She seemed to be free in her expressions at this point, demonstrating increasing confidence as she improvised her lines and rhythms with my support. I echoed her expressions both verbally and with musical accents, while keeping a steady beat.

Finally, we spontaneously (though possibly induced by me in order to bring closure to the session, as the session's end was approaching) transitioned into a fervently dynamic musical climax as we began to play as fast and as loud as she could, until together shouting and pounding out a final six beats to the words: "NO MORE! NO MORE! NO MORE!"

Case Summary

Teresa seemed to swell with pride as her fear dissipated. With the expression of her anger, she completed a needed defensive action and reinforced a sense of her independent self. Her spine had straightened and her head was held high; clearly "*pronking*," which refers to the large and graceful movement animals make when they are essentially celebrating their successful escape from a predator. I find that this particular phenomenon of behavior is readily observable in humans and it is also commonly presented in musical terms, as in this case with my client. Certainly, we can feel the pomp and power expressed by an orchestra, often at the end of a symphony or the climactic ending of a lively jazz or rock music performance. This behavior seems to have a dual function: it importantly utilizes surplus energy liberated during the fight or flight experience and also serves to fuel the expression of a personal victory. This might include the relief or joy (as often with humans) of escaping to freedom, or perhaps the social display of prowess that often accompanies victory in mating rituals and other fights for dominance. In Teresa's case it was, I believe, a mixture of all of these expressions, as it served to complete the act of standing up for herself and expressing her needs in the face of an apparent, or rather, *a parental* threat.

I was gratified to notice Teresa's uplifted, bouncy, and bright-eyed energy as she left this session. She expressed her gratitude, saying she felt "really great," and I could see her obvious sense of liberation. This session served to culminate several weeks of work amidst an added sense of time pressure, as Teresa's course of therapy was limited by her plans to move to the west coast in one month's time. It was also gratifying to hear Teresa report the following week that her vomiting had stopped after our previous session. Interestingly, Teresa's vomiting ceased to be an issue for the rest of our time together. She continued to describe a shift in her being which supported the rejection of her father's advances and a capacity to properly nurture herself. While Teresa's long term outcome is unknown, our work together clearly provided a step on the road to her recovery and self-regulation.

Conclusion

I have always appreciated the creativity, freedom, and adventurousness of taking different paths to get to the same "place." In working with trauma, that place is a return to *the rhythm of life*. The many paths I have explored both personally and professionally have led me back to an inner truth: that music is my most fundamental resource for dealing with life's many traumas. The paths described in this chapter for providing a process for resolving trauma have consistencies and differences which can be creatively manipulated to benefit clients in a course of therapy. Traumatization involves a form of loss and can be likened to losing a sense of how to get home. Therapy cannot tell traumatized individuals how to return home – especially if they do not possess a sense of ever having been there – but it can provide a map to guide them and to keep them moving in the right direction, helping to release the stuck or constricted sense of feeling lost and hopeless when off "in the woods" on their own.

This chapter endeavored to present an understanding of how SE and gestalt therapy can be integrated to help people metaphorically and literally find their way through their trauma. Two familiar quotes from the respective founders and cofounder of these two approaches help to summarize this connectedness: Peter Levine's "No one can do it for you but, you can't do it alone," (Becker, personal communication, July 10, 1998) and Lore Perls' "Do as little as possible and, as much as is necessary," (Ruella Frank, personal communication, 2002). Both of these quotes seem to share philosophical ground in terms of understanding the limits of a therapist's power when attempting to assist a client in their personal exploration or journey. I see their statements as being in alignment with the famous Taoist philosopher, Lao-Tzu's sentiment: "The Sage reigns over the people by humbling himself in speech; and leads the people by putting himself behind," (1990, p. 98).

My philosophy involves letting music be my guide, as it has never failed to keep me moving, unstuck. Music's capacity to motivate movement makes it ideal for use in trauma work. Peter Levine (2002) states:

Traumatized people tend to get stuck – stuck in their trauma, stuck in the sensation of emotions and the feelings. The beauty of music and rhythm is that they allow people to move through the trauma at a fundamental bio-social level freer of second guessing and critical self-judgment. (Levine, 2002, p. 152)

The clinical illustration presented here demonstrates this point of view clearly. Perhaps another client of mine said it best at the conclusion of an experiment in a recent session: "I can't collapse and play the drum at the same time."

References

Becker, C. (1998, July). *Symptoms as bound energy: Resolution of symptoms – Resources needed for successful resolution of threat.* Paper presented at the meeting of the Foundation for Human Enrichment's Somatic Experiencing Training: Beginning Level, New York, NY.

Bosco, F. (1997). Sensing and resonating with pain: A process-oriented approach to focusing the body/mind using music therapy. In J. V. Loewy (Ed.), *Music therapy and pediatric pain* (pp. 7-21). Cherry Hill, New Jersey: Jeffrey Books.

Bosco, F. (2002). Daring, dread, discharge, and delight. In J. V. Loewy & A. Frisch Hara, (Eds.), *Caring for the caregiver: The use of music and music therapy in grief and trauma* (pp. 71-79, 176). Silver Spring, MD: American Music Therapy Association, Inc.

Clynes, M. (1977). *Sentics –The touch of emotions.* New York: Doubleday.

Descartes, R. (1998). *Discourse on method* (3rd ed.) (D. A. Cress, Trans.). Indianapolis, Indiana: Hackett Publishing Company, Inc. (Original work published 1637)

Jacobs, L., Philippson, P., & Wheeler, G. (2007). Self, subject, and intersubjectivity: Gestalt therapists reply to questions from the editors and from Daniel Stern and Michael Mahoney. In D. Bloom, M. Spagnuolo Lobb, & F. Staemmler (Eds.), *Studies in Gestalt therapy: Dialogical bridges* (pp. 13-38). Instituto di Gestalt, HCC, Siracusa, Italy: Instituto di Gestalt, HCC.

Kohler, W. (1947). *Gestalt psychology.* New York, NY: Liveright Publishing Corp.

Lao Tzu (1990). *Tao teh ching.* (John C. H. Wu, Trans.). Boston: Shambhala Publications. (Original work published ~500 B. C.)

Levine, P. (1997). *Waking the tiger.* Berkeley, California: North Atlantic Books.

Levine, P. (2002). Trauma, rhythm, contact and flow. In J. V. Loewy & A. Frisch Hara (Eds.), *Caring for the caregiver: The use of music and music therapy in grief and trauma* (pp. 148-153). Silver Spring, MD: American Music Therapy Association, Inc.

Perls, F., Hefferline, R., & Goodman, P., (1951). *Gestalt therapy: Excitement and growth in the human personality.* Highland, NY: The Gestalt Journal Press, Inc.

Poole Heller, D., & Heller, L. (2001). *Crash course: A self-healing guide to auto accident trauma and recovery.* Berkeley, CA: North Atlantic Books.

Porges, S. (1995). Orienting in a defensive world: Mammalian modifications of our evolutionary heritage. A polyvagal theory. *Psychophysiology, 32,* 301-318.

Chapter 3. Pain and Beauty: From Psychopathology to the Aesthetics of Contact
Gianni Francesetti

Chapter Introduction

"Pain and beauty" is a paper that I consider a theoretical development of Gestalt therapy's basic concepts. It is the result of my exploration of psychopathology and aesthetics from a Gestalt therapy perspective and testifies the attempt to set up an understanding in this field consistent with our core theory and epistemological foundations. Our core concepts — such as contact and contact boundary, self, field, intrinsic criteria, phenomenological method — are the basis for this exploration. From this journey, a new light provides the possibility to have a further glance: to distinguish different kinds of suffering on the basis of the quality of absence; to propose an understanding of psychotic experiences; to distinguish different kinds of beauty, objectual and emergent; to look at one possible meaning of evil; to propose the aesthetic criteria as a criteria for evolution; to connect aesthetics and ethics. The main and old problem in diagnosis and psychopathology is methodological: the risk to approach people as objects. One hundred years ago, Karl Jaspers opened a new path making it possible to escape from this objectification: the psychopathologist is not studying patients as objects any more, but is interested in patients' experience understandable by *Einfühlung*, empathic attunement. I suggest some other steps on this path, consistent with Gestalt therapy principles: to consider the suffering as a cocreated phenomenon, expressing the suffering of the field, creatively expressed by the individual, detectable by senses and transformed in the process of contact by creating beauty. That means that suffering does not belong to the *other* that I meet as psychotherapist: it is an emergent phenomenon cocreated by both therapist and patient, and more severe is the suffering, more radical is the need to plunge in a preverbal dimension where subjects and objects are not defined yet, but still in the process of emerging. Throughout this path we can pass from an objectual perspective to a radical field perspective in psychopathology.

I consider this effort to expand our theory and practice and remain faithful to our foundations as the specific characteristic of the NYIGT. I am an associate member of it, a non-local or far-flung member, so I don't participate in the meetings and in local issues. Nevertheless, I feel part of this institute because I share with the community this intentionality: to continue to study and chew our foundational theory and to expand it in new understandings and applications, inside and outside our network. This is the common ground that supports me in my commitment in therapy, teaching, theory development, organisational and political work. This is why it is so meaningful to me to be a member of this community, and why I am honoured and proud to be part of this book. This paper has been fostered by this ground, throughout the nourishing contacts I continuously have with friends and colleagues of this Institute.

"Pain is nothing
but the surprise
of not meeting each other" [4]

Pain and Beauty: From the Psychopathology to the Aesthetics of Contact [5]

Abstract
The concept of beauty in Gestalt therapy is explored, underlining the central importance of the aesthetic criterion for this model. Aesthetic evaluation, which is an essential component in the work of any Gestalt therapist, is a prereflexive and preverbal process, located at the root of the *Gestaltung,* in the dimension in which the subject and the world emerge. An original conception of psychopathology and psychotherapy is discussed: psychopathological suffering is conceived as an absence at the contact boundary. Therapy therefore consists in restoring presence to the encounter, through a process which transforms absence into pain and pain into beauty. The therapeutic engagement in "distilling beauty" from the relational histories and dynamics narrated by the patient is considered from an existential perspective, seeking to make sense of human suffering and of our work as therapists. Finally, in this light, we consider the ethical ground of psychotherapy, which permits us to avoid the risks of reductionism which we face at present – namely the risk of reducing the psyché into a biological or intimistic event.

Key words
Beauty, pain, aesthetics, contact, Gestaltung, intrinsic evaluation, psychopathology, ethics, existentialism, reductionism

"Of all of psychology's sins, the most mortal is the neglect of beauty"
J. Hillman

François Cheng opens the first of his five meditations on beauty with these words:

> In these times of universal suffering, random violence, and natural and ecological disasters, to speak of beauty could seem incongruous, improper, even provocative – almost scandalous. But this is precisely why

---

[4] Alda Merini, *Aforismi e magie*, Rizzoli, Milan, 1999
[5] Opening keynote lecture at the third Conference of the SIPG (Società Italiana Psicoterapia Gestalt – Italian Gestalt Psychotherapy Society), Palermo, 9 December 2011. Published in Italian in: Francesetti G., Ammirata M., S. Riccamboni, N. Sgadari, M. Spagnuolo Lobb (Eds), Il dolore e la bellezza. Dalla psicopatologia all'estetica del contatto, F. Angeli, Milano, 2013.

we can see that beauty, as evil's opposite, really is situated at the other extreme of the reality we must face. (Cheng, 2009, 5).

Is it inappropriate, then, to speak of beauty? Is it superficial, useless, almost an idle diversion from that which really counts, is it important, concrete and urgent? As a tribute to Palermo, home to the third SIPG Congress, I will quote, by way of answer, a passage from the film *I cento passi* (*The Hundred Steps*)[6], which tells the story of Peppino Impastato, a young man from Cinisi (Palermo) who took on the mafia and was killed in 1978. Peppino, seated with a friend on the mountains overlooking the Punta Raisi airport, looking down on the ugliness of the illegally constructed houses below, remarks: "It takes nothing to destroy beauty... Instead of political struggles, of demonstrations, we should help people to recognise beauty, to defend it. Beauty is important: everything else flows down from it."

Coming from Peppino Impastato, symbol of the civil struggle against the mafia, this is not the statement of someone concerned with matters that are futile or cosmetic. In a completely different context, James Hillman (1997, 56) writes, "Of all of psychology's sins, the most mortal is the neglect of beauty." Beauty, then, may be considered a central concern for psychology and ethics, as François Cheng himself affirms in the continuation of the passage cited above, stating that the consideration of beauty is no idle game but rather "our urgent and ongoing task" (Cheng, 2009, 5). Yet in what sense can beauty be so important? And then, to what kind of beauty are we referring?

In the present discussion, I intend to explore the theme of beauty in Gestalt therapy, thus focusing and subsequently seeking to extend on a concept which constitutes one of the cornerstones of our model.

My paper will cover four main points:

1. Beauty: a cornerstone of Gestalt therapy theory
2. Pain: psychopathological suffering as absence rather than pain
3. From psychopathology to the aesthetics of contact. Distilling beauty: an existential perspective.
4. Aesthetic Ethics: Ethos and Polis as roots and horizons of aesthetics.

1. Beauty: a cornerstone of Gestalt therapy theory

> *Beauty is truth, truth beauty, - that is all*
> *Ye know on earth, and all ye need to know."*
> (J. Keats)

---

[6] *I cento passi (The Hundred Steps)*, 2000, directed by M.T. Giordana

As therapists we witness the transformative effects of our work on a daily basis. There are times when a Gestalt intervention proves truly enchanting in the magic that emanates from it and the traces of beauty which it creates and leaves behind itself. Feedback such as the following is frequent in groups after therapy: "Now that you've worked everything through you're really beautiful: the lineaments of your face have never been so relaxed and harmonious, you've got a new light in your eyes and your body has acquired a new grace."

1.1. Intrinsic or aesthetic evaluation

We start out from the consideration that our founders located beauty at the very heart of the theory of Gestalt therapy and did so identifying an intrinsic criterion for evaluating human health:

> There are two kinds of evaluation, the intrinsic and the comparative. Intrinsic evaluation is present in every ongoing act; it is the end directedness of process, the unfinished situation moving towards the finished, the tension to orgasm, etc. The standard of evaluation emerges in the act itself, and is, finally, the act itself as a whole. In comparative evaluation, the standard is extrinsic to the act, the act is judged against something else." (Perls et al, 1994, 65-66)

This is one of the concepts, which makes our approach so revolutionary, even today, sixty years on. It means that the health of a human being may be expressed and recognised through the quality of contact, without any recourse being made to any external criteria of comparison: the strength, grace, rhythm, fluidity and intensity of the organism's contact with its environment, the process whereby a figure comes to form itself against a ground – the beauty of contact, in sum, is the measure of health. What has been identified, then, is an aesthetic criterion for the evaluation of contact, of the encounter underway, of the situation and of health (Joe Lay in Dan Bloom, 2003; Robine, 2006; 2007; Spagnuolo Lobb, 2011)[7]. As Gestaltists, we are all engaged in the pursuit of good form – alchemists seeking out the precious metal which emerges spontaneously from contact, the good form which is its beauty (Zinker, 1978). Laura Perls (1992), indeed, maintains that the fundamental concepts of Gestalt therapy are at once philosophical and aesthetic.

It is at this point that an initial problem arises: comparative evaluation – which we, in a revision of the concept of diagnosis in Gestalt therapy (Francesetti, Gecele, 2009; 2010), referred to as extrinsic - lies on a predominantly reflexive

---

[7] See also the *International Gestalt Journal* specific Issue on Aesthetics, Vol. 30, N. 1, 2007.

level. Yet is intrinsic evaluation, too, inasmuch as it is nonetheless a form of evaluation and therefore a judgement, also a reflexive phenomenon? It is at this point that the concept of aesthetics proves useful. Intrinsic evaluation is, in fact, "aesthetic" and this is a concept which we must explore in further depth.

In the eighteenth century, the founder of aesthetics as a discipline, Alexander Gottlieb Baumgarten, defined it as the "science of sensible cognition." This is clearly an oxymoron, in which the term "cognition" seems to sit awkwardly with the adjective "sensible," but it refers precisely to a "knowing with the senses" (Desideri, 2011). The Age of Reason saw the emergence of the dignity of knowing through feeling, not just through reason. The word "aesthetics" — ancient in its etymology, modern because created in the 1700s — came into extensive use, indicating a research approach applied in particular, but not exclusively, to the fine arts. This term has come to be applied in two main senses: the first is the reduction and restriction of aesthetics into reflection on art, the second the application of this concept to consumer items and in particular to the human body itself. Both of these tendencies are based on a conception of aesthetics and of beauty applied to an object. I, however, will here steer clear of this meaning seeking out the sense of beauty in a region which transcends the object and the subject.

The term "aesthetics" was coined by Baumgarten himself, who used it for the first time in a 1735 volume entitled "Reflections on Poetry" in which he put forward the idea that, just as there exists a science of intellectual contents, namely logic, so there should exist a science of the sensible data of knowledge, which would be termed aesthetics." (D'Angelo, 2011, 16).

Indeed, the ancient Greek *aisthesis* means sensation and aesthetics thus constitutes knowledge through the senses. That which is *An-aesthetic*, instead, is a pharmaceutic product or a procedure which dulls the senses. Hence we can immediately connect the aesthetic phenomenon to the gestalt conception of awareness – that is to say, with the conception of awareness as the capacity to be awake to one's own senses, to feel the excitement at the contact boundary. As Margherita Spagnuolo Lobb (2003a; 2004) reminds us, the English adjective awake shares roots with the noun awareness.

1.2. Aesthetic evaluation at the root of Gestaltung: a prereflexive and preverbal emerging process

If aesthetics is not a reflexive process but rather constitutes knowledge through the senses, what is it that we encounter in our senses at the contact boundary? Where can we place the aesthetic evaluation? The natural (as Husserl would call it) empiricist, positivist, scientific stance would tell us that there is an already-constituted organism which, encountering an already-constituted world, gets to know it. The senses of the organism register the objects present in a given world. The phenomenology, together with Gestalt psychology, tell us that this is not the case. Rather, we co-create a world and a subject in our senses, to such a radical extent that one world and one subject only exist in one unrepeatable sensation:

> Being strictly, the first, last and only of its species, each sensation is a birth and a death. (Merleau-Ponty, 2003, 293).
> Perception does not come to us as an event in the world, to which we can apply the category of causality, but rather as a re-creation or a re-construction of the world at every moment. (ibid., 283).

Again: "sensation is literally a communion" (ibid, p. 289). One of the biggest revolutions in phenomenology is the realisation that the apparent stability of "a myself" and "a world" is, instead, the fruit of a continuous creation: "the subject is not a secure possession, but to possess it we need to continuously reconquer it" (von Weizsacker, quoted by Ballerini, 2011, 107). We are particularly well aware of this when we live through or encounter a psychotic experience, which reveals this creation grasped in its instability. The obvious stability of the world, usually taken for granted, comes to the fore in psychotic experiences precisely because it is this that is lost. To quote Husserl:

> The real world exists, only on the continually delineated presumption that experience will go continually in the same constitutional style." (Husserl 1969, pps. 251-2)

This does not mean that we should fall into an *ab-solutus*[8] postmodern relativism, where the individual creates her/his own reality at her/his own pleasure. Co-creation is not a self-sufficient form of generation, but rather a process in which the subject her/himself emerges from the ground, at once generating it and being generated her/himself [9]. In the senses, then, there is not a "distinct ego" which encounters "defined objects." There is rather the root of the Gestaltung: a process of co-creation of experiential phenomena, in which a not yet distinct ego and not yet defined objects are continuously emerging.

---

[8] Etymologically, *absolved of every constraint, of every limit.*

[9] This concept seems to me to avoid falling into the contemporary revival of the *new-realism* (Ferraris, 2012) which reaffirms a dichotomy between events and their interpretation in favour of the former, in contrast to the Nietzschian assertion that "there are no facts, only interpretations," one of the slogans of post-modernism. Both of these positions seem to propose a dichotomous and simplistic logic in drawing a distinction between facts and interpretations which can be overcome through a logic of co-creation whereby subjective interpretation and objective events are co-created, thus being neither factually given nor interpretatively free.

With regard to this dramatic perspectival transformation – from that of me/given world to that of the incessant co-creation of the me and world — I will here bring into focus just one point: namely, that this creation comes about without deliberation and is pre-verbal. That is to say, it is not a result of the ego function: no one gets up in the morning needing to say, "now I'll create myself" (except in cases of severe depression). It comes about, moreover, at a pre-reflexive moment, in a region of experience in which words have yet to emerge. We should state that it regards in primis neither the ego nor the personality function of the self, but is placed exactly in what Goodman refers to as the id of the situation (Robine, 2006; 2011; Wollants, 2008), what Minkowski would term the "vague and confused" background, the locus of "perceptive communion" (Merleau-Ponty), of what Desideri astutely terms "perceptive commerce."

In the senses, more than encountering each other, organism and environment create each other: they co-emerge [10].

Aesthetic evaluation, then, occurs at a moment of the formation of experience that precedes reflexive working through. It is an immediate and preverbal knowledge. Aesthetic judgement has its genesis before language: it is rather the precondition thereof, dwelling in the realm of the implicit (Stern, 2004). It is born, therefore, in a chiaroscuro, nuanced moment, prior to the separation of subjectivity from objectivity:

> Subjectivity itself cannot be thought of as being constituted and formed prior to the emergence of an aesthetic curvature in the perceptive fabric of experience. We might even go so far as to reverse this relationship and see the sphere of subjectivity, with the sensus sui which it necessarily implies, as an immanent "response" to the emergence of an aesthetic attitude. (...) We must refer, then, to an aesthetic genesis of subjectivity, rather than to a subjective genesis of the aesthetic."(Desideri, 2011, 78)

We are referring, then, to how we immediately feel as events unfold, not to how we judge them a posteriori – to how we feel them as we co-create them and give them form. We cannot evaluate aesthetically without being involved in the object's creation. There is no such thing, in this sense, as objects that are beautiful *per se*. There is only the experience of generating beauty in the presence of something that becomes a fount of beauty. This does not mean that beauty is in the eye of the beholder, as Hume asserted, since beauty is a phenomenon which emerges from experience and therefore belongs to a dimension ingeniously brought into focus by our founders, who trod a fine line, falling into neither

---

[10] Our phenomenological understanding seems consistent with the concept of *proto-self* introduced by Damasio (2010)

subjective relativism nor realist objectivism[11]. In beauty, thus understood, we may grasp the epiphany of the lifeworld, the manifestation of the productive fault which precedes the emergency of the "me" and the "world," the only safeguard against losing ourselves in the objectivisation of the other or her/his relativistic denial.

Aesthetics is thus a knowledge which is already in tune, already emotionally attuned, already, *in-tended*[12]: an awareness of what is going on at the contact boundary, in the co-creation of experience, of what is being moved during the encounter and of the extent to which we are moving together, co-moving each other and being emotionally moved together. Emotional co-moving, indeed, consists in being touched by what is happening to the other and thus is a moving-with the other. Resonance is a co-influenced movement.

In his last book, Daniel Stern (2010) identifies as fundamental units of experience what he calls *dynamic forms of vitality*: on these units, or Gestalten, the affective intersubjective attunements are based. This line of research seems to support our thesis: vital forms are evaluated in a prereflexive way, are perceived as holistic wholes (Gestalten indeed), are emergent properties of the experience itself. Their parameters are: strength, movement, space, time, direction/intentionality, the same that are relevant in the process of good form's intrinsic evaluation.

Aesthetic knowledge is emergent (it is born at a given instant), ephemeral (it only lasts as long as a given experience), bodily (it is incarnate in the senses and in the resonance of the body). It is neither objective nor subjective. This last point is central because it suggests a third dimension, which is neither objective, nor subjective, which is rich in its implications: "Between the two poles of absolute subjectivity and objectivity, aesthetic experience occupies a middle ground, that of intersubjectivity." (D'Angelo, 2011, 116).

What happens in a session, be it with a couple or in group settings, and which we feel to be "beautiful" is neither objectively beautiful (it is not a quality of the object) nor subjectively beautiful (for me alone, as if it were a question of personal tastes). It is, indeed, present for whoever is present in their senses — who is, therefore, aware and participating, implicated in the situation. It is beautiful for us to be present inasmuch as we are touched by what is happening. We are not, in fact, referring to the beauty of either an object from which we can

---

[11] I am referring here to the concept of a self that emerges in the situation (see Spagnuolo Lobb, 2001; Wollants, 2008, and Philippson, 2009).

[12] Note the Italian verb *intendere*, from the Latin *in-tendere*: tuning an instrument, making its strings resonant with the heart.

be detached, nor of something that is "nice," gracious, comforting and cosmetic[13]. When involved in contemplating beauty our eyes change, our breath changes: the beauty does not belong to the object or to the subject, but is an emerging contact phenomenon. We are rather concerned with a phenomenon which transforms and seizes us, whose power can have the emotionally disruptive force of a tidal wave or the subtle, penetrating quality of the air high up in the mountains. Moreover, because it transforms, it leaves behind a trace of itself. It is a power which is always inevitably transformative, and consequently de-structuring: nothing good and new emerges without a reciprocal *ad-gressive*[14] destructuring of those involved in the contact. The link between aesthetics, awareness, the lifeworld and transformation emerges even more clearly if we probe the etymology of the word in further depth, as did the classical philologist Richard Onians:

> The Greek verb *aisthanomai* (long form of *aisthomai*: "to perceive"), from which *aisthesis* derives, is the middle of the Homeric *aisto*, which means "I gasp," or "breathe in." In its affinity with terms indicating the "breath" of the living, *aisthesis* shares the same root as *aion*, meaning time which regenerates itself and, prior to that, the "vital force" which flows through bodies (...) (Desideri, 2011, 74-75).

Beauty, then, transforms and leaves a trace of itself. Another central relationship also emerges here: the link between beauty and presence. This is a link that brings us to the other crossroads of our discussion: pain. And along this path we will encounter the essence of psychopathology.

2. Pain: Psychopathological Suffering as Absence Rather than Pain

> *When we admire the beauty of the pearl, we must never forget that it originates in the sickness of the shell.*
> K. Jaspers

2.1. Pain as a criterion for suffering in medicine and absence as a criterion for suffering in psychopathology

In medicine, the opposite of life is death. In psychotherapy, which is phenomenologically and existentially oriented, instead, the opposite of life is not

---

[13] This distinction is also relevant in the aesthetic evaluation of a work of art, as the trial of Pygmalion teaches us: we can enjoy the beauty of something which would be monstrous if it became real, like a painting of a devil or a sculpture of a dragon.
[14] *Aggression* comes from the Latin *ad-graedior* – to move towards.

death. Death is rather something that plays a constitutional part in life, inasmuch as it determines the uniqueness and preciousness of every moment. It is life's vital companion, precious and necessary. The opposite of life, which is presence, is, instead, absence. In the tragic words of a patient living with what is perhaps the most extreme condition of absence, namely melancholic depression:

> "Everything is dead in me. There is no life any more. Everything is mechanical. My movement is no longer my own. It is dead. I am dead."

In medicine, the opposite of well-being is ill-being, where the suffix "ill" refers to physical illness and pain. To avoid pain, the surgeon operates by administering an an-aesthetic. Dentists teach us that if a tooth hurts, it means that something is wrong and needs taking care of. This is also the function of pain in physiology: it is a signal that care is required.

In psychotherapy, which is phenomenologically and existentially oriented, pain is not the opposite of well-being. Pain is an intrinsic and indefeasible part of life. The opposite of well-being is, once again, absence.

Indeed, the apex of the beauty of an encounter, and therefore of its health, sometimes coincides with the apex of the pain which is unleashed through the contact. During a patient's therapy, the unleashing of an acute pain may correspond to the aesthetic apex of the encounter.

Herein lies the anthropological vision of Gestalt therapy: an individual who is healthy and vital must be fully present in her/his senses, not anaesthetised. If it is painful to be present in one's life, then it is healthy to feel this pain. Indeed, beauty is not always easy, "nice" or attractive. In the words of a patient, at a moment when we had reached a therapeutic breaking point:

> (...) at this point I'm going to pick up a pen and write to you. Beauty takes a bit of energy. As a look at it, I can see that it's made up of tears, saliva, sweat and vomit ... To tell the truth, I'd have thought it would be made of light. Maybe this was my mistake?

Something radical happens when we pass from the domain of medicine to that of psychopathology: with this transition we make a quantum leap that has perhaps yet to be sufficiently discussed. We pass, indeed, from a dimension where we may (often usefully) reason in terms of individuals and objects to one in which it is impossible to abstract the individual from the relational field by which (s)he is constituted. To say that "(s)he is immersed" therein will not suffice. The relational field is veritably that "by which "(s)he is constituted."

This is the point which reductionism tends to obscure. At worst, it fails to take into account that as subjects we are not "abstractable" from the relational situation and abstracts us away from our bodies, reducing us to mere brains. As

Alva Noe (2010) asserts, we are no more our brains than the cellulose molecules of banknotes are money.

Anaesthesia is a watershed which draws a line between the two dimensions, the medical domain of the body-object and the psychotherapeutic vision of the living-body (Galimberti, 1987; Borgna, 1988). Anaesthesia may be a component in the well-being of a *Körper* (a body in the anatomical sense, such as a dentist sees in her/his chair), but not of a *Leib* (a living body). How can one love if anaesthetised?

Psychopathology, then, unlike medical pathology, cannot overlook the relational dimension without giving itself over to the objectivization of the subject (as we have known at least since Jaspers' work) and to paradox (Jaspers, 1963). If we locate ourselves in a relational dimension, the psychopathological event is not a subjective pain. For example, the pain of bereavement is healthy and is a sign of health. The absence of pain in the narcissistic impossibility of loving constitutes a psychopathological and existential tragedy.

The psychopathological event constitutes an absence at the contact boundary. This absence manifests itself as something *an-aesthetic* and *a-poetic*. Anaesthesia is not feeling, the a-poetic (*poiesis*, from Greek, making) is not being creative. Aesthetics and poetry, in this recess of the lifeworld, are inextricably bound together in their coexistence. Poetry is the specific activity of the psychotherapist: her / his healing words are *poietic* words, words which have a body, tactile words which touch and transform because they are vehicles infused with beauty right from the moment of their inception. Yet there are also gestures that speak, silences pregnant with contact and communication.

2.2. Three forms of absence

Let us examine the various kinds of absence and therefore of psychopathology (Francesetti et al., forthcoming). We can identify three fundamental forms.

2.2.1. First Form

From our first meeting, her presence in contact with mine immediately created an intense atmosphere of suspense, of tension – a climate in which anything could happen. Tragedy hung like an axe over our heads. There was a sense that the unthinkable, the catastrophic might be upon us at any moment.

I breathe … I try to bear up against the anxiety and to endure this oppressive, sinister atmosphere, but every now and then I succumb to sudden moments of giddiness. I constantly recall a session with another patient, years before, in which I suddenly felt the room (or myself) shake. For a fraction of a second I was disoriented and then, looking at each other, we both realised that there had actually been a small earthquake. Such was the climate in which the session with Maria began:

T: Good morning.
M: Good morning.
Silence
T: How did you get here?
M: My daughter brought me here ... Yes, I think it was my daughter ... As far as I know, it was she.
The way in which she says these words, which are something of a verbal tic of hers, plunges me into a universe in which nothing is stable or consistent. It is a whirlpool of fragile, papier mâché objects which are continuously falling to pieces. Truly and ontologically, there is no certainty.
T: Your daughter Anna?
M: Yes, my daughter's name is Anna, as far as I know...
M does not pass via her body in seeking out these answers. It is as if nothing has settled in the certainty of memory, of experience, of feeling. Everything is concretely possible, so nothing is acquired, and her answers spring from deductions which are not rooted in anything which we can, in a shared way, call body or reality.

The first kind of absence therefore consists in not being constituted as subjects. This is what happens in psychotic experiences (Spagnuolo Lobb, 2003; Spagnuolo Lobb and Francesetti, forthcoming). Paradoxically, in this absence there lies a unique and extremely powerful form of presence. When we encounter it – if we do not withdraw from the contact boundary – it immediately seizes, infects, overcomes or overwhelms us. Therein lies the non-constitution of the subject but also a powerful atmospheric presence, since the subject is potentially there, the urge to constitute it is incredibly strong but the path leading to its constitution, at least in this relational field, is materially lacking. If we look into the eyes of an individual in a state of psychotic anguish, we see something beyond, an abyss. We in turn feel naked, as if we have been bypassed. The psychotic's glance is deconstructive, because it immerses us in a dimension in which subjectivities have not been constituted. There, it is impossible to co-create ourselves in any definite way, but the work of co-creation may be powerfully active, although impeded from attaining to the definition of subjects. We are immersed in a continuous and continuously futile endeavour to constitute a world with clear and connected boundaries, in a crucible of white heat in which every possibility is created and dissolves. This is a land of lunatics, forsaken by constituted subjects and objects, since this world precedes the constitution of the definite. Yet it is this special quality of absence and potent presence, which at times permits us to be artists, poets, extraordinarily creative. And, following Heidegger, this is the secret truth which is the exclusive preserve of lunatics, poets and children (Blankenburg, 1971; Salonia, 2001; Borgna, 2011): it is a testimony to the miracle with which we throb in the dimension of the between (Buber, 1996; Francesetti, 2008), of the interest (note the Latin root, *inter-esse*, 'to be in the between') which denudes and disarranges the arrogance of individuality. Before being defined subjects we are a field-emerging phenomena, pulsing with life.

2.2.2. Second Form

A man in his fifties says to me: "I don't have any problems in particular, just life's usual little worries. But it seems to me that I am not living. I'm 50 years old and my life has no flavour. I'm always dissatisfied. Recently I've felt a kind of happiness welling up in my throat momentarily, but it stopped there. My body stiffened up, went cold and I couldn't feel anything any more."
"And how do you feel now, as you tell me about it?"
"Nothing ... I'm ok... normal, I guess."

The second way in which we may be absent is when we constitute ourselves as subjects but are absent to our own senses, anaesthetised. This is the absence that we experience during our neurotic experiences[15]. Here it is difficult to define ourselves through a process of co-creation and therefore the potentialities of the field are only partially embraced. The field is weak because it is anaesthetised.

Both in the first and in the second kinds of absence, protective modalities geared towards making this unbearable suffering bearable intervene, rendering this absence unknowing. Absence disappears into the oblivion of itself.

It is at the contact boundary that the therapist encounters these absences, and (s)he encounters them aesthetically – with her / his senses.

The therapist – present to her / his senses, fully engaged in the co-creation of contact, enmeshed in the weaving together of the fabric of the relationship – feels these absences. This sensation is already a therapeutic act, since it causes the forgotten absence to emerge once more as a figure in the relational field. It does not matter if this is not yet the case in the patient's mind. An absence recalled is already a presence. It is worth bearing in mind that the Latin verb *ricordor* from which the modern Italian *ricordare* derives actually means to "bring back into the heart." The very fact of relocating the absence between us performs the miracle of transforming it into a presence. *Aisthesis* here becomes *poiesis*, feeling becomes creation.

2.2.3. Third Form

---

[15] These absences, which Gestalt Therapy refers to as contact interruptions, are *felt aesthetically* in contact as absences in the co-creation of experience which is, as we have seen, occurring incessantly.

P. is a 35 year old man, very tense in his posture, the smile on his lips strangely discordant with the hardness of his stare. If I allow myself to feel, I feel afraid. I can feel his sarcasm[16] clawing at my flesh. P. has been sent to me after abusing his girlfriend.

He tells me with a sardonic coldness: "When I go with a woman, I don't feel anything except my own pleasure. What I'm interested in is my own pleasure. At the beginning there aren't any problems. Then at a certain point she always contradicts me, and I can't stand that. There's no reason for it, so I get angry. Then she wants to go. Doesn't she understand that she has to stay there? And if she can't understand it the easy way, perhaps she can understand it the hard way."

"And you say that this always happens at a certain point in your relationships?"

"Yeah ... But you should know that I basically treat women like prostitutes, because they're all whores. They don't realise it, because I'm smart, but I take advantage of them. And in the end when they realise it, it's already too late. I've already taken advantage of them ..."

This third form of absence often occupies a very marginal place in psychotherapy, because those involved are far less likely to ask for help and their treatment is very difficult. This is the experience of an absence that has no sense of the suffering of the other. It is the sense of those who, having no sense of suffering, inflict it. Severe narcissistic and sociopathic conditions fall into this category, as do antisocial behaviours. This is the tragedy of those who do not feel the other's suffering and therefore inflict it. The pain of those who do not feel pain becomes a suffering provoked, a pain which emerges in the other. Those who torture express their own absence in inflicting pain on the tortured. It is a transformation of *suffering-absence* into *suffering-inflicted* and of this into *suffering-pain*. This condition – the experience of which is deprived of any possibility of feeling the other's pain – should be fully acknowledged in psychopathology. As a student once said during a seminar: "And where are we going to put the bad people? They exist, too!." In these experiences there may be the anaesthesia of the pain of the other or alternatively even an experience of enjoyment in inflicting pain on other.

3. From Psychopathology to the Aesthetics of Contact. Distilling Beauty: an existential perspective.

> *I don't know how a poem*
> *takes form.*
> *I take the mud*

---

[16] From the Greek, *sarkaizein*, i.e. to lacerate the flesh (Cortellazzo e Zolli, 1983).

of my life
and feel
like a great sculptor.
　　　　　Alda Merini

3.1. Emerging and objectual beauty

The beauty to which we are referring emerges from presence at the contact boundary. It is neither pre-existent nor subsistent. It is ephemeral, transient, non-objectual. It is like a melody in the air which is irreducible to the vibrations of strings and drums: even though it is dependent on these, it breaks free into intersubjective space-time and consumes itself. It does not, then, persist. To what end, then, do we seek it out and create it? Because, as we have said, it transforms us and leaves behind a trace of itself. With the fullness of the encounter, which we feel as beautiful, we generate relational goods (Cavaleri, 2003; 2007). These are produced through an experience which may involve pain or pleasure – which does not matter – but which is always aesthetic: felt and real.

Being emergent, it does not belong to the individuals who encounter each other, but rather generates itself as a realisation of the potentiality at the contact boundary. It belongs neither to me nor to you. It is a breath which is generated between us. Breath in Greek is *Psyché*, i.e. *psyché,* soul. *Psyché* (in Apuleius' story) is the most beautiful figure in the whole of classical mythology (Hillman, 2002, 12). We are animated by this event which vibrates between us at the culmination of our encounter, nourished as much by our limitations as by our potentialities. The soul of our touching each other is this event which exists but does not persist. As therapists, we are creators of beauty. In this sense, we are soul-makers. What relationship can be identified between the beauty which emerges and the beauty of the object?

An objectual work of art – Monet's *Water Lilies*; Gaudì's *Sagrada Familia*; Michelangelo's *Pietà*, or the poem by Merini cited at this convention – may be understood in terms of the miraculous capacity of the form of the material to serve as a vehicle for this momentary nub of vibration in the soul, carrying it through space and time. Yet it always requires a co-creator – who is never a mere receiver in the field – i.e. (s)he who, savouring the work, vibrates in its form. This individual acts as a re-creator who generates the work anew (and it is literally new, an unheard-of novelty) in the present of the situation, since in savouring the work (s)he resuscitates, once more, the breath contained therein. (S)he nourishes the work. A work of art, without anyone who falls in love with it for just a moment, remains a mere possibility, its breath mortified, awaiting resurrection. Living art reveals itself in contact. To pass it by without embracing its beauty is to mortify it. When a work's beauty is embraced, it is revived. And, as Denham-Vaughan writes (2009), the contact with beauty can support us in our darkest hours.

3.2. Distilling beauty

If we draw nourishment from contact with beauty – that we always co-create - and this is the end to which contact and intentionality teleologically spurs us, we are also moved by another equally strong impulse, namely, the urge to enshrine the degree of beauty and of absence encountered in our moments of contact. In this sense, we are living works of art, since we act as vehicles through space and time for the ephemeral breath produced by our encounters[17]. I have written "the degree of beauty and absence" because it is in our nature to conserve both. Indeed, not only is beauty never lost, but neither is absence (which, as we have seen, constitutes psychopathological suffering). This latter remains as a form of living suffering which is carried forward into subsequent moments of contact, seeking out the right moment to be seen and transformed into the beauty of an encounter. As therapists, we are co-creators of such propitious occasions, of such kairòs[18] . To carry interrupted intentionalities through to their conclusions is to bring about their transformation into beauty. This may perhaps transcend the limits of individual existences and also make sense when the intentionality is launched by one party and followed through by another. This concept might explain some transgenerational loyalties, how some individuals seek to conclude tasks begun by their ancestors, or to undertake new ventures of which they will never themselves see the fruits. A few months ago a patient of mine told me about one example of this which I found particularly beautiful. Last summer an old man arrived on foot at a farm house in the Cuneo province and asked to be put up in the barn for one night. He told his hosts that he had come from France, travelling on foot for what was now over a month in order to become a Pélerin Fou – a mad pilgrim. The mission which he had undertaken was the following: eight centuries ago, a group of pilgrims set off from France for the Holy Land. They crossed France and Italy on foot then set sail from Puglia. Unfortunately, they suffered a shipwreck in which many died. The survivors were taken as slaves and none ever reached their destination. This "mad pilgrim," then, had set off for Jerusalem in order to retrace and, finally, to complete their journey. Is such an undertaking really foolish or does it rather display a loyalty to the fabric of life as it unfurls across history? Is the pilgrim a fool or does he stand as witness to the possibility

[17] "A novel, poem, picture, a mmusical work are all individuals, that is, beings in which the expression is indistinguishable from the thing expressed, their meaning, accessible only thruogh direct contact, being radiated with no change of their temporal or spatial situation. It is in this sense that our body is comparable to a work of art" (Merleau Ponty, 1962, 175, quoted in Dastur, 2007, 36)
[18] Kairòs, from the Greek, means 'the right moment'

that our interrupted journeys may also come to be followed through after us by others than ourselves?[19]

During a seminar on bereavement, I treated the grieving process in relational rather than individualistic terms (Francesetti, 2011) and I presented the idea that this process consisted in giving to life the relational goods which have built up with the deceased. I underlined, moreover the fact that this is a powerful impulse which we experience in various different ways, feeling, for example, the need to introduce the gestures, objects and teachings of the person who has left us into our own lives. A participant had an insight: she said that her grandfather died before she was born, but in the family nobody talked about him and she was secretly curious about everything regarding him. She collected all the information regarding her grandfather and all his belongings in a hidden place: 'it was a secret obsession for me!'. She abandoned this 'obsession' when she was seventeen, for no apparent reason. Only many years afterwards did she find out that her father went into therapy when she was seventeen in order to work through his father's death. During the seminar she realized that when she was seventeen her father took care of the memory of his father and in the family field she was relieved from the task of keeping his memories.

As Cavaleri (2007) states, we cherish our relational goods. But these also include the suffering of the relationships we have lived through: we carry both the good and the bad with us, as radiant potentialities of our own presence. Our radiance springs from the beauty encountered (and always co-created). However, it is also the potential radiance that springs forth in exact proportion to the suffering which we cherish. The suffering that we have been through is the potentiality for an explosion of light.

As Alda Merini writes, the weight of one is precisely the weight of the other: beauty is nothing other than the unveiling of a fallen shadow and the light that has been released from it. Ultimately, we all carry with us traces of suffering from the fields that we have crossed, seeking out the right moment to transform them from pain into beauty. This process consists in distilling pain from absence, beauty from pain and can be considered to represent the essence of our work in psychotherapy. In therapy, two people meet in a room. Starting from the fabrics of their lives, they take up their wounded and interrupted intentionalities so as to revive the naked fibres of the portion of life given to them, weaving new threads. They perform their distilling function so attentively that, as one of my patients put sit, "sometimes you can hear the grass growing." They distil pain as if it this were "their sole possible mission."

---

[19] The word history comes from the Greek *histor*, meaning witness (Cortellazzo, Zolli, 1983).

This is why we are ineluctably involved in working on the grief process. This is the period over which pain is distilled into new life, over which two distinct loyalties are elaborated: to life which continues to flow forward to the beat of our hearts, and to the relationship through which we have lived, which must continue to flow through our arteries (Vázquez Bandín, 2009; Francesetti, 2011).

Pain is presence, while psychopathological suffering is absence. Paradoxically, the more suffering, and therefore the more absence and numbness, the more potentiality there is for pain, and therefore for presence. The more psychopathological suffering is present, the more pain has been carried forward, ready to fertilise the shared ground. Suffering becomes a living pain and a new breath where there is the relational support necessary for this to unfold. It proves harmful, instead, where this support is lacking. That those who distil pain into presence cannot do so alone would seem to be a general rule in life. As Paul Valéry writes, we do not arrive at our destination alone – a position that stands in marked contrast to the narcissistic refrain, "We are born and die alone."

3.3. A difficult challenge: what relational meaning in inflicting pain?

Yet what can be said of the pain of those who inflict pain on others? Of those who torture, abuse, rape and kill? What relational meaning can we discern in such cases? In a radically relational vision we can come to grasp the vital intentionality of this act: the pain which cannot be felt by oneself is made to be felt by another creature. This other creature has the possibility to transform it. Such behaviour obviously arouses a sense of repulsion in us, since we react to the intrinsic perversion of the process: an innocent party is made to suffer violence and pain so as to transform the pain of another. The following words by Simone Weil are enlightening on this point:

> The innocent victim who suffers knows the truth about his executioner. The executioner does not know it. The evil which the innocent victim feels in himself is in his executioner, but this[20] cannot feel it. . The innocent victim can only know the evil in the shape of suffering. That which is not felt by the criminal is his own crime. (…) It is the innocent victim who can feel hell. (…) All crime is a transference of the evil in him who acts to him who undergoes the result of the action." (Weil, 1952, 122; 124).

On the transformation of absence into pain and beauty, Weil writes:

---

[20] The executioner

The false God changes suffering into violence. The true God changes violence into suffering. (...) Patience consists in not transforming suffering into crime. That in itself is enough to transform crime into suffering. (...) Purity is absolutely invulnerable as purity, in the sense that no violence can make it less pure. It is, however, highly vulnerable in the sense that every attack of evil makes it suffer, that every sin which touches it turns in it to suffering. (...) Evil is carried out by those who have no knowledge of this real presence. In that sense it is true that no one is wicked voluntarily. (...) That which gives more reality to beings and things is good, that which takes it from them is evil. (*Ibidem*, 122 ff.).

Beauty is necessity which, while remaining in conformity with its own law and with that alone, is obedient to the good." (*Ibidem*, 204).

Pain is transferred until it is transformed: as Jean Paul Sartre reminds us, it matters not so much what has been done to us as what we ourselves do with it.

Considering psychopathology as absence permits us to distinguish it from existential pain, and therefore to distinguish our clinical operations from the accompaniment of individuals experiencing existential suffering. From this perspective, nonetheless, the symptom is a crystallised individual expression of an absence which, once deconstructed in therapy, takes us back to existential and relational events. A panic attack, for example, is an incomprehensible individual clinical symptom, but once it is deconstructed it leads us back to an unknowing and unbearable relational solitude (Francesetti, 2007). In their psychopathological suffering patients carry their suffering relational fields with them into the therapeutic clinic with a request for care that comes, through them, from the very fabric of life itself (Francesetti, 2011):

Those who suffer from depression make a figure of the pain caused by the absence of the other. They thus bring this suffering from the relational field into the open, helping us to recognise and cure it. This healing process touches the relational field in general and thus the very ground of the world itself. Every such healing process has the potential to protect all human beings. Patients suffering from depression (although to a certain extent the same could be said for all human suffering) bear a burden on their individual shoulders which far transcends them. They are afflicted with a pain which belongs to the whole world and which has been transferred to them in their relational interactions. Every time they manage to transform this suffering into awareness, resourcefulness, a new creative adjustment or love, to whatever extent, they cure the suffering of the whole world. They break the chain whereby suffering is transferred across relationships and generations, through a marked accomplishment which is fundamentally ethical in its character.

3.4. An existential perspective: beauty as a driving force of evolution

This clinical vision of suffering and the quest for beauty is in tune with a historical perspective of a teleological character – of a perspective, in other words, which involves the concept of evolution and evolutionary criteria. We might liken this perspective to Alfred Whitehead's conception (1979) according to which the teleology of the universe is directed towards the production of beauty. This is a Darwinian conception of evolution with a different criterion: the winner is not the fittest but the one most able to transform pain into new life. Modern biology has stressed that other criteria should be considered as influencing driving evolution – the criteria of cooperation above all, whose importance grows with the degree of evolutionary complexity (Keltner, 2009; Nowak and Highfield, 2012). In this perspective, (s)he who survives is not the strongest, but the one most capable of creating cooperation, of forging bonds. Yet let us now try to push this idea even further, proposing a new criterion of evolution: beauty. As the anthropologist Francesco Remotti (2011) reminds us, Darwin himself was ultimately struck by the quantity of energy expended by animals and above all by mankind in the production of beauty. Darwin, however, left the question of the evolutionary meaning of this incessant endeavour, which also cost lives, unanswered. From the perspective that I am here presenting, we could affirm that our lives are made for distilling and creating beauty. This is what survives us. It is stronger than our lives because it at once belongs and does not belong to us. It is created with the other and the other will carry it forward, together with us, as it has become the flesh and blood with which (s)he is animated. It will be fertile at every subsequent moment of contact. It will guarantee our presence even in our absence: that which is con-signed (i.e., marked, together) transcends us forever. The passage from pain to beauty is, indeed, also a passage from an individual to a relationship: while pain is of the individual, beauty is co-created.

Why should we not consider the generation of beauty as the driving force of evolution? And, following Whitehead, see evolution as a creative distillation of pain into beauty, in which we are all involved?

One patient, who had been severely abused as a child one day said to me, in extreme anger: "What can you do? What do you think you can do? In the face of all the evils of the world you can't do a thing! What you do is irrelevant in the face of all this horror!" At that moment she was right. Yet it was that very patient who, some years later, defined therapy in the terms of distillation to which I have referred above: as a process of distilling pain from absence and then life from pain. That we might witness life's miracles, every day and as our "sole and possible mission" is a notion which ends a further and fundamental meaning to our everyday therapeutic activities. In my patient's own words: "Distilling: it's an ancient and mysterious art. Yet that's our real and possible mission. We distil pain in order to savour the fragrance of joy."

This outlook also recalls a fundamental existential question with which our founders were much concerned (Laura Perls, 1992; Goodman, 1968a; 1968b): the crucial question of theodicy[21]: "unde malum?." This is the question raised by Job, the innocent and righteous man from whom God took everything: wealth, children and health (Poma, 2005). If God is good and omnipotent, why, then, should the good suffer? This is a question that belongs to all of us when we find ourselves in a state of suffering.

One possible and radical answer is that without evil there could not exist the fruits of that transformation which comes to "distil" suffering into beauty, absence into presence. Through this process, a special and unique quality of love is created which can only be born in limited beings such as our human selves. No God, precisely because of his omnipotence, could produce this love. Indeed, if a God exists he needs us to produce it for him. The creation of love from impotent pain is only possible for a limited creature, which is constitutionally immersed in, and therefore has the possibility to distil such suffering. This vision reveals an endeavour to which all humankind contributes: the production of a unique love which we alone are able to create. And, inasmuch as we are inclined to pursue beauty, we are inevitably creative. In the words of the *Bhagavad Gita* (4:11): "Wherever they may be, men follow in my footsteps."

The following passages from the letters of Emmanuel Mounier (1995), whose seven month old daughter was left in a vegetative state after contracting encephalitis, seems to me to provide a magnificent expression of an encounter with pain and its transformative power. As he is experiencing what is one of the greatest forms of existential suffering, Mounier writes:

> 11 April 1940: (...) Like you I feel a great weariness and a great calm, mixed together. I feel as if the real and the positive are given to us by the calm of the love of our daughter, which is sweetly transformed into an offering, into an transcendent tenderness, which is part of her, which comes back to her and transforms us with her. It seems to me that weariness belongs only to the body, which is so fragile in the face of this light and due to the fact that everything that was habitual, possessive for us with our daughter is now being consummated in a more beautiful kind of love. (...) (62)

---

[21] The term theodicy, coined by Leibniz, refers to a branch of theology. Its etymological meaning derives from the Greek *théos* (god) and *díke* (justice). In other words, it treats of the "doctrine of the justice of God." Leibniz uses the term *theodicy* to refer to the doctrine of the justification of God for the evil present in creation.

28 August 1940: (...) I felt a sadness which touched me deeply, but it was lighter and as if it had been transfigured. And I cannot describe my response thereto as anything other than adoration. (...)(66)

4. Aesthetical Ethics: Ethos and Polis as Roots and Horizons of Aesthetics

*Beauty is necessity which, while remaining in conformity   with its own law
and with that alone, is obedient to the good*
S. Weil

We have discussed how beauty lies at the heart of Gestalt psychotherapy, and the relationship between aesthetics, psychopathology and therapeutic praxis. We have also outlined some bases for the inclusion of the aesthetic criterion as a guide to therapeutic intentionality (Bloom, 2010; 2011). Let us now consider what kind of relationship can be traced between these concepts and the ethical dimension of psychotherapy. Right from its origins, our model has been the incarnation of a vision which is, amongst other things, social, ethical and political. What relationship can be traced in Gestalt therapy between aesthetics and ethics, ethics being, that which guides all our actions, including the therapeutic? And what is the relationship between therapeutic actions and the community?

We have seen that to embrace beauty at the contact boundary is already to orient oneself towards action. In fact, it is already an action in itself. Here, diagnosis and therapy coincide. Just as we can identify an extrinsic and an intrinsic diagnostic process (Francesetti, Gecele, 2009; 2010), so we can also refer to an extrinsic and an intrinsic ethics. The former guides our therapeutic behaviour on the basis of the guidelines set out by the professional community in rules and codes of practice. The second emerges as an orientation directly from the contact (Bloom, forthcoming). Aesthetic evaluation is already an orientation to therapeutic action: we have no need of any external reference to know what to do in the encounter. For this reason, as Sichera (2001) notes, citing Aristotle, our therapeutic work is *phronesis*. It is neither *episteme* (i.e. it does not descend from general principles on the basis of which we decide what to do at a given moment, as might a mathematician), nor is it *techné* (we do not reproduce a proven technique, as might an artisan). A therapeutic action is phronesis – the ability to act in the right way on the basis of the new orientation which emerges from every new situation. Any action, with its correct therapeutic conduct, its ethos, its goodness, springs from aesthetic evaluation at the contact boundary.

For this reason, when we are involved in a pursuit whose beauty touches us we immediately feel that what is happening is good and true. In our experience of beauty thus understood – i.e. not as objectual but rather as emergent and relational – the beautiful coincides with the good and the true. From the Greeks onwards in our culture, and in the languages of many others, such as Chinese

(Cheng, 2009) and Hebrew[22], beauty, goodness and truth do not only correlate but are also indissolubly implicated in each other to the extent that they coincide. The Italian word *bello* derives from the Latin as a diminutive of *bonus* – i.e. good. And it is perhaps no idle chance that in Gestalt psychotherapy we refer to "good form,"

As Laura Perls observes, good form springs from a commitment: from our commitment to make contact, a commitment of our own creation energy and aggressiveness – our willingness to deconstruct and to allow ourselves to be deconstructed, to accept the limits and constraints of the situation, to assume them so as to transform them creatively. All of this makes Gestalt therapy experiential, experimental and existential (Laura Perls, 1992; Bloom, forthcoming).

The right action that emerges from the aesthetics of the moment is born neither by chance nor in isolation from the rest of the world: the background, too, is implicated. The more the ground is rich in the sediment of her/his own experience, of her/his theoretical approach, of her/his relationship with her/his own professional community etc., the more the therapist will be able to nourish her/his presence. All of this functions as a necessary *third party*, which nourishes and stabilises the therapist, that (s)he does not lose her/himself, either in a narcissistically savage form of therapy or in a confluent *folie à deux* with the patient. Intrinsic ethics is born the twin of intrinsic evaluation. In this sense, in Gestalt therapy, we can lay claim to an aesthetic ethics, in which feeling is doing, *aisthesis* is *poiesis*. Both spring from the generation of experience, where subjects form themselves and generate their own unique and unrepeatable contact. Ethics is intrinsically incarnate in the situation. Ours is a *situated ethics* (Bloom, forthcoming).

In considering the therapeutic situation as being constituted – always and inevitably – by the third party present as the ground, we come, finally, to its relationship with politics, since the *polis* represents the third party *par excellence*. And it is this which saves psychotherapy from two risks present in our time: the reduction of the *psyché* to either a biological or to an intimist phenomenon.

4.1. First form of reductionism: Psyché as a individual biological event

The former kind of reductionism is biased towards one or another of the various scientific forms – pharmo-therapeutic, statistic, diagnostic or correlative to biological data. These include the recent "*neuro-mania*" as it has been called by Legrenzi and Umiltà (2009), two neuroscientists who warn against recent

---

[22] I thank Nurith Levi for having focused the Hebrew word 'Yoffi', meaning both *beauty* and *good*.

attempts to explain all human phenomena and behaviours by reducing them to neuronal circuits. As Luciano Mecacci, another neuroscientist who studied under Alexander Luria, has acutely noticed, the majority of neuroscientific research adds nothing to our knowledge of psychology. It rather only describes the biological correlates for processes which psychology has already described[23]. The fact that neuroscientists themselves have been the ones to reveal the abuses being made of their disciplines in the psi- field clearly bears witness to the existence of a temptation to biological reductionism. Too often neuroscientific findings are dragged in to explain things we already know as if they were something new or to unnecessarily introduce experimental data on a different level. With this criticism, I do not mean to cast any doubt on neuroscientific research – which is in fact doing much to corroborate Gestalt theory - *per se*. I would rather advise caution against the aspects of epistemological slipperiness by which it is at times accompanied. For example, there is a tendency to consider a phenomenon "true" if it has a measurable biological correlate, as if only that which is detectable from a third person perspective is true, first person experience being insufficient to grasp experiential phenomena (Skonick Weisberg et al., 2008; Gallagher and Zahavi, 2009; Spagnuolo Lobb and Francesetti, 2010a; 2010b). As Monti and Motterlini write (2012, 29):

> Behind the appeal of neuro-babble lies nothing other than the age-old trap of reductionism. The neuroscience of neuro-images seduces us with the illusion of being able to trace (and therefore to explain) a psychological macro-phenomenon back to its neural micro-components, a behavioural phenomenon back to its concrete and tangible basis. It offers, therefore, not so much any understanding as the illusion thereof, which is produced by confusing the level of description – i.e. of the image – with that of explanation. (...) Indeed, as we gaze in fascination at results in the form of colourful images of the brain, it is important that we do not forget to keep our own brains switched on.

If we forget that "we are not our brains" – i.e. that we cannot have the experiences which we have without a body and a world – this seeking out of neuronal correlates for our experiences comes to represent an undue reduction of life to electro-chemical circuits. The presence of the third party – the world always present in the ground, implicated and implicit in each of our moments of contact – helps us to avoid falling into this kind of reductionism.

---

[23] Paper given at the Expert Meeting of the FIAP (Federazione Italiana delle Associazioni di Psicoterapia – Italian Federation of Psychotherapy Associations), Rome, 6 May 2011.

4.2. Second form of reductionism: psyché as an intimist event

The other kind of reductionism, which is perhaps more dangerous because it is less evident, being intrinsic in the very birth of psychotherapy, reduces the *psyché* of the individual and our encounter with it to whatever happens in the therapy room Our psychic life – our soul, we might say (in an etymological sense, indicating that which renders us animate, alive) – instead comes into being as an emergent phenomenon in the relationship. Yet to consider the *psyché* as a phenomenon emerging from a dyadic relationship is still reductive. The dyadic relationship, in turn, draws its consistency and boundaries from being rooted in a third party ground, made up of the many: of the polis with its myriad and, at times, significant variations. The experiences of individuals become manifest in the single person, but they feed on the whole world.

In our therapeutic practice, we support and distil beauty, but, returning to the objection of my patient, cited above, this can only be meaningful if we do not forget what is going on outside. If the therapist agrees to take care of the psyché in her/his own room without asking him/herself on the meaning of this activity in a broader, global context, (s)he lacks awareness of her/his social role and might even end up maintaining the status quo, becoming an accomplice in keeping the psychic life isolated and cut off from the world, building it a golden cage in the therapeutic practice. (S)he will thus betray fail to live up to the political commitment of psychotherapy, which Laura Perls (quoted by Kitzler in Spagnuolo Lobb and Amendt-Lyon, 2003, 105) summed up, saying that "real psychotherapy is always somewhat subversive of the existing order." Psychoanalysis has been considered as some as the necessary manifestation of a nineteenth century culture which needed a space for those aspects of the psychic life which could not be expressed in society and provoked unease. Psychoanalysis can be thus seen as a social tool for adapting society to bourgeois civility. Aside from the various matters which this reading overlooks, it is nonetheless true that if psychotherapy loses its conscious connection to the third party, if it is unaware of its social position, it risks nowadays becoming the accomplice of a consumerist society which is once again shutting authentic vitality off from the world, protecting it by constructing a *buen retiro*, while the world instead needs its creativity. How can Gestalt therapy reconnect to the political impulse which marked its birth? Perhaps the answer is to insist on a greater communication between the therapist's practice and the world: to bring psychotherapy out of the closed space of the two-way relationship in the room and the world within the therapy. In addition to being aware of the political role we are playing (Robine, 2012), another concrete solution might be to start doing group work again, from small groups to those Life Focus Groups to which Erving Polster (2007) makes reference. At this time of social disconnection, self-improvement groups are again proving relevant, as they did in the 1970s. There is, however, the fundamental difference that, in the 1970s, these groups were responding to the impulse towards the expression of subjective experiences and of freedom. Nowadays, the impulse is radically different: there is a need to experience connections, networks of belonging and constraints and, through these, to discover new paths to follow and the strength and the right to act in the world. Another approach might be to work in public institutions, such as schools. Why should we limit ourselves to treating one teenager with panic attacks when, after a long series of vicissitudes, (s)he finally makes it to our private practice, rather than going directly into schools to teach pupils that, in order to cope with their fear as they go out into the world, they need only take care of their own networks of belonging (Francesetti, 2007)? And even before this, it is necessary to teach children to recognise and value their own sensations, experiences and roles and to use this awareness in their being with others. We might also take Gestalt praxis to organisations and into the world of work. Gestalt therapy is a wider and broader field than Gestalt psychotherapy. Finally, on another level, it is important to find ways to make psychotherapy accessible to more people. It is paradoxical in a market society that although there is a widespread need for support and therapy there is also, at the same time, a growing number of psychotherapists who are struggling to find work. In consumer terms, we need to bring together supply and demand. In other words, to adopt Paul Goodman's political angle, we need to bring psychotherapy to the people, onto the streets, into the squares, to invent an *agorà-therapy* for our times.

4.3. *"Beauty is important: everything else flows down from it."*

After 30 years, the house of the mafia boss that ordered the killing of Peppino Impastato is now part of a foundation that welcomes young people coming from all over the world to learn how to protect civil rights with non-violent methods. To reach this transformation, of course, there has been a lot of pain and struggle. Against this ground, we can rediscover the political relevance of aesthetics, that to which Peppino Impastato referred and lived to the end. An an-aesthetised, in-animate individual may be an efficient producer and consumer (a consumer who uses aesthetic objects to stay an-aesthetised), but not a citizen. How can one be a citizen, if one does not resound with the social field in which one lives, does not feel passion, indignation, does not feel the necessity and the beauty of belonging, of shared soul-making?

"Beauty will save the world," wrote Dostoevskij. I have here sought to define what kind of beauty may save us. Now, to conclude, I would stress that beauty works through us, through the aesthetics of our commitment (Laura Perls, 1992). The world can only be saved through our incessant, passionate, shared seeking out and nurturing of beauty, which is the sensible form of our relational heritage.

As Gestalt therapy teaches us, this is exactly what human beings are made for.

Bibliography

Ballerini A. (2011), *Esperienze psicotiche: percorsi psicopatologici e di cura*, G. Fioriti Ed., Roma.

Bhagavadgita (1999), ed. Marcello Meli, Mondadori, Milano.

Binswanger L. (1960), *Melancholie und Manie,* Neske, Pfullingen (it. trans. Melanconia e mania, Bollati Boringhieri, Torino, 2006).

Blankenburg W. (1971), *Der Verlust der naturlichen Selbstverstandlichkeit. Ein Beitrag zur Psychopathologie symptomarmer Schizophrenien.* Enke, Stuttgart (it. trans. *La perdita dell'evidenza naturale,* Raffaello Cortina Editore, Milano, 1998).

Bloom D.J. (2003), "Tiger! Tiger! Burning Bright." Aesthetic Values as Clinical Values in Gestalt Therapy, in Spagnuolo Lobb M. & Amendt-Lyon N., eds., , *Creative License:. The Art of Gestalt therapy*, Wien-New York, Springer, pp. 63-78.

Bloom D. (2010), The Phenomenological Method of Gestalt Therapy: Revisiting Husserl to Discover the "Essence" of Gestalt Therapy, *Gestalt Review,* 13 (2).

Bloom D. (2011), Sensing Animals/Knowing Persons: A Challenge to Some Basic Ideas in Gestalt Therapy, in Levine Bar-Yoseph T. ed., *Advanced Gestalt Therapy.* Routledge, New York.

Bloom D. (1013), Situated Ethics and the Ethical World of Gestalt Therapy, in Francesetti G., Gecele M., Roubal J., eds., *Gestalt Therapy in Clinical Practice. From Psychopathology to the Aesthetics of Contact*, FrancoAngeli, Milano.

Borgna E. (1988), *I conflitti del conoscere*, Feltrinelli, Milano.

Borgna E. (2011), *La solitudine dell'anima*, Feltrinelli, Milano.

Buber M. (1923, 1996), *I and Thou*, New York, Touchstone.

Cavaleri P. (2003), *La profondità della superficie*, FrancoAngeli, Milano.

Cavaleri P. (2007), *Vivere con l'altro*. Per una cultura della relazione, Roma, Città Nuova.

Cheng F. (2009), *The Way of Beauty: Five Meditations for Spiritual Transformation,* Inner Traditions, Rochester.

Cortelazzo M. & Zolli P. (1983), *Dizionario etimologico della lingua italiana*, Zanichelli, Bologna.

D'Angelo P. (2011), *Estetica*, Laterza, Roma-Bari.

Damasio A. (2010), *Self Comes to Mind. Constructing the Consciuos Brain,* Pantheon.

Dastur F. (2007), The Importance of the Concept of Form in Psychopathology, *International Gestalt Journal*, Vol. 30, N. 1, 31-52.

Denham-Vaughan S. (2009), Ravishing beauty: in our darkest hour what will sustain us?, *British Gestalt Journal,* 18, n. 2, 28-29.

Desideri F. (2011), *La percezione riflessa*, Raffaello Cortina, Milano.

Ferraris M. (2012), *Manifesto del Nuovo Realismo*, Laterza, Roma-Bari.

Francesetti G. (2007), *Panic Attacks and Postmodernity, FrancoAngeli*, Milano (Or. Italian ed. 2005; French ed., 2009; Macedonian ed. 2009; Spanish ed. 2012; Russian ed. forthcoming).

Francesetti G. (2008), La sofferenza della Zwischenheit. Una lettura gestaltica di 'Colpa e sensi di colpa' di Martin Buber, in: *Bertolino L., a cura di, Colpa e sensi di colpa*, Apogeo, Milano.

Francesetti G. & Gecele M. (2009), A Gestalt Therapy Perspective on Psychopathology and Diagnosis, *The British Gestalt Journal*, 18, 2: 5-20.

Francesetti G. & Gecele M. (2010), Psicopatologia e diagnosi in psicoterapia della Gestalt, *Quaderni di Gestalt*, 23, 1: 51-78.

Francesetti G. (2011), Alcune Gestalten delle esperienze depressive, in: Francesetti G. e Gecele M., *L'altro irraggiungibile. La psicoterapia della Gestalt con le esperienze depressive*, FrancoAngeli, Milano.

Francesetti G., Gecele M., Roubal J. (forthcoming), *Gestalt Therapy in Clinical Practice. From Psychopathology to the Aesthetics of Contact*, FrancoAngeli, Milano.

Galimberti U. (1987), *Psichiatria e fenomenologia*, Feltrinelli, Milano.

Gallagher S. & Zahavi D. (2nd ed. 2012), *The Phenomenological Mind*, Routledge, London.

Goodman P. (1968a), Human Nature and Anthropology of Neurosis, in Pursglove P.D., *Recognitions in Gestalt Therapy*, Harper Collins, New York.

Goodman P. (1968b), The Age of Gold, in Pursglove P.D., *Recognitions in Gestalt Therapy*, Harper Collins, New York.

Hillman J. (1997), *The Soul's Code: In Search of Character and Calling*, Bantam Books, New York.

Hillman J. (2002), *Politica della bellezza*, Moretti e Vitali, Bergamo.

Husserl E. (1969), Formal and Transcendental Logic, Martinus Nijhoff, The Hague.

Jaspers, K. (1963), *General Psychopathology* (Trans. from German by J. Hoenig & M.W. Hamilton), Machester University Press, Manchester.

Keltner D. (2009), *Born to be good. The science of a meaningful life*, W.W. Norton &C., New York.

Kitzler R. (2003), Creativity as Gestalt Therapy, in Spagnuolo Lobb M. & Amendt-Lyon N., eds., *Creative license: The art of Gestalt Therapy*. Springler-Verlag, Wien-New York.

Legrenzi P. & Umiltà C. (2009), *Neuro-mania. Il cervello non spiega chi siamo*, Il Mulino, Bologna.

Merini A. (1999), *Aforismi e magie*, Rizzoli, Milano.

Merleau-Ponty M. (2003), *Phenomenology of Perception: An Introduction*, Routledge, New York and London (Or. Engl. Ed.: 1962, Humanities Press, New York)

Monti M. & Motterlini M. (2012), Tutti i colori della neurotruffa, *La Domenica del Sole 24 Ore*, 15 aprile 2012, 29.

Mounier E. (1995), *Lettere sul dolore*, BUR, Milano.

Noe A. (2010), *Out of Our Heads: Why you are not your Brain and Other Lessons from the Biology of Consciousness*, Hill and Wang, New York.Nowak M.A., Highfield, R (2012), *Super Cooperators: Altruism, Evolution, and Why We Need Eachother to Succeed*, Free Press.

Perls F., Hefferline R.H., Goodman P. (1951). *Gestalt Therapy: Excitement and growth in the human personality*, Julian Press, New York.

Perls L. (1992), *Living at the boundary*, Joe Wisong ed., The Gestalt Journal, New York.

Philippson P. (2009), *The emergent self. An existential-Gestalt approach*, Karnac Books Ltd, London.

Polster E. (2007), *Psicoterapia del quotidiano*, Centro Studi Erickson, Trento.

Poma A. (2005), *Parole vane*, Apogeo, Milano.

Remotti F. (2011), L'enigma dell'ornamento. Appunti su alcune pagine di "The descent of man" (1871), *L'ateo*, 3: 19-24.

Robine J.-M. (2006), *La psychothérapie comme esthétique*, L'Exprimerie, Bordeaux. Engl. Publ. (2007) Gestalt Therapy as Aesthetics, *International Gestalt Journal*, Vol. 30, N. 1, 9-30.

Robine J.-M. (2011), *On the Occasion of an Other*, Gestalt Journal Press, Gouldsboro ME (it. trans. *Il dispiegarsi del sé nel contatto*, FrancoAngeli, Milano, 2011).

Robine J.-M. (2011), Psicoterapia della Gestalt 'e' psicopatologia. Nove proposizioni per pensare questo 'e', in La creatività come identità terapeutica. Atti del II congresso SIPG, Torino, 10-12 Ottobre 2008, FrancoAngeli, Milano.

Robine J.-M. (2012), *Le changement social commence à deux*, L'Exprimerie, Bordeaux.

Rossi Monti, M. (2002), *Percorsi di psicopatologia*, Franco Angeli, Milano.

Roubal J. (2007), Depression. A Gestalt Theoretical Perspective, *The British Gestalt Journal*, 16, 1, 35-43.

Salonia G. (2001), Disagio psichico e risorse relazionali, in *Quaderni di Gestalt*, 32-33: 13-22.

Salonia G. (2008), La psicoterapia della Gestalt e il lavoro sul corpo. Per una rilettura del fitness, in S. Vero, *Il corpo disabitato. Semiologia, fenomenologia e psicopatologia del fitness*, FrancoAngeli, Milano.

Sichera A. (2001), A confronto con Gadamer: per una epistemologia ermeneutica della Gestalt, in Spagnuolo Lobb, *a cura di, La Psicoterapia della Gestalt. Ermeneutica e clinica*, FrancoAngeli, Milano.

Skolnick Weisberg D., Keil F.C., Goodstein J., Rawson E, Grey J.R. (2008), The Seductive Allure of Neuroscience Explanations, *Journal of Cognitive Neuroscience*, 470-477.

Spagnuolo Lobb M. (2001). The theory of Self in Gestalt Therapy: A Restatement of Some Aspects, in: *Gestalt Review*, Vol. 5, No. 4, pp. 276-288.

Spagnuolo Lobb M. (2003a), Therapeutic meeting as improvisational co-creation, in Spagnuolo Lobb, M. and Amendt Lyon N., eds., Creative license: The art of Gestalt therapy, Springer-Verlag, Wien-New York.

Spagnuolo Lobb M. & Amendt-Lyon N. (Eds.) (2003), *Creative license: The art of Gestalt Therapy.* Springer-Verlag, Wien-New York.Spagnuolo Lobb M. (2004), L'awareness dans la pratique post-moderne de la Gestalt-thérapie, in Gestalt, Societé Français de Gestalt ed., XV, 27: 41-58.

Spagnuolo Lobb M. & Francesetti G. (2010a), Fenomenologia, *Quaderni di Gestalt*, 23, 127.

Spagnuolo Lobb M. & Francesetti G. (2010b), Metodo fenomenologico, *Quaderni di Gestalt*, 23, 129.

Spagnuolo Lobb M. (2011), *Il Now for next in psicoterapia. La psicoterapia della Gestalt raccontata nella società post-moderna*, Franco Angeli, Milano.

Spagnuolo Lobb M. & Francesetti G. (forthcoming), Behind Hercules' Columns. Gestalt Therapy with psychotic experiences, in: Francesetti G., Gecele M., Roubal J. (2013), *Gestalt Therapy in Clinical Practice. From Psychopathology to the Aesthetics of Contact,* FrancoAngeli, Milano.

Stern N. D. (2004), *The present moment in psychotherapy and everyday life,* W.W. Norton & C. Inc., London, New York.

Stern N. D. (2010), Forms of Vitality: exploring Dynamic Experience in *Psychology, the Arts, Psychotherapy, and Development*, Oxford University Press, Oxford.

Vázquez Bandín C. (2009), Espérame en el cielo, in *Buscando las palabras para decir, Ed. Sociedad de Cultura Valle-Inclán*, Colección Los Libros del CTP, Madrid, pp. 81-106 [Eng. Trad.: Wait for me in Heaven].

Weil S. (1952), *Gravity and Grace*, trans. Arthur Wills, Putnam's Sons, New York.

Whitehead N.A. (1979), *Science and the Modern World*, Macmillan, New York.

Wollants G. (2008), *Gestalt Therapy. Therapy of the situation*, SAGE Publications Ltd., London

Zinker J. (1978), *Creative Process in Gestalt Therapy*, First Vintage Books Edition, New York.

Acknowledgments I wish to thank the editorial board of the *British Gestalt Journal* and their anonymous referees for having improved the present article through their useful suggestions and insights.

Chapter 4. Developmental Somatic Psychotherapy: Developmental Process Embodied Within the Clinical Moment
Ruella Frank

Chapter Introduction

I became a full-member of the New York Institute for Gestalt Therapy in 1987, about six months after beginning my training with Laura Perls. It was my fascination with infant movement patterns in the first year of life that led me to the study of gestalt therapy. I wanted to further my understanding of these movements from a psychological perspective. Although I had completed a four year gestalt training program elsewhere, it was in Laura's Tuesday morning theory/practice group, and later in my weekly theory-supervision classes with Richard Kitzler that I found the solid ground on which to develop my interest — the integrating of movement from a developmental perspective into the therapy experience.

It soon became clear to me that unlike most contemporary psychotherapies, gestalt therapy has always lacked a consistently conceived theory of human development. At the time of gestalt therapy's founding in 1952, human development was regarded as occurring in discrete and linear phases, an assumption that was always disputed by our founders. And although Laura did introduce the beginnings of a developmental theory from her ideas regarding "dental aggression" — the progression of sucking to chewing and its role in introjection — these concepts remained embryonic. To compensate for this deficiency, I saw that many of my gestalt colleagues were turning to developmental theories of other psychotherapy modalities. These other linear, normative and cause and effect based theories do not seamlessly integrate into gestalt therapy's emergent experiential process, leaving practitioners standing on unstable ground. The 1980s brought with it ground breaking infant research, which allowed researchers (Daniel Stern, Ed Tronic, Alan Fogel, Berry Brazelton, et. al.) to begin theorizing that an organizing of self emerges in overlapping waves rather than discrete stages. An ongoing interaction with the past exists in all present experience and moves us toward the future. A developing self was now clearly seen as interactive and dynamic from the very beginning. With this latest infant research, an understanding of contemporary motor theories (Esther Thelen, et.al), my background in somatic therapies and a deeper understanding of gestalt theory, I began to formulate what later became an expansion of gestalt therapy using a developmental, somatic and relational lens.

Although my work has grown and changed since the writing of this chapter (2004), the primary principles of development presented here as well as the two case vignettes that elucidate these principles continue to be germane to our gestalt theory and practice. I cannot imagine an understanding of human development without a comprehension of movement.

I am grateful for the ongoing support and encouragement from my teachers and colleagues at the New York Institute for Gestalt Therapy and am delighted to be part of this book.

Developmental Somatic Psychotherapy: Developmental Process Embodied Within the Clinical Moment[24]

Introduction

As one of the contributing authors to *New Dimensions in Body Psychotherapy*, I am pleased to be part of a project that brings together diverse and novel explorations within the field of psychotherapy. A pre-requisite for any work to be labelled a new dimension is that new parts have been integrated into what is already known in such a way as to create a different and unique whole.

This is certainly true of Developmental Somatic Psychotherapy. Inspired by the work of somatic/developmental practitioners and theorists, this *new dimension* is a relational and movement-oriented approach to psychotherapy within a Gestalt therapy framework. In pulling together these dynamic strands, a template for understanding and working with early psycho-physical blocks as they arise within the here-and-now of the adult therapy session has emerged.

In any process-oriented, present-cantered therapy, embodying developmental theory within session must be firmly grounded in the data of experience, the world of phenomena — what we see, what we hear, what we sense and what we feel. What was *then and there* is an abstraction or cognitive construct and can offer relevant and viable information only if observed in the *here-and-now* of therapy. Developmental Somatic Psychotherapy proves a comprehensive system of phenomenological analysis for practitioners to diagnose and treat their clients through explorations in developmental movement patterns. Simply put, it is a new way of observing and working with the unfolding, moment-to-moment unspoken dialogue of therapy. It is only by understanding how early experiences arise through a variety of phenomena within the client/therapist relationship that we gain access to them.

Developmental Somatic Psychotherapy is not only an expansion of Gestalt therapy — a novel approach within its theory and practice — but also can be quite usefully combined with other psychotherapy models, even those models which do not attend to movement processes. It offers a frame-work for understanding clients' pre-verbal experiences that are often over-looked or misunderstood and left unattended. Thus, existential issues with roots in early life surface with great immediacy. These issues would not emerge as easily, if at

---

[24] *Excerpted from: Totten, N. (Ed.), (2005), New Dimensions in Body Psychotherapy, Developmental Somatic Psychotherapy: Developmental Process Embodied within the Clinical Moment,* Berkshire, England, Open University Press/McGraw-Hill Education. Pgs. 115-127.

all, in other psychotherapies. Fleshing out the greater background from which present behaviors arise enhances the narrative developing within each session, as well as throughout the course of therapy.[25]

Developmental Roots

The origin of my work is in the mid-1970s, when I was introduced to Bonnie Bainbridge-Cohen. An occupational therapist with a background in dance and movement, Bainbridge-Cohen spent years studying and working with developmentally delayed infants. Her keen eye for movement analysis led to unique observations of infant patterns; then applying her observations to their treatment. Knowing that early infant movements also underlie movement possibilities for adults, Bonnie taught her work to dancers and movement therapists; analyzing and working with their movement patterns to provide integration and balanced alignment.

At the time, I was teaching dance and developing a private practice in movement therapy. I was so intrigued with developmental movement that I taught the patterns to my students and private clients, many of whom were Gestalt psychotherapists. They were equally fascinated and reported a variety of changes in their emotional, physical, and psychological states that were difficult for them to verbalize. Interested and encouraged by their reactions, and wanting to make further sense of what was happening, I enrolled in a Gestalt training program. From what I had read and from my personal experience as a client in Gestalt therapy, I believed its holistic approach and use of experiment would enable an almost seamless inclusion of infant developmental patterns within its practice. My intention was to integrate developmental patterns within the psychotherapy session as a means to facilitate insight and change.

After my four years of training were completed, I continued my studies with Laura Perls, co-founder of Gestalt therapy along with her husband Fritz Perls and Paul Goodman. In Laura's weekly group, we focused on the central and unifying concept of Gestalt therapy theory, contacting — the quality of being in touch with ourselves and our environment.

Laura taught that the processes of contacting were primarily and fundamentally supported by coordinated movements. Contacting could not occur without accompanying sensorimotor support. The quality of sensorimotor support influences the quality of contact and vice/versa. Both exist simultaneously and are the essential structure of experience. This was my "Aha!" moment. I now understood that infant developmental patterns, which underlie all possible movement, are also primary supports for contacting.

---

[25] For further information, please see my book, *Body of Awareness: A Somatic and Developmental Approach to Psychotherapy*, GestaltPress/Analytic Press, 2001.

In the 1980s, Daniel Stern and many other researchers and theorists (C. Trevarthen, A. Fogel, B. Brazelton, B. Beebe), brilliantly observed parent-infant interactions in detail. Whereas former psychoanalytic thinking described infant development in discrete stages, these researchers described the emergence of self as a co-creation — a relational event occurring throughout the course of a lifetime. The organizing self arises in overlapping waves and is dynamic. Past continually interacts with present, shaping and being shaped by it. This process-oriented approach supported Gestalt therapy theory's original assertion that self is the interaction of individual and environment in ongoing sequences of creative adjustment, that self is, in fact, co-created by individual and environment.

Almost a decade later, another important piece came together as I discovered the work of Esther Thelen, a motor-developmental psychologist. Thelen challenged former understanding that had dominated the field since the 1950's — that infant movement patterns were a product of brain development alone — a genetically driven perspective. Creating elegant infant experiments, she demonstrated that early movements arise in relation to the environment — gravity, earth and space — as well as the infant's biomechanical potential, and physiology in relation to tasks the infant was exploring and accomplishing. The brain was one of many sub-systems that contributed to these developing patterns, no one more important than the other. Thelen believed that infant patterns of perception and action — developmental patterns — were fundamental to the evolution of the child's mental and social life. From this, I added that the tasks infants explore and accomplish are generally in relation to their primary caregivers and through such dynamic, interaction patterns, the infant's body takes shape — breathing, gesture, posture, and gait — reflecting and expressing that relationship.

My work since then has expanded Laura Perls' concept of sensorimotor support within the client-therapist field with a new emphasis on its developmental roots within the infant-caregiver dyad. Based on the findings of a variety of contemporary researchers, I elaborated the theoretical basis for support from a developmental and relational perspective and have explored its relevance within the client-therapist field. A new approach for psychotherapy emerged, an approach rooted in human development, attending to actual phenomena and drawing on the richness of direct experience, Developmental Somatic Psychotherapy.

It is impossible to go into a detailed explanation of Developmental Somatic Psychotherapy within the confines of these pages, yet this chapter may give the reader some idea of its primary concepts and theoretical underpinnings. The case study at chapter's end demonstrates theory into action.

Developmental Movements: Primary Patterns of Response

If you carefully observe an infant and caregiver relationship, you see the graceful and fluid emerging of ongoing non-verbal interaction. Subtly, yet powerfully, each partner influences the other so that every exchange builds upon that which has occurred just moments before. Patterns of movement begin to form from these creative, spontaneous connections. Each pattern that develops between the partners has its own unique rhythm and style, a kind of improvised dance, reflecting the nature of every interaction. There are as many varied rhythms and styles of movement pattern, as many dances, as there are different relationships.

Developmental patterns are seen most clearly in a variety of transitions in functioning — sucking to chewing, grasping to releasing, sitting to creeping on all fours, toddling to walking. They organize within the daily tasks of caring for an infant: carrying them from one place to another, feeding, hugging, rocking, changing diapers, playing with, etc. Such fundamental exchanges between baby and caregiver contribute to the physiology of the infant and manifest in his individual pattern of breathing, gesture, posture and gait. And because movement patterns are social by nature — meaning that they emerge in relation to another — they accompany the infant's evolving psychosocial experience. Every developmental pattern that emerges, therefore, is a primary response within the relational field and expresses a dominant need at the time of its emergence. *The infant's developing psychological functioning is experienced and expressed through movement.*

Movement patterns form in overlapping sequences throughout development. Earlier patterns do not appear, then disappear, but rather serve as supports for later patterns to surface. One pattern integrates another, creating larger and larger supporting structures contributing to the whole experience. The earlier pattern remains, therefore, part of later and more highly organized experiential processes —sucking provides the foundation for chewing while crawling underlies and supports walking. What came before provides the background for what is next to come. In this way, each developing movement appropriates the structure or internal coherence of the earlier pattern, as well as lends its structure to the forming of the next. Because the infant (and adult) can move from chewing to sucking or walking to crawling at any given moment, background patterns continue to be available and ready for use.

Spontaneously emerging movement patterns become essential supports for contacting and are integrated into the developing nervous system – the quality of being in touch with one's body (me) and the environment (not-me). Contacting is not possible without underlying sensorimotor support, and the sensorimotor system functions only in contacting. They are an indivisible unity. Throughout the process of early development, a newly organizing experience of self – including the differentiation of me and not me — gradually comes into being through movement. It cannot be otherwise.

Patterns take their own form and shape through rhythms emerging over time. Rhythms are seen in the visible changes in bodily tensions[26] as the infant (or adult) moves, and are heard through changes in breath and patterns of speech. Individual rhythms articulate patterns as they develop dynamically within the relational field. Rhythmic patterns that arise between infant and caregiver create emotions as well as characterize them.

We can look at an infant's developing rhythm and style of moving and learn about her contacting style or how she organizes experience. We are able to see her preferences for either high or low intensity of stimulation; how she will live through and express her emotions, how her emotions are sustained and how they dissipate; how she will move toward or away from that which she prefers or does not prefer; her sense of personal space, her preference for relational space; and the energetics (the flow and quality of outward moving energy) she uses in relation to the task she performs.

Fluid functioning and Patterns of Disruption

When the relationship between infant and caregiver is well matched, such that each partner is sufficiently met often enough, movement patterns emerge as graceful and fluid. This does not mean that every infant and caregiver dialogue goes smoothly. Times of difficult adjustments are vitally important in allowing both parties a function in co-creating their relationship. For the infant, especially, these moments of discomfort provide him the opportunity to exercise newly developing functions. This may be learning to tolerate a moderate amount of frustration and accompanying anxiety. The infant also learns something about how to signal his needs most effectively to another and how to cope when they are not met. The caregiver gains similar skills and learns to tolerate her own levels of frustrations and anxieties in adapting to the infant. For both parties, these mildly difficult adjustments are an essential aspect of learning, so necessary to the process of growing.

When too many difficulties occur within the relationship and neither partner is satisfied enough of the time, the infant's emerging movement patterns begin to demonstrate anxious, troublesome disruptions. They appear awkward and less effective in achieving the task at hand. Even in the seemingly simple patterns, for example, rolling from back to belly, the infant cannot easily find the coordination between one part of his body and the other, and in relationship to the environment. The patterns that emerge during these chronically difficult encounters disrupt the infant's maturing neuro-muscular system and inhibit his capacity to be in touch with his body and the environment. When the infant-

[26] J. Kestenberg-Amighi, S. Loman, P. Lewis, M. Sossin (1999). *The Meaning of Movement*, New York, Brunner-Routledge, pg. 24.

caregiver field does not sufficiently mature over time, the inharmonious patterns that develop overpower the infant's newly emerging and highly sensitive system.

Because all patterns are supports for one another, the disrupted pattern comes to dominate the preceding pattern, and influences subsequently emerging patterns. The impediments to movement echo at every level of functioning as contacting episodes emerge without sufficient support. This can appear as diminishing sensory experience, repressing and displacing of affect, inability to regulate emotions, distortion in perception, and difficulty in organizing meaning.

Developmental Pattern and the Adult Therapy Client

Looking — once more — at Laura Perls' notion that sensorimotor supports (or coordinated movements) underlie contacting, it becomes clear how rhythmic patterns organize within the infant-caregiver dyad. Patterns provide flexibility for creative adjusting over time. Similarly, we see how patterns organize in chronic disruptive infant-caregiver fields and produce inhibition and fixation.

Developmental patterns are the foundation for all possibilities of movement, and form not only the body of the infant, but also are present in the structure of adult experience. Watching adults move, therefore, gives us much the same information as to their adult organizing capacities as directly observing infants gives us knowledge about theirs. In fact, with a thorough understanding of how infants develop through movement, we can know something profound about how adults assimilate experience in the here-and-now of therapy. Because patterns organize relationally, they provide psychological material for investigation within therapy. With this knowledge, the therapist now has sufficient ground to understand how his or her clients' movement patterns have emerged in infancy and how they have adapted over time.

When therapists apply this relational and developmental approach, they analyze subtle, rhythmic patterns that continually arise within the client/therapist field. They notice not only the client's fluid and alive movements, supporting clarified and spontaneous experience, but also those movement patterns that do not complete themselves easily, inhibiting experience. Therapists have the ability to not only observe, but breakdown movement patterns into their most basic components and utilize developmental patterns as experiments within session.

This opens the possibility for a variety of explorations. Attending to the incomplete pattern, the client's primary style of contacting is revealed and the function of the chronically fixed pattern becomes known. For example, how does this disrupted pattern support some belief the client has concerning him or herself in the world? In the discovery process, the habitual disruption, initially taken on by the infant or child as temporary assistance, becomes available for use. The existential issue that accompanies the fixation of pattern moves foreground to be worked with and through. And when the client explores a more fluid variation in movement pattern, another choice in contacting is made available. How does the client experience the novelty in contacting —with what degree of curiosity and excitement and what degree of anxiety? In each case, the client's psychological organizing reveals itself through the primacy of movement.

All patterns continue developing in the here and now. They are fundamental to contacting and are present in all experience, forming the present/past and present/future.

Developing Supports for Contacting: Rhythmic Diagnosis

The Story of Jenny

To carry us into the moment of the therapy session is to pull us away from the concept of what is done into the actuality of how it is done. This case study has been distilled from my recollection and detailed notes taken after each session.

These sessions were part of an intensive where my client Jenny and I worked 1 1/2 hours daily for five days. Six months prior to this series of sessions, we had done another five-day series. In general, my psychotherapy practice is conducted on a one-hour-per-week basis. As Jenny lived in Europe, this was certainly not possible so a change in format was necessary. These meetings were the first time that we had seen each other since the fall series. Jenny had come to work with me only months after the sudden, accidental death of her adult daughter. The reader will notice that each of Jenny's movements to emerge during our sessions — her breathing, her gestures, her gait, her posture — express some meaning and communicate how she lives within her world.

In our initial phone conversation, Jenny told me that although her husband and colleagues were very willing to comfort her, she was not experiencing their support. At a loss for words, Jenny wanted to work through the language of her body.

"I just can't talk about this anymore" she had said, "I have to do something else."

"Well, we will have to experiment and see what happens," I told her.

Day One of the Intensive

As the session begins, I take a moment to focus on my body and sensitize myself to my breathing, the level of my muscle tension, any organic stirrings, my state of alertness, etc. All these experiences will become supportive background to the developing session. In placing the locus of attention on my self, my sensory system fine-tunes and allows me to move into a state of readiness – able to flow in any direction with my client. Only now do I turn my attention to Jenny.

Sitting, Jenny appears motionless. Her arms gently rest on her lap. When she moves them, the action is from her wrist and hands alone, while her forearms and upper arms remain sedate. As Jenny breathes, each shallow inhale carves a slender, vertical path from the base of her breastbone upward to her collarbones. Her exhale is even less perceptible. The movement of her abdominal area appears held on both inhalation and exhalation.[27] Now aware of increasing tension in my chest, I take several deeper breaths.

Jenny tells me of an image from a dream that she had after our last series of sessions. Although the dream was many months ago, the image has stayed with her. It is that of a red suitcase. I ask Jen if she might like to unpack her suitcase in order to discover what might be within it. Jen closes her eyes and slowly moves "inside" the image and "inside" herself.

After some time, she tells me that she can visualize the lining of her suitcase. It is "… sort of red. The walls are red, but I can't touch them. They seem far away." Jenny's arms reach out as if to touch the walls on either side of her suitcase. With a perturbed look she continues, "I can't touch them." I watch as she rubs the pads of her fingertips with her each of her thumbs in a constant and easy rhythm.

I invite Jenny to become acutely aware of this motion, "Put all your consciousness into this experience," I say. As she explores her patterning, eyes closed, I notice that her head gradually circumscribes small, subtle circles in the air. Within moments, her lips appear to purse and release, purse and release. I ask her to notice the movements of her lips and, if she is interested, to exaggerate them. At first, Jenny opens and closes her mouth almost imperceptibly, then more boldly. Her tongue stirs and I say, "If you want to, you might include more of your tongue in this motion," and she does.

We sit there for what seems to be quite a while until Jenny's feet begin a pulsation – she broadens and condenses the surface of her soles and her toes stretch and flex. After some moments, Jenny's torso and pelvis become part of the action and begin to twist and compress – one upon the other. Now, a whole-body phenomenon has emerged. Again Jenny says, "I can't touch the lining," sounding more and more frustrated — more and more strained. I notice that her breathing is held or bound on the inhalation and she begins to gasp. While I sit at the edge of my chair, Jenny lives at the edge of her experience.

I have the impulse to reach over and offer my physical presence as a container. I take a few breaths to make sure that this is not my need alone and then take the risk. Moving to the edge of my chair, I place my bare feet on either

---

[27] Fluid inhalation begins at the naval and simultaneously expands upward and outward to the collarbones and downward and outward into the abdominal cavity. Fluid exhalation simultaneously condenses inward and downward from collar bones to naval and inward and inward from pubic bone to naval.

side of Jenny's feet, giving her a boundary that she can press into. My wordless intervention is welcomed. "Please don't leave me," Jenny cries out. I move out of my chair and crouch onto the floor in front of her. I hold the outside of her lower legs with my hands, while my feet remain on either side of hers. Now sobbing Jenny repeats, "Please don't leave me." "I'm here. I'm not leaving," I respond. She moves towards me and we embrace. Her heaving sobs are punctuated by several sharp, staccato inhalations. I feel as if her heart might break — and my own. "I'm here. I won't leave you. I promise." Jenny and I hold onto each other until our breathing has steadied. Only then do I return to my chair as she settles into hers.

Jenny monitors her breathing rhythm and notices that it is now without her familiar gasping. She tells me that the gasping that she felt just moments ago, when she was crying, had been with her all her life. When she was a young child, a teenager, and young mother, she suffered panic attacks. And even now, when she feels unsteady, the gasping returns.

She tells me that on two occasions, one when Jenny was approximately seven months old and the other during her early childhood, her mother had been hospitalized for some months. At that time, Jenny was left with her aunt until mother was well and could return home. And when mother was home, Jenny experienced her as critical and distant. "Your gasping pattern seems to be similar to that of an infant or young child who has been left for too long and is terrified." I say. Jenny says that the experience of not feeling the lining of the suitcase was, indeed, terrifying, and although she did not have the words to really describe what was happening at the time, this experience was familiar to her.

With both arms around her, Jenny holds herself tight. I bring this to her attention. "Now you are providing the kind of container that I provided for you," I say. Jenny rubs her hands up and down her arms in a soothing rhythmic way, breathes deeply and whispers to herself, "I won't leave you."

Structural Analysis:

The work looked as though it was intuitive on my part, but it was merely my attending to what became most obvious within the relational field. The emerging rhythm told me what went before and what will be next — what has been and what will come. I kinesthetically attuned to the field and waited for the rhythm to clarify and to pull me inside itself.

The first rhythmic patterns to clearly grab my attention were observed through the steady, circular movements of Jenny's fingertips and hands, the circling motions of her head, the almost imperceptible opening and closing of her mouth, a stirring/reaching action of her tongue, joined by the broadening and condensing of her feet.

At first, the movement's rhythm was even in its flow and had a low intensity to it and appeared graceful. Then its intensity heightened and the rhythmic flow lost the even quality and grew abrupt and strained. Jenny's breathing became shallow and tight. She gasped repeatedly and I felt my concern build. I sensed where the rhythm was moving and intervened non-verbally, providing support for the next relational step to emerge. In other words, I met and contained her anxious reach and offered her my resistance — something/someone to press into. As Jenny accepted my support (my feet on the outside of each of her feet, my hands placed on the outside of each of her legs), the relevant existential issue underlying the repetitive rhythm spontaneously expressed itself – now that you are here with me, I can feel my terror of your not being here. She then sobbed and continued gasping.

Jenny's primary pattern — sucking/swallowing/breathing— that emerges immediately after birth with its accompanying predominant need (to be met, to incorporate, to feel soothed) was often left unsatisfied in an earlier relational field, and predictably enough, restated itself in the present. It is, in fact, the present/past. As in the infant, the pattern originated at her mouth and spread to her head, hands and feet which expressed a similar rhythmic flow.

The frequent loss of Jenny's primary caregiver now expressed itself as a pattern of reaching/straining with the mouth, hands and feet, gasping for air and, alternately, holding her breath. The breathing pattern, set early in the client's history, was the primary adjustment. Over time, a pattern of depression, punctuated by moments of panic, emerged as a repetitive, "preferred" rhythm. Jenny's movement pattern reflected some deficiency in the satisfaction of sucking/swallowing/breathing. The rhythm restated the world again and again, "I cannot feel you, touching me, touching you." The redundancy shaped and shaded a habitual emotional tone — terror. This emotional constancy forged identity — something to hold onto in an unsteady world. With the repetition of pattern, the entirety of the earlier environment came back each time. Behind this adjustment, the prior waves of panic collided with an exhausted depression and expressed that which had not been adjusted to – a devastating abandonment.

Jenny, now stroking her arms and breathing deeply at session's end, was able to give herself the support that had not been provided by the prior, historic environment and that was essential for her to move through her grief-filled present situation — the accidental death of her daughter.

Day Three of the Intensive

Jenny begins the session with a familiar, agitated depression. "I don't know why I came here....after all......I always return to this experience..... my depression...... it's always the same......I feel so heavy....and weighted down." Each phrase seems to drift out of her mouth and suspend in space.

The recent and devastating loss of her daughter has brought the earlier experiences of abandonment and the accompanying sensations of depression and panic to the foreground. With a lighter, steady, gradual rhythm and firm tone, I tell her, "Of course you're depressed. It seems so natural at this time. As you work through your earlier losses, it will help to heal this recent loss of your daughter. And, as you mourn her loss, it will help to heal your prior losses." I say this with conviction, having been through a similar process.

Jenny looks directly at me. "I believe you," she says, and appears to take heart. She reports that now she has a light and airy feeling inside her chest and abdomen. "I'd like to follow these sensations," she tells me, and closes her eyes. Jenny stays with the novelty of lightness/airiness and reports feeling both excited and "a little scared." Moments pass and I watch as her mouth begins a sucking/reaching movement; her hands/fingers, feet/toes join in the process as they flexibly expand and condense in a gentle, even rhythm; and her torso wriggles as if looking for something to snuggle into. Jenny's movements are flowing and graceful. I roll up several thick, cotton blankets and tuck them along either side of Jenny's torso, giving her something to resist. "This feels right," she says.

After some time, Jenny's arms, which were held close to her body, start to reach out to either side and behind her. She moves forward in her chair and now reaches in my direction, her eyes remaining closed. I have the impulse to extend my hand and meet hers, but wait until I know that it is not my wanting to make something happen, but rather my being part of a larger happening. I move to the end of my chair and grab onto her hand. At that same moment, she also moves forward as if to rise, and we both use each other to pull ourselves onto our feet. Standing, we hold each other's hands and begin to sway side to side. It is unclear which one of us began this rhythmic movement. What is clear is that we both enjoy it. As we sway, I experience the tension held in Jenny's shoulders in my hands.

I now include my feet (separated from each other by about 24 inches) in the sway, and shift my weight from one foot to another exaggerating and slightly changing the movement's rhythm – lift/drop, lift/drop. Then I stamp each foot onto the floor – lift/stomp, lift/stomp, making the movement more of a march as I draw my feet closer together. Jenny opens her eyes and joins me in this different beat. Letting loose our hands, we march away from the chairs and into the studio to use the larger space.

Marching consists of an even up-down rhythm in the vertical plane. I notice that Jenny's march has much more emphasis on the down rather than the up-beat. This creates intensity to the rhythm and gives it a held rather than free quality. Once brought to her attention, Jenny exaggerates this downward movement and finds words for her experience. "I won't. I won't," she shouts. Jenny realizes that she is saying this to the mother of her childhood. "I feel such defiance when I say this. It's very familiar. This describes my relationship with her," she says. I ask her to pay attention to her throat as she shouts "I won't," and she senses a familiar tension there – part/whole of her pattern of defiance.

I invite Jenny to try something different. I ask her to give more emphasis to the up-beat while she marches. This will make the pattern more even and free flowing. Jenny practices this new pattern and soon "I won't" changes to "No." which she speaks with a newly freed energy. Now there is no holding in her throat.

In a prior session, Jenny told me how difficult it had been to express the depth of her grief about her daughter's death to her colleagues and friends. She would start to tell them how she felt, and soon would begin to worry about their needs, putting her own in check. I found a phrase that might serve as her mantra — "Right now, this is more about me than about you."

In this session, I ask Jenny to march right up to her colleagues and friends and repeat her mantra. "Right now, this is more about me than about you," she says several times and with great enthusiasm. Jenny then decides to say this to her mother. This time she not only enjoys the statement, but the presence of her mother as well.

Structural Analysis

The first rhythm to organize our relational field was Jenny's vocal pattern of drifting/suspending — I don't know why I came here...I always....my depression.....it always...etc. I chose not to echo what I sensed was habitual, but rather to influence the pulse of the relational field by creating a different rhythm (and tone). I met the low intensity of her drifting/floating rhythm with one that was lighter, steady and gradual. This shifted Jenny's experience from "heavy and weighted down" to "light and airy."

Following this experience, Jenny moved into a flowing rhythm of sucking/swallowing/breathing that moved throughout her entire body. Her reach extended beyond the environment of her body, and towards me. I reached back offering leverage and assistance. For a reach to emerge as fluid, there must be an appropriate source of response. We grasped onto each other, pulled ourselves up and out of our chairs, and easily fell into a swaying rhythm with our arms – side to side. Jenny had moved smoothly from the earlier suck/swallow/breath rhythm of an infant to the later soothing swaying rhythm of a young child. Sensing the tension in Jenny's shoulders, I took the initiative to start a different rhythm – the march.

The even up/down vertical rhythm of the marching pattern has its roots in the chewing or dental aggressive pattern (beginning in the sixth month to the 24th - 30th month). It is a pattern of differentiation — push/release, push/release. I thought that the chewing/marching pattern would more clearly diagnose the interruption that I noticed in Jenny's sway — her unaware and held shoulders that prevented her feet from fully contacting the earth and supporting her — and it did. Jenny's emphasis on the down-beat of the march demonstrated a lack of rebound (push/release) in the pattern. There was much intentionality in the intensity of the rhythm's downward stroke.

When she experimented with the emphasis on this downward stroke, her defiance emerged. It was not merely a chronic physical pattern, but rather part of the entirety of experience — the mother/daughter dyad of her childhood, which was reinforced with her every step. As Jenny balanced the upward/downward stroke, the pattern lightened in intensity and became more symmetrical. (Her push was now freed). Defiance transformed into a more fluid "No!" A change of rhythm changed the quality of the whole and a new relation emerged.

Post-Script

At the end of our five-day series, Jenny stated that she would not be coming back to see me. She had accomplished what she had wanted to do, and believed that now she could do the remaining work of her mourning with friends, family and colleagues. And I agreed.

References

Bainbridge-Cohen, B. (1993). *Sensing, Feeling and Action*. Northhampton, MA: Contact Editions.

Frank, R. (2001). *Body of Awareness: A Somatic and Developmental Approach to Psychotherapy*. MA: Gestalt Press/Analytic Press.

Kesternberg, J. (1965). The Role of Movement Patterns in Development II: Flow of Tension and Effort. *Psychoanalytic Quarterly* 36, 356-409.

Kestenberg-Amighi, S. Loman, P. Lewis, M. Sossin (1999). *The Meaning of Movement*, New York: Brunner-Routledge.

Perls, F., Heffeline, R., and Goodman P. (1951). *Gestalt Therapy: Excitement and Growth in the Human Personality*. New York: Julian Press.

Perls, L., (1993). *Living at the Boundary*. New York: Gestalt Journal Press.

Stern, D. (1985). *The Interpersonal World of the Human Infant*. New York: Basic Books.

Thelen, E., Smith, L. (1993). *A Dynamic Systems Approach to the Development of Cognition and Action*. Cambridge, MA: MIT Press: Bradford Book Series in Cognitive Psychology.

Chapter 5. Aggression and Conflict in Post-Modern Society and in Psychotherapy

Margherita Spagnuolo-Lobb

Chapter Introduction

When I think of my relationship with the NYIGT, many vivid memories crucial to my contribution to gestalt therapy come to my mind.

First, I think of my therapist and former trainer, Isadore From. He introduced me to the Institute, and to the book by Perls, Hefferline and Goodman.

But my "official" story with the Institute started in 1997 when the NYIGT and my Italian "Istituto di Gestalt HCC" organized the "transatlantic dialogue," conference in New York. There all of us, Italians and New Yorkers, presented their ideas in written form. There I met Ruella Frank, Dan Bloom, Joe Lay, Richard Kitzler, Lee Zevy, Gail Feinstein, Karen Humphrey, Susan Gregory, Carl Hodges, and many others. I joined the institute in that year.

In 1998, I organized the 6th European Conference of Gestalt Therapy, as chair of the European Association. I think 14 people from the NYIGT participated. Carl Hodges supervised the work with group process— first time this was used in a European conference. I nominated the NYIGT to become an honorary member of the European Association. The Europeans didn't agree with that proposal. The "split" between Californian Gestalt therapy, the Cleveland and New York models was still deep. Many Europeans, ignoring the early history of the EAGT, continued to think that Gestalt therapy hadn't been founded in New York, but in California, by Fritz Perls,

In 2001, the NYIGT and my institute did a fantastic experiment— what was then called "the miracle of Lipari." Some 14 members of each gathered on Lipari, one of the Aeolian Islands close to Sicily. The experiment was to be in a leaderless group for 7 hours a day for 5 days. Not all of us could speak English or Italian, so much of the interaction was through our non verbal contact. The "miracle" was that at the end we all experienced a great personal power in the group setting, the freedom to be spontaneous and in contact with all the others. We ended with the magical sense of being recognized and seen at a group level and of being deeply rooted in that group event. It as in 2001 that I had the honor of becoming a full member of the institute.

After Lipari, I did many things with the Institute and its members. Richard Kitlzer and Dan Bloom were part of a conference in Naples (organized partly by me) in 2002. Dan shared the plenary events with Claudio Naranjo, who accused the NYIGT of having spoken badly of Perls at his New Yorker funeral—among other things. I and members of the NYIGT, presented together at the EAGT conferences in Prague, Athens, and Berlin. Dan Bloom (editor-in-chief), Frank Staemmler, and I co-edited the International journal *Studies in Gestalt Therapy.*

Dialogical Bridges, from 2007 to 2009. That journal was co-published by the NYIGT, Zentrum für Gestalttherapie, and the Istituto di Gestalt HCC.

The NYIGT is one of the very few places where it's possible to talk of serious theoretical matters and then go to dance and feel free in our bodies and our minds. It's my home.

My recent book *The Now-for-Next in Psychotherapy. Gestalt Therapy Recounted in Post-Modern Society*, published in 2013 in its English edition, expresses my model and the NYIGT is its natural home. I'm proud now to "donate" part of a chapter of that writing of mine, to this book edited by Dan Bloom and Brain O'Neill (whom I heartily thank) in honor of what the Institute has become now. I'm proud of being a Gestalt therapist and Full Member of the NYIGT.

Aggression and Conflict in Post-Modern Society and in Psychotherapy[28]

> The relations that exist between individual and society, and between social groups, cannot be understood without considering the problem of aggression. . . . [T]he remedies prescribed for aggression are always the same old ineffective repressive agents: idealism and religion. We have not learnt anything about the dynamic of aggression in spite of Freud's warning that repressed energies not only do not disappear but may even become more dangerous and more destructive if driven underground (Perls, 1969b, p. 7).

1. Aggression[29] and Conflict: Anthropologies Compared

Work on the feeling of aggressiveness and on conflict in Gestalt therapy deserves a discussion of its own. All psychotherapeutic approaches give their own answers to these questions: What is the role of conflict in human relationships? Is it always a sign of dysfunction? Is aggressiveness always a destructive, negative feeling? The answers have to do with the idea that each approach has of human nature and of the relationship between individual and society.

Aggressiveness is seen in Gestalt therapy as a primary positive strength in that it is linked to the vital energy of biting, to the ability to deconstruct realities in order to create (or co-create) a new reality. It resides above all in the body and for this reason may be disturbing. Powerful anger (whether triggered by the religious, ideological, or amorous need to belong, or by the need for power) may carry us beyond any logic belonging to the categories of social living.

That aggressiveness is part of human nature is obvious, but this does not guarantee that it will be considered as positive. Psychological theories, in fact,

---

[28] This chapter is part of my recent book *The Now-for-Next in Psychotherapy. Gestalt Therapy Recounted in Post-Modern Society*, Milan: Franco Angeli, 2013 (in this chapter referred as "the book"). Most of the content is a part of chapter 5, other parts are taken by the Introduction. The whole book treats core concepts of Gestalt therapy in nowadays society, then offers a new perspective on the Oedipus complex (transformed by the triadic phenomenological field), and my models of Gestalt therapy with couples, families, groups, and training. The book can be ordered at www.amazon.com in, both electronic or paper versions.

[29] I use the word "aggression" here to be coherent with Perls' language (*Ego, Hunger and Aggression*, 1942). Perls referred to the act of "*ad-gredere*" (from the Latin, "going to-wards"), stressing the need of society and human beings to deal with aggression as a real act, a movement not a mentalized feeling. Aggression refers to the act of ad-gredere, while ag- gressiveness is the related feeling. I use the two terms in this sense.

generally consider it a destructive force because it conflicts with the demands of social living. It is clear that this perspective has at its base a certain kind of anthropology. This anthropology is fundamentally pessimistic in that it does not consider the possibility of self-regulation and dichotomizing in that it polarizes realities and experiences between good and bad, individual and social, mental and bodily, political and private, etc. Considering aggressiveness rather as a strength that is fundamental for the survival of the human being and also for a solution of social problems that does not *a priori* sacrifice individual needs, implies a positive anthropology that is open to the possibility of integration of physiology with respect for the social rules, hence with faith in the human being's ability to self-regulate even at a social level.

The reason why Frederick Perls detached himself from psychoanalysis (cf. Perls, 1942) was precisely because of his conception of aggressiveness that was different from that implicit in Freudian theory. He understood aggressiveness as a biological strength fundamental for survival, not only physical/ animal survival, but social too. It was precisely through this consideration of the physiology of the experience that the founders of Gestalt therapy (appealing to the European tradition of phenomenology and of existentialism and to the American tradition of pragmatism[30]) proposed to go beyond the dichotomies between the mental event and the physical experience, between individual and social needs. In the concept of "experience of contact in the here-and-now," the two poles are integrated, and physiology fully reclaims its place in the phenomenological field of being-with, of social reality.

In practice, Perls linked what were traditionally defined as the "individual experience of aggression" and "social experience of conflict" in a conceptual continuum. Aggressiveness permits us to reach not only an object useful for survival (food), but also the Other, a part of the environment that is equally useful for survival. *Ad-gredere* the Other means reaching her/him, "biting her/him" to make her/him one's own, not to annihilate her/him. Perls' epistemological operation was not easy. In fact, his idea of dental aggression as criticism of the developmental theory of psychoanalysis was unsuccessful when he presented it at the Marienbad congress of the International Association for Psychoanalysis in 1936. It implied liberation from the concept of the death drive, and hence from the super-ego and from many other theoretical and methodological frameworks that were holding up the structure of a culture based on the dichotomies of good-bad, healthy- sick and so on.

From introjection as a fundamental method of learning (and of change) proposed by the post-Romantic culture of the early 20th century (which was the cradle of dictatorships, of the patriarchal family, of the sense of belonging as obedience) in which psychoanalysis was born, the focus was moved to "dental

---

[30] See Chapter 2 of the book, dedicated to the theory of self (Spagnuolo Lobb, 2013, pp. 67-93).

aggression," to rebellion and to the differentiation of the self as a model of *normal* growth. The child's physiological ability to bite was considered to correspond to the psychological ability to deconstruct reality. So the patient, in order to grow, must be able to say no, must be able to rebel, even against the psychotherapist. This was precisely the opposite formulation to the psychoanalytic, which instead considered it necessary for the patient to accept the analyst's interpretation, with a view to ensuring the positive transference and therefore the cure.

The developmental evidence for dental aggression became the link to propose a different, more positive anthropology which made it possible to pass from the polarization between individual needs and social demands to their integration, by way of a process of deconstructing and reconstructing the meanings created in the relationship (see Spagnuolo Lobb et al., 1996).

We may schematize the difference between the two anthropological trends as follows:

From intrapsychic anthropology....	*....to Gestalt anthropology*
Human being – culture separation Nature – culture separation	Unitary nature of the developmental processes among human being – nature – culture
Pessimistic perspective on the human being	Positive perspective on the human being
Aggression as destructive, negative strength	Aggression as indispensable strength for survival

The conflict between persons, the social result of aggressiveness, is seen in Gestalt therapy as part of normal development of relationships. This offers the possibility of working through the differences without any one emerging at the cost of others, reaching a new, unimaginable co-created reality, in which each can emerge with her/his own individuality and with the satisfaction of having "won" a unique sense of being-there in the social community. In every aggressiveness, then, it is possible to trace an intentionality of contact, and in every conflict that results from it there is a potential for improving the contact[31]. The question the Gestalt therapist asks her/himself in situations of conflict is: what intentionality for the co-creation of the contact is there in the parts involved in that particular conflict?

---

[31] We shall see how, in the clinical example that follows, the patient does not intend to destroy the therapist, but to emerge with his own energy and individuality.

At the origin of the conflict, in brief, is the desire to make a positive contribution to the situation. Going through the conflict means having faith in the self-regulation of the relationships. This is what the founders of Gestalt therapy themselves have to say, "Our differences were many, but by bringing them forth rather than politely concealing them we many times arrived at solutions that none of us could have anticipated." (Perls, Hefferline and Goodman, 1951, p. 13)[32].

2. The Role of Aggression in the Social Context and the Concept of Psychopathology as Unsupported "Ad-gredere"

Fritz Perls' intuition on childhood development, which gives value to the deconstructing implicit in the development of the teeth (*dental aggression*, Perls, 1942), is based on a conception of human nature as capable of self-regulation, a positive concept as compared with the mechanistic conception in force at the turn of the 19th-20th century (with which Freudian theory was imbued) which gave no room for individual creativity. The child's ability to bite supports and accompanies her/his ability to deconstruct reality. This spontaneous, positive, aggressive strength has a function of survival, but also of social interconnection, and allows the individual to actively reach what in the environment can satisfy her/his needs, deconstructing it according to her/his curiosity.

The physiological experience of *ad-gredere*, which supports the more general organismic experience of going towards the other requires oxygen. It has to be balanced and supported by exhalation, a moment of trust towards the environment in which the organism relaxes its tension and control, to go on to take another breath (and oxygen) in a spontaneous, self-regulated manner. The pause in control, letting oneself go to the other or to the environment, is the fundamental cue for the control/trust rhythm to be able to occur spontaneously, in order to reach the other balancing active and restraining presence, creativity and adjustment, assimilating the constitutive novelty of contacting the other.

When this support of oxygen is lacking, excitement becomes anxiety. The definition we give of "anxiety" in Gestalt psychotherapy is in fact "excitement without the support of oxygen." The physiological support to reach the other is lacking. The contact comes about in any case (it could not fail to come about as long as there is the self, or as long as there is life), but the experience is characterized by anxiety (Spagnuolo Lobb, 2004). This implies a certain desensitization of the contact boundary, In order to avoid perceiving anxiety, it is

---

[32] Ed Nevis (2003, p. 293) relates, "What I remember most from my early studies with Fritz Perls, Laura Perls, and Isadore From is the almost relentless way they pushed me to look at my objections to considering a thought, an action, or an insight. Fritz kept asking: "And what are your objections...?"... "And what are your objections...?," on and on. It was not required that I change my attitude or behavior; but it was imperative that I achieved enriched awareness of the potential to be different, if I so desired."

necessary to put to sleep part of the sensitivity in the here and now of contacting the environment; the self cannot be fully concentrated, awareness decreases, the act of contact loses the quality of awareness and of spontaneity[33] .

For this reason, the Gestalt therapist looks at the bodily process of the patient-in-contact, and suggests breathing out in the event that s/he sees that, concentrating on a significant experience, s/he is not exhaling fully. The therapist knows that in this case the patient's physiological experience is of an excitement without the support of oxygen, s/he knows that the patient is distracted at that moment from the therapeutic contact and cannot assimilate any novelty contained in it. In other words, the therapeutic contact cannot come about without the support of oxygen, in that the change for Gestalt therapy concerns all the psycho-corporeal and relational processes. It is necessary to suggest to the patient that s/he breathe out in order to have the support of oxygen to accept the novelty brought by the therapeutic contact.

Gestalt therapy thus wonderfully puts together the "animal" soul and the "social" soul, for centuries considered mutually antagonistic in western philosophical culture: if the contact is a super-ordinate motivational system, there is no separation between instinctive motivation for survival and social gregarious motivation[34].

The emphasis Gestalt therapy puts on relationality thus has an anthropological valence in considering self-regulation (between deconstruction and reconstruction) of the organism/environment interchange and a socio-political valence in considering creativity a "normal" outcome of the individual/society relationship. Creative adjustment is in fact the result of this spontaneous strength of survival that allows the individual to be differentiated from the social context, but also to be fully and importantly part of it. Every human behavior, even pathological behavior, is considered a creative adjustment.

The concept of *ad-gredere* finds its Gestalt application in the formation of the contact boundary.

3. Aggression, Conflict and Intentionality of Contact in Post-Modern Society

What has been said thus far briefly summarizes the revolutionary perspective of Gestalt therapy has on aggressiveness and conflict. The crucial part of this is the faith in the individual's intentionality of contact, in the desire of

---

[33] These concepts are the basis of the theory of Gestalt psychopathology (see Francesetti et al., eds., 2013).

[34] Daniel Stern's theory of implicit relational knowledge as a superordinate motivational system in humankind confirms the intuition of the Gestalt theory of contact, brought to light a good 50 years earlier (see Spagnuolo Lobb *et al.*, 2009).

every human being to be seen and recognized for the *positive* contribution s/he wants to make to the conflict with her/his full, spontaneous presence, and above all in the conviction that this implies a self-regulation of social relationships. The social community should therefore accept the *uncertainty* that derives from this trust[35] : the regulation of the group is in fact autogenous, it does not require a control of good and evil with rules imposed from outside.

The good is trust in human nature.

This perspective is profoundly ethical[36] (Bloom, 2013) and probably cannot be maintained from the point of view of political power since political power it is the opposite of trust in human nature. This perspective challenged society in the years of "new age" (the slogan of the disciples of Gestalt in the 70s was "Gestalt is a way of being, not just a psychotherapy") and followed perfectly in the footsteps of the narcissistic society, which sought support for individual autonomy[37].

Today, this perspective on aggressiveness and conflict continues to challenge society in a twofold sense. On the one hand, post-modern society is familiar with the sense of uncertainty that derives from the lack of stable points of reference, and hence is readier to accept the idea of self-regulation. In a society in which there is no longer certainty about anything, in which even the respectable next door neighbor may turn out to be a terrorist, or the air we breathe may be poisoned, self-regulation is the form that may be taken by the need to believe in something positive.

On the other hand, the feeling of aggressiveness no longer has the emotional structure that it had 60 years ago, As a social feeling it actually seems to be detached from conflict, which is its relational context. People are aggressive for no reason. Aggressiveness is felt without the perception of an experiential background that might contain it and give it direction. Aggressiveness has become dangerous precisely because it is not supported by the sense of the relationship to which it belongs. One may kill at any age and for any futile reason (or without reason).

As we shall see better further on in this chapter, young people today, when they are aggressive, seem angry with the world (understood in undifferentiated terms), they have a psycho-physical disturbance typical of those who are not nurtured, contained, calmed by the arms of someone who loves them. The negative energy unleashed in their bodies unheard, unseen, gallops unreined and strikes someone at random, in the hidden hope of being stopped (Spagnuolo Lobb, 2009). Since the lack of relational containment has not

---

[35] For a definition of the concept of uncertanty, see Staemmler (2006),

[36] See Chapter 10 of the whole book, *Training in Gestalt Therapy*, Spagnuolo Lobb, 2013, pp. 252-274.

[37] See *Introduction* of the book, Spagnuolo Lobb, 2013, pp.21-33.

permitted the differentiation of the self in the growth of the young, now, in consequence, they behave in a confluent manner: shooting or killing is unsubtle, makes no distinctions: it strikes in the mass, in the fog of a confluent perception.

These young people must be provided with strong arms that can contain and relax the terrible stress they feel at having to live without the nurturing other in an agonizing solitude in which everything is a demand for performance, arms that can make them rest and concentrate on the emotions, on the direction of the excitement they feel, so that they may finally identify "who I am and what I want of you."

4. Working Through Conflict in the Therapeutic Contact: a Clinical Example

I should now like to give a paradigmatic example of classic Gestalt work with aggressiveness and conflict. [38]

P.: I know I have to choose whether to spend the evening with my girl¬– friend or with my friends... (his breathing is strained and he does not look at the therapist).
T.: What do you feel now?
P.: Anger.
T.: Can you look at me?
P.: (looks at therapist)
T.: What do you feel?
P.: (continues looking at the therapist, breathes deeply, then) When I look at you my anger grows. That scares me...
T.: What do you think?
P.: On one hand I think that– like everybody – you expect me to choose. On the other I think you could understand me...
T.: And what do you feel in your body?
P.: If I look at you, I feel anger growing in me...
T.: Where, in what part of your body do you feel anger?
P.: In my chest and a bit in my legs.
T.: Let's stand up.
(They stand facing each other).
T.: Plant your feet firmly on the ground, breathe deeply and feel your pelvis... look at me and let your anger move your body.
P.: (Breathes, concentrates, looks at the therapist, then...) I'd like to stamp my feet...
T.: Do it... and add words for me.
P.: (Stamps his feet, first slowly, then increasingly within the movement, which becomes rhythmic, intense, looks intensely at the therapist, breathes and...) I don't

---

[38] Later in the book I offer a proposal for clinical intervention with more problematic cases of a-contextualized aggressiveness, typical of the "liquid" society.

want you to decide for me... I don't want anybody to decide for me... I want to be the one that chooses my life... I want to be the one that chooses what to do.

The rhythmic movement is in complete harmony with the increase of anger and with the trust felt by the patient that this anger can be accepted by the therapist. The therapist, with her glance and her own breathing, in tune with him, supports this development of the patient's physical and relational experience. When the wave of the experience is calmed, the patient seems exhausted, but whole.

T.: What do you feel now, in your body and towards me?
P.: I feel more myself... my body is part of me now... towards you I feel... peace... and I thank you for being with me.

The patient's face is more luminous and his body more harmonious (Bloom, 2003). The space between therapist and patient is clearer and breathing is easier.

The creative solution is achieved only after the divergences have been gone through, and is always a new, unexpected solution.

5. From the Need for Aggression to the Need for Rootedness: a New Clinical and Social Perspective on Conflict

Returning to the problems of aggressiveness in contemporary society, psychosocial analyses today reveal a change in relational capabilities. As described in the Introduction, to my book after what was called the "narcissistic society" (1970s-1980s) (Lasch, 1978), which later developed into what some defined as "borderline society" and others "technological" (Galimberti, 1999) (1980s-2000), today the term used is "liquid society" (Bauman, 2000), characterized by the lack of relational support and consequent lack of self-support. This development of social needs influences both the perception of people in general and the individual experience of conflict.

Some decades ago, in the period of greatest diffusion of Gestalt therapy (1960s-1970s), the feeling of aggressiveness was linked to the fulfillment of the self and associated to the capability of independence from authoritarian figures. Today aggressiveness is perceived by individuals with a certain "liquidity," without the support necessary to make its expression functional in contact. What is missing is the ground of taken-for-granted certainties that derives from earlier assimilated contacts. For this reason the act of deliberating (identifying oneself with or alienating oneself from parts of the environment, *ego-function* of the self) cannot be clearly defined against the experiential background (*id-function* and *personality-function* of the self)[39].

Social feelings become increasingly "liquid." They may take many forms and at the same time have neither containment nor structure. Children at school, for instance, cannot stay still, they have to keep moving continually, they are not accustomed/brought up to concentrate and breathe. Their breathing has no container; the experience of a whole body that contains the emotions is lacking.

This experiential system seems not to give place to a positive anthropology of self-regulation. It is difficult to speak today of positive aggressiveness. Anything at all may be done at the instant of aggressiveness, even killing. The 21st century is strewn with acts of violence by young adolescents, often from families that seem beyond suspicion. Simply by way of example, I mention the case of Erika and Omar, two teen agers of 14 and 16 who, after ferociously killing Erika's mother and younger brother, went out for a beer[40], or the case of Lorena, the 14-year-old Sicilian girl murdered with cold brutality by three youngsters of the same age with whom she had begun an adolescent sexual game (see Spagnuolo Lobb, 2008) or Kim, the German boy who in a moment of madness used his father's weapons to kill 15 innocent youngsters, ex-schoolmates, and a passer-by (see Spagnuolo Lobb, 2009). We might relate many similar episodes, in which, faced with the question "Why did you do it?" The youngsters often answer "I don't know."

It appears, then, that aggressiveness is experienced without conflict, an unreined aggressiveness, without relational intentionality.

5.1. The Social Denial of the Need for Rootedness

Western society has moved from the *denial of aggression* (lamented by Perls) to *the denial of the need for rootedness*. In the modern era, idealism and religion have been the two great systems of removal of opposition and of individual criticism (see Galimberti, 2006, but also Perls, Hefferline and Goodman, 1951, pp. 9-11). If this leveling of individual difference responded to the social and cultural strategy of denying aggression, a parallel leveling carried out by contemporary society may be identified in the denial of people's need for rootedness. I am referring to the move away from mass communications and legislative commitment in young people's need for work. Most of young people are only temporarily employed or are without work; again, the need of immigrants to find a place to live, the need for primary good relationships for

---

[39] I develop a clinical and theoretical descripton of these terms in Chapter 2 of the book (Spagnuolo Lobb, 2013, pp. 67-93).
[40] On this, see the opinion of Umberto Galimberti on the anesthetized state of the young (Spagnuolo Lobb, 2010).

children, who very often suffer from the physical or relational absence of their parents (who are away from home or distracted), irrespective of whether they are separated or not. I do not think we are sufficiently aware of (nor have we been helped to realize) the degree to which children, from birth, live in a condition of affective abandonment, of how rare it is for parents and children to have a close physical relationship 24 hours a day, which should be normal at least in the first year of life. Children today grow up adjusting to the absence of caregivers, developing anxiety towards the containment of their emotions and accustomed to not sharing them (the other is not there or is always busy, or may be a pedophile whose intentions are evil).

This condition does not improve as the years go by. Indeed, society shows itself to be increasingly demanding and falsely nurturing. The school demands the ability to concentrate and devotion to study; entering a university is sometimes a gamble; work, if one finds a job, requires notable sacrifices and offers few guarantees. Affective relationships, in these conditions of stress, are an optional extra that is not always relaxing, or a niche in which to rest and sleep (instead of exercising one's relational creativity).

The experiential condition of young people today is that of having to find one's direction very quickly in a complex world, in which the educators – parents and teachers – know less than those they are educating (Spagnuolo Lobb, 2011). Think of the world of internet and of those working relationships that are based on values very different from those of 20 years ago. Young people have to find their way without a clear perception of where they are going, of the balance between themselves and the environment, and they have to do this quickly. The videogame goes ahead without pause and waits for no one. They learn to face up to this emergency by means of trial and error and cannot waste time between one match and the next. Sometimes they do not even know whether they have won or lost the "matches" they find themselves playing. They cannot relax, there is no orientation phase in their lives - too many emergencies, too little time and no adult who knows more than they do.

Patients today are "liquid" too. They suffer from disorders that have to do with the lack of the ground of taken-for-granted experiences –panic attacks, PTSD, eating disorders, serious psychopathies (see Francesetti, 2007). Their experience is characterized by a lack of relational support and, consequently, a lack of self-support.

In short, if 50 years ago society showed insensitivity to individuals' need for differentiation and rebellion against pre-established authority, today it shows insensitivity towards individuals' need for rootedness.

5.2. The Co-Creation of the Ground as Rootedness

What is missing in our society is the ability to be in a relationship starting from *the containment of the initial chaos*, which would allow individuals to experience that sense of taken-for-granted security that comes from the "obvious" presence of the significant other and from which the differentiation of the self may emerge. The relational ground on which the experience of novelty can rest is missing. The experience of the aggressive emotion needs to be supported with a relational ground, in such a way that it can lead to contacting the other rather than to its indiscriminate destruction. Without the sense of solidity of the ground, the figure cannot be clearly formed.

Going back to the experience of a healthy conflict, young people must be made able to experience their *ad-gressing* with the strength that comes from (physiologically and psychologically) feeling that one is rooted in the earth, and from a harmonious, spontaneous sense of self. One example might be having children at elementary school start the day with a bodily relaxation exercise, rather than with a task to which they immediately react with distraction and hyperactivity. This basic experience would allow the children to be in the classroom with a more boundaried sense of self. Another example in the working world might be starting the day in the factory with a briefing time, in which anyone who wished to do so could tell the group of colleagues what bodily sensations and relational emotions s/he has at the start of the day. And so on. All the agencies of socialization and work ought to bear this need for rootedness in mind.

6. Conflict in the Therapeutic Relationship Today: from the Support of the Figure to the Support of the Background

The therapeutic relationship, like any other, must face up to this sense of emergency by containing the chaos that characterizes the beginning of every experience. Further, it must be based on procedural and aesthetic aspects, defined elsewhere as implicit narrative aspects (Spagnuolo Lobb, 2006; Stern, 2006) capable of building the ground of acquired certainties from which the figure can then emerge with differentiated clarity and relational strength, with that charm that characterizes the harmony of opposites in the figure/background dynamic. Without the sense of solidity that comes from the earth, the ground, it is impossible to find direction in relationships – especially in difficult relationships – with clarity, and with the security that acceptance of the different (the novelty) requires.
The feeling of aggressiveness, the positive strength of survival that F. Perls (1942) indicated as what society needed to recognize in order to support the creative power of every individual and to solve the problem of managing social, personal

and group conflicts, has to be rethought today in terms of the lack of ground in the experience of contact[41] .

The clinical problem is no longer that of supporting aggressiveness in the contact, but of supporting the "being-with" of the patient with the therapist, (Bloom,forthcoming) so that the feeling of aggressiveness can find a solid relational containment in order to orient itself in the contact. The therapeutic relationship must therefore provide not so much the courage to break authoritarian pre-established rules, but rather the sense of security in the relationship and in the other, which permits a clear perception/differentiation of the figure and a clear ability to decide, as an aware co-creation supported by the curiosity towards the other.

Listening, the strategy ordinarily proposed for the resolution of conflicts, must be supported today by listening to one's own body, by a kind of sensation – like the sense of rootedness, the experience of being there in a boundaried, powerful manner – which, if a few decades ago was taken for granted, today has given place to the experience of "liquidity." It is becoming even more important today to support everything that allows one to remain concentrated on oneself within significant contacts[42].

---

[41]My colleague and friend Frank Staemmler (2009) has also tried to rethink the concept of aggression in Perls, reaching a different position. He proposes to replace the word "aggression" with a varitey of alternatives such as motivation, interest and so on.

[42] The original chapter (Spagnuolo Lobb, 2013, pp. 134-150) continues with clinical examples of several shapes of *ad-gredere* according to the patient's contact style.

References

Bauman, Z. (2000). *Liquid modernity*. Cambridge: Polity Press.

Bloom, D. (2003). "Tiger! Tiger! Burning Bright" – Aesthetic Values as Clinical Values in Gestalt Therapy. In: *Creative License: the Art of Gestalt Therapy*, Spagnuolo Lobb M., Amendt-Lyon N., (Eds.), Wien, New York: Springer, 63-78

Bloom, D. (2013). "Situated Ethics and the Ethical World of Gestalt Therapy. In: *Gestalt Therapy in Clinical Practice, from psychopathology to the aesthetics of contact*, Francesetti G., Gecele M., Roubal J., (Eds.), Milan: FrancoAngeli, 131- 145.

Bloom, D, (Forthcoming) "Reflections on Phillip Lichtenberg's 'Inclusive and Exclusive Aggression: Some (Gestalt) Perspectives' – A Window to the Next Resistance? *Gestalt Review*, 17.3

Francesetti, G. (2007). *Panic Attacks and Postmodernity. Gestalt Therapy Between Clinical and Social Perspectives*. Milano: FrancoAngeli (or. ed: *Attacchi di panico e post-modernità. La psicoterapia della Gestalt tra clinica e società*. Milano: FrancoAngeli, 2005).

Francesetti, G., Gecele, M. and Roubal, J. (Eds.) (2013). *Gestalt Therapy in Clinical Practice. From Psychopathology to the Aesthetics of Contact*. Milano: FrancoAngeli.

Galimberti, U. (1999). *Psiche e techne. L'uomo nell'età della tecnica*. Milano: Feltrinelli.

Galimberti, U. (2006). L'uso della ragione. *La Repubblica delle D* 499: 274.

Lasch, C. (1978). *The Culture of Narcissism: American Life in an Age of Diminishing Expectations*. New York: Norton.

Nevis, E.C. (2003). Blocks to Creativity in Organizations. In M. Spagnuolo Lobb and N. Amendt-Lyon (Eds.), *Creative License: The Art of Gestalt Therapy*. Wien-New York: Springer, 291-302.

Perls, F. (1942/1947/1969a). *Ego, Hunger and Aggression: a revision of Freud's Theory and Method*. London: G. Allen & Unwin, 1947; New York: Random House, 1969.

Perls, F. (1969b). *Gestalt Therapy Verbatim*. Moab, UT: Real people Press.

Perls, F., Hefferline, R., Goodman, P. (1951). *Gestalt Therapy: Excitement and Growth in the Human Personality.* Highland, NY: The Gestalt Journal Press, 1994.

Spagnuolo Lobb, M. (2004). L'awareness dans la pratique post-moderne de la Gestalt-thérapie. *Gestalt* (*Societé Française de Gestalt* ed.) XV(27), 41-58 (it. trans: La consapevolezza nella pratica post-moderna della Gestalt Therapy. In P.L. Righetti with M. Spagnuolo Lobb (Eds.), *Psicoterapia della Gestalt*. Percorsi teorico-clinici. Rassegna di articoli dai *Quaderni di Gestalt.* Padova: Upsel Domeneghini Editore).

Spagnuolo Lobb, M. (2006). La psicoterapia tra il dicibile e l'indicibile. Il modello della psicoterapia della Gestalt. In M. Spagnuolo Lobb (Ed.), L'implicito e l'esplicito in psicoterapia. Atti del Secondo Congresso della Psicoterapia Italiana. Milano: FrancoAngeli, 19-27.

Spagnuolo Lobb, M. (2008). Il trauma di scoprirsi genitori di assassini. La Sicilia July 12th.

Spagnuolo Lobb, M. (2009). *Adolescenti assassini*. La Sicilia March 26th.

Spagnuolo Lobb, M. (2010). La vita e il dolore nell'arte dello psicotera¬peuta. Intervista a Umberto Galimberti. *Quaderni di Gestalt* XXIII(1), 15-34.

Spagnuolo Lobb, M. (2011). L'adattamento creativo come compito tera¬peutico nella società liquida. in G. Francesetti, M. Gecele, F. Gnudi and M. Pizzimenti (Eds.), *La creatività come identità terapeutica.* Atti del II convegno della Società Italiana Psicoterapia Gestalt. Milano: Franco¬Angeli, 23-43.

Spagnuolo Lobb, M. (2013). *The Now-for-Next in Psychotherapy. Gestalt Therapy Recounted in Post-Modern Society*. Milan: FrancoAngeli (orig. Italian Ed. 2011; Spanish Edition, 2013, Los Libros de CTP).

Spagnuolo Lobb, M., Salonia, G. and Sichera, A. (1996). From the 'Discomfort of Civilization' to 'Creative Adjustment': the Relationship Between Individual and Community in Psychotherapy in the Third Millennium. *International Journal of Psychotherapy* 1(1), 45-53 (ilt. trans: Quaderni di Gestalt 24/25, 95-105, 1997; Spagnuolo Lobb M. (Ed.). *Psicoterapia della Gestalt. Ermeneutica e clinica.* Milano: FrancoAngeli, 2001, 180-190; sp. trans: *Psicoterapia della Gestalt. Ermeneutica y clini*ca. Barcelona: Gesida, 2002, 209-219).

Spagnuolo Lobb, M., Stern, D.N., Cavaleri, P. and Sichera, A. (2009). Key moments in psicoterapia: confronto tra le prospettive gestaltica e inter-soggettiva. *Quaderni di Gestalt* XII(2), 11-29.

Staemmler F.-M. (2006). The willingness to be uncertain: Preliminary thoughts about interpretation and understanding in gestalt therapy. *International Gestalt Journal*, 29 (2), 9-40.

Staemmler, F-M, (2009), "Aggression" in *Agression, Time, and Understanding*. Santa Cruz, CA & Orleans, MA: Gestalt Press. 3-186.

Stern, D.N. (2006). L'implicito e l'esplicito in psicoterapia. In M. Spagnuolo Lobb (Ed.), L'implicito e l'esplicito in psicoterapia. Atti del Secondo Congresso della Psicoterapia Italiana, with DVD, Milano: FrancoAngeli, 28-35.

Chapter 6. Contact, at the source of experience
Jean-Marie Robine

Chapter Introduction

My first article about Gestalt therapy more than 30 years ago and after a few years of practice was about contact. My second article, shortly afterwards, was about psychotherapy as aesthetics. Today, these two topics reaminremain my idiosyncratic interests about Gestalt Therapy. Iin my opinion, they are the very core of our theory and practice. Not only as fundamentals but as a radical shift in paradigm for psychoptherapypsychotherapy. And I still consider that most of our other concepts are nothing but outcomes of these ones.

Of course, my understanding of these concepts evolved as the years went by and this chapter below is my last last working-out about centrality of "contact." I hope it could contribute to a further elaboration of our fundamentals because I consider that most of them have been insufficiently explored.

For instance, as Gestalt therapy today refers more and more to its relational dimensions as if it were implicitly contained in our theory of contact, we can see inside our community much skidding, as if what is said or written about contact could be transferedtransferred as such about relationship.

Of course, contacting a chair, contacting environment, contacting any object — or being contacted by — does not imply exactly the same parameters as contacting an Other, and this is the epistemological complement I (we) still have to elaborate.

And I think that one the main missions of New York Institute for Gestalt therapy is to keep the flame, to study our original concepts and to offer further developments consistent with the fundationalfoundational proposals. That's also why, even though not living in New York City, even though not being a native English speaking speaker but a French one, I like being a member of this community.

I am pleased to see that this chapter has met a worldwide use and that it's used in many training programs: after having been published in French in 2010 in *Cahiers de Gestalt-thérapie*, it has been translated into English to appear in the online Brazilian journal *aw@re* (www.aware.psc.br) with comments from Dan Bloom, Lillian Frazão and Selma Ciornai, in Russian (www.geshtaltart.dp.ua) and in Spanish (CTP editions). I do hope it would will open more debate not only about this topic but about many other which have be considered as obvious but which, as many so-called obvious concepts, need to be unfolded.

Contact, at the source of experience[43]

Pre-

Contact is the most important organizing concept of Gestalt therapy theory. *Contact* refers to all the movements of a given organism and its environment, that is, all the field movements the field Contact is therefore the phenomenon that precedes any organization of experience: pre-Oedipal, pre-object, pre-conscious pre-representation, pre-emotional, pre-psychic.... Becoming sedimented in a "psyche," experience was and will be again contact, for it is in and through contact that the psyche will exist and preside over future experiences. The *pre* is both genesis and structure.

This concept originates and confirms the shift of paradigm, the radical brought organized by Perls and Goodman with the creation of Gestalt therapy. Before them, the psyche was the lens and object privileged by the "psy"s **psy**chotherapy, **psy**chology, **psy**chiatry, **psy**choanalysis... However, since the first words of their founding text, our authors have relocated experience because "Experience occurs at the boundary between the organism and its environment."[44] Contacting and being contacted are the actions operating at the boundary and thanks to which the field differentiates into an I and a not-I.

This concept, doubtlessly because of its apparent simplicity and common usage, became increasingly distorted, little or not all differentiated from that of relationship. It has been used for an ethics of dialog, an ideology of relationship, or for inscribing Gestalt therapy in the premier ranks of "relational psychotherapies."

Certainly, as much research confirms, an important factor, essential even, that determines the success of a psychotherapy, whatever that may be, resides within the quality of the relationship created between the therapist and the client, as well as with the quality of their therapeutic alliance. But Gestalt therapy is *not primarily* centered on the quality of the relationship between therapist and patient for that is not an end in itself but the means. It is the means of exploring, working and transforming as much as necessary the qualities of an individual's relationship with what is 'other' and his environment, human and non-human.

With

> *If a red surface and a blue surface are in contact with each other, a blue line and a red line coincide.*
>
> Franz Brentano

---

[43] This article and the following response first appeared in *Aw@re*, 2(1), 2011.
[44] PHG, p. 49

Certainly, if a red surface and a blue surface are in contact, they do not create a violet line when they are united, even if this is hallucinated through an illusion of perception. Contact is not a mutual or reciprocal experience because we can be in contact with someone or something, for instance by gaze or by memory, without this person or object being in the least bit of contact with us. The very definition of reciprocity implies the equal exertion of an action by the first to the second as by the second to the first.

However *con*-tact implies *with*. Touch with. It is definitely this "with" that generates shifts in meaning there being so many possibilities of being "with." "I am so *with* this film I saw last week...," "I'll go for a ride *with* my car," "I am and will be *with* you in this difficult time...," "I'd love to live *with* you..." The etymological reference to tactility increases ambiguity because touching is the only one of the five senses that implies reciprocity: I can see you without being seen, hear you without being heard... I cannot touch you without being touched. When I touch a keyboard I am simultaneously touched by it, but this does not at all refer to a *lived* experience, a fundamental aspect when the contact is interhuman. I experience touching a keyboard, but the keyboard does not *live* this experience with me. Contact is therefore also a form of consciousness, a "knowing with."

If I establish physical contact with someone, like pinching their arm, their probably painful experience with this contact will be fundamentally different from the one I lived through. Even if contact is an act that puts into play a "with" and a "being," the lived experience cannot be considered the same because "with" does not mean "sameness." On the contrary, in this example, it allows differentiation.

All contact implies placement being in the presence of otherness, of *two*. Maybe it is better said as: *experienced as two*. When some therapists suggest to their clients to "get in contact with their feelings," it shows that these therapists, in their anthropology or their weltanschauung[45] , consider feelings as separate and distinct from the self, and they transmit this implicit notion to their client. It is paradoxical for those who mean to unite experience into a single Gestalt!

Sometimes it may indeed make sense for patients to express themselves in this way, like when parts of their own body are experienced as strange or foreign. Perls and Goodman cite the case in which a pain is localized in a body part and not experienced as "me," but as something that happened to me, as if it came from "outside"... and that does not belong to me.

Sometimes the therapist's language can help the client re-appropriate their experience as well as it can create, amplify, or support the separation or splitting.

---

45 World view

Contact as awareness

> *Awareness is characterized by contact, by sensing, by excitement and   by Gestalt formation.*
>
> Perls, Hefferline and Goodman[46]

For Perls and Goodman, the connection between awareness and contact was established with the introduction of *Gestalt Therapy* when they affirm "contact as such is possible without awareness, but for awareness contact is indispensible."[47] I am in contact with the ground, with the seat on which I sit, with the air that I breathe. These forms of contact are sometimes called "physiological" or "physical" and are opposed to "psychological" forms that imply consciousness—even if implicit—and the construction of a figure. However, the patterns of this "physiological" contact (I maintain this mediocre terminology for lack of a more satisfying one) are not in opposition to the "physiological" modalities. There really and truly is a continuation from one to the other: my manner of being in contact with the ground is related by analogy to my roots; my manner of breathing is coherent with my other exchange modalities of taking and giving with the environment. These   apparently distinct planes can be legitimately approached as *consistency[48]* of experience. They should be considered as a continuity within the breadth of experience and not as a distinct modality.

> Thus the connection between the world and awareness is one of contact. The world exists for the awareness in so far as the world is concretely and singularly what the awareness is not. The awareness touches the world since its partial neutralization can establish exteriority without distance between them. The world is neither subjective nor objective: it is the 'it-self' that invades and contacts the awareness, just as the awareness passes the world in its nothingness, [49]

wrote J.-P. Sartre.

Non-awareness and non-contact are called *confluence[50]* in Gestalt therapy. This non-awareness consists of habits and knowledge, of facts gathered throughout experience and through introjects. Certain confluent experiences remain potentially contactable. For example, it is possible to question the

------

[46] Perls, Hefferline, Goodman (hereinafter : PHG), p. 39

[47] ibid.

[48] For more on the concept of consistency, see Robine J.-M. (2008)

[49] J.P. Sartre, p. 400

[50] PHG pp.303-4

legitimacy of a spontaneously used word, that is, to bring the word into figural while I am in a relationship of confluence with my mother language. Other experiences are harder to contact because of repression or other modes of fixation. [51]

A figure/ground relation

> *Contact [...] is the forming of a figure of interest against a ground or context of the organism/environment field.*
> Perls, Hefferline & Goodman [52]

This awareness, or, relying on the works of Brentano and then Husserl, this *intentionality*, builds figure/ground relationships. It brings to the foreground and selects within the field of possibilities excerpts that can become significant.

Contact, therefore, aims and builds meaning. *Contacting* is building a form. "Form is where organism and its milieu meet," Weizsäcker wrote already in 1940 and, as a consequence, Maldiney[53] was able to advance that the formation of forms creates existence.

To be certain of using the concept of contact in a coherent manner, it would be preferable to systematically add to the word "contact" not just "with whom or with what" but "through which modalities."

Regarding the question "with whom or what?" I would readily suggest to come back to the introduction of Perls', Hefferline's, and Goodman's book. "The crucial question is: with what is one in contact? The spectator of a modern painting may believe that he is in contact with the picture while he is actually in contact with the art critic of his favorite journal."[54] This raises, among others, the question of transference: beyond perceptual and sensorial contact, with whom is my client in contact?

Touching, seeing, hearing... are regular modes of contact, but so are remembering, fantasizing, thinking, being excited, singing, writing, dreaming, being moved and so on. I can contact a friend by looking at him, hearing him, telephoning him, touching him, going to see him, remembering him, anticipating him, imagining him, and so on.

We can use as a basis the principle of noetic-noematic variations as elaborated by Husserl regarding consciousness to apply to contact. When I establish contact with someone, like a patient, I contact this person and this

---

[51] For more: Robine J.-M. & Lapeyronnie B. (1996)

[52] PHG, p. 54

[53] Maldiney H. (1990)

[54] PHG, introduction, pp. 39

person contacts me. We do not have the same contact "object," the same contents or even the same objective. (This is the noematic aspect of experience: the other as *noema*).

"Thinking," "loving," "hating," "imagining"... they are all verbs for what the mind does. Walking, breathing, feeling, thinking, hearing, going to, fantasizing, dreaming... are contacting types or modalities (*noesis*). With the same "object" (the "other," for example), I can have different types of contact: touching, hearing, looking, remembering him/her, feeling, projecting, cautioning, thinking of him/her, loving him/her, and so on.

But the contacting modalities can be united around two axes, two essential movements: going towards or distancing. Or, in other words, integrating or differentiating; fusing or separating; linking or unlinking; belonging or diverging... "(Contact) leads to touching and uniting [...]. The stakes of contact and its risks will be as much about leading to an encounter where a separation occurred as being able to separate from an integral union right down to the fusion," wrote Lekeuche.[55] It is also the double movement of contact introduced in the bipartition brought by Imre Hermann in "clinging" and "going out to search." This will be extended by Balint in his description of "ocnophile" types (to cling, to hang on) and "philobate" (going out to search). [56]

Inflexions of contacting

> ...the soul is wherever the action is, that's where the soul is, where the action is.
>
> P. Goodman [57]

And since each situation is new, even if it has similarities to previous encounters, each contact will be at the time adjustment and creation. The forms that can entail creative adaptation within a given situation are many, but the forms that can take on the interruptions, distortions, inhibitions, and fixations of this creative adjustment are limited. It is precisely towards these "inflexions" of experience that the therapeutic act will be focused.

Rather than using the phrase "interruptions of contact," a concept that generates ambiguities, I proposed in 1997[58], following Binswanger's tradition, the use of the term "inflexion." This term, borrowed from linguistics, refers to the ensemble of modifications of a word to express different grammatical categories such as tense, grammatical voice, gender and so on. Transposed to the topic that

---

[55] Lekeuche, p. 34

[56] I examined these two notions in relation to the dynamic of contact in Robine J.-M., 1990

[57] P. Goodman interview with Glassheim E., in Glassheim (1973)

[58] Robine J.-M. (1997-98) p.125

interests us, the modality variations, the deformations and other fluctuations in contacting are thus not subject to the opprobrium that the idea of interruption can bring. However, when Perls & al. discuss interruptions of contact, it is important to keep in mind that they believe that "the on-goingness of the process will not be lost."[59] They believe that, in the sequence of contacting, creativity can be interrupted by certain modalities and that therefore contact can eventually be carried on within routines or acted by a reduced self (i.e., losses of ego-functions of the self).

If contact accompanies each movement between a subject and its environment, which is to say all movement OF THE field, contact is an act, not a result. It is therefore more relevant to speak of contacting because actions are better expressed through verbs than nouns. Gestalt therapy promotes a culture of verbs over that of nouns, adjectives or adverbs.

When I listen to a patient, it is the verbs of his narrative that I most eagerly listen to. This is because they describe the processes, actions and contacting according to modalities that can often be considered his experiences as such, if not, sometimes, as a metaphor or metonym of his experience.

About contact at the contact-boundary

> *To appear means, for a singular essence or being, its coming into the open, its advent between sky and earth, in space-interval and time-interval.*
> Eugen Fink [60]

The concept of contact-boundary is a direct consequence of contact and represents a specific practical interest. Nonetheless, there is often confusion between "contact-boundary" and "boundary" or "boundaries" in the use of this concept that resembles that of, for example, structural family therapy: limits, contours. This is the case of the different boundaries Erv and Miriam Polster described, which have little connection to Perls' and Goodman's concept of contact-boundary, which can cause much confusion. "Contact-boundary" is a sort of epistemological abstraction, such as with "self." There is no good reason to reify or to transform an experience into an object and thereby justify speaking of "one's" contact-boundary as could be said of actual boundaries.

When teaching this concept, I sometimes use an analogy drawn from the way the famous philosopher Merleau-Ponty taught his own difficult concepts. Most of the time, I am not aware of my hand because I do not feel any specific sensation there. When I lay my hand on an object or on somebody's shoulder, through the same act I feel my hand and I feel the object or the other. Touching

---

[59] PHG p. 301
[60] Fink E., pp.. 70-71

this object gives it existence in my tactile experience and, through the same operation, it gives sensations, thus existence, to my hand. It's contact that simultaneously gives existence to the other and to me and which, by the same token, differentiates one from the other. The same operation, the same act, separates and joins. Contact creates a boundary and boundary creates contact as well. Without contact, there is no differentiation; without differentiation, there is no contact, thus no experience. [61]

"Contact is touch touching something."[62] Sight is neither the eye nor the object but the "oval of vision"[63] . It thus links the eyes with the world that is seen. At work is a process similar to that shown by Husserl when he said that there is no "consciousness" but only the "consciousness of" something.

An experience can seem to be intrapsychic when it actually is a contact-boundary event. An event continues because we are always engaged in one contact or other.

This has many consequences for psychotherapy. Every client describes the majority of their experiences as an intrapsychic suffering: shame, guilt, hatred, neglect, rejection, anger, conflict, and so on. These experiences should be considered as contact experiences. By considering them not as solipsistic phenomena but as contact-boundary phenomena, it changes the perspective and has an extremely powerful therapeutic impact. If "the contact-boundary is the organ of awareness,"[64] then contact-boundary, as experience, is the prime "location" where the therapist and client should work together.

Post

After some sixty years of Gestalt Therapy, which has been marked by the introduction of "contact as first experience" that brought multiple practical and methodological consequences, it is surprising that the Gestalt community should be little interested in refining, enriching and differentiating this concept. It was an important concept in the works of the Hungarian School of Psychoanalysis (Hermann and Balint, whom have already been mentioned, as well as Spitz, Mahler, and especially Szondi, whose work was continued by Jacques Schotte). This concept would today benefit from the enrichment through the works of Todorov; Bin Kimura's concept of *aïda*; Winnicott's concept of betweeness; Lacan and other psychoanalysts; and Merleau-Ponty's and Maldiney's works... It is also important to articulate the concept of contact within the context of relationships,

---

[61] Robine, 2007

[62] PHG, p. 217

[63] PHG, p. 269

[64] PHG, p. 85

particularly of therapeutic relations, which are non-reducible to contact, transference, projective identification, interaction, communication, dialogue or intersubjectivity.

> But if we must investigate "action-passion" and "'combinatio," we must also investigate "contact." For action and passion (in the proper sense of the terms) can only occur between things which are such as to touch one another; nor can things enter into combination at all unless they have come into a certain kind of contact. Hence we must give a definite account of these three things—of "contact," "combination," and "acting."
>
> Aristotle

Bibliography

Aristotle, On Generation and Corruption, English trans. Oxford, 1922 (Book 1, ch. 6, §3)

Balint M. (1959), Le*s voies de la régression*, Paris, Payot, 1972

Binswanger L. (1947-55), *Introduction à l'analyse existentielle*, French trans. Paris Ed. de Minuit 1971

Binswanger L. (1947-57), *Discours, parcours et Freud*, French trans. Paris, Gallimard, 1970

Brentano F. (1914), On What is Continuous in *Philosophical Investigations of Space, Time and the Continuum*. London : Croom Helm, 1988.

Fink E., l'analyse intentionnelle et le problème de la pensée spéculative, in *Problèmes actuels de la phénoménologie*, Paris, Desclée de Brouwer, 1952,

Glassheim E., The movement towards freedom in Paul Goodman's *The Empire City*. Dissertation of Ph. D., The University of New Mexico, 1973

Hermann I. (1943), *L'instinct filial*, Denoël, Paris, 1972

Husserl E. (1913), *Idées directrices pour une phénoménologie*, French trans. Paris, Gallimard, TEL, 1985

Kimura B., *Ecrits de psychopathologie phénoménologique,* Paris, PUF-Psychiatrie ouverte, 1992

Lekeuche in *Le contact*, Schotte & al., Le contact, Bruxelles, DeBoeck-Wesmael, 1990

Maldiney H. (1990), "La dimension du contact au regard du vivant et de l'existant," in Schotte J. (Ed). *Le contact*, Bruxelles, DeBoeck-Wesmael.

Perls F.S., Hefferline R., Goodman P., (1951), *Gestalt-thérapie*, French trans. Bordeaux, l'exprimerie, 2001

Polster E. & M. (1973), *La Gestalt, nouvelles perspectives théoriques et choix thérapeutiques et éducatifs*. Montréal, Le Jour, 1983

Ponge Francis, *La fabrique du pré. Les sentiers de la creation* Skira, 1971, p. 191

Robine J.-M., (1990) "Le contact, expérience première," *Revue Gestalt*, n°1, *Société Française de Gestalt, reédité p.64 sq in Robine J.-M., Gestalt-thérapie, la construction du soi*, L'Harmattan, Paris 1998

Robine J.-M. & Lapeyronnie B. (1996), "La confluence, expérience liée et expérience aliénée." *Cahiers de Gestalt-thérapie* n°0, 1996 and reedited p.105 sq in Robine J.-M., Gestalt-thérapie, la construction du soi, L'Harmattan, Paris 1998

Robine J.-M. (1997), "Anxiété et construction des Gestalt," in *Cahiers de Gestalt-thérapie* n°1, reédité p.125 sq in Robine J.-M., *Gestalt-thérapie, la construction du soi*, L'Harmattan, Paris 1998

Robine J.-M., Melnick J., Schack M.-L., Spinelli E. (2007), "Contact and Intrapsychic Perspectives : Gestalt Therapists Reply to Questions From the Editors and From Ernesto Spinelli," *Studies in Gestalt Therapy: Dialogical Bridges*, vol. 1, n°2

Robine J.-M., Le maintenant a-t-il un avenir? in Goriaux P.-Y. (sous la direction de-), *Le maintenant*, Minibibliothèque de Gestalt-thérapie, n°110, IFGT, 2008

Sartre J.-P., *Carnets de la drôle de guerre.* Gallimard, Paris 1995, pp. 400sq.

Schotte & al., *Le contact*, Bruxelles, DeBoeck-Wesmael, 1990

Todorov T., *La vie commune*, Paris Seuil,

Weizsäcker V. Von (1940): *Le cycle de la structure.* Paris, Desclée de Brouwer, 1958

A Response to "Contact, at the Source of Experience" – Dan Bloom joins Jean-Marie Robine in a "duet" (abridged)

Dan Bloom

Jean-Marie Robine's essay, "Contact, at the source of experience" is an important essay that takes "contact," gestalt therapy's core concept, and opens it up for us to look at it in different ways. I am happy to offer my response to his essay.

Jean-Marie and I "grew up" as gestalt therapists on different continents but as students of the same teacher, Isadore From. Isadore taught precise understanding of gestalt therapy in New York City and in Europe. So it should be clear from what follows that we have much in common in our understanding of gestalt therapy even though our differences should be equally clear. We are in tune so often that most of my response will focus on areas of our differentiation, of contact, where our ideas may be more clearly distinguishable.

Since I call us "in tune," let me offer this metaphor. Consider what follows as my part in a "musical duet"[65] with Jean-Marie, where I will take –up some of his themes in "musical" variation, harmony, accompaniment, and counterpoint.

At times I will take an idea in a different direction. Sometimes I will question something I "hear." And sometimes my response will differentiate my perspective from his.[66]

And then, I will add my own ideas relevant to the central theme of his essay, as if stepping out from this duet and playing a solo.

His essay has so many melodies that I must select among them. Hopefully, our "music" will be a whole different than the sum of its parts.

I divide my part of this duet into "movements" to correspond to the named sections of Jean-Marie's essay. And within these movements, I number my responses into sections.

Opening Movement: "'Pre'"

1."Contact is the most important organizing concept of Gestalt therapy theory," begins Jean-Marie.

I broaden his declaration with my own to underscore the relevance of our concept of contact to phenomenology and to all phenomenological or experiential psychotherapies:

---

[65]The Gestalt psychologists frequently use music as an example of gestalt formation.

[66] Jean- Marie's other writings often give a more extensive presentation of the complex ideas he summarizes here. To some extent, then, my responses to this essay suffer from are subject to this limitation.

Contact[67] is experience in its immediacy, its imminence, prior to any organizing or further development; and before the emergence of figure/ground itself.

In the terms of generative phenomenology (Steinbock, 1995), (Zahavi, 2005) contact is pre-reflective and the supra-sensible substrata from which all forms of consciousness are emergent. Experience, contact, is "pre-gestalt." If the personalist William Stern's comment makes sense[68], "There is no gestalt without a gestalter," there is no "gestalter" without contact. Contact precedes the organizer/organizing of experience.

Contact is "pre," as Jean-Marie observes. I state this phenomenologically in order to historicize gestalt therapy, to situate it in the tradition of thought from which it developed. I believe it is important for gestalt therapists to understand our place in the history philosophy and psychology. I will return to this theme several times.

2. Jean-Marie: "…experience was and will be again contact, for it is in and through contact that the psyche will exist and preside over future experiences."

Again, I expand to widen this other remarkable declaration phenomenologically:

Contact as a process is an ongoing further developing temporal sequence of experience itself, with contact opening to and creating a world of sensation, feeling, emotion, movement, thought, action and meaning, which reflexively is the further basis for contact. Contact and continuing contact is a functioning of the organism/environment field *and of the self/lifeworld field.* Lifeworld (E. Husserl, 1936/1970), (Binswanger, 1963; Heidegger, 1962), (Boss, 1983), (Steinbock, 1995) is an expansion of gestalt therapy's "field " in a phenomenological direction, and I will and I will take this further in my solo part of this duet.

3. When gestalt therapists write about the inspired originality of contact and consequently of gestalt therapy itself, there is a possibility that this might be encourage "gestalt therapy exceptionalism" — a way of thinking about gestalt therapy that sees it as having a savior's mission. This might be one to steps away from a gestalt fundamentalism or even fanaticism. This can be avoided by our understanding the context within which contact and our other ideas emerged.

Perls and Goodman's "contact" was an inspired *synthesis* of concepts from American pragmatism, Gestalt psychology, and phenomenology. They brought

---

[67] While Jean-Marie and I use the term "contact," it should be understood as "contacting," as well. Experience is on going, processual. Jean-Marie directly addresses this in his essay. "Contact" is also precise moments in the sequence of contacting (PHG. 403). Further details are not necessary in this response.

their synthesis into the psychotherapy world and radically reorganized the prevailing psychoanalytic emphasis on a one-person intrapsychic paradigm; their feat cannot be overstated. While Daseinanalysis, for example, situated a patient as a person-in-the-world (*Umwelt, Mitwelt, Eigenwelt,* being-in-the-world) and brought an existential-phenomenological focus to psychotherapy (May, Angel, & Ellenberger, 1958), in principal ways it was committed to an intrapsychic model.

By the time Goodman and Perls presented "contact" as the pre-cursor to the psyche or mind, the Cartesian "ghost in the machine" monadic mind had been under assault from all directions. Not only had the American pragmatists done their work, but in Europe, phenomenologists, famously from Husserl, Heidegger, and Merleau-Ponty drawing on substantial roots in previous centuries presented a unifies notion of human experience emergent of interaction with the world. Self, subject, Dasein, Ego, or the subject developed from a previous undifferentiated world.

Here are specific examples from sources Goodman undoubtedly knew. In 1934, the well-known American pragmatist John Dewey, wrote, "Experience is a matter of the interaction of organism with its environment, an environment that is human as well as physical." *Art as Experience,* p. 246. (Dewey, 1934/1980. In lecture courses given at the University of Chicago, George Herbert Meade developed the concept of contact in *The Philosophy of the Act* (Mead,1938) as part of his own explanation of the social self. Goodman was familiar with the words of both Meade and Dewey.

We can read Perls and Goodman and be caught up in the reformist fervor of their argument since it is directed at the orthodox psychoanalytic establishment, which was indeed wedded to the Cartesian tradition. We can also be thrilled by Perls and Goodman's utopian and trenchant social criticism of the conformist authoritarian post-World War II society. It is easy to decontextualize gestalt therapy and attribute more originality to our founders than deserved. Gestalt therapy exceptionalism — the idea that gestalt therapy has a special truth and we are its "missionaries" — actually trivializes gestalt therapy' significance.

I am confident Jean-Marie and I agree about that Perls and Goodman worked within a context, as the references in his essays to Eugen Fink and Jean-Paul Sartre, for example, show. And as Jean-Marie observes elsewhere[69], Perls and Goodman's theory of self as organized contact was a radical de-centering of self from its autonomous independence and re-situated self as a field function. Perls and Goodman's work was a deliberate and creative contribution within a context of which both of them were knowledgeable. The more we all know of the context, historical and theoretical, the more we can appreciate the complexities of

---

[69] Robine, J-M (2011. *On the Occasion of the Other.* Gouldsboro Me.: Gestalt Journal Press

our theory and its contribution. And the more we can reach through Perls and Goodman's ideas into the background from which they themselves drew inspiration, the further we can develop our own grounded contemporary understanding of gestalt therapy.

4. Jean-Marie and I are distressed at the widespread misunderstanding of gestalt therapy terms among gestalt therapists.

None of gestalt therapy's core ideas are simple to understand. Jean-Marie observes that the names we have for these concepts are easily confused with words in everyday common usage. "Contact," "self," "boundary," and even "field," are ordinary words in everyone's ordinary, non-clinical, vocabulary.

Many of us regret that trainees too often fail to take the time to learn these how these words have special meanings in our concepts and make-do with superficial misunderstandings. They mistake the common usages of the terms with their technical meaning. While this must be true for all modalities, it is hard for me to think that psychoanalytic candidates understand that "drive theory" has something to do with how one steers an automobile.

How many definitions do gestalt therapist have for "contact" and "boundary" and how many of them are so diluted by common usages that our theory itself lacks becomes thin and lacks coherence? And how many definitions are simply wrong? These abominable misunderstandings inevitably neutralize the radical move represented by "contact" that Jean-Marie describes so well in his essay. This is a theme Jean-Marie repeats in his essay; following his repetitions, I will repeat this theme as well. It is a theme that needs repetition.

5. Contacting is a function *of* the boundary – the phenomenal boundary of contact: Jean-Marie and I are in unison; and, of course, not confluent since our voices are distinct.

Since the Perls and Goodman text was written in my native language, I can be more directly critical of it than non-native English speakers. Some of the original text's writing is an invitation to the many of the errors among our trainees (and trainers) that I referred to above.

"Experience occurs at the boundary *between* the organism and its environment..." (Perls, Hefferline, Hefferline, & Goodman, 1951 emphasis added) The boundary of contact is *not* a place of separation, as Perls and Goodman otherwise make clear. That quoted description uses a common English preposition that marks physical separation, "between this and that." The authors ought to have chosen more carefully — and our students ought to be warned – because this sloppy English led to a major confusion in gestalt therapy. This is not an insignificant confusion — as Jean-Marie observes and as I emphasize.

When "boundary" is a place of separation, gestalt therapy becomes one more psychotherapy of isolated human beings interacting *across* a boundary of separation. The locus of therapy shifts *from* the boundary of contact *to* the independent psyche of the patient — a gestalt therapy version of an intrapsychic model. It is no longer psychotherapy of the contact-boundary (Francesetti & Gecele, 2009) or "the situation." The social phenomenal field is not where human beings roam as isolated animals. Rather, gestalt therapy understands contact as a differentiation of "I and not-I" at the boundary, as Jean-Marie writes, and, as I add, within the social field of the human animal organism. The *lifeworld.* It is not the differentiation of a solitary I from a not-I, which I will prefer to write as "I/not-I," but an emergent process of a socially situated person. This is a process of self emergence, where self is the structure/function of contact, emergent of the field. I will expand this in my solo movement, below.

6. While gestalt therapy is psychotherapy *of* this boundary — phenomenologically, there is "nowhere else" — gestalt therapy is not a therapy of the psychotherapy relationship, as Jean-Marie observes. A person seeks a psychotherapist for treatment for his or her own particular distress and expects to return to life with improved functioning. A person in therapy properly expects her or his own experience to be figural in the session. While the therapy relationship is the means by which a person's relationship with "what is 'other'" is transformed, it is not the goal of the therapy. The therapist/patient relationship facilitates he psychotherapy; it is not its purpose. Contacting is in and of itself the method and cure. (Perls, et al., 1951)

As Jean-Marie observes in a later section, "About contact at the contact-boundary: If "the contact-boundary is the organ of awareness," then contact-boundary, as experience, is the prime "location" where the therapist and client should work together." I add, and modify: There is no "patient." There is a "patient-in-therapy" at the contact-boundary.

I am think he and I agree, yet I need to address a few sentences in his paper, which might point to an area of distinction between our views.

7. Jean-Marie suggests that the distortion of "boundary" as a place of differentiation of I and not-I somehow becomes lost in "relational psychotherapies," "an ethics of dialogue" and "an ideology of encounter." Such distortions must be corrected or gestalt therapy becomes muddled. Yes, I say, we must be careful not to lose the richness of the contact-boundary in gestalt therapy.

Yet is Jean-Marie is unduly dismissive of "an ethics of dialogue," and perhaps some of the other develops of the relational perspective in gestalt therapy? The relational attitude is very popular among gestalt therapists and, like Jean-Marie, I am also critical of some aspects of the relational turn in gestalt therapy. But for the most part (or among the best of its practitioners) the relational perspective is not based upon a misunderstanding of gestalt therapy. Jean-Marie explains this point better elsewhere. (Robine, 2011). He argues that relational gestalt therapy assumes a dialogue of two *already differentiated* "I's."

This neglects contact, which is pre- "I," as he describes here. I won't address whether or not this is a fair characterization of the relational approach, but I will offer this on behalf of the relational perspective as I understand it:

Contemporary gestalt therapy's emphasis on the ethical, intersubjective, relational, or dialogical aspects of gestalt therapy *is implicit in contact as the pre – and on-going structuring of experience* —of the boundary of contact, the patient/therapist field.

A patient's therapeutic insight in any gestalt psychotherapy session is a function of this field, facilitated by this dialogical relationship with the therapist, supported by this relationship's ethical framework, without which this openness of contact cannot develop. There is no "patient," as such; there is no "therapist, " as such." There is a "this- patient-with-this-therapist-in-this-session." Attention to this aspect of the gestalt therapy is an ethical turn away from a therapist-patient relationship where the therapist "acts" upon the patient. These gestalt therapist are known to view the patient as "manipulating," "resisting," and so on, and more or less discount the significant factor of the therapist's own felt presence in the field.

While there may be relational gestalt therapists who neglect the pre-ego contact foundation that constitutes any possible intersubjectivity, they, as Jean-Marie, notes, grossly misunderstand a core concept of gestalt therapy – contact. The Ego function, the "I" of self functioning is only one aspect of the contact process. To think otherwise is to ignore the fullness of contact.

Second Movement: With

1. Contact is never by "itself." "All contact implies being in the presence of otherness," writes Jean-Marie. "Otherness" is any kind of human contact since contact can be an action in the physical, biological, phenomenal, or a combination of these "regions" or "domains" (my terms). The use of a single term across so many different domains or regions might seem to be misuse of a word that muddles our theory; I will show in the next "movement" how it is quite the opposite — that it is part of the radical revolution of gestalt therapy theory. In whichever region the concept is used, contact is always a situated or worlded event: always "with," intentionality, directed toward, open to and within the world, or more rudimentarily, a sensed response of the field.

2. Jean-Marie gives examples of contact with things and persons.

I quibble with one of his example's potential implication only insofar as I want to amplify the implicit relationality of experience and, consequently, of contact. He writes:

If I establish physical contact with someone, like pinching their arm, their probably painful experience with this contact will be fundamentally different from the one I lived through. Even if contact is an act that puts into play a with" and a "being," the lived experience cannot be considered the same because with' does not mean 'sameness.' On the contrary, in this example, it allows differentiation.

We can easily identify this from our everyday experience of contact with persons.

Yes, the experiences of the same things by two people *are* different. This is one of the elements of our difference or differentiation as I/not-I, using his terminology, how often do we innocently touch a friend and find him recoil to what he calls a "tickle?" Our experiences are different. When is a touch (our experience), a tickle (his different experience)?

But the *experience* is not just a "touch" and a "tickle," unless those aspects of a whole experience are separated out the one event from the other, as if one turned a continuous line into a series of points. It is a touch/tickle linked in a circuit of responses where I-and-my-friend have an experience in common *and* have our own experiences. My touch immediately becomes a touch/tickle. An "I" experience and a "We" experience alternate as figure/ground and are inseparable.

Jean-Marie's example isolates a moment from more complex experience. Yes, that moment is of different figural experiences, but the figure and ground quickly alternate. There is no actual "here-and-now" independent instant empty of the previous moment and without an expectation of the next. (Zahavi, 2005) Contact is not only never without "an other," it is never outside of time consciousness or the temporal sequence of contact. The pinch and my touch example includes the sense of the other's reaction to me reacting to the other's reacting to me and so on in the alternating figure/ground in the flow of experience. While our experiences are not the same, we are also in a common experience of the emerging inter-human event of which each of us is an indivisible yet different part. Empathy — not confluence — plays an important part in this alternating figure/ground since our sense of one another (as empathy) is a component of our sense of the situation (Robine, 2011)

Further, as Jean-Marie observes, there is never merely contact, but always a contact of, to, or with. I amplify: Contact-with is an I/ not –I differentiation. It is also a functioning of the field. I repeat: It is a differentiation of an "I" in the context of the "We." An "I" cannot differentiate except from a field of which the other is always already a part — a social constituent of the lifeworld. Contact is of the organism/environment field, as Perls and Goodman write. The human "environment" is not unpopulated.

Lest I be unclear, the toucher and the tickled know they are different and have different experiences; and they also have a common, changing, experience.

Movement Three: Contact as Awareness.

The spontaneous consciousness of the dominant need and its organization of the functions of contact is the psychological form of *organismic self-regulation.* p, 274 (Perls, et al., 1951)

1.The section, "Contact as Awareness" is a brief section in Jean-Marie's essay. It is a short continuation of "With," and he remarks that,

"Physiological" contact (I maintain this mediocre terminology for lack of a more satisfying one[70]) are not in opposition to the "physiological" modalities. There *really and truly is a continuation from one to the other:* [emphasis added] my manner of being in contact with the ground is related by analogy to my roots; my manner of breathing is coherent with my other exchange modalities of taking and giving with the environment. These apparently distinct planes can be legitimately approached as *consistency* of experience. *They should be considered as continuity within the breadth of experience and not as a distinct modality.* [Emphasis added]"

I restate and take this further: human beings are beings-in-the-world (Heidegger, 1962), as human animal organisms practically engaged with the world in an embodied indivisible process of awareness, consciousness, knowing, acting, and meaning-making.

2. [Section omitted]

Movement Four: A figure/ground relation and Inflexions

"Language is the house of being.,"
(Martin Heidegger, 1964)

1. Jean-Marie's original idea, "Inflexions of contact," is a brilliant development of our classical model. It shines a new light, a welcome light on contact. It is an idea to be celebrated. He adds a new perspective to a familiar idea and transforms it.

How true it is that we orient ourselves towards the world in gestures of language, pre-verbally and with silence. (Heidegger, 1962) To Heidegger and his intellectual descendants in the German and French tradition, we are always articulated in the world through the mode of understanding — and this involves

---

[70] Perhaps "biophysical contact" could be a more satisfying to Jean-Marie than "physiological contact.

language, discourse, silence, the saying, the unsaid, the said, and so on. We are interpretative beings, to out it hermeneutically.

How fitting that our modes of contact be described with the grammatical term, inflexions. As beings-in-the-world, we are always alive in language I add: the embodied creative conversation of contacting-in-the-world is without end.

2.The traditional term, "interruptions of contact" can lead to the misimpression that contact is like an electric circuit that can switch on and off, be broken, rather than a process of experience that flows and shapes with differing modalities varying creatively with the opportunities and limitations of each situation. An interruption ends the human conversation abruptly; inflexion changes its mode. An interruptions of contact model rather than an inflexion model can lead to a notion that contact can be either good or bad, rather than intrinsically evaluated within its inflexions, on its own terms. The classical interruptions actually break or rupture nothing, but only affect the direction of contact — that is, inflect it as one would inflect the case of a word in a sentence — but without awareness.

3.Contact is creatively ongoing, but its clarity can be diminished by virtue of unaware bending or modifying — Jean-Marie's inflexion. Inflexion is more than mere changing direction; it is changing the "grammar" of contact itself, its functioning in the field — its "grammatical" case, its dynamic, its mood, its relationship to the entirety of which it is a part and which it forms. The parallels with the nuances of language itself seem to be endless, as they ought to be.

4. Jean-Marie draws on Husserl's careful distinction between the *noema* and *noesis* of intentionality in his discussion of contact. I would like open his ideas in my own words and see if I understand Jean-Marie correctly. As I understand Husserl, the *noema* is the object intended; the *noesis* is how I intended it — Jean-Marie's "modality of contacting." That is the candy I see; an intentional object of consciousness. This might be called the *noematic* object of contact. The "that" is a candy I want; my wanting is the how of I perceive it, in my mode of wanting. Let us say contact and intentionality are equivalent, which is defensible statement.[71] And since, as Jean-Marie explains in this paper contact is always "contact-with," intentionality must also be "with." This is consistent with both Husserl's later theory of intentionality as situated in the lifeworld (Welton, 2000) and Heidegger's discussion of being-in-the-world. (Heidegger, 1962)

---

[71] If intentionality is directed toward an object, however, it would be inconsistent with contact's field emergent properties. The object of contact as much "calls out" to to the "arc" of contact is its passive target. Intentionality as "openness" is a better beginning for our consideration.

To return to Jean-Marie's inflexion more explicitly: my manner of intending this object is through my mode of inflexion. I may turn towards it, away from it, like it, dislike it, and so on.

Movement Five

I am in so much agreement I pass over it.

Movement Six: *About contact at the contact-boundary*

1.In this movement Jean-Marie and I again play mostly in harmony. I can underscore agreement line after line in this section.

Ordinary everyday living shows us actual physical boundaries that separate, not boundaries that create, and selves who have names and pay taxes, and are not always in the process of reconfiguring. We do notice our phenomenological world of spatiality or temporality. Husserl referred to this world of our common conceptions, "the natural attitude."(Edmund Husserl, 1973) Heidegger described this as our everyday being-in-the-world of *Das Man,* The They. (Heidegger, 1962) This everyday world is a world of the famous "splits" described by Perls and Goodman — most importantly, body and mind; self and external world. This is the world of Descartes, and, of course, not the world of gestalt therapy. Following the argument of Perls and Goodman, these ordinary conceptions that include the misunderstandings of boundary, self, contact-boundary, and perhaps even contact itself, are imbedded in our adjustment to the inescapable dangers and frustrations of being human animal organisms whose impulses towards satisfaction are always restricted by anti-human social structures. Chronic frustration and danger cause these common sense and immediate impressions of our everyday world.

We gestalt therapy trainers come up against our students' everyday conceptions when we teach the phenomenological concepts of gestalt therapy. As the phenomenologists always knew, it is difficult to acquire the phenomenological attitude; it is similarly difficult to understand "boundary" as a locus of meeting or in Jean-Marie's words, that

> It's contact that simultaneously gives existence to the other and to me and which, by the same token, differentiates one from the other. The same operation, the same act, separates and joins. Contact creates a boundary and boundary creates contact as well.

3. But if we are to think of contact in terms of differentiating me from this table, for example, and me from another person, are we describing the same process? Jean-Marie does not make address this question clearly enough in his essay. Let me address this in my terms, which might be different from his, were he to describe it.

144

The "otherness" of the table is a different ontological category from the "otherness" of another person. It is perhaps too simple to consider contact as only an I/not-I event. Differentiating I/not-I is not sufficient to describe an inter-human process; the human other is not a person differentiated from me as a *negation,* that is, in terms of *not* being me. Only objects exist through negation. This desk is not me, of course, but it becomes mine when I identify it, name it, possess it, use it.

The human other as subject is *other* than me — but not a not-me. If I define the other as "not me," I am taking over the otherness of the other through my definitions. The other becomes "mine" as being "not-me." I see the other in terms of myself — as a negative, a not-me. The other is "thematized," overtaken on my own terms. (Levinas, 1981) In gestalt therapy terms, by calling the other, "not-me," I have placed the other into a familiar category, assimilated the novelty or mystery of the other into my understanding of the world of me and not-me's. To resist the desire to understand the other as a not-me requires a felt sense one's own existential ground—an id of the situation that, perhaps is an id of the lifeworld. This underlying "pre-structure" of the lifeworld may very well be a condition of contact itself. For nothing can emerge from itself and contact cannot be without ground.

If I accept the human other as "Other" — on his or her own terms and not as a negative of me — a unique interhuman contact is possible, dialogical contact.

We reach the human other through language, the language of speech and silence, poetry and gesture, glance and caress. These are the inflexions of dialogical contact that make no sense when made toward inanimate things. Language is a constituent of our being. (Heidegger, 1962)

Movement Seven: Post

Jean-Marie has presented many of the ideas that continue to make gestalt therapy a direct challenge to contemporary psychotherapy theory and practice. He doesn't simplify these ideas — our world is complex and to understand our world we need to reach out and match its complexity within our own understanding. In doing this we make a uniquely human contact.

I have responded to some of the ideas in Jean-Maries paper, "Contact, at the source of experience." I doubt I have done them justice considering their depth and nuance. Sometimes I've taken the liberty to expand my ideas in directions beyond the scope of a simple response. This is a measure of how Jean-Marie welcomes us into new frontiers of gestalt therapy.

References

Binswanger, L. (1963). *Being-in-the-World* (J. Needleman, Trans.). New Yor, & Evanston: Harper & Row.

Bloom, D. (2005). A Centennial Celebration of Laura Perls: The Aesthetic of Commitment. *British Gestalt Journal, 14*(2), 81.

Boss, M. (1983). *Existential Foundations of Medicine & Psychology*. New York: Jason Aronson.

Dewey, J. (1934/1980). *Art as Experience*. New York: Penguin Putnam.

Francesetti, G., & Gecele, M. (2009). A Gestalt therapy perspective on psychopathology and diagnosis. *British Gestalt Journal, 18*(2), 5 - 20.

Friedman, M. (1955). *The Life of Dialogue*. London: Routledge and Kegan Paul Limited.

Gallagher, S., & Zahavi, D. (2008). *The Phenomenological Mind: An Introduction to Philosphy of Mind and Cognitve Science*. London: Routledge.

Heidegger, M. (1962). Being and time (J. Macquarrie & E. Robinson, trans.): New York: Harper & Row.

Heidegger, M. (1964). Letter in Humanism (F. A. Capuzzi, Trans.). In D. F. Krell (Ed.), *Basic Writings* (pp. 217 - 265). New York: Harper Collins.

Husserl, E. (1936/1970). *The Crisis of European Sciences and Transcendental Phenomenology* (D. Carr, Trans.). Evanston: Northwestern University Press.

Husserl, E. (1973). *Logical Investigations* (J. N. Findlay, Trans. 2nd Revised ed.). London: Routledge.

Levinas, E. (1981). *Otherwise than Being or Beyod Essence* (A. Lingis, Trans.). The Hague: Marinus Nijhoff.

Lewin, K. (1951). *Field Theory in Social Science: Selected Theoretical Papers*. New York: Harper.

May, R., Angel, E., & Ellenberger, H. F. (1958). *Existence*: Basic Books, Inc.

Mead, G. H. (1938). *The Philosophy of the Act*. Chicago, Ill: University of Chicago Press.

Merleau Ponty, M. (2002). *Phenomenology of Perception*. London: Routledge.

Perls, F., Hefferline, R., Hefferline, R., & Goodman, P. (1951). *Gestalt therapy: Excitement and growth in the human personality*: Julian Press.

Philippson, P. (2001). *Self in Relation*. Highland, New York: The Gestalt Journal Press.

Philippson, P. (2009). *The Emergent Self*. London: Karnac Books.

Robine, J.-M. (2011). *On the Occassion of the Other*. Goudsboro, Me.: Gestalt Journal Press.

Spiegelberg, H. (1972). *Phenomenology in Psychology and Psychiatry*. Evanston, Ill,: Northwest University Press.

Staemmler, F. M. (2006). A Babylonian Confusion?: On the Uses and Meanings of the Term "Field" [Festschrift for Malcolm Parlett]. *British Gestalt Journal, 15*(2), 64-83.

Staemmler, F. M. (2007). On Macaque Monkeys, Players, and Clairvoyants: Some New Ideas for a Gestalt Therapeutic Concept of Empathy. *Studies in Gestalt Therapy, 1*(2), 43-63.

Steinbock, A. J. (1995). *Home and beyond: Generative phenomenology after Husserl*: Northwestern Univ Pr.

Thompson, E. (2007). *Mind in Life: Biology, Phenomenolgy, and the Sciences of Mind*. Cambridge, MA: Harvard Universitiy Press.

Welton, D. (2000). *The Other Husserl*. Bloominton, Ind: Indiana University Press.

Zahavi, D. (2005). *Subjectivity and selfhood: Investigating the first-person perspective*: MIT Press.

Chapter 7. Practice-Based Evidence
Philip Brownell

Introduction

In choosing this chapter for the book I am pointing to the contemporary world in which the New York Institute for Gestalt Therapy (NYIGT) has an influence. In most places where psychotherapy is practiced people demand that therapists use methods that have been demonstrated to be effective. That leads to discussions of the philosophy of science behind research, research methodology, and the understanding and utilization of research findings. Increasingly, research findings will not only support what gestalt therapists have sensed for decades concerning the effectiveness of the approach, but they will also help refine gestalt therapy theory itself. As one of the leaders in gestalt therapy theory development, the NYIGT has an opportunity to extend its influence through the research activities of its members.

This chapter, taken from the *Handbook for Theory, Research, and Practice in Gestalt Therapy* (2008, Cambridge Scholars Publishing), describes a contribution to the larger field, not just the field of gestalt therapy, that gestalt practitioner-researchers can make. This is an opportunity to dialogue with clinical and professional colleagues from other perspectives so that the gestalt approach continues to affect the evolution of psychotherapy in general. The NYIGT, like other gestalt organizations, has an opportunity to build on its heritage as it moves into the twenty-first century through encouraging practice-based research, thus bridging between the clinic and the university. I hope the reader glimpses from this chapter how that might be so.

Related to these things is my own place at the NYIGT. I am a relatively new member, and I do not reside in New York City; so, I am a member at a distance. However, I associate with many of the longstanding members of the institute, and I value their commitment to, based on their interest in, the development of gestalt therapy theory. I respect their intelligence, and I value their input in my own work. I hope to make a contribution to the work of others.

Let me also say that I have many other interests. I could have chosen very different subjects and provided an entirely different contribution. I am interested in spirituality, and I have been writing extensively in the genre of the psychology of religion (an example being a book I am currently working on concerning spiritual competency in psychotherapy). I could have provided an article on executive functions and how they relate to self-regulation. I could have provided something on the gestalt approach to treating chemical dependency. I could have given an article describing the self-conscious emotions of shame, guilt, embarrassment and pride and how they relate to gestalt therapy. I could have provided something on the use of gestalt therapy theory in organizational development. I could have given something on field theory, phenomenology, or experiment. I could have provided something about what I believe our core theory to be.

Instead, I gave this chapter, which I believe to be on a subject absolutely essential to the survival of gestalt therapy as a viable and contemporary approach to psychotherapy. Without research, gestalt therapy will continue to become marginalized throughout the world, and it will be assimilated into the larger field without its own distinction.

Practice-Based Evidence[72]

> How to find truth, that is the question, and how to know that one has
> found it. Nothing has so occupied reflective men and women for as long as
> we have record; nothing has elicited more anguish and struggle. Nothing,
> also, has created such a climate for despair and irresponsibility as the
> modern conviction that the word no longer has much meaning.
> —Daniel Taylor

In the beginning of this book we raised the issue of warrant: what
constitutes sufficient justification for the practice of gestalt therapy? Might it be
the so-called evidence provided through randomly assigned clinical trials
(Goodheart, Kazdin and Sternberg 2006, Nezu and Nezu 2008)? Might it
reasonably include other types of "interventions," treatments, and techniques like
those listed by the American Psychological Association (APA 2006)? Indeed, what
constitutes the "evidence" in the construct of "evidence-based practice?" Is it
process outcomes studies, such as those Leslie Greenberg advocates in chapter
four? Is it gestalt-informed qualitative research, such as Paul Barber advocates in
chapter three? Is it the common factors research or the practice-based or client-
centered outcomes such as those suggested in the writings of Barry Duncan and
Scott Miller (2000) or Hubble, Duncan and Miller (1999)?

Relative Evidence

Certainty "is either the highest form of knowledge or is the only epistemic
property superior to knowledge" (Reed 2008, np). In a world in which certainty
escapes us, no form of evidence can rise above the need for degrees of confidence
and measures of error, or random variance. In such a world, we can only have
relative forms of support and more or less warrant.

Thus, while we may have a sense of the truth of a reality that is objective
and independent, we only have a relative understanding of it, and even that
comes from a subjective experience within it. This is the critical realism
suggested by Alan Meara in chapter one. With such a perspective as ground, what
are acceptable ways of justifying one's interpretation of experience and thereby
supporting one's beliefs?

---

[72] Originally published in Brownell, P. (Ed), *Handbook for Research, Theory, and Practice of Gestalt Therapy*, pp., 90 – 103, Cambridge Scholars Publishing, Newcastle: UK,.

Personal Experience and Assertion

One way is that people can contemplate the assertions of others regarding what they have experienced. This is what resides behind the use of self-report tests and the testimony of witnesses-of-fact in forensic psychology.

The main epistemological problem of testimony is that an enormous number of our beliefs originate in the assertions or testimony of speakers, but our accepting or believing those assertions merely on the word of the speaker does not seem sufficient for those beliefs to be justified, warranted, or knowledge. The problem is diminished but not eliminated if it is assumed, as is standard, that the speaker is justified or warranted in the beliefs that his assertions express, and even if he knows them. Assuming that the answer to this problem is positive, not skeptical, how do we account for this positive answer? Testimony depends upon other fundamental sources of epistemic warrant like perception or memory, but not conversely. A testimonial chain of knowledge must eventuate in a speaker who knows directly by, say, perception. Can the reliability of testimony be justified by appeal to just these other sources along with familiar forms of inference, especially induction? The view that it can be is called reductionism, and it is opposed by anti-reductionists who hold that testimony is a source of warrant in itself, not reducible to warrant derived from these other sources, even if empirically dependent on them. Anti-reductionists typically offer various kinds of a priori justifications for the acceptance of testimony. Anti-reductionists also view reductionists as holding to an individualist epistemology, which grants knowledge only if the putative knower autonomously evaluates and endorses testimony. By contrast, they favor a social epistemology, which holds that the possibility of the vast knowledge we gain from testimony depends essentially on our membership in an epistemic community. (Adler 2006, np)

Thus, testimony is relative, not only in terms of absolute truth, but also in terms of its context and etiology in an "epistemic community."

People in such a community ask if there is social validity associated with any given inquiry (Gresham and Lopez 1996). How does it fit? Is there social significance and importance associated with research and are the interventions and procedures socially acceptable? Some will say one thing and others will say something else.

There will be those who emphasize the need for internal validity (the context of the laboratory) versus those who emphasize the need for external validity (the context of the clinic).

What people say arises out of the relational matrix in any given research or epistemic community. Gestalt therapists recognize this as reference to the spheres of influence that comprise the field. Thus, the evidence of testimony is relative to a context.

The report from personal experience, in and of itself, is often regarded by some as constituting sufficient warrant; however, it is insufficient for others.

When gestalt therapists assert the effectiveness of gestalt therapy and refer to their clinical experience, that would be acceptable to some, but when the lens of the field is widened it would be insufficient to others. Testimonial is a means for establishing warrant, but its degree of relativity is so high that it cannot stand alone to provide sufficient warrant.

Rejection of Warrant Based on Foundationalism

Sometimes people will attempt to justify one belief or assertion based on another (more foundational assertion), but if that supporting assertion is not warranted, one simply creates an epistemic regress. The skeptic would maintain that such regress is inescapable, that it constitutes an infinite regress, and therefore warrant is impossible. That would make all research futile, and therein resides the flaw in the skeptical stance. It is practically unacceptable, because within limits we can justify various kinds of beliefs and assertions and we simply must be responsible. Thus, Kvanvig (2007, np), speaking of coherentist epistemic justification stated,

> This version of coherentism denies that justification is linear in the way presupposed by the regress argument. Instead, such versions of coherentism maintain that justification is holistic in character, and the standard metaphors for coherentism are intended to convey this aspect of the view. Neurath's boat metaphor—according to which our ship of beliefs is at sea, requiring the ongoing replacement of whatever parts are defective in order to remain seaworthy–and Quine's web of belief metaphor–according to which our beliefs form an interconnected web in which the structure hangs or falls as a whole — both convey the idea that justification is a feature of a system of beliefs.

This is an attractive way for gestalt therapists to consider the construct of warrant, because holism is already a central component in the belief system inherent to gestalt therapy. Thus, research in support of gestalt therapy would be most helpful if it provided many strands and intersected many other strands at points in such a web of meaning.

The Rejection of Conclusive Evidentialism

There is no way to escape the point that all "evidence" in support of practice is relative. At this point it might be helpful to establish some of the implications of that statement. Evidentialism in psychotherapy claims that unless there is conclusive evidence for the efficacy of a certain practice, one lacks warrant and should not engage in that form of practice. Addressing evidentialism in religion, Forrest (2006) observed:

Evidentialism implies that it is not justified to have a full religious belief unless there is conclusive evidence for it. It follows that if the known arguments for there being a God, including any arguments from religious experience, are at best probable ones, no one would be justified in having full belief that there is a God. And the same holds for other religious beliefs, such as the Christian belief that Jesus was God incarnate. Likewise, it would not be justified to believe even with less than full confidence if there is not a balance of evidence for belief." (np)

This is the crux of the problem. Some might claim that belief in gestalt therapy's efficacy/effectiveness is not justified unless one has conclusive evidence to support its practice. When put that way, the EBP movement is evidentialist in its approach to warrant.

I once met a psychologist trained in a strict application of such evidentialism. She found herself in a dilemma. She needed to conduct assessments for, and provide therapy to, an offending population, but she could not find specific instruments and interventions that were documented in the research literature for her particular population (a certain culture of people on a particular island nation where virtually no specific research had been conducted). Thus, she needed to operate with a relative degree of confidence, extrapolating from the research literature that she could find. This, however, flew in the face of her training, a training asserting the limits of application based on the model of empirically supported treatments (ESTs). ESTs not only describe intervention procedures, but also describe the appropriate populations for which such procedures apply. Thus, she was lost. She could not, in good conscience, do the job for which she was hired in accord with the training she had received.

Consequently, the magnitude of evidence necessary to attain warrant is a relative quantity, and it cannot be ascertained in isolation. In every case, it must be assessed in connection with other components of a given situation. Warrant is contextual and the evidence that is available and applicable is relative to one's context.

Evidence-Based Practice

The American Psychological Association adopted a working definition of evidence-based practice, and they asserted that evidence-based practice in psychology (EBPP) is the integration of the best available research with clinical expertise in the context of patient characteristics, culture, and preferences (APA 2006). They went on to make a critical distinction between empirically supported treatments and evidence-based practice and to open up multiple and relative streams of support as "evidence:"

It is important to clarify the relation between EBPP and empirically supported treatments (ESTs). EBPP is the more comprehensive concept. ESTs start with a treatment and ask whether it works for a certain disorder or problem under specified circumstances. EBPP starts with the patient and asks what research evidence (including relevant results from RCTs) will assist the psychologist in achieving the best outcome. In addition, ESTs are specific psychological treatments that have been shown to be efficacious in controlled clinical trials, whereas EBPP encompasses a broader range of clinical activities (e.g., psychological assessment, case formulation, therapy relationships). As such, EBPP articulates a decision-making process for integrating multiple streams of research evidence—including but not limited to RCTs—into the intervention process." (*APA* 2006, 273)

The APA task force pointed to a range of research designs that all contribute to the body of knowledge relevant to evidence-based practice. They include clinical observation, qualitative research, systematic case study, single-case experimental designs to examine causal factors in outcome with regard to a single patient, process-outcome studies to examine mechanisms of change, effectiveness studies in natural settings, Random Controlled Treatments and efficacy studies for drawing causal inferences in groups, and meta-analysis for observing patterns across multiple studies and for understanding effect sizes. With regard to any particular treatment intervention, the task force identified two considerations: does the treatment work–a question of its efficacy, which is most related to internal validity, and does it generalize or transport to the local setting where it is to be used–a question of its effectiveness, which is most related to external validity.

In spite of the variety of these methods, globally a number of problems have been observed with EBPPs. They are limited in regard to the generalizability of the results in their empirical supports, and that leaves a lack of confidence in them among clinicians. Furthermore, clinicians are often distant in many ways from the processes involved in such research, and the results have low transportability to clinical practice. In addition, evidence-based movements overemphasize treatments and treatment differences, ignoring outcome results on psychotherapy demonstrating variation among psychologists, the impact of relationship, and other common factors (Wampold and Bhati 2004).

In contrast, Practice-based Evidence (PBE) provides a bridge for this gap between research and practice (Evans, Collins, Barkham, et. al. 2003).

Practice-Based Evidence

Practice-based evidence is a useful model and not just a play on words. It has been characterized as a bottom-up process of gathering data that relies on the experience of practicing clinicians to inform treatment (Dupree, White, Olsen and

Lafleur 2007). Practice-based research networks (PBRNs) have been utilized to cooperate among clinician-researchers across diverse organizations in preventative medicine (Green 2007); such PBRNs seek to increase external validity and the generalizability of results. The mental health system in one locality, for instance, discovered that linking EBP with the research strategies associated with practice-based evidence (PBE) could improve service to clients. Outcome measurements were used to bridge between EBP and PBE, and they were based upon objective factors and clients' perceptions of care, often utilizing standardized measures at referral, during moments of assessment, the beginning of therapy, at discharge and then again at some interval following. In the agencies in question, this process became systemic and often provided useful clinical information as well as a read on client progress (Lucock, Leach, Iveson, et.al. 2003). Wade and Neuman (2007) found that integrating research skills into clinical processes could correlate clinical practices with treatment outcomes, providing helpful feedback to clinicians regarding the effectiveness of their methods. Unfortunately, they also observed that the average clinician lacks the time, resources, and expertise to work out such an integration without support. Several studies in the United Kingdom argued for utilization of an outcomes instrument known as the Clinical Outcomes in Routine Evaluation (CORE) to assess the effectiveness of treatments from such a bottom-up, practice-based perspective (Barkham, Mellor-Clark, Connell 2006; Stiles, Leach, Barkham, et.al. 2003; Barkham, Margison, Leach 2001, Mellor-Clark, Barkham, Connell, et.al. 1999).

Although many people have bridged the gap between EBP and PBE with outcome studies, surveys, and qualitative studies to discover patterns in actual practice, one of the research designs identified by the APA task force serves as both a form of evidence in support of EBPs and as a form of PBE. That is the single case time trial, otherwise also known as case-based time-series analysis. (Borckhardt, Nash, Murphy, et.al. 2008) pointed out that the

> ...practitioner-generated case-based time-series design with baseline measurement fully qualifies as a true experiment and that it ought to stand alongside the more common group designs (e.g., the randomized controlled trial, or RCT) as a viable approach to expanding our knowledge about whether, how, and for whom psychotherapy works.(77)

They also pointed out that the APA Division 12 Task Force on Promotion and Dissemination of Psychological Procedures recognized such time-series designs as important and fair tests of both efficacy and/or effectiveness. Thus, the single-case research design can do a great deal for gestalt therapists. It is a design individual gestalt therapists can utilize at the level of the clinic to track the process of therapy with individual clients, and if they collect the data across several clients, they can make observations about patterns emerging in the way they practice. Further, aggregates of several gestalt therapists using the same designs could be used to observe still larger patterns.

Would these patterns provide conclusive evidence that gestalt therapy worked? No. However, they would contribute to a growing body of relative warrant.

The Role of Common Factors

The research in support of common factors is an example of coherent justification. The "common factors" themselves form a web of meaning, a contextualized, interlocking network of features. The research on common factors provides warrant for the belief that psychotherapy works because it "rides on the back" of these mechanisms of change that serve as ground for all forms of psychotherapy (Sprenkle and Blow 2004). Common factors are decidedly practice-based in nature. Furthermore, some of the elements in that web of common factors are particularly consilient with gestalt therapy theory (see below).

Asay and Lambert (1999, 30) claimed that "common therapeutic factors can be divided into four broad areas: client factors and extratherapeutic events, relationship factors, expectancy and placebo effects, and technique/model factors." They attributed about 40% of positive effect to the first category, client factors and extratherapeutic events, and about 30% to the second, relationship factors. In the same volume, while examining qualitative research, Maione and Chenail (1999) corroborated such a delineation by identifying client factors, therapeutic relationship, and technical or model factors. Drisko (2004) asserted that common factors in clinical social work included the client and the client's context, the therapeutic relationship, and expectancy. Bickman (2005) organized the common factors somewhat differently and identified five categories of factors: client characteristics, therapist qualities, change processes, treatment structure, and therapeutic relationship. An Italian study (Gallo, Ceroni, Neri and Scardovi 2005) identified six common factors, three of which overlap other studies: therapeutic alliance, communicative style, regulation of expectancies, setting building, collecting personal history, and to keep the patient in mind. In a comparison of cognitive-behavioral, psychodynamic and interpersonal therapies, Bernard Beitman (2005) concluded that common factors accounted for most outcomes. Technique was important but accounted for about 15% of outcome while 55% of the change was attributable to patient variables.

In a commentary on Saul Rosenzweig's classic article on common factors (1936/2002) Barry Duncan concluded that

. . . .because all approaches appear equal in effectiveness, there must be pantheoretical factors in operation that overshadow any perceived or presumed differences among approaches. In short, he discussed the factors common to therapy as an explanation for the observed comparable outcomes of varied approaches...in the spirit of Rosenzweig's legacy and the wisdom of the dodo, this article suggests that psychotherapy abandon the empirically bankrupt pursuit of prescriptive interventions for specific disorders based on a medical model of psychopathology. Instead, a call is made for a systematic application of the common factors based on a relational model of client competence. (Duncan 2002, 34)

In 1997 Bruce Wampold et al. published the results of a meta-study of effect sizes of various treatments described in six professional journals. His findings indicated that the treatments sampled all had about the same effect sizes, thus corroborating Rosenzweig's early thinking. As has been seen above, other research has extended these findings to identify some of the common factors in question. Of course, it should be noted that some have found flaws in Wampold's research,[73] but that is to be expected when the discussion is still fully engaged and there are diverse theories all competing for attention.

Reading Rosenzweig's original article, though, it becomes apparent that predating Frederick Perls and Paul Goodman, he had caught sight of some of the salient and important elements that eventually came to hold prominence in gestalt therapy theory. These were a shift to the present, the influence of the therapist's personality, the organizing influence of a well-developed theory, the mix between the personality of the therapist and that of the client–what is now known as an intersubjective relationship–and an emphasis on holism:

> ...in attempting to modify the structure of a personality, it would matter relatively little whether the approach was made from the right or the left, at the top or the bottom, so to speak, since a change in the total organization would follow regardless of the particular significant point at which it was attached." (Rosenzweig 1936/2002, p. 8)

Common Factors and Gestalt Therapy Theory

Various researchers have identified common factors and in the process a few factors have emerged as a little more "common" than others. These are what the client brings to therapy (client factors and extra-therapeutic events), therapist qualities, the relationship between the therapist and the client, specific methods used by the therapist, and expectancy factors.

An experienced gestalt therapist would immediately recognize these features as belonging to gestalt therapy theory and practice.

---

[73] See Crits-Christoph 1997, Howard, Krause, Saunders and Kopta, 1997

Client and Extra-Therapeutic Factor

This is the field–all things having affect, and especially so this is the view of the field most associated with the client's life space. This is what the client brings to therapy that bears on the process of therapy and the issues to be visited during that process. This includes the client's cognitive-intellectual capacities. It includes those elements of culture, history, financial resources, and legal impact that affect the course of therapy

Therapist Qualities

This relates to the presence of the therapist as an authentic person, the capacity of the therapist for contact, and his or her training and experience. It includes the life space of the therapist.

- *Relationship:*

This concerns the relational qualities of the working alliance, and it relates directly to the gestalt therapy concepts inherent to dialogue–presence, inclusion, commitment to dialogue, and the creating of conditions permissive and conducive to dialogue.

- *Specific Method*:

Certainly, this encompasses the aspects of theory referred to above, but more specifically this also relates to gestalt therapy's reliance on a phenomenological method and experiment, for gestalt therapy is decidedly phenomenological and experiential.

- *Expectancy:*

This relates to faith in the paradoxical theory of change; it is a faith position more generally as well in that gestalt therapists trust that what is necessary will be supplied by the field (Brownell 2008).

Conclusion

Warrant pertains to the justification for beliefs and actions. The practice of gestalt therapy is warranted because of the testimony of satisfied clients and gratified therapists and the coherent nature of its holistic web of meaning. Where the field of gestalt therapy is currently focused is in the provision of evidence to support the theory and practice of gestalt therapy; however, such evidence can only be relative and can never be conclusive. Furthermore, the source of the evidence that does emerge needs to be from a mix of research procedures and methods so that the evidence-based practice of gestalt therapy is soundly based in practice-based evidence. Several considerations for bridging the gap between these two often polarized perspectives have been offered, and one of them, the observation that common therapeutic factors reside behind the effectiveness of psychotherapy, in a pantheoretic manner, holds promise for significant support for gestalt therapy because, among other things, the consilience that exists between some of the most common factors and the basic tenets of gestalt therapy bodes well for the soundness of gestalt therapy theory.

Resources

Adler, Johathan. 2006. Epistemological problems of testimony. In the *Stanford Encyclopedia of Philosophy,* Edward Zalta, ed. Stanford: Stanford University.   Accessed   March   25,   2008   from http://plato.stanford.edu/entries/testimony-episprob

APA Presidential Task Force on Evidence-Based Practice. 2006. Evidence-based practice in psychology. *American Psychologist.* 61(4) 271-285

Asay, Ted and Michael Lambert. 1999. The empirical case for the common factors in therapy: Quantitative findings. In Mark Hubble, Barry Duncan, and Scott Miller, eds., *The heart and soul of change: What works in   therapy,   33-56. Washington: American Psychological Association.

Barkham, Michael, John Mellor-Clark, Janice Connell and Jane Cahill. 2006. A core approach to practice-based evidence: A brief history of the   *origins   and applications of the CORE-OM and CORE System. Counselling & Psychotherapy Research* 6(1) 3-15

Barkham, Michael, Frank Margison, Chris Leach, Mike Lucock, John Mellor- Clark, Chris Evans, Liz Benson, Janice Connell, Kerry Audin, and Graeme McGrath. 2001. Service profiling and outcomes benchmarking using the CORE-OM: Toward practice-based   evidence in the psychological therapies. *Journal of Consulting and Clinical Psychology.* 69(2) 184-196.

Beitman, Bernard. 2005. To The Editor: Defining the Core Processes of Ppsychotherapy. *American Journal of Psychiatry.* 162(8) 1549-1550

Bickman, Leonard. 2005. A Common Factors Approach to Improving Mental Health Services. *Mental Health Services Research.* 7(1) 1-4

Borckardt, Jeffrey, Michael Nash, Martin Murphy, Mark Moore, Darlene Shaw and Patrick O'Neil. 2008. Clinical practice

Brownell, Philip. 2008. Faith: An existential, phenomenological and biblical integration. *In Miracles: God, science, and psychology in the paranormal, vol.2, medical and therapeutic events*, J. Harold Ellens, ed.   Westport: Praeger-Greenwood.

Crits-Christoph, Paul. 1997. Limitations of the dodo bird verdict and the role of clinical trials in psychotherapy research: Comment on Wampold et   al. (1997). *Psychological Bulletin.* 122(3) 216-220

Drisko, James. 2004. Common factors in psychotherapy outcome: Meta-analytic findings and their implications for practice and research. *Families in Society.* 2004 Jan-Mar Vol 85(1) 81-90

Duncan, Barry. 2002. The legacy of Saul Rosenzweig: The profundity of the dodo bird. *Journal of Psychotherapy Integration.* 12(1) 32–57

Duncan, Barry and Scott Miller. 2000. *The heroic client: A revolutionary way to improve effectiveness through client-directed, outcome-informed therapy.* San Francisco: Jossey-Bass, Inc.

Dupree, Jared, Mark White, Charlotte Olsen and Camille Lafleur. 2007. Infidelity treatment patterns: A practice-based evidence approach. *American Journal of Family Therapy.* 35(4) 327-341.

Evans, Chris, Janice Connell, Michael Barkham, Chris Marshall and John Mellor-Clark. 2003. Practice-based evidence: Benchmarking NHS primary   care counseling services at national and local levels. *Clinical Psychology & Psychotherapy.* 10(6) 374-388

Forrest, Peter. 2006. The epistemology of religion. In the *Stanford Encyclopedia of Philosophy.* Edward Zalta, ed. Accessed March 26, 2   008,   from http://plato.stanford.edu/entries/religion-epistemology

Gallo, Eugenio, Giuseppe Ceroni, Cecilia Neri and Andrea Scardovi. 2005. Specific common therapeutic factors in psychotherapies and in other treatments. *Rivista di Psichiatria.* 40(2) 63-81

Goodheart, C. D., A.E. Kazdin and R.J. Sternberg. (2006). *Evidence-based psychotherapy: Where practice and research meet.* Washington: American Psychological Association.

Green, Lawrence. 2007. The prevention research centers as models of practice-based evidence: Two decades on. *American Journal of Preventive Medicine.* 2007 Jul Vol 33(1, Suppl) S6-S8

Gresham, Frank and Maria Lopez. 1996. Social validation: A unifying concept for school-based consultation research and practice. *School   Psychology Quarterly*, 11(3) 204 – 227

Howard, Kenneth, Merton Krause, Stephen Saunders and S.Mark Kopta. 1997. Trials and tribulations in the meta-analysis of treatment differences: Comment on Wampold et al. (1997) *Psychological Bulletin.* 122(3) 221-225

Hubble, Mark, Barry Duncan and Scott Miller. 1999. The heart and soul of change: What works in therapy. Washington: American *Psychological Association.*

Kvanvig, Jonathan. 2007. Coherentist views of epistemic justification. In the *Stanford Encyclopedia of Philosophy.* Edward Zalta, ed. Stanford: Stanford University, accessed March 25, 2008 from http://plato.stanford.edu/entries/justep-coherence

Lucock, Mike, Chris Leach, Steve Iveson, Karen Lynch, Carrie Horsefield, and Patricia Hall. 2003. A systematic approach to practice-based evidence in a psychological therapies service. *Clinical Psychology & Psychotherapy*. 10(6) 389-399.

Manderscheid, Ronald. 2006. Some thoughts on the relationships between evidence based practices, practice based evidence, outcomes, and performance measures *Administration and Policy in Mental Health and Mental Health Services Research*. 33(6) 646-647

Meione, Paul and Ronald Chenail. 1999. Qualitative inquiry in psychotherapy: Research on the common factors. In Mark Hubble, Barry Duncan, and Scott Miller, eds., *The heart and soul of change: What works in therapy*, 57-88. Washington: American Psychological Association.

Mellor-Clark, John, Michael Barkham, Janice Connell and Chris Evans. 1999. *Practice-based evidence and standardized evaluation: Informing the design of the CORE system*. 2(3) 357-374

Nezu, Arthur and Christine Maguth Nezu, eds. 2008. *Evidence-based outcome research: A practical guide to conducting randomized controlled trials for psychosocial interventions*. New York: Oxford University Press.
Reed, Baron. 2008. Certainty. In the *Stanford Encyclopedia of Philosophy*. Edward Zalta, ed. Stanford: Stanford University.. Accessed March 25, 2008 from http://plato.stanford.edu/entries/certainty

Rosenzweig, Saul. 1936/2002. Some implicit common factors in diverse methods of psychotherapy. *Journal of Psychotherapy Integration. 2002*, 12(1) 5–9 (first published as "Some Implicit Common Factors in Diverse Methods of Psychotherapy," by Saul Rosenzweig, 1936, *American Journal of Orthopsychiatry*, 6, 412–415).

Sprenkle, Douglas and Adrian Blow. 2004. Common factors and our sacred models. *Journal of Marital & Family Therapy*. 30(2) 113-129
Stiles, William, Chris Leach, Michael Barkham, Mike Lucock, Steve Iveson, David Shapiro, Michaela Iveson and Gillian Hardy. 2003. Early sudden gains in psychotherapy under routine clinic conditions: Practice-based evidence. *Journal of Consulting and Clinical Psychology*. 71(1) 14-21

Wade, Kathleen and Karen Neumann. 2007. Practice-based research: Changing the professional culture and language of social work. *Social Work in Health Care*. 44(4) 49-64

Wampold, Bruce and Kuldhir Bhati. 2004. Attending to the omissions: A historical examination of evidence-based practice movements. *Professional Psychology: Research and Practice*. 35(6) 563-570

Wampold, Bruce, Gregory Mondin, Marcia Moody, Frederick Stich, Kurt Benson, and Hyun-nie Ahn. 1997. A meta-analysis of outcome studies comparing bona fide psychotherapies: Empirically, "all must have prizes." *Psychological Bulletin* 122(3) 203-215

Chapter 8. Seán Gaffney
The Cycle of Experience Re-Cycled:
Then, Now...Next

Chapter Introduction

I have selected this paper for a small number of simple reasons:

1) In the historical context of NYIGT, it is a provocation;

2) In that same context, it is indicative of the freedom of expression that is both in the history of the institute and is its current and future strength;

3) In its original publication (Gaffney et al, 2009) it brought together schools of Gestalt therapy theory, methodology and practice that had been divided and divisive since the late 1950s in the USA – and, by association, internationally.

To expand and clarify: NYIGT was founded in 1952. What was eventually to become GIC (the Gestalt Institute of Cleveland) was founded in 1955. In between these two events, original members of NYIGT travelled to Cleveland to train the collection of clinicians, organizational psychologists and management trainers who had a network there, partly based on them having been through NTL (National Training Laboratories) together. NTL had been envisioned by Kurt Lewin, realised by his doctoral graduates and colleagues, and at the heart of applications of humanistic psychology in the USA.

GIC had moved effortlessly from individual applications of Gestalt therapy into couples, family and group therapy as well as sensitivity training for managers and group and organisational applications of the core theory, methodology and practice of Gestalt therapy. In NYIGT, the focus long remained on individual therapy. The Organisational and Systems Dynamics Center at GIC was founded in 1975, by which time the two institutes had long gone in different directions, with all the value-judgements such divisions can engender.

The two first institutes drifted apart, and supposed ideological differences – a clinical focus only versus a clinical, social and organisational range – supported the taking of sides. Some old colleagues and friends had not even met for some 25 years. In 2006, a Colloquium was held in New York with such stalwarts of GIC as Edwin and Sonia Nevis along with NYIGT stalwarts like Richard Kitzler, Karen Humphrey, Zelda and Norman Freeman and Bud Feder.

At that time, I represented GIC OSD Center as a faculty member and presented the GIC specialty, the "Cycle of Experience." My friend and colleague and former NYIGT president Dan Bloom presented the original "Sequence of Contact," of which the Cycle is seen as a variation.

I later wrote the following piece, published in the Gestalt Review with commentaries by Edwin Nevis (formerly Director of GIC, and then Director of GISC, (Gestalt International Study Center Cape Cod) and Dan Bloom, NYIGT).

Currently, I have the unique position of being a full member of NYIGT, a faculty member of GIC OSD Center and a Senior Professional Associate/Program Director of GISC.

In this way, my paper represents a contribution from the "out-crowd" by a member of the "in-crowd" on a subject still sensitive for many NYIGT members, and still a defining difference between non-USA practitioners trained by NYIGT or alternatively, GIC or GISC.

In choosing to publish this paper here, I am honoring both of my Gestalt traditions – GIC and NYIGT as well as GISC which deliberately represents a non-polemical perspective.

The Cycle of Experience Re-Cycled:
Then, Now...Next?

ABSTRACT: This paper is an attempt to present a contemporary version of the Cycle of Experience, grounded in the context of its history and development, and explicitly adding considerations of a field perspective. The focus is on the heuristic value of the model as a pedagogical support in the training of Gestalt practitioners in all applications.

KEYWORDS: Contacting Sequence, Cycle of Experience, field perspectives, organism/environment, person/environment.

INTRODUCTION – A RECENT 'THEN'

At the April 2005 Conference on Roots of Gestalt Therapy in Antwerp, organized by the Gestalt International Study Center (GISC), Edwin Nevis and I, in a foolhardy moment, agreed to develop a contemporary version of the Cycle of Experience (CoE). Edwin, and his wife Sonia March Nevis, were founding members of the Gestalt Institute of Cleveland (GIC), where the CoE was created. Since 2005, Edwin and I have regularly exchanged and discussed our ideas, occasionally supported by the presence of Sonia, with her first-hand experience of the Cycle and her own distinctive approach.

At the same time, Dan Bloom of the New York Institute for Gestalt Therapy (NYIGT) and I, together with others – principally Peter Philippson – were engaging in energized debates on the GSTALT-L mail list about the relative merits and or demerits of the CoE in comparison with the Contacting Sequence (CS) - the latter as explicated in the foundational Gestalt therapy text Gestalt Therapy (PHG, 1994 p.179)[74]. This debate continued between Dan and me during a visit I made to NYIGT early in 2007. Out of these rich initiatives came a proposal by Susan Gregory (current President of NYIGT) to hold a colloquium at NYIGT to compare and contrast the two models[75].

This article emerged from my experience at the colloquium, as my thinking and teaching came together in a new synthesis. The paper is not in any way an attempt to report in full on the proceedings; nor is it intended to compare, contrast and discuss the two schemas – I leave that to others. Rather, it is my

---

[74] This work is generally referred to as PHG, the first initials of the last names of its authors: Frederick Perls, Ralph Hefferline, and Paul Goodman.

[75] The colloquium was held on December 8, 2007. In addition to the discussion of the two models, Sonia and Edwin Nevis led a discussion of personal memories of Paul Goodman. This was followed by a ceremony honouring senior members of the Gestalt Community: Phillip Lichtenberg, Richard Kitzler, Bud Feder, Norman Friedmen, Zelda Friedman, Sonia Nevis, and Edwin Nevis.

attempt at fulfilling my part of "The 2005 Antwerp Agreement," energized by having had the opportunity to participate in and learn from such an exciting event as the NYIGT Colloquium. In other words, the principal focus of this paper is to re-cycle the Cycle of Experience. Edwin Nevis has advised me on the historical aspects of an earlier draft, and generously offered a commentary on the finished article, thus completing the task we had set ourselves.

SOME HISTORICAL AND THEORETICAL BACKGROUND

Origins of the Colloquium Topics

The Cycle of Experience (CoE) was created by the faculty of the Gestalt Institute of Cleveland (GIC) around 1960. It was also sometimes referred to as the Cycle of Awareness. Outside the USA and the rest of the Anglo-Saxon world, where translations of "experience" can be imprecise and limited in scope – Scandinavia, for example - it is also known as the Cycle of Energy, or sometimes the Cycle of Contact, and even the Energy Circle. Over the years since its creation – originally as a heuristic for teaching core Gestalt constructs - much has been made of the distinctions and/or similarities between the CoE and the original "process of contacting," or Contacting Sequence (CS), still most closely associated with NYIGT. The sequence was intended as a "description of experience"[76] while the Cycle was a modification of the basic human process implied in the contacting sequence. The Cycle was initially developed as a teaching aid. Each of these proposed "models" is widely established and used by Gestalt training institutes and practitioners around the world, and the preference for one or the other – and its proposed legitimacy as standard Gestalt theory – can usually be traced back to the influence of one or other of these two institutes in the training of the founding members of the local institute, the work of traveling trainers, or advanced training programs taken by individual practitioners.

The Two Institutes & Their Teaching Styles

NYIGT, formally established in 1952, is the first Gestalt therapy institute. It was founded by the original "band of blessed and rebellious outcasts"[77]. GIC began as an informal small group in 1954 and formalized in 1956 as the Ohio Institute for Gestalt Therapy. In 1958 "Cleveland" was substituted for "Ohio," and five years later the group was incorporated as the "Gestalt Institute of Cleveland." Its founders – mostly academically trained clinical and organizational psychologists - were trained by the original NYIGT group of Fritz and Laura Perls,

---

[76] Dan Bloom, personal communication

[77] Elliott Shapiro, quoted by Richard Kitzler, 2006.

Paul Goodman, Paul Weisz and later their adept, Isadore From, each of whom conducted the Cleveland training workshops in the early years.

The Siblings Develop

The move from the anarchic exuberance and "apprenticeship" training approach of NYIGT to the academic tradition of the Cleveland group, and their institute, was, perhaps a larger step than those involved may have appreciated there and then. At the same time, the Cleveland group shared the social and political radicalism of the NYIGT members, and members of both institutes often found themselves at the same protest-rallies and demonstrations. Nevertheless, many of the GIC founders already had established backgrounds in university teaching, and this formalized training and educational focus soon emerged. Whilst NYIGT was offering free-standing workshops and the opportunity for apprenticeship training in its unique teaching/learning community, GIC turned naturally to designing formal training programs with both experiential and didactic elements. In other words, while NYIGT was creating something of a guild of master practitioners, each of whom could then take on apprentices, GIC was busy formalizing itself as an accredited educational institute, offering open professional training programs.

Perhaps the biggest difference between the two institutes was the application of the Gestalt Model by GIC to working with couples, families and organizations. In 1960 Sonia Nevis, Edwin Nevis, and William Warner began doing workshops for couples, Warner and Sonia Nevis expanded their work to include couples and family therapy. Shortly thereafter, Virginia Satir and Carl Whitaker were brought in to train faculty in doing family therapy.

Likewise, Richard Wallen and Edwin Nevis began in 1960 to use Gestalt awareness methods in sensitivity training groups and in leadership development programs for corporations. By 1974, robust training programs in couple and family therapy and in organization and system development were being offered, while NYIGT maintained its original focus on individual therapy. And, finally, while NYIGT has steadfastly stayed with the Contacting Sequence as originally presented, the new GIC programs were built around a cornerstone of the Cycle of Experience.

As reported at this Colloquium by Sonia March Nevis and Edwin Nevis, the standard NYIGT training of a line-by-line hermeneutic reading of PHG was not applied in the training of the GIC founders. While they were, of course, encouraged to read the book – and they did – it was not the core training content: this was, rather, in an experiential group with theoretical inputs from PHG to illuminate the experiences. Indeed, Fritz Perls actively encouraged the trainees to forget what they had heard on his most recent visit since his current perspective was more relevant! This can be contrasted with the more 'orthodox' PHG approach of Isadore From, and his focus on individual therapy.

And so to the Cycle...Then and Now?

Perhaps the most influential and lasting of the didactic inputs in GIC and later in GISC was and maybe still is the CoE. This was originally intended for heuristic applications as a cognitive support for experiential learning of the core constructs of PHG, such as contact, awareness, figure-ground and field. As such, it was a teacher's version of the CS as described in PHG (pages 179 – 209, 1994 Edition), Figure 1:

Fore-Contact/Contact (A & B)/ Full Contact/Post-Contact.
Figure 1.

This is the "description of experience" that NYIGT used and still uses as its basic orienting principle.

A comparison between an early-published version of the CoE (Zinker, 1977) and the CS may be helpful here. According to Zinker (who uses the title "Awareness – Excitement – Contact Cycle"), the cycle is as follows (Figure 2):

Mobilization of Energy
Awareness   Action
Sensation   Contact
Withdrawal   Withdrawal
Figure 2.

This is sometimes presented as a circle (Figure 3), as in Nevis (1987, p.2):

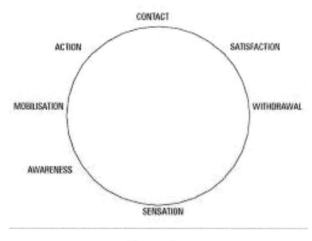

Figure 3

Figures 2 and 3 – and the many variations on them – can be regarded as containing the basic elements of both the CoE and the CS as originally formulated. It will hardly take much imagination to relate the two schemas in the following manner (Figure 4), though not all adherents of the CS might agree with me doing this. Most see the two as intrinsically different.

Post-Contact..........Withdrawal
Full Contact..........Action/Contact
Contact A & B..........Awareness/Mobilization of Energy
Fore- Contact..........Sensation

Figure 4

Comment

Zinker (1977) presented his version as a prescriptive and normative model, including details of the "interruptions" in terms of "psychopathology," much as Isadore From had proposed in NYIGT with regard to the Contacting Sequence [78]. (Each of these is fully in line with the discussion of interruptions to contact in PHG (1994, p. 227)). Regrettably, Zinker's psychopathological version became fixed in the minds of many of his readers, so that the CoE soon became some sort of model of an ideal experience, and by extension, a diagnostic instrument for less than ideal, psychopathological behaviors – far from the heuristic intentions of its creators.

And it seems to be partly this inclusion of very specific psychopathological "interruptions" at very specific points in the wholeness of the cycle - despite the similar schema in PHG - which has given rise to some of the objections to the CoE. In addition, there is an understandable misunderstanding about its wholeness. Some commentators seem to take Zinker's – and others' – use of the CoE as a model with distinguishable interfaces between phases as evidence of an unintegrated approach[79] which proposes dividing human experience into a segmentable model and therefore an inaccurate representation of what is an integrated event. Worthy of note here is that Nevis refers to the "Flow of Continuous Experience" when presenting the Cycle (Nevis 1987, p. 3). He also introduces "The Interactive Cycle" (Nevis 1987 p.29 - 40). Indeed, the Cycle has variously been depicted visually as a circle, a cycle and a sine curve (Nevis 2007), each of which can be seen as an attempt to capture something of the integrated nature of the Cycle.

My own experience of using it heuristically is that it is an aid to supporting the understanding of the integrated wholeness of our experience, both as organisms and persons as we live our integrated physiological/psychological experience of the field of which we are so

[78] Richard Kitzler, personal communicarion

[79] Bloom and Phillipson, personal communication

169

inextricably a part. As an aid to supporting our understanding, the Cycle is not a model or description of experience - it is a hypothetical schema against which the trainee as a person can check her own experience of being in the world. It is a heuristic, not a once-and-for-all description of that person's reality. That belongs to them, and not to any model or external map. As a Gestalt trainer internationally, I use Figures 1, 2, 3 and 4 above (with my own variation of the CoE: see Figure 5) along with a series of experiential exercises and discussions. I will expand on this in a later next section of this article. But first...

A Theoretical Diversion – Then becoming Now

An important contextual or field comment is necessary at this point. Where the ground of the two models is concerned, there seem to be three constructs of field theory involved, often overlapping[80] . In summary, with my own extrapolations: Fritz Perls brought with him to New York a biological field, that of organism/environment possibly emerging from his time as assistant to Kurt Goldstein, whose seminal work is entitled "The Organism" (Goldstein 1934,1995), as well as the ecological field of organism/environment as portrayed in the holism of Jan Smuts (Smuts, 1926/96), which Fritz Perls had read in Germany and had time to further pursue during the sojourn of the Perlses in South Africa immediately prior to their further emigration to New York. To these can be added the psychological field of person/environment as proposed by Kurt Lewin (Marrow, 1969). We know from Staemmler (ibid) that Fritz Perls had heard of Lewin's work from a fellow assistant of Kurt Goldstein. Each of these approaches to field can be seen in the context of the field perspectives of such Gestalt psychologists as Wertheimer, Koffka and Köhler. As conceived by these pioneers of Gestalt-psychological research and experimentation, theirs is primarily a psychological field, that of person/environment, though the work of Köhler with apes (Köhler 1957) emerges from an organism/environment field. The research and thinking of these Gestalt psychologists was known to Laura and Fritz Perls in the intellectual and academic circles in which they moved between the wars in Germany – indeed, Laura Perls studied Gestalt Psychology with Max Wertheimer. Paul Goodman was acquainted with their work – Wertheimer, Koffka, Köhler, Lewin and Goldstein had all been living and working in the USA since fleeing Germany in the 1930s. Goldstein had been recommended to go to Goodman for his training in English, which he did.

In other words: there was a dynamic richness of field perspectives, all shaken and stirred in the synthesising mind of Fritz Perls and offered as a cocktail to Paul Goodman, which he imbibed, further distilled through the filters of his

---

[80] I am indebted here to the stringent analysis of "field" in Gestalt therapy theory and practice by Frank M. Staemmler in a recent issue of *The* British Gestalt Journal (Staemmler, 2006)

own considerable and fertile intellectual heritage, and then poured into PHG. A heady mixture in many respects!

THE CYCLE RE-CYCLED – NOW, NEXT?

To begin with, I do not share the opinion of my colleagues in NYIGT that the two schemas are oppositional to each other. I sincerely trust – in the wake of the Colloquium - that some sort of foundational ownership of the "original and best" is not any longer at work. That would not only be regrettable in general for the practice and theory development of Gestalt, it would be unworthy of us as Gestalt practitioners and contrary to the wholeness, in name and nature, of the Gestalt approach. In this regard, the recent discussion of the themes of this paper in *Studies in Gestalt Therapy: Dialogical Bridges* (Robine, Schack, Melnick & Spinelli, 2007) represents both the necessary differentiations involved, as well as the opportunity for an open exchange in the spirit of the Colloquium. Nevertheless, what is for me an obscure side-issue also made a regrettable appearance: the semantics of 'sequence' versus 'cycle'. To throw out the baby with the bathwater of a name given to a diagram almost 50 years ago, and which subsequently became common currency amongst many practitioners and trainers in the history of the development of Gestalt in all its many applications, is for me a weak justification for any unwillingness to even consider that the Cycle may have theoretical, practical and heuristic value.

Having dispensed here with my minor polemics, allow me to offer a summary of the core considerations involved in my proposal:

• The CoE was originally designed as a pedagogical support when teaching such core Gestalt therapy constructs as contact, awareness, figure-ground and field. As a teaching aid, it is open to adaptation by any teacher to fit their teaching styles and interactive field sensitivities. To paraphrase Laura Perls, there may well be as many Cycles of Experience as there are Gestalt trainers using it. As such, it is, very appropriately, anything but a fixed gestalt.

• Organism-environment: the field of all animate and maybe even inanimate things – rocks for example change structurally in changing temperature environments.

• Then person-environment, the psychological field - or better, life space of the animal in general (organism/environment), and we human beings in particular (both organism/environment as a biological/ecological model and person/environment as a psychological model).

• The Two Kurts – Goldstein and Lewin - as the research-based explicators in effect of the holistic thinking of Jan Smuts, and all three emerging from Fritz Perls via Paul Goodman. And then via NYIGT to Cleveland, the latter with its academic ground of clinical and organizational psychology as well as its various connections to the national training laboratory (NTL) and thus also to Lewin.

• The person as embodied self...the embodied self as organism...the person as organism...the organism as person...

• As organisms, we are always in contact with our environment – though not necessarily always contacting it. As organisms, we are always aware of our environment – though not necessarily psychologically conscious of it. As bodies, we sense and respond to our environment. As persons, we make meaning, sort, select, are reactive, proactive. As organisms, we are constantly in flux. As persons, we like to think we can direct and control this change through our choices.

Much of this is neatly summarized in the bold statement that "Gestalt is the original, natural and undistorted approach to life" (PHG, 1994 p. XXIV). I used to question what I regarded as the un-necessary anthologizing implicit in the use of the word "undistorted"...more recently, I am inclined to see this as a reference to the tension between the embodied self construed as organism of the biological/ecological organism-environment field, contrasted with the person of the person-environment field, and the consequences of dealing with this tension. Can this be the tension between field-emergent self as we construe it in Gestalt and its ego-functioning when a part (Ego) presumes to be the whole (Self)? Maybe a topic for the next colloquium?

Allow me here to present my current version of the Cycle of Experience and how I use it as a trainer, keeping close enough to some recognizable original version so as not to confuse either its fans or its detractors. In other words, I have been less concerned with changing the form for the sake of change, and more interested in explicating and re-stating the rich ground from which my version has emerged.

A TYPICAL TRAINING SESSION ON THE CYCLE

I like to open by presenting the Cycle as a general hypothesis, for teaching purposes, of the process of the self as it emerges as an evanescent figure of the physical and social field, and how the aspects of the self in gestalt therapy theory– Id functioning, Ego functioning and Personality functioning (PHG 1994, p.156 – 161) - are involved in this process, in one way or another. I continue by introducing the organism-environment and person-environment constructs referencing Goldstein, Lewin and Smuts as distilled through Perls and Goodman, including the Contacting Sequence. I claim that we are always in contact with, though not always "contacting," our environment and always from some position on an awareness continuum between that of organism (the embodied self in its Id functioning) and/or the person (the psychological self – in its Ego and Personality functioning). As such the Cycle is a support to exploring the movement between the two. The Cycle is a whole here presented in its parts as a teaching aid, which is as useful to understanding our experience as we find it to be – no more, no less. It is a biological model, an ecological model, a figure-ground model, a life space model, a field model. It is intended as a heuristic supporting the wholeness of the gestalt of Gestalt.

And since it is intended to aid our understanding of our own and others' experience of the field of us/environmental other, then it is natural that I now turn to the experiential. A note here: I will sometimes choose to start directly with the experiential – related here to the interactive sensitivity of the teacher, mentioned above. This also means that I am open to finding myself following the dynamics of any process which emerges, rather than any planned sequence. Whatever, this training session will usually be within the format outlined below. For the purposes of this article, and to avoid the fixity of an instruction manual, I am choosing here to present this in direct speech, and will include process comments both from memories of recent sessions and also from my experience as I write:

> "I would now like to guide you through a connected series of experiential exercises, small group reporting and discussion, and whole group discussions. There will also be a piece of theory teaching, and I will end with a summary of theoretical points. Please be prepared to allow the flow of the session as a whole to eventually make sense or not for you, and to allow your combined sharing to be part of the experience. Trust that you will remember what you need to remember, if not today, then maybe tomorrow, or next week, or whenever. This experiential session will take the time it takes, so please also be prepared to support the wholeness of the session by using the transitions from one activity to another as opportunities for any short breaks you may need. In this regard, I will work – within reason – at keeping us in sync with each other."

I always feel excited when opening this piece of work –with its complexity, its unpredictability and the richness of possible learning available to all, including myself. I am also aware of how important it is for me to be clear, tracking the group to catch any confusion and repeating and emphasizing as the need arises. A clean and clear start is a necessary support for all that follows...so I have sometimes summarized the main points on a whiteboard or flip-chart as a permanent reminder throughout.

> "Please divide into two equal groups (should there be a person over, I will already have suggested agreeing with a fellow-member to switch places during the first four short exercises). Arrange two rows of chairs facing each other, about a yard/meter apart. Will one group please fill the row to my left, close your eyes and simply notice your process as this exercise unfolds. Will the others now please take a seat in the row to my right, and

also simply notice your process. Those with your eyes closed, please now open them at whatever pace suits you and all of you go with the flow of whatever happens."

As do I – and the flow of whatever happens is always so unique. I have seen chairs being moved forwards or backwards, attention focused on the person diagonally opposite, waves from one end of a row to the other, spontaneous hugs, a smile followed by total silence, even people who never open their eyes...I sometimes need to bracket my directive streak as an academic teacher and focus on letting them get on with whatever is happening – the temptation of the "perfect" exercise for the "perfect" learning outcome of my former days can still catch me by surprise!

"Will you now please bring this activity to an end, and include me saying this as part of your experience. Will those on my left again close your eyes, please...and those on my right please quietly change places with each other...and all just simply stay with your experience...now again, I invite those with their eyes closed to open them at their own pace and all of you to simply go with whatever happens."

I am noticing as I write how strong my need is to capture the flow of the session, while the accuracy demanded by writing a readable text in the context of this article means that I am being less spontaneously creative than in any of the sessions of this nature that I have run. A genuine dilemma –with no solution but to get on with it!

"Can you all now bring your exchanges to a close, again including my directions as part of your experience in this session. Will those on my right please close your eyes and those on my left quietly change places with each other, and again all simply stay with your experience. Will those with your eyes closed now please open them at your own pace..."

(I then do the basic exercise twice, the same way as before. In this way, each group member will have unexpectedly met up to four people as their environmental other as well as me as trainer, in the context of the physical room, and any and all other environmental influences).

"Thank you. Will you now please form groups of minimum three and maximum five, and share your experience with each other. And just notice how this experience of being in a small group of three or five differs from that of the pairs in the opening exercises. And remember that everything we are doing here is part of the whole. Take a maximum of twenty minutes, please."

I am now preparing for some teaching, and processing any events of the exercises which are particularly figural for me and which I may use as examples to illuminate some point or other.

When the groups are finished with their sharing, I offer an opportunity for anyone who needs to say something, to do so and add that we will have plenty of further time for discussion.

Then I move into the didactic session, asking the group members to constantly check their own experience in relation to the theory – experience always comes first. Theory – any theory – is a simplified generalization of discrete events, not automatically applicable to individual experience. One of the reasons, maybe, why we humans have so many discrete theories of just about everything! Including, of course, experience...

Anyway, I then briefly present or summarize (depending on the order in which the elements of the session have been taken) the history of the models as outlined above, as well as my summary of the core elements as I see them (see "THE CYCLE RECYCLED – THEN, NEXT?" above). And so to my latest (though not final) version of the Cycle of Experience (Figure 5):

Contacting/Changing.......A New Cycle Emerging OR

Energized Moving   The Figure Dissolving

Figural Awareness   Reflective Awareness

Sensory Awareness   Withdrawal

Ground   New Ground

Figure 5:
The Cycle of Experience: Awareness, Contact and Change.

I will generally offer the following inputs about each aspect of the wholeness of the Cycle, while stressing that our experience is an integrated whole and that it is the wholeness of each trainee's own experience which is paramount here:

1) Ground – the full potential of the organism-environment, person-environment field from which figures will emerge.
2) Sensory Awareness – how we as organisms sense our presence of the organism/environmental field and how we experience the influence of that environment. So what we see, hear, smell, taste, touch, our proprioceptive experience. (Id functioning). For example, what we see rather than look at; what we hear rather than listen to.

3) Figural Awareness –how the organism organizes its experience and/or how the person makes meaning of her sensory experience. The self-energized emerging figure (organism/environment – id functioning) – beginning to look at and listen to; the fast figure (ego functioning) – instantly looking at and listening to compared with seeing and hearing; the habitual figure (personality functioning) - what we usually see/look at or hear/listen to.

4) Energized Moving – the field-emergent self in its spontaneity OR the ego/personality functioning in action. For example, as an organism, I need nourishment. As a person, I want a medium rare steak with garlic potatoes on the side, and a 1996 St. Emilion. In my personality functioning, I go happily along with "the usual, sir" as a re-enforcement of an established pattern of a customer/server relationship, and how I see who I am in that relationship. Moving here can be towards or away from the environmental other in the context of the figure, whether self-energized or by an act of will as may be the case for the habitual or fast figure.

5) Contacting/Changing – the whole of who I am meets the environmental other, and who I am is changed as self emerges in and from that meeting – or my ego or personality functioning act as if they are that wholeness of field-emergent self. The other is also involved in the same process, with me as environment.

6) Either a new energized Cycle emerges spontaneously (the emergent self process continues) OR I move to

7) The Figure Dissolving – the energy evoked by and carried by the figure has been expended in contacting/changing and dissolves.

8) Reflective Awareness – I make meaning and sense of my experience and add it to who I think I am (Personality functioning).

9) Withdrawal – self and all of its aspects have finished the previous figural business and integrated its learning and change.

10) New Ground – a new ground, enriched by our experience, learning and integration is now available for new figures to emerge.

As such, the cycle is a recurring sequence of elements, though not of content. The content is always unique to any field, whether physical or social, and our behavior is always a specific of that particular field. I then propose that each person spends maximum 10 minutes in a pair with each of two of the maybe four others they met in the facing chair, exploring, comparing and contrasting their experience with and of each other and the relevance of the model to that experience.

I will then throw this open to the group members to discuss, in new 3 – 5 person sub-groups, related to their own experiences of the exercises - and in general - and what meaning they are making of it all. This is followed by a plenary session where members are invited to share their experience and learning.

I will usually end the exercise by offering the following as a summary of both the exercise as a whole and the full Cycle:

A)   Sensing – unfocused awareness

B)   Figure – focused awareness : emerging, fast, habitual?
C)   Energized Moving – towards or away from
D)   Contacting/Changing – start of a new cycle OR
E)   Meaning-making – reflective awareness

I close the training session with a review of the core Gestalt constructs involved and suggest new 3 – 5 person configurations to take an hour or so discuss their understanding of them:

- Figure – Ground
- Organism – Environment as Field
- Person – Environment as Field
- Awareness
- Contact
- Self and its Functions
- Change

SOME APPLICATIONS

The experiential and didactic session exemplified above has been used with both Gestalt therapist and Gestalt in Organizations training groups, as well as with organizational clients. In all contexts, the heuristic value of the Cycle is apparent. With its focus on experiential learning and interactive teaching, on core Gestalt constructs, and on de-anthologizing human behavior, it provides a supportive ground for the integration of theory and practice.

When teaching the Cycle, I like to evoke reactions to the impact of sensory and figural awareness on the nature of contacting the environmental other of the person/environment field; and also the impact of reflective awareness on allowing the integration of our experience into who we now are, post contact.

The full excitement of contact is in the realization that, from the perspective of the environmental other, she is person to me as environment. This is one of the reasons why I have developed the construct "contact boundary dynamics" (Gaffney, in press) - to get to the heart of this meeting, in which all behaviors have intentionality with respect to the environmental other. Behaviors are thus emergent from and always of the person/environment field. In person to person contact, where each is both person and, at the same time, the other's environment, "contact boundary dynamics" is intended to capture the mutuality and unpredictability of such contact.

I now use "contact boundary dynamics" to replace such typical constructs as "interruptions" or "disturbances" to contact, or even contact "functions," "styles" or "modalities." All of these seem to me to posit a discrete individual behaving as if in a vacuum, and are counter to Gestalt thinking where self is field-emergent.

As Lewin has pointed out (Lewin 1935, p. 71 - 73), behavior is a function of person/environment, which is in turn, fully congruent with the fundamental field perspective of Gestalt, however presented. Embedded as it is in a field perspective, the re-cycled Cycle is always relational, as is Gestalt in its foundational theory and the various explications and applications of its the core existential, phenomenal and field-emergent values.

I and my environmental other share in the emergent creating and temporary maintenance of our contact boundary dynamics. Some of this excitement and complexity can become figural as participants in the session outlined above process and share their experience in the various configurations. And then reflect on that experience...

Experiential teaching of the Cycle promotes an understanding of the field of me/other, where awareness, contacting and change are interactive, mutual engagements. Whether as a therapist with a client or as a consultant with an organization, this understanding will have professional consequences, since our aware presence and use of self with the environmental other is a distinctive core competence of Gestalt practitioners in whatever modality they practice.

The session as outlined above also lays the ground for follow-up training work on "contact boundary dynamics," interweaving the awareness continuum with contact – from being in contact to actively contacting, whether through need, want or choice. Combined, these two sessions firmly place the Cycle in its pedagogical context as a heuristic in teaching Gestalt. And not only in Gestalt institute training settings: as Edwin Nevis points out (Nevis 1987), part of the work of the Gestalt practitioner is to teach our clients – especially perhaps couples, families, groups and in organizational settings – alternative perspectives which will allow alternative choices to emerge.

SUMMARY – NOW AND NEXT?

This article is an explicit attempt to restore the Cycle as a heuristic, and to more overtly connect the process of the Contacting Sequence with the Cycle of Experience, in a contemporary context.

I am fully aware of having removed the anthologizing of human behavior so intrinsic to both the Contacting Sequence and its interruptions as well as the version of Zinker – and many others – of the original Cycle of Experience. Some may assume that I have here removed, or anyway moved away from Gestalt therapy. As a practicing Gestalt therapist myself, let me assure the reader that I have not done so. I have simply moved from training models which start by assuming pathology, to a training model that assumes nothing other than that we human beings do what we do, most of the time as best we can in our perception and understanding of ourselves as one agent of a field of agencies.

For many years, the Cycle – minus the inserted psychopathologies – and leading up to the version presented here, has supported me and my gestalt trainees in understanding something of:

- the complexity of our existence as embodied beings.
- the nuances of the Gestalt theory of self.
- the multiple realities of a social field where the environmental other is a function of who I am, as well me being a function of who she is.
- how the apparent chaos of ground organizes around the order of an emerging figure.

And more, and more as the learner makes his meaning of his experience. My assumption is that such understanding is a solid ground for our work, whether as therapists, facilitators of personal development groups, or organizational consultants, all from a Gestalt perspective.

I believe that the Cycle of Experience has always been a useful heuristic in supporting understanding of core Gestalt constructs. As presented here, in a synthesis of practice and theory, I hope that it may long continue as such. Only time will tell...

References

Gaffney S. (2008). Gestalt in Society – The North of Ireland. *Gestalt and Social Change*. Melnick & Nevis Eds. GISC Press. Cape Cod, USA.

Goldstein, K. (1995). *The Organism*. New York, USA, Zone Books.

Kitzler, R. (2006). The Ontology of Action. *International Gestalt Journal*, Vol. 29, 1/2006, pp. 43 – 100. IGJ, Gouldsboro ME. USA.

Köhler, W. (1957). *The Mentality of Apes.* Harmondsworth, England, Penguin Books.

Lewin K. (1948). *Resolving Social Conflicts*, New York, Harper and Row.

Nevis, E. (1987). *Organizational Consulting – A Gestalt Approach.* GIC Press, Cleveland, Ohio, USA.

Nevis, E. (2007). *Training materials*, GISC, Cape Cod, USA.

Perls, F., Hefferline, R., Goodman, P. (1994). *Gestalt Therapy – Excitement and Growth in the Human Personality*. Gestalt Journal Press, Highland NY, USA.

Smuts, J. (1926/96). *Holism and Evolution*. Gestalt Journal Press, Highland, NY, USA.

Robine, Schack, Melnick & Spinelli, (2007). *Studies in Gestalt Therapy: Dialogical Bridges*. Siracusa, Italy, Istituto di Gestalt.

Staemmler, F.M. (2006). A Babylonian Confusion? – The Term "Field." *British Gestalt Journal*, Vol 15/2, pages 64 - 83. Bristol, England

Zinker, J. (1977). *Creative Process in Gestalt Therapy*. New York, Vintage Books.

Chapter 9. Sensing Animals/Knowing Persons: A Challenge to Some Basic Ideas in Gestalt Therapy
Dan Bloom

Chapter Introduction

Choosing a contribution that represents my association with the institute wasn't especially difficult.

Who I've been, am, and will be as a psychotherapist are inextricably linked with the New York Institute for Gestalt Therapy. I've been a member of the NYIGT since 1975, joined before I was a therapist and matured as a psychotherapist and person within its community. My history and its are interwoven.

To my understanding, the institute is *alive in history*. I experience us as an institute that not only traces itself back 60 years to its emergence nearly coeval with gestalt therapy itself, but as an institute of persons living-through our own history in an experiential self-reflective way; in an existential way. We are not a museum of the history of gestalt therapy or, worse, a mausoleum for its founders. We are the institute in which gestalt therapy is lived and discovered within the experienced history that is our, foundation, our source. We bring our history forward into our present explorations of gestalt therapy theory/practice; we understand contemporary developments in the context of our history. Lived-history in the present is a double helix of our foundational theory and contemporary insight, which continuously co-creates new figures of theory/practice. This being alive-in-history is a sustaining support for my explorations of gestalt therapy.

There is an implicit polarity or tension in this approach. On the one hand, by continuing to honor the basic model presented in *Gestalt therapy, excitement and growth in the human personality* (Perls et al., 1951), we appear to be conservative. Our reputation not unfairly is that we defended this model for decades against its possible dilution. On the other hand, our history is one of radical questioning. Our founders challenged the status quo. Challenges are at our core: How can we teach the traditional model and yet not reify it and reinforce a status quo? How can we keep gestalt therapy theory/practice from being introjected ideas and imitated techniques while still being clear that gestalt therapy has an important, serious, and essential theory to be studied? How can we keep our history alive, that is, experientially present?

Different members of the institute deal with this tension differently. As I came to settle myself at home in the NYIGT, I found my own ways to balance this tension. One of these ways is to be both an iconoclast who challenges the often-unquestioned assumptions of gestalt therapy and a conservative who preserves and draws inspiration from our foundation.

In the paper I selected, I question some basic taken-for-granted concepts of gestalt therapy and by questioning them I ask gestalt therapists to pause and re-consider some of our accepted concepts —and to reconsider them from within our own model, as expanded.

My teachers at the NYIGT were Laura Perls, Richard Kitzler, Isadore From, and Patrick Kelley. Richard was my therapist, supervisor, mentor and friend. He died in 2009 at age 81. Nothing I think or write these days is free of his mark. This chapter is no exception and to know that is gratifying, indeed. Richard. The iconoclast and conservative, *par excellence.*

Reference

Perls, F., Hefferline, R. and Goodman, P. (1951). *Gestalt therapy: Excitement and growth in the human personality.* New York: Julian Books.

Sensing Animals/Knowing Persons: A Challenge to Some Basic Ideas in Gestalt Therapy[81]

Abstract: Gestalt therapy is the psychotherapy of "awareness," yet "consciousness" is given a secondary role. This chapter reconsiders these concepts and offers an alternative, the "awareness-consciousness continuum within the sequence of contacting." Additionally, the sufficiency of the organism/environment field is considered. The "self/world field" is offered as a supplemental phenomenal field that provides an understanding of the "person." Finally, contact is suggested as the link that unites the "organism/environment" and "self/world fields" of the "human animal organism."

This chapter is a cannon shot across the bow of conventional gestalt therapy and asks gestalt therapists to rethink some basic ideas. I ask us to reconsider how we have been using "awareness,[82]" "consciousness," and the "organism/environment field." I offer alternatives.

Gestalt therapy is the psychotherapy of awareness (see, for example, Yontef, 1993). From the simplest activity of the cellular membrane to the complex achievements of a human being, awareness is the thread that knits the sequence of contacting[83] into a whole experience, culminating in an actual moment of integration — itself also called "awareness." We are human animal organisms (Isadore From, personal communication to author) — biological creatures with "awareness." This description expresses our need for a theory of holism. It may even be gestalt therapy's unique identifier in the world of psychotherapy. It might be folly for me to ask us to reconsider this.

"Awareness" served gestalt therapy well. I will argue here that as it has been used, it limits gestalt therapy's ability most fully to address human experience. Consciousness is being studied in many different disciplines. (Dennett 1991) "Consciousness [is] just about the last surviving mystery" (Dennett 1991, p. 21) and it is one of the central concerns of contemporary psychology, cognitive

---

[81] This chapter was originally published in *Gestalt Therapy —advances in theory and practice*, (2012),Talia Bar-Yoseh Levine (Ed,) pp. 71-82. New York: Routledge

[82] This paper does not discuss consider "mindfulness" in gestalt therapy, which would be another matter altogether. Definitions of "mindfulness" vary and often use awareness, consciousness, conscious awareness, and attention in differing ways. See *Studies in Gestalt Therapy: Dialogical Bridges*, 3(2), specifically dedicated to "Attention, Mindfulness, and Awareness."

[83] As used here, "contacting" refers to an entire process — the sequence of contacting (Perls et al., p. 403), while "contact" refers to a moment in that sequence.

neuroscience, and philosophy. Sometimes in the literature "consciousness" is called "conscious awareness." Sometimes "awareness" is not even mentioned at all. And sometimes no distinction is even made between the two. But according to gestalt therapy, "consciousness" is *only* a functional hesitation within human experiencing. "Awareness" is *the* transformative process of experience. Since gestalt therapy gives its own meanings to "awareness" and "consciousness," contemporary discussions of consciousness in psychology and philosophy are not readily understandable within gestalt therapy's terms — and vice versa. So long as we gestalt therapists speak our own language, we speak only to ourselves. Unnecessarily private terms ought to be re-defined to enable a broader conversation between gestalt therapy and other approaches. When redefined, "awareness" and "consciousness" more effectively can be used experientially and be more valuable phenomenological tools in our psychotherapy practice than they are now.

Even more problematic for us as clinicians than our relationship to the larger world is that we reach the limit of "awareness's" usefulness when we try to address relationship and dialogue, or consider existential questions of meaning, freedom, and responsibility *within* gestalt therapy itself. Of course we are animals biologically coupled to our environment in our embodied functioning. Yet, using Aristotle's classic phrase, human beings are *zoon logon politikon echon* — reasoning, speaking, social animals. Of course, self emerges at the contact-boundary of the organism/environment field. Yet human *beings* — as *existential-phenomenal* beings —are persons in a social world of values and meaning who know the finitude of their own lives. Humans are socially related persons with bonds of trust and love not only instinctually driven organisms. "Awareness" and the "organism/environment field" are insufficient concepts to address these further dimensions.

In this chapter, then, I challenge the primacy of "awareness" in gestalt therapy. I question the sufficiency of "awareness" to account for our *human* animal's fullest nature and offer alternatives. I ask that "awareness" share its central position with "consciousness" so that the "awareness continuum" (L. Perls, p. 13) may become the "awareness-consciousness continuum" of experience. Further, I propose that the organism/environment field be *supplemented* with another field, the self/world field, which I will describe below, so that the fullest measures may be taken of the human *knowing* animal organism.

An historical expedition

But where did gestalt therapy's "awareness alone" model originate? This is easy to answer: Gestalt therapy's founding text, *Gestalt Therapy, Excitement and Growth in the Human Personality* (Perls et al., 1951), which remains the most influential presentation of gestalt therapy's metatheory to this day. It establishes the centrality of awareness. In the following section, I will critically examine Perls et al.'s treatment of consciousness and awareness. Perls et al. unnecessarily exaggerated the split between awareness and consciousness, leaving us with a theory that insufficiently accounts for such significant matters such as intersubjectivity, relationship, responsibility, dialogue, and the fullness of being human — of being a person.

Gestalt therapy begins

In developing their own modality, the founders of gestalt therapy were understandably eager to establish their alternative to psychoanalysis. They had a specific dragon to slay, which was the central place of *the* conscious and *the* unconscious mind in psychoanalysis. "Consciousness" denoted the "conscious mind." They had to find a more distinctive concept than "consciousness." They needed a concept to announce gestalt therapy as different — without the seemingly cerebral and abstract connotations of the psychoanalytic model. That concept was "awareness." Perhaps they thought "awareness" fit nicely within the biological holism of Gestalt theory or of Kurt Goldstein's theory of the organism — although Goldstein himself apparently did not use that term. Or perhaps "awareness" appealed to Paul Goodman's Aristotelian holism, in which the soul and body constitute a single substance. (Crocker, 2008; Kitzler, 2007).

Whatever the reason, they chose "awareness." Perls et al. describes it expansively: "[A]wareness is characterized by *contact,* by *sensing,* by *excitement*, by *Gestalt* formation." (Perls et al., p. x). "It is orientation, appreciation and approaching, choosing a technique; and it is everywhere." (Perls et al., p.385.) And "every contacting act is a whole of awareness, motor response, and feeling" (Perls et al., p. 258) Continuing to build their concept, they write, "[T]he contact-boundary is the specific organ of awareness." (Perls et al. p. 259) And "Aware response in the field ...is a creative integration of the problem," (Perls et al. pp. 230,232) — not a thought about it.

Consciousness? It is a functional delay in the sequence of contact to solve a problem of adjustment (Perls et al, p. 259). Or, when referring to the "conscious mind" in psychoanalysis, it is a *passive* associator, rationalizer, or talker. (Perls et al, p, 239) Was Perls et al.'s unique distinction between awareness and consciousness well founded?

At the time Perls et al. was written, the study of introspection was supplanted by the dominance of behaviorism. (Güzeldere, 1999) Yet in continental Europe, the study of consciousness and subjectivity continued to flourish. (Spiegelberg, 1972) Except for references to Gestalt psychology and psychoanalysis, Perls et al. ignore these developments since, I argue, this served their goal of founding their own method. Despite some brief references to the Harry Stack Sullivan's Washington School, it was as if psychoanalysis were the only game in town.

The authors claim that from the beginning psychoanalysis was hampered because it neglected Gestalt psychology's "adequate" theory of awareness (Perls et al, p. 239). Gestalt psychology for its part failed to make a "rapprochement" with psychoanalysis. "The lack of daring to do it must be attributed to the Gestaltists, for the psychoanalysts have not lacked daring." (Perls et al., p. 398) But gestalt therapy *will* have the courage to do what the gestalt psychologists lacked courage to do: to take an "adequate theory of awareness" from Gestalt psychology and integrate it into their new psychotherapy. Yet on what basis can the authors claim that Gestalt psychology concerned itself with "awareness" at all?

The English translations of the Gestalt psychologists exclusively use the word "consciousness"– not "awareness." German has different words for "awareness" *(Bewusstheit)* and "consciousness" (*Bewusstsein*). Evidently "awareness" was *not* of interest to Gestalt psychologists -- "consciousness" was. On what basis can the founders rest their claim of psychology "having an adequate theory of awareness"? Looking at our founders' sources for another possible reference, "awareness" does not appear anywhere in Jan Smuts' *Holism and Evolution* (1926) either, although here, too, there are discussions of *consciousness.*

Perls et al. then proposes a definition of consciousness:

> [C]onsciousness is the result of a delaying of the interaction at the boundary. . . . [C]onsciousness is functional. . . [I]f the interaction at the contact-boundary is relatively simple, there is little awareness ...; but where it is difficult and complicated, there is heightened consciousness." (Perls et al., p. 259)

Consciousness *emerges from* awareness when functionally necessary. This seems to be a casual point to the authors; it is a significant point here since I propose that awareness and consciousness are *inseparable* within the sequence of contacting as the *awareness-consciousness continuum.* I go further: *contact, not awareness, is the creative integration of experience.* Contacting is the process that includes *both* awareness and consciousness as phenomenal elements of the emerging figure/ground within the flow of experience. Contact, not awareness alone, is the basis for gestalt therapy's theory of self. Contact is the heart of gestalt therapy. The awareness-consciousness continuum is the sequence of contacting. I will return to this shortly.

Consciousness is more than a delay. It is knowing.

But if consciousness is just a practical delay, it has not much use in an uncomplicated world. Its function is to solve problems and in simple worlds there are simple problems. Small problems, little difficulties: minimal delays, barely any consciousness – but without much consciousness there is not much knowledge. Does gestalt therapy seriously propose a model of human functioning where knowledge would be superfluous? Or where knowledge is only "a delaying of interaction," rather than that which enables and enhances human interaction, or the basis for interest or curiosity? To be sure, "delay" has practical advantages. Matters come to our consciousness, we notice what we need, get it, and then go on our way.

Awareness, that which guides a plant to light, a bee to a flower, rules the biological domain. Yet this world for a biological organism is different from that for a human being. Consciousness as a functional delay must be from William James's *Principles of Psychology* (1981). His insight was a watershed contribution to philosophy that reverberated through American pragmatism and Continental philosophy (Heidegger. 1927/1962). Later, in, "Does 'Consciousness' Exist?" James added some further considerations,

> [T]*here is a function in experience which thoughts perform. That function is knowing.* 'Consciousness' is supposed necessary to explain the fact that things not only are, but . . . are known. *(James, 1987*, p. 1142, emphasis added)

Consciousness is a function and this function is *knowing*. Human beings thrive on knowing. Knowledge is our species' achievement. Consciousness is human knowing. Our sense of ourselves as persons in relationship to one another would be impossible without consciousness — as knowing. Our being in relation to one another is on the basis of our knowing one another —with hesitations and interruptions as well as grace and satisfactions. It More radically, consciousness as knowing is constitutes our being amidst one another since understanding — knowing, consciousness — is a function of our being-in- the world (of others). (Heidegger, 1927/1962) Understanding is an element to intersubjectivity. (Orange, 1995) It is a good deal more than delay. Yet, awareness has been the cornerstone of gestalt therapy from Perls et al. onward. (Klepner, 2005) The goal of gestalt therapy is the heightening of awareness (Yontef, 1993) so that the sequence of contacting may proceed without unaware interruptions.

Reconfiguring Awareness and Consciousness

By the continuing to use Perls et al.s' definition of consciousness without critical examination, gestalt therapy is missing an opportunity more finely to address the nuances of lived experience. So long as awareness alone is the template for the gestalt therapy process, gestalt therapy is locked in the organism/environment field model, which implies *individual* animals driven to satisfy biological needs. Yet awareness and consciousness can be understood as different yet integral components of gestalt therapy -- unified by the crucial concept of contact. By reconfiguring consciousness as a function of the human knower, gestalt therapy opens to wider notions of the person situated in a world of other persons. An *awareness-consciousness continuum* integrates awareness with consciousness within the sequence of contacting and self. Further, it has the advantage of opening the barriers of gestalt therapy's private language so that gestalt therapy might join other contemporary inquiries into consciousness, subjectivity, and intersubjectivity — in which gestalt therapy has a good deal to contribute.

To this end, I suggest the following reconfiguration of awareness and contact. Awareness is our sense of the situation. It is the sensible ground of our experience, the *incarnate* domain of self, or the "id of the situation," (Robine, 2003) without which we would be disembodied specters. Awareness is our felt ground as our "sense" of the social field. (Spagnuolo Lobb, 2007) Awareness is our *sense of one another*, as the ground for whole "intersubjective" experience. Awareness can also be thought of as "embodypathy," "*Einleibung*," (Staemmler, 2007, p. 53)

Awareness is our initial awakening to what is, from the first barely focused seeing of our waking eyes, to the background throb of a sore limb in our dim awareness, or the background as we attend to figural concerns of which we are conscious. It is the fringe around the focus of our consciousness. Awareness can shift in and out of consciousness with the direction and re-direction of our attention. Awareness "could be described as the fuzzy twin of attention. Awareness is more diffuse than attention — it implies a relaxed rather than a tense perception by the whole person." (Perls, p. 10, 1973) Consciousness emerges from awareness within the sequence of contacting. (Perls et al., p. 403) We act with conscious deliberateness. We draw on knowledge to guide us and to widen our perspective of the world. Without consciousness, awareness is empty sensation. Awareness and consciousness develop across the sequence as a continuum, remaining connected in the developing figure/ground process.

Often awareness functions without consciousness, as many of our activities do not need conscious attention. But awareness is the scaffold upon which consciousness rests. It is its ground, as in figure/ground. Consciousness cannot stand securely without this foundation. Awareness, to some degree, is always present. But if dim, a person would then be on insecure ground. Consequently, contacting might become more fixed than fluid; hollow abstractions of egotism might develop and these might increasingly become distant from lived experience. A person might become rigid, and stiffen as against the unaware ground. With diminished awareness, consciousness is short-sighted, lost in a dark world. This is one of different possibilities when consciousness is separated from awareness.

Consciousness with awareness is, of course, embodied consciousness — an experience of contact, which brings the fullness of human knowing and the possibilities of personhood and intimate relatedness. We approach one another with conscious knowledge gained from previous contact, not just with isolated aware sensation. We knowingly form relationships and forge bonds of community. The more seamlessly awareness and consciousness are connected, the more solidly — the more contactfully — these are built. Of course, we often approach one another with knowledge that limits the possibilities for creative new experience. Our experiences enrich our future powers of contacting as well inhibit us from necessary risk taking. The figure of contact is at its brightest to the extent it is unfettered by unnecessarily restricting prior "knowledge." Of course everything we do is not a result of conscious deliberation. We act skillfully in the world with a familiarity most often transparent to us. We know how to do things without being conscious or aware of how we do them. (Heidegger, 1961) This "understanding" is neither phenomenally aware nor conscious, but available to either in the sequence of contacting.

Familiar Concepts "Re-Tooled"

I now offer a brief review and modification of gestalt therapy's core theory that, I suggest, enables it to more suitably address the fullness of human experience.

"Experience is ultimately contact," and "self . . . [is] the function of contacting the actual transient situation." (Perls et al., p.229, 371), and the other (Philippson, (Philippson, 2001 p, 20) "Self[84] . . . is aware and orients, aggresses and manipulates, and feels emotionally the appropriateness of environment and organism." (Perls et al., p.373.) It is both aware and conscious. Self emerges as the awareness-consciousness continuum from aware sensed id functioning though conscious deliberate, knowing ego and personality functionings. Self is contact in its immediacy and contacting in its entire process.

As a process, self develops within the temporal sequence of contacting as three partial elements functions: id functioning, ego functioning, and personality functioning. This is significant since awareness and consciousness are aspects of these functions. Id functioning is the sentiency of the situation — sensations, urges, and tensions. This is awareness par excellence. Ego functioning is the process of self exercising conscious choice, agency, taking meaningful actions — with consciousness, par excellence. For ego functioning to function, so to speak, the "I" must know what to choose, how to orient, with what to identify. Awareness and consciousness go hand in hand as qualities of self functioning — the awareness-consciousness continuum.

Personality functioning is the consequence of previous contacting. It is the self function for what we have learned from prior contacts and now know,

---

[84] By no means do all gestalt therapists accept this theory of self. Lynne Jacobs, for example, is a major critic. (Jacobs, personal communications, and in press)

including — and importantly — what we have learned from social contacting. Through continuing social contacting, interpersonal knowledge increases. We acquire personal and shared history, values, culture, and so on. Personality functioning is the responsible structure of self. Personality functioning allows for personal continuity. It is the basis upon which further contact intelligently can be made. Were it not for our having an identity, remembering our likes and dislikes, how could we make choices? At the risk of invoking homunculi, how could ego functioning function without being able to "consult" the results of previous contacts while also trusting the felt senses of id functioning? *Self functions are inseparable.* Contacting, then, is of the actual indivisible situation. (Bowman, 2012)

We ask, "Who are you?" A person answers — Organism/environment field to self/lifeworld field – to person

Gestalt therapy originally proposed that all experience is a function of the organism/environment field. This remains the bedrock of gestalt therapy — and it should remain so. But it is an incomplete foundation. Human beings are animals; we are also persons. The organism/environment field fully accounts for our *biological* nature as the necessary fundament of life. The organism/environment field is not the phenomenal field; it is not the psychological field. (Staemmler, 2006) The organism/environment does not — and cannot — fully account specifically for us as persons. The meeting of an organism with its environment is a biological interaction, and although it is absolutely necessary for experience, it itself is not an *experiential* event. To the extent that gestalt therapy is a psychotherapy that focuses on human *experience*, it ought to address the phenomenal field — which is not the organism/environment field, though inextricably coupled to it. The exclusive use of the organism/environment field in gestalt therapy is biological reductionism (Staemmler, 2006). It is time to consider a supplemental "field."

Criticism of the organism/environment model's sufficiency is not new. For example, in 1928, the Hamburg professor William Stern proposed specifically that the Gestalt theorists' emphasis on the interaction of the organism and the environment was insufficient to account for human experience, including meaning-making and personality. Stern proposed the "person" as a solution (Ash, p. 314)[85].

"Person" bears self's temporal continuity, carries knowledge and memory, and enables personal responsibility. Without personhood, we would be unable to enter into relationships. "In the conscious living of human beings," writes gestalt therapist Sylvia Fleming Crocker, an advocate of organismic holism, "one of the major ways in which affecti*vity shows itself is in the personhood of the person, since persons both originate* and bestow *value* upon certain things and events and strive to realize their desire for them." (Crocker, 2008, p.131) Gestalt therapy's self is emergent of the organism/environment field; and as a structure and function within the stream of experience, self is of the phenomenal field as well. The person/world might be this phenomenal field. Person usefully may be understood as the human being as rational, knowing agent (Sokowlowski, 2008). And "world" may be understood as the phenomenal world of which the person is a part: *lifeworld* (Gallagher & Zahavi, 2008), *Umwelt* (May, Angel, & Ellenberger, 1958, p. 54), *lifespace* (Lewin, p, 43 (Lewin, 1951) 43 ff) or World (Heidegger, 1827/1961, Buber, Rosenzweig in Friedman, 1955), each of which concept is different yet sufficiently similar not to require further discussion here. Each describes a world constituted by and constituting the human being. The word "person" carries the further weight of no less of authorities than Martin Buber, Kurt Goldstein, and Kurt Lewin. Person/world field, then, is a candidate for the phenomenal field emergent of the organism/environment field.

Yet there is a better gestalt therapy alternative. Since self, not person, is the *immediately* emergent phenomenal structure of the organism/environment field, *self/world field* is a better name for the human being's phenomenal field. Self as a phenomenal structure is always in-the-world since, in gestalt therapy terms, self is constituted by contact. "World" is that "other" whose meeting at the boundary is the phenomenal contact-boundary of self emergence — Philippson's self/other. (Philippson, 2001, 2009) "World" is simultaneously constituted by self as its world of experience and constitutes self as contract. Self is in-the-world, [86] and this is the self/world field.[87]

"Person" then emerges of the self/world field as a result of *social* contacting as self accumulates its own "personality" through experiencing its relational history. This is the personality functioning, functioning. Self emerges. Person develops. "Person" is not a split-off "entity," but remains integral to the self/world field. "Person" is not gestalt therapy's version of "the subject" in a subject-object social field.

Awareness in the biological and phenomenal fields

Every living cell adjusts to its environment with *biological* awareness. But do humans directly experience cellular activity? For the most part biological

---

[86] This is a variation of Heidegger's concept of Dasein's being-in-the-world.

[87] "I/world" (Stemberger in Amendt-Lyons, 2002) is similar concept but insufficient since it apparently refers only to the "I" or ego functioning of self. See also Wollents' (2008) "person/world" and "situation," with which I have reservations as raised, above.

awareness is beyond our possible experience. The human being as *sensing* organism perceives and adjusts to its environment in *phenomenal* awareness. The human being as *knowing* person also adjusts to the world with consciousness. However, biological awareness and phenomenal awareness are different yet inextricable. Phenomenal awareness is a function of the *lived body* (*Leib*) (Welton p. 227); biological awareness is a function of the physical body *(Körper)*. Awareness, then, is actually a concept that can cross domains. It is a quality of the biological and phenomenal fields. That is, *in contact* the environment of the organism/environment field also becomes the phenomenal world of the self/world field. Said differently, the experiential world that gives "breath" to the person emerges from the natural environment that provides oxygen to the cells of the organism. The natural body of homo sapiens becomes the phenomenal lived body of the human person. These are coupled by awareness and contact.

Contact with its consummation through the sequence of contacting is the transformative experience central to gestalt therapy: the reconfiguring of new wholes of feeling, thought, and action. Contacting as a biological process and as a phenomenal event is of the *awareness-consciousness continuum* that crosses two domains of one whole human process. (Kitzler 2009) It is inconceivable that contacting can proceed without the accumulation of knowledge. Contact is not merely awareness, but a whole experience integrating awareness with consciousness — and action. In contact, awareness as a biological process of the organism/environment field becomes a felt, *aware* sensation of phenomenal self/world field. *Contact is the hinge within gestalt therapy; contact enables awareness to cross the organism/environment to the self/world fields and thereby establish a unity of the human animal organism.* The person is emergent of this process and gives contacting its human face.

When gestalt therapy supplements the organism/environment field with the self/world field, awareness and consciousness may be re-defined to become more precise descriptors of experience. Awareness (first as biological responsiveness and then as sensing) and consciousness (now as embodied knowing) are experienced as the *awareness-consciousness continuum* in the developing sequence of contacting. These terms are more fitting a relational, dialogical, and field-emergent self perspective than awareness taken alone.

Let me take this further. Social contacting transforms the human animal's environment into the world of the person, the world of personal *experience*. This "*world is the structure of meaningful relationships in which a person exists and in the design of which he] participates.*" (May, p, 59).

Self/world field and the organism/environment field, then, are aspects of one another, "two sides of the same coin." Whatever occurs in one occurs in the other, yet they are *different*. Self/world field can neither separate from self nor can self, as contacting, separate from the organism/environment field. Self is always in-the-world and always a function of contacting — *a process of the organism/environment and self/world fields.* We human beings are biological aware creatures and simultaneously phenomenally aware *and* conscious beings for whom own being is of concern to us. (Heidegger, 1927/1962)   We are existential-phenomenal beings. Persons.

"A person is not a substance or an entity that we perceive as a thing. A person is like an eddy in a stream, a vital locus of centering in the flow of all that enters a human's system: the physics and chemistry, the biology, the psychology, the culture that enters into each of us, and their relevant history as well." (Hefner, p. 76)

Personhood crowns our humanness.

We are sensing/animals knowing/persons alive in the organism/environment *and* self/world fields: the indivisible world of the human being in which awareness (biological as well as phenomenal) and consciousness have central roles. The organism/environment field and the self/world field are unified by contact across the awareness-consciousness continuum.

Conclusion

Gestalt therapy has an important theory relevant to contemporary phenomenology and psychology that can contribute to in those fields. But so long as we unnecessarily use a private language with idiosyncratic definitions we discourage communication with those outside our "hideout." We keep our treasures hidden. I have attempted to show how the awareness-consciousness continuum and contacting are important phenomenological concepts. I hope they can be exported from gestalt therapy to the wider world. Our usage of awareness and consciousness, on the other hand, is idiosyncratic and serves to reinforce our isolation as a modality.

I have also proposed that the basic organism/environment field is insufficient to account for the wealth of human experiences. I have offered a supplemental field for consideration: the self/world field. This supplemental field brings to gestalt therapy more of the depth of phenomenology.

This cannon shot across the bough of mainstream gestalt therapy thinking will not likely have much effect. Even if my points are well founded and my argument strong, to budge the weight of tradition takes great effort. But if I've given some readers cause to pause or question, I will have succeeded sufficiently to have warranted this effort.

References

Amendt-Lyon, N. (2005), Book review – Stemberger, G (ed.) *Psychischestörungen im Ich-Welt-Verhältnis. Gestalttheorie und psychotherapeutische Krankheitslehre.* (Psychological disorders within the I-World relationship: gestalt theory and psychotherapeutic pathology) Wien: Verlag Krammer, 2002, in *International Gestalt Journal*, vol. 28, no.1, 131-135.

Ash, G. (1998) *Gestalt Psycholology on German Culture, 1890-1967*, Cambridge University Press.

Bowman, C. (2012) "Reconsidering holism in gestalt therapy: a bridge too far", in *Gestalt therapy: Advances in theory and practice,* (ed) Bar-Yoseph, T, London: Routledge

Crocker, S. F. (1983/2008) "A Unified Theory", In P. Brownell (ed.) *Handbook for theory, research, and practice in gestalt Therapy* (pp. 124-153) Newcastle, UK: Cambridge Scholars Publishing

Dennett,D. (1991) *Consciousness Explained*, Boston, MA: Little, Brown, and Co.

Friedman, M. S. (1955), *Martin Buber— The life of dialogue*, University of Chicago Press, Chicago, IL, USA

Gallagher, S. and Zahavi,D (2008) *The Phenomenological Mind: An Introduction of Philosophy of Mind and Cognitive Science*, London: Routledge.

Güzeldere G (1999), "Approaching consciousness," in N. Block, O. Flanagan & Güzeldere (eds.), *The nature of consciousness*, pp. 1-68. MIT Press, Cambridge,

Heidegger, Martin, (1927/1961), *Being and time*, J. Macquarrie & E. Robinson (trans.), Harper San Francisco, New York MA

Hefner, P. (2000), "Imago dei: The possibility and necessity of the human person", *In the human person in science and theology*, N.H. Gregerson, W.B. Drees, & U. Görman (eds.), (pp. 73-94) T James, W. (1987), "Does consciousness exist?" in *William James writings 1902-1910,* pp. 1141-1158, Library Classics of the United States, New York.

Kitzler, R. (2007), "The ambiguities of origins: pragmatism the University of Chicago, and Paul Goodman's self", *Studies in Gestalt Therapy: Dialogical Bridges,* vol.1, no. 1. pp. 41-65.

Klepner, P, (1995), "Awareness, consciousness, interpretation", paper presented at the New York Institute for Gestalt Therapy

Lewin, K. (1951), "Defining the "Field at a Given Time." K Lewin, & Cartwright (eds.), *Field theory in social science*, Harper& Row NY, NY, USA. (pp. 44-59).

May, R. (1958), *Contributions of existential psychotherpy.* in *Existence,* R May (Ed.), Basic Books.New York, NY, (pp. 37 - 91).

Orange, D, (1995), *Emotional understanding*, The Guilford Press, NY

Perls, F. S., Hefferline, R.F. & Goodman, (1951), *Gestalt therapy: excitement and growth in the human personality*. The Julian Press. New York.

Perls, F. (1973), The gestalt approach & eyewitness to therapy. Science & Behavior Books, Palo Alto, CA.

Perls, L. (1992), *Living at the boundary*, Gestalt Journal, Highland, NY.

Philippson, P. (2001), *Self in relation.*: The Gestalt Journal Press, Highland, NY,

Philippson, P. (2009), *The emergent self.* Karnac. London, UK.

Robine, J.-M. (2003), "Intentionality in flesh and blood", *International Gestalt Journal,* vol. 26, No. 2, pp. 85-110.

Smuts, J. (1926), *Holism and evolution.* Viking Press, New York.

Sokolowski, R. (2008), *Phenomenology of the human person*, Cambridge University Press. Cambridge, UK.

Spagnuolo Lobb M. 2007, "Being at the contact boundary with the other: The challenge of every couple," *British Gestalt Journal*, vol. 16, no.1, pp.44-52.

Spiegelberg H. (1972), *Phenomenology in psychology and psychiatry, a historical introduction*, Northwestern University, Press. Evanston, Ill.

Staemmler F.-M. (2007), "On Macaque monkeys, players, and clairvoyants: Some new ideas for a gestalt therapeutic concept of empathy," *Studies in Gestalt Therapy: Dialogical Bridges,* vol. l , no. 2 pp. 43-64.

Welton, D. (1999), The essential Husserl, Indiana University Press. Bloomington, IN

Wollents, G. (2008) Gestalt therapy, therapy of the situation, Faculteit voor Mens Samenelving, Turnhout, Belgium.

Yontef, G. (1993), Awareness, dialogue, and process, The Gestalt Journal Press, Highland, NY.

Chapter 10. The Self and the Skin

Peter Philippson

Chapter Introduction

Why this piece? How does this connect to the particular concerns of the New York Institute for Gestalt Therapy?

As I understand it, the major theme of the Institute has been to provide a continuity between the founding theory and more recent thinking and practice. That is what attracted me to it in the first place.

So this piece for me stems from an important part of that foundational heritage: the principle that mind and body, inner and outer, must not be separated. The problem is that the theory also says that self and other arise relationally in the contacting process, and much of the writing about this in the Gestalt field has been influenced by a very disembodied psychoanalytic approaches to intersubjectivity. Meanwhile the embodied Gestalt approaches were, in the main, approaches to the individual.

My aim and wish has been to find or clarify a theory and clinical practice that combines the relational with the holistic. I realised that the approach to theory in my previous writing (*Self in Relation and The Emergent Self*) provided a template for holding these two together. What is more, I found that by going this way, I could gain a new understanding of the process of eating disorders, especially anorexia, processes that I had been working with for many years with more or less success, but with a background sense that I didn't really understand it.

So part of the development of these ideas was discussing them with clients, trainees and supervisees with a history of eating disorders and applying them in my clinical practice. I found that they immediately made sense to people from all these groups, and that seemed to me a good support for the theoretical approach.

I realised early on that the idea of the Self and the skin flowed so quickly out of the previous theory that it was not amenable to publication as a separate book. I was pleased to be able to place it in the book *Continuity and Change*. However I am also pleased to be able to include it in this book.

> *Experience occurs at the boundary between the organism and its environment, primarily the skin surface and the other organs of sensory and motor response... We speak of the organism contacting the environment, but it is the contact that is the simplest and first reality.* (Perls et al., 1994/1951: 3, hereafter called PHG)

As we slip towards a language of motion and process, we slide away from words which remember the fleshy, bone-filled human animal caught up in the throes, passions, and suffering of life – the very animal sitting in the chair across from us, and to whom all these impersonal processes refer. (Roberts, 1999: 134)

The Self and the Skin[88]

Experience occurs at the boundary between the organism and its environment, primarily the skin surface and the other organs of sensory and motor response... We speak of the organism contacting the environment, but it is the contact that is the simplest and first reality. (Perls et al., 1994/1951: 3, hereafter called PHG)

As we slip towards a language of motion and process, we slide away from words which remember the fleshy, bone-filled human animal caught up in the throes, passions, and suffering of life – the very animal sitting in the chair across from us, and to whom all these impersonal processes refer. (Roberts, 1999: 134)

Introduction

In its original foundation, Gestalt Therapy was a very heavily physically/biologically based approach, rooted in the functioning of a human organism in its environment, and the specifics of the physical capacities and limitations of the human animal.

In this paper, I develop my understanding of the Gestalt theory of relational self to take greater account of the physical aspects of relational selfhood.

I argue that there is a danger of the body being sidelined in a relational approach, and that this would compromise the holistic nature of Gestalt therapy. I outline the implications of making a clear distinction between the embodied level of organism/environment, and the personal level of self and other, and apply this specifically to work with people with eating disorders.

Relational selfhood

Now the "self" cannot be understood other than through the field, just like day cannot be understood other than by contrast with night. If there were eternal day, eternal lightness, not only would you not have the concept of a "day," you would not even have the awareness of a "day" because there is nothing to be aware of, there is no differentiation. So, the "self" is to be found in the contrast with the otherness.' (Perls, 1978: 55)

---

[88] Originally published in Bloom, D,. Brownell, P, *Continuity and Change: gestalt therapy now* (2011), Cambridge Scholars Publishing, Newcastle upon Tyne, UK, pp. 334-352

Gestalt therapy is a therapy of boundaries, understood in a particular way. What something is always seen as outlined and limited by what it is not, and it is the processes by which the *is* and the *is-not* both remain separate and interact that the Gestalt approach explores. In Gestalt Psychology for example, perception is the process by which a figure is formed against a (back)ground, and the figure has meaning in relation to its background (the note 'G' has a different significance in the C major scale and the E minor scale). Rather than taking self as being some kind of essence of a person, Gestalt Therapy theory takes it as always pointing to a co-creation of self/other, and explores the boundary processes that support the self/other differentiation in the moment rather than exploring self in isolation. Change in self always emerges from experience at the organism-environment boundary, new ways of engaging with the environment or new possibilities offered by the environment.

My previous books, *Self in Relation* and *The Emergent Self* describe this process in detail. However, my aim in this present writing is to put the emphasis on the significance of this understanding for ourselves as embodied (or, possibly better, 'embodying') beings. I have been concerned about the way body experience has been discussed completely separately from discussions of relational or intersubjective therapy approaches. I think that it is very easy for us to come to a kind of formal dualism: of mind, which is now seen as intersubjectively constituted, and body, which belongs to the individual.

The human being as an organism has a physical boundary with its environment, particularly at the skin surface and the sense organs, as PHG says. The skin separates the organism from its environment and maintains its physical integrity: as the Alan Sherman song goes, 'Skin's the thing that if you've got it outside, it helps keep your insides in'. It is also where organism and environment interact in a number of different ways. It allows air, sun's rays and moisture (sweat) to pass to maintain body homoeostasis. Its sensitive nerve endings register the impact of the environment on the organism. And its texture is affected by both the organism (nutrition, ways it is used etc.) and the environment (some environments lead to rougher or smoother skin, or puncture, blister, or damage it), so that the way it performs its other interactions are changed in changing environments and by organismic factors.

This relationality is at the heart of our embodiment. While we only know and experience the world around us through our bodies, it is equally true that we only know our bodies, our physical capabilities and fragilities, through their engagement with the world. We measure our strength and weakness in our physical abilities: to lift, to change, to navigate in the world. But we also experience our physicality in our relating: when teaching about the body in therapy, I often encourage people to pair up, stand a distance apart, and then one moves steadily closer to, then further away from, the other. I ask both to check on the changing experiences of their bodies. They usually find this changes during the experiment.

In the Gestalt understanding, self is not known in itself, but through a boundary of self/other, and what is taken as other is an inherent factor in what I identify as self. In a very real sense (though I shall expand more on the complexities of this later), I cannot be 'self-aware': I am that which is not other. As such, self takes its form not only though the process of 'selfing' but also of 'othering', and the contours of the other engaged with are also the contours of the self emergent from the engaging. This is an existential view of self, arising in the course of engaged existence. As Sartre wrote:

> But it is actually a question of fact, which may be formulated thus: is the I that we encounter in our consciousness made possible by the synthetic unity of our representations, or is it the I which in fact unites the representations to each other? (Sartre, 1957: 34)

Sartre identified with the first formulation, as do I, and identified the second with Husserl's view of 'transcendental consciousness'. This is the meaning of Sartre's view that existence precedes essence. It is in the engagement of existence that the consciousness arises of an 'I' that is the 'doer' of this engagement.

So we have two descriptions of boundaries: one of organism/environment, the other of self/other. The question arises of how these interrelate, and that – together with a third boundary – is the subject-matter of this paper. Put otherwise, what is the relation between the self and the body, or the self and the skin? It turns out that this question is a very fruitful one, and illuminates therapeutic work with people with eating disorders and body dysmorphias, as well as more general therapeutic issues. It has the further advantage that the theory is not disembodied, as can easily happen in my experience with a relational or dialogic approach to theory and practice.

This relationship between self and skin is far from simple. While in a moment of sensing (touch, sight, hearing, smelling, tasting) we could say that self is at the skin surface, there are many times when this is not the case. Much of the time, for example, we regard our clothing as part of ourselves, and the rubbing of our clothing against our skin, when noticed at all, becomes a kind of proprioception. Meanwhile the clothing we choose to wear becomes a statement of ourselves in a quite chameleon-like way. At other times, we objectify an aspect of ourselves, e.g. a sore finger, or even cut away parts of our bodies in ways that range from the simple (cutting hair or nails) to the radical (amputation, surgery, gender reassignment).

In fact, the latter, gender reassignment, points to another complication: body dysmorphias, where my felt sense of my body as encoded within my brain does not align with the physical actuality. While we could see this as a problem, and of course it is for those who experience it, from this perspective we could find the wonder in how often we can have such an exact knowledge of our bodies in space, so that gymnasts and acrobats can interact with their surroundings with grace and skill (graceful movement depends on such accurate orientation in space). The times when this does not happen merely points to the complexity of this ability to match proprioception and sensing of the world.

I experience my body simultaneously in proprioceptions, in touching the world, in showing me to the world, and in seeing the world seeing me. None of these has any necessary connection to any of the others, and 'body-experience' is an interaction between all of these.

The contacting body

I have developed a reformulation of the Gestalt theory of self in contact, or id, ego and personality, one that hopefully avoids some of the contradictions in the Gestalt literature, over the course of my books and articles. I will state it here in a form that emphasises what this means for a Gestalt understanding of the body in relation to the self and contacting.

Let us start with an experiment. I would ask you to shut you eyes, then when you are ready, open them but without immediately focusing on something. Keep your vision a bit fuzzy. Slowly let whatever seems organismically most interesting become your figure along with your sense of how your body registers your interest. Let that figure and body excitement develop in its own time, and be aware it might involve movement either of your head or of your whole body towards the object of your interest. Discover what the culmination of your interest is: looking, touching, smelling, hearing or whatever. And in its own time, let yourself move away from the figure to a sense of you now that contact has happened, and then back to the 'fuzzy' openness to what will be next.

It is worth taking several tries at this, slowing down the sequence of contacting, giving it its time rather than hurrying to a figure or to a pre-ordained result. In the sequence, your experience of your body is likely to change several times, ranging from something vaguely sensed (PHG says 'the body looms large', p. 159), to more definite and responding to its figure of interest, to being engrossed in the contact, to separating and experiencing the assimilation of the contact, and back to vague sensing.

You might find interesting difficulties in doing this. For some, staying vague rather than moving quickly into finding something to pay attention to produces anxiety, and they keep their bodies energised and their eyes focused towards making habitual figures. For some, being willing to focus and declare a solid interest is what produces anxiety, and they would rather keep a wide focus and a low level of energisation. Some avoid movement towards the object of interest, some find difficulty in moving away once contact has been made and returning to the void.

Three boundaries of self

As I describe these boundaries, maybe take time to compare them with your experience in the experiment above.

An underlying theoretical understanding, which I explain at some length in my book (Philippson, 2009), is that of emergence and complexity. Complexity theory shows how a comparatively simple system with feedback loops can lead to the emergence of a more complex system. Such emergent complex systems are found everywhere in nature. A good example is a weather system, say a hurricane, formed by the interaction between sun, sea, rotation of the earth and atmosphere. Other examples are population fluctuations, the Gulf Stream, evolutionary changes and many other systems. The primary characteristic of complex emergent systems is that they do nothing that disobeys the physical laws of the simpler system from which they emerge (and of which they also stay part), but they also have their own laws which are not derivable from the simple system. Cars, for example, are emergent from the physics of their components, and their components can be studied in isolation as they function in a car, yet nothing in their components give an understanding of a finely tuned engine, let alone traffic flow. In fact, the parts are subservient to the running of the car, in that components are changed in order to keep the car running without a sense of the identity of the car changing. Thus you cannot reduce consciousness and selfhood to physical interactions, but you can also not disconnect them, and the state of the physical interactions inherently affects consciousness and the experience of being oneself (for example chronic pain states or hormonal conditions), or even makes consciousness impossible in states of death or unconsciousness.

1.   *Organism/environment; It/not-it*

This is very much the base level. If there were no physical boundary at which interactions happen that can be registered in some way that is beyond the immediate interactions (i.e. the boundary is sensitive), there would be nothing on which to build a sense of a person engaging in a world. There is enough difference in the process across the boundary that there can be some 'rubbing up' that can be experienced. Moreover, there is enough coherence and continuity in that experience to sustain a sense of a person 'in' a world. But that person, who is not reducible to an organism in an environment, has not yet entered our picture. Conventionally, we would speak of 'my experience', but this is not the way I want to go, and that is the import of the Sartre quote above. At this level it is important to notice that we are not speaking about the definite identifications and alienations required to say 'I experience this'. Nor is there a defined sense of body, or what belongs 'inside' or 'outside', nor a sense of deliberate choosing or focusing. Rather there is just the vague experiencing of the 'is-ness' of the moment. In a language where every verb has a subject, like English, it is difficult to get a sense of this. When Descartes said 'I think therefore I am', he was putting forward an 'I' (which he saw as separate to the world of matter) that then applied itself to thinking or other activities. Thus he was assuming in his choice of grammar exactly what he was trying to prove! However from this present perspective, all we can really say is that there is thinking (or seeing or hearing etc.) going on, and there is some system which can register this rather than it just happening.

We all have experienced a vague discomfort in our bodies, moved around to try to get comfortable without paying much attention, and only through this moving and attending (if it happens: sometimes the discomfort is resolved without ever needing conscious attention, especially in sleep, but also while awake) do we get any sense of the 'meaning' of the discomfort as say a stone in my shoe or a bruise on my foot, i.e. inside or outside. Neurologically, we all have systems for reflexive activity that were central to the functioning of our evolutionary ancestors, systems that do not involve or require consciousness. The delay between experiencing and 'my experience', however brief, is central to this paper, and I will now go on to describe the next stage.

2.   *Self/other I/not-I. The ego boundary.*

This is the level where we bring awareness to experiencing, and which we usually see as the beginning of our experiencing. It is at this level that the raw 'rubbing up' becomes identified as 'I am doing and experiencing this' and 'this' becomes alienated as 'other': the 'I' forms out of identification as the one who experiences and 'other' forms as that experienced, and is alienated as not-I. Notice also that there is a double level of identification and alienation. As the gestalt psychologists point out, the act of noticing involves the formation of a figure of interest (identification) against a background of what is not currently of central interest (alienation). I form self in relation to the other that I now both alienate/make other and make figural.

The function of this boundary is contact, a meeting of self and other rather than of an organism and an environment. It is only now that we can speak of choosing and intention in relationship, and it is in this 'self-other space', which can be quite distinct from the organism-environment space, that I can get a sense of where I end and other begins. The body experience here is much more solid, in engagement with an equally solid 'outside world' separate from me.

It is central to this way of understanding body process to realise that I have a range of possibilities for the relationship between these two boundaries: self/other and organism/environment, between the self and the skin. In much of everyday engagement, we are most balanced and embodied when we align these boundaries, identifying 'my experience' with experience at the skin surface, the seeing of the eyes, the hearing of the ears, the tasting of the mouth, the smelling of the nose. These then become 'my skin', 'my eyes', etc. Fritz Perls' insistence on the use of 'I', 'me' and 'my' aims precisely at such identification.

204

However, there are also many meaningful situations where it helps us if we make different identifications and alienations. If we look at skilled tennis players, golfers, woodcarvers, sword fighters, pinball players, we see how they make their tool or game implement a part of themselves, moving it as part of a whole-body movement. Conversely, if my finger is hurt, I can study the damage as if it was some object, potentially even to the extent of surgically removing some part of it. At a less extreme level, we cut our hair and nails, identify our surface with our clothes or make-up.

Furthermore, there are specific brain structures involved in our proprioceptive sensing of our bodies, which sometimes function in such a way that we are not able to comfortably align the self and the skin. Some people experience themselves as a different gender to that implied by their body shape (transgender). Some people feel a profound wrongness in the existence of a second arm or leg and feel more authentic if they can persuade someone to remove it (body dysmorphism). From this perspective, as I wrote above, rather than such dysmorphias being difficult to understand, they point to the wonder of how often there is a close 'cross-modal' matching between the body as we see it and feel it (see also Stern, 1979). It is no more complicated to understand on a physical level than the awkwardness pubescent children experience as their bodies change shape quite rapidly, changing the length of their reach, their centre of gravity, their stride length etc.

Finally, we all operate with a sense of 'personal space', the point at which we feel invaded by someone coming closer. For some people at some times, this is quite far out from their body as they hold people at a distance; for other people or at other times, it is fine and pleasurable for them to share their bodies intimately and sexually with another person.

All these point to a converse situation to that which Perls emphasised in requiring clients to make owning statements about the body: where it is vital that enough space is given to the first stage, the experiencing body-in-environment, to allow the self-identification to occur in a way that best fits our purposes in the moment. If we do it too quickly, we can lose some of the subtle relationships between self and skin that are the (completely unverbalised) prerequisites to skilful use of tools or personal space. If we move into identification as 'my body' too quickly, our body-sense becomes rigid.

All these variations of self in relation to skin are normal adjustments in specific situations. While they may cause problems for people, they are problems to come to terms with, whether the problem is a body dysmorphism or the loss of a favourite tennis racquet that easily becomes identified as a body part.

There are other situations where I take actions to confuse the relationship between the self and the skin in order to defend against difficult situations. In a situation of abuse, for example, a child may disown the painful or invaded skin surface and 'regroup' to somewhere experienced as beneath the skin which can be experienced as unaffected by what is happening 'further out'. Meanwhile the abuser experiences the child as an extension of his/her desires without any independence and separateness. In this way, at great cost to the child, there is no longer any dangerous conflict between the self-identifications of the abuser and the child. Conversely, someone can enlarge their sense of themselves to include other people. For example, someone who abuses children can act as if they are merely extensions of their own desires. I shall have a lot more to say on this subject, but now need to introduce the third boundary significant for the formation and maintenance of relational self.

The personality boundary. Me/not-me

While the vague experiencing of the organism/environment boundary and the more solid contacting of the self/other boundary are events of the moment, this boundary acts as a ground for both experiences and contacts over time. It is described in PHG as the 'verbal replica of self', but I would take it as much more than that. It is certainly verbalisable, a representation of self that I can know and describe to others. (And it is the only level at which I can be 'self-aware': at the other boundaries, self arises in contacting otherness.) It involves my identifications, e.g. as therapist or writer or husband or father, and also my values and commitments to relationships and home.

From the perspective of this paper, the familiar body is an important part of personality. I know the feel of my body, my physical capacities and limitations. I know the look of my body, its shape and size, scars, eye colour etc. I know the memories of my body, remembered pleasures and pains, smells and textures. I know my assimilation of how others have responded to my body, whether with affirmation or criticism - and also how I imagine others see me. I know what attracts me, and what repels me: my taste for food and physical surroundings, my sexual preferences, my cultural interests (books, music, visual arts).

It is worth noticing that all these will have changed in a number of ways during my lifetime, and will continue to change. My body shape, capacities and limitations, memories, preferences and responses from others all continue to develop. This is characteristic of personality: our stable ground is itself not stable unless we stabilise it! Our sense of continuity is an achievement, not a given, and is even in some ways a story imposed on a situation. From this perspective, a criticism of the psychoanalytic emphasis on narrative is that it treats something changeable as being fixed enough to base a treatment on. Sometimes a unifying narrative (just like an owned, known body) can be a support; at other times it is an imposition on a situation that needs to be fluid and described (if at all) in many different ways.

Personality always has two faces: the assimilations that guide and support our lively and flexible engagement in the world, and our fixed defensive ways of limiting our relational possibilities to what is familiar and unchallenging. In bodily terms, this is also true. We can orientate towards our physical preferences and take into account our physical limitations, while remaining open to new experiences and possibilities, learning new tastes and practicing new skills. We can conversely limit ourselves to a very small range of experiences, and set ourselves to fear and dislike whatever lies outside this range. Physically, the former can be seen in practiced and graceful movements towards lively expression; the latter can be seen in low energy, shallow breathing, areas of immobility (often in the lower body), habitual defocusing in general or not looking at the other person in particular. In these ways, sensation and emotion can be kept to a minimum and set within bounds that seem tolerable.

The interaction of the three boundaries

All these boundaries intersect and interact in various ways with each other. The state of the organism/environment boundary affects both the self/other formation and what is assimilated to personality. If I am physically unwell, for example, or my skin has been roughened by my work or lifestyle, that will affect the physical experiences on which I base the other boundaries. The figures I form at the self/other boundary affect the assimilations I make to personality, but also affect how the world responds to me, and thus what is experienced at the organism/environment boundary. The personality assimilations will affect my physical position in the world, and thus both experiencing and self formation.

In the same way, disruptions of any of these boundaries affects the others. If I disrupt the experiencing at the first boundary by moving too quickly into purposeful activity, that activity will need to be based on some habitual/personality preferences, something I look out for in a variety of situations (criticism, praise, money, sex, for example) rather than being responsive to the situation at that moment. Such overdependence on self/other and personality leaves the person resourceless in situations outside their familiar relational terrain. They usually come into therapy when they are faced with such unfamiliar situations. If I disrupt the contacting at the second boundary, either by staying uncommitted at the first boundary or by fixed introjects (or superego demands) at the third boundary, I will find my life deprived of intimacy and human warmth. Such people usually come into therapy through their isolation: while they may be resourceful in their known world, they feel depressingly trapped in that world.

All of these situations have physical presentations connected with them, and can be explored therapeutically on a physical level.

Case examples

Tim comes to therapy with a sense that his life is going nowhere. He has fallen into a job that gives him no satisfaction, has no close friends and no particular interests. His handshake is limp, his eyes are not completely focused on anything and his language is vague with little sense of any part of his speaking being emphasised any more than anything else. If given a choice of seating, he finds it difficult to choose where to sit, and the offering of choice causes him anxiety. When he sits, he slumps listlessly and with very little body movement. His sense of his physicality is tenuous.

He is operating mostly at the first boundary, and feels fear at the prospect of being accountable for his more choiceful movement into the second boundary: stating a preference, finding his own interests, telling someone he wants to be closer to them. He has little sense of his third boundary: his familiar sense is of vagueness.

Tim could be helped in therapy by anything that firms up his experience into figures of interest. This could be anything from telling the therapist what he is aware of moment-to-moment, or making firm physical contact with the therapist (grasping hands or pushing) or doing definite movements. I would say that there is a need to explore active physical contact at some stage in the therapy: developmentally, this presentation emerges from an early life where physical (rather than verbal) engagement is either unavailable or dangerous and painful. As a rule of thumb, those who have assimilated reasonable physical connectedness in their most formative years can summon up a felt sense of physical relating if prompted by words; those who have not will not, and will need to be supported to a new process of assimilation of physical contacting before touch-words will be able to point to touch-experience.

Jane comes to therapy with a very different presentation. Her presenting issue is difficulty with a demanding boss. Her eyes are quite focused and her voice is firm. She sits upright. Her focus is so strongly on her problem that she can speak of little else, and the therapist is only there as a means to an end, of solving the problem. The way she presents this problem situation though gives the sense of her as trapped in an impossible maze. She's 'tried everything and it doesn't work'. Jane experiences her body, and her body-sense is of tension (that she associates with her work situation) and continuous anxious arousal.

She is operating mostly at the second boundary. She has a fixed identification of herself as the person trapped in her problem, and engaged mostly with the reality or fantasy of her boss (even in her dreams!). This could well be a repeat of a familiar situation in her earlier life, a transference of an overbearing parent maybe. But it could also be the reverse of that: a wish to be given firm boundaries that she has never experienced. She is geared towards fight or flight in a way that does not allow the relaxation of the first boundary, which also allows for an appreciation of novelty and possibility.

Jane would benefit in therapy from ways of working that support her to relax her deliberateness: attention to breathing, relaxing her looking and widening her focus to take in a bigger scene. The therapist being silent would be challenging for Jane, as it would disrupt her habitual focussed engagement, but sometimes would be the only alternative to joining her in an anxious talking-about her 'problem'. And her anxiety in the silence could be made a figure for awareness in its own right.

At a later stage of therapy, a physical intervention could be to ask Jane to let herself lean back into my arms, something she is unlikely to easily trust me to engage in with me, as she does not understand or experience the world as willing or able to support her safely. Once again, if the assimilated experience of safe, supportive touch is largely absent, there will be a need for actual exploration of touch.

A basic model

I now want to present a model of a situation I see very frequently with clients, especially those with eating disorders. This is the situation where the client identifies self as beneath the skin, and alienates the area between the skin and the body identified as self.

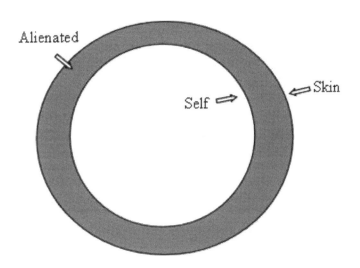

Diagram 1

Doing this essentially alienates the person from her physical experience, which happens to a body surface that is not her. It also alienates her from her active touching of the world, which is done by her skin surface on her behalf. The body surface is treated as a physical engine with a more etherial self inside. Interestingly, Aldous Huxley suggested that early severe physical punishment predisposed to a sense of mind/body duality and disembodied spirituality.

The next stage is that the disowned outer segment receives projections of fear, anger, or disgust, and is acted upon accordingly by the identified self. Unsupported engagements with the environment become transformed into internal battles with this segment.

In anorexia, a prime example of this process, the segment receives all the annihilating rage and disgust the person would otherwise express towards her environmental situation. The overwhelming urge is to get rid of its badness and ugliness. This seems easily done, and not eating at first produces a sense of satisfaction. In fact, the sense is that the one who eats is the disgusting outer segment, and the eating is one of the disgusting things that segment does. There is often a sense of a split between the mental/spiritual and the physical/animal: I think of something an anorectic client said to me when she finally allowed her hunger: 'You must help me - I'm eating like an animal!' However, the other side of the dilemma is that the person still wants to avoid identifying right up to the skin surface, and therefore reinstates the disowned segment, 'pulling in' even further. Now there is another 'bad/ugly' thing to be annihilated, and so round the circle, often until death.

Treatment often tries to convince the anorectic client to eat, and that she is actually very thin, not fat. But when any weight put on (and even the act of eating itself) is not experienced as hers, but as that of her mortal enemy, such a strategy often fails, with the client seeing the therapist taking the segment's part against her, and therefore as an enemy to be fought and lied to.

The situation is not very different with someone who compulsively overeats and puts on weight. Again there is a disowned segment between the self and the skin. Usually in this case the person experiences the outer segment as a protection, a buffer zone between the person and a world that seems overwhelming. Sometimes the fat outer layer is disliked, sometimes not, but mostly such considerations are irrelevant: you do not choose a bodyguard for his looks! And of course you would need some convincing that your bodyguard is unhealthy for you.

Coming to the skin

The general statement of how to work with both of these situations can be simply put, though the practice is more difficult, particularly for the client. The therapist needs to help the client to resensitise and reown his body right up to the skin surface, where he can make a sensory connection to otherness. The difficulty, of course, is that the client is frightened enough of the consequences of skin contact with the world that he will bring all his defences into play to avoid doing it. A further complication is that the client will often come into experiential contact with mishandling, neglect, or abuse of his body, which he has put aside by pulling away from the skin surface, and will experience the therapist as being abusive or invasive. The therapist will need to ensure as much as possible that

210

she stays in contact with the client, so that sense of invasion is experienced alongside a sense of the mutuality of the present relating. Of course, if the therapist and client don't manage to maintain this contact, it could well be that the therapist does go further than the clent consents to, and is actually therefore invasive. I usually check with clients at various points how they experience my looking at them, because I am of course paying attention to their whole bodies, not just their faces, and our interactions round this looking and being looked at will need to be explored just like any other interactions.

At some points in these explorations, the client will move away from the skin surface. Usually, at least at first, he will not be aware of doing this, but the therapist can often pick up the signs of this happening: a ceasing of movement (of, say, the client's legs, hips, or head) or of breathing, or the client's eyes losing focus or wandering around. When I bring a client's attention to this, she can often notice a loss of sensation. The therapist can encourage the client to stay in eye-contact, moving away and back when necessary. Physical resensitization can be encouraged by physical contact (reasonably firm, as the aim is to reawaken, not to soothe, but of course not so firm as to be painful), or, if this is too much for the client (or too challenging for the therapist!), she can do this for herself by stroking, or firm tapping. I will say more about the latter. A very common process with clients who move away from the skin surface is that they find it difficult to hold a sense of physical contact, and crave a contact that they can continue to feel. This is a common motivation in cutting, and also for entering violent relationships or engaging in masochistic activity. Unfortunately, the level of pain also encourages a moving away from the skin in the longer term. There is a kind of middle path, firm continuous patting, that never becomes painful, and yet has an 'afterglow'. As I wrote above, clients can do this for themselves, or the therapist can do it. In a group, people can choose several other group members to pat them simultaneously. Their reported experience is that they feel more alert, connected and differentiated. Significant exercise can also help, but has the problem that many anorectic people can have patterns of exercise taken to the extent of physical harm.

Perls and Reich

The history of Gestalt thinking about bodywork is bound up with the history of its major founder, Fritz Perls. The two major strands of this are Perls' work as an assistant to Kurt Goldstein in his work with brain-damaged soldiers after World War 1; and his analysis with Wilhelm Reich, who was developing his analytic approach to body analysis and bodywork, with strong support from Freud (at that stage). It is also important to be aware where Perls parted company from his mentors, particularly Reich.
In fact it is useful to see how there is a difference in approach between Goldstein and Reich in the area where their ideas intersected: the relationship between self

and other. For Goldstein, self actualizes and in actualizing self, the environment also actualizes.

> The environment of an organism is by no means something definite and static, but is continuously forming commensurably with the development of the organism and its activity. One could say that the environment emerges from the world through the being or actualization of the organism. Stated in a less prejudiced manner, *an organism can exist only if it succeeds in finding in the world an adequate environment* – in shaping an environment (for which, of course, the world must offer the opportunity).' (Goldstein, 1939:88, italics in the original)

That is, there is for Goldstein and Perls no separable environment to defend against, whereas Reich saw the 'muscle armouring' as being a defence against the environment. Thus Perls, working from Goldstein's assumptions, understood the process behind chronic muscular tensions as an attempt to force oneself into a mould acceptable to an overwhelming environment (turning aggression against the self) rather than mould a growthful environment out of the possibilities of the world.

> The system of muscular contractions by which the neurotic attacks and squeezes his spontaneous impulses is called (by Wilhelm Reich) his "character-armor." This gives it the status of an objective barrier that must somehow be attacked and broken through. Actually it is the person's own aggression turned against himself. Instead of regarding this armor as a dumb object, a shell or rigid crust to be crushed, surely the appropriate therapeutic technique is to interpret it as misdirected activities of the person himself. (PHG: 463)

> We have seen that, identifying with the authority, the self wields its aggression against its alienated drives, e.g. its sexuality. It is the self that is the aggressor; it conquers and dominates. Yet strangely, when the character-analysts come to speak of the boundary between the self and the alien, they suddenly mention not the "weapons of the self" but the "defenses of the self," its "defensive armor" (Wilhelm Reich).'(PHG: 145-6)

Self beyond the skin

We can now look at the opposite picture: where the self is habitually taken as wider than the skin surface.

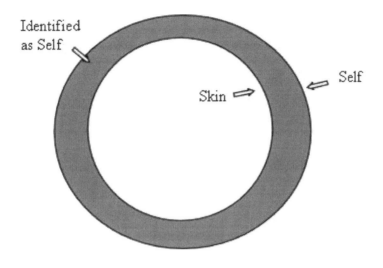

Diagram 2

So what would this mean? Again, the skin surface would not take its primary role as the source of experience and orientation. This time though, there would be a sense that part of the world is self, and that what happens to that part of the world is happening to me and I would be totally identified with it.

Let us take a simple example of this to start with. We usually identify with our clothes, so what happens to the clothes happens to us. If somebody responds favourably to them, we take that as a favourable response to ourselves. Similarly with an unfavourable response. And of course we are mostly in a position to choose our clothes, so they are an expression of ourselves. If our clothes are damaged, we have a sense of damage to ourselves.

More seriously, we might extend our self-boundary to include another person or group of people, and be totally identified with them. While the ability to do that is an important one as we identify with our family, friendship circle, co-workers etc., a habitual identification can become for example stalking behaviour, a denial of the other person's separate existence. Even where the behaviour towards the other is to look after them, the other person will experience it as taking over and manipulative.

In a family, a parent who treats partner and children as extensions of him- or herself creates a highly destructive family environment where other family members will find it difficult or impossible to individuate. Bob Resnick (personal communication) speaks about one-power and two-power systems. In a one-power system, only one person can assert his/her will at any time and the others must follow. In a two-power system, people can differ and conflict at times and the system can hold this creatively. While in some families the one power can

213

move between family members, and the aim is to avoid conflict, where a parent brings the rest into his/her sense of self there is no space for negotiation.

Therapy with people with this process

Once again, the aim is to support and challenge the client to stay at the skin surface. However this works differently here. The client is not disconnected from the skin surface. Rather the experience at the skin and sensory organs is treated as a proprioception, an internal experience rather than a relational one. In the case of a sexual abuser, for example, the attention is on his/her sensation, not the experience of the child being abused. The other only comes into the picture if s/he refuses to fit into the abuser's pleasures. People with this process will often give priority to how something 'feels' to them over what is actually happening (e.g. 'I feel like you hate me' if someone has disagreed with them).

The holding of the boundary here is achieved, if it can be achieved at all, by the therapist holding his/her side of the boundary, neither entering the client's self-space nor letting the client enter his/hers.

For the client this process can be unbearably hard and equates to a sense of loss of part of self. For the therapist, it will also be hard: it is not pleasant to sit with someone who doesn't see you as a separate human being, but as part of his/her self-gratification.

Why would someone with this process come into therapy? There seems to me to be two reasons. The first is that they face an ultimatum from their family, work, or thwarting courts. In this case they will come to therapy but not have any motivation to engage. The question is whether they are more willing, in the short and medium term, to tolerate the pain of therapy or the consequences of leaving (although I have come across a situation where the person pretended he was still coming to therapy while not attending). If the client stays, in the longer term s/he will hopefully find something worth staying for.

The second motivation is a pervasive sense of emptiness and depressed mood. At times this is a strong enough motivation to stay with the process. There usually in my experience needs to be a sense that the client cannot tolerate where s/he is.

Conclusion

I have found this way of exploring self and organism fruitful and exciting. Since the AAGT conference, I have presented it a number of times on training workshops, and people have always found ways of relating to it. I am glad to have this opportunity to show it in a wider context.

References

Goldstein, K. (1939) *The Organism*. American Book Company, Boston.

Perls, F.S. (1978) Finding Self through Gestalt Therapy. *Gestalt Journal* I, 1: 54-73. Highland, NY.

Perls, F., Hefferline, R., Goodman, P. (1994/1951) *Gestalt Therapy: Excitement and Growth in the Human Personality*. Gestalt Journal Press, New York.

Philippson, P. (2001). *Self in Relation*. Gestalt Journal Press, Highland, NY.

Philippson, P. (2009). *The Emergent Self: An Existential-Gestalt Approach*. UKCP/Karnac, London.

Roberts, A. (1999). Digging up the Bodies. *British Gestalt Journal*, 18, 1: 134–137.

Sartre, J.P. (1957). *The Transcendence of the Ego: An Existentialist Theory of Consciousness*. Noonday Press, New York.

Chapter 11. Dramatic Gestalt Dreamwork
Sylvia Crocker

Chapter Introduction

I chose this expanded version of my article on Dramatic Gestalt Dreamwork because I am anxious to share some of my amazing experiences with this method. My hope is that other Gestalt therapists will discover for themselves the transformational power of Gestaltdrama by using it in working with dreams in groups settings.* [Note: the method can also be used in individual sessions through the use of empty chairs and role-reversals.]

My first career was in philosophy, yet after moving with my family several times I realized that I needed a new career, which I found — most happily — in Gestalt therapy. My development as a Gestalt therapist was strongly influenced by many of the same thinkers and approaches that influenced *Paul Goodman:* Aristotle, Kant, Freud, Husserl, Kierkegaard, The Tao Te Ching; many that influenced *Fritz Perls:* Freud, Moreno and the theater, Goldstein, body-oriented approaches, Buddhism; and influences on *Laura Perls:* the Gestalt psychologists, Buber, Goldstein, Heidegger, Tillich, the arts. When I began to read the Perls, Hefferline, and Goodman text (1951) I felt an immediate kinship with its ideas and its approach. Then as I became close friends with Richard Kitzler I realized that my understanding and practice of Gestalt therapy had a very close affinity with that of the New York Institute. Although I trained with the Polsters and at the Gestalt Therapy Institute of Los Angeles, when I later became a full member of the New York Institute I felt I had "come home."

Many members of the New York Institute are currently engaged in deepening our understanding and the connections and implications of Gestalt theory, while others are expanding Gestalt practice and applications to a widening range of client populations. Some are involved in empirical research, which will become increasingly important as we are able present empirical evidence of the efficacy of Gestalt therapy. Further, we have moved increasingly into a deeper understanding of relationships, not only between client and therapist, but also those between members of families, relationships within organizations, and between persons as citizens and the wider societies in which they live. I have been involved in a number of these expansions of Gestalt theory and practice. And through my teaching in various places in the world many other therapists have been and will be influenced by the New York Institute's approach to Gestalt therapy.

Dramatic Gestalt Dreamwork

Abstract: The purpose of this article is to encourage the use of a dramatic method in working with dreams. It stresses the importance of the holism of the organism. It locates dreaming as a manifestation of the organism's capacity for self-regulation and of its compulsion to integrate everything in its experience into a functional whole. Using a Gestalt version of Psychodrama, this method employs other group members to play parts that appear or are implied in the dream, but unlike Psychodrama Gestaltdrama uses role-reversal so that all of the verbal and non-verbal comes from the dreamer.
The existential meaning of a dream emerges as the dreamer has dramatic contact with each part of the dream.
Keywords: dreamwork, Gestaltdrama, Psychodrama, holism, post contact, assimilation, phenomenological method.

Part One

Introduction

My first Gestalt training workshop was with the late Leon Fine, a therapist training in both Gestalt and Psychodrama. He himself had trained in Gestalt with both Fritz and Laura Perls, and was a certified trainer in Psychodrama who had studied with Jacob Moreno. One of the things I learned from Leon was a way of doing group work that employed a version of Psychodrama that--as described by Richard Kitzler when he saw it demonstrated at a *Gestalt Journal* Conference in the early 1980's — is "pure Gestalt."

Over the years since then I have used this dramatic form of Gestalt many times in working with dreams in a group setting, and these have been among the most amazing and awe inspiring experiences I have had as a Gestalt therapist. While Gestaltdrama is not restricted to dreamwork, in this paper I want to share some of the experiences I've had with it as a method of working with dreams. My hope is that other therapists will begin to experiment with this approach to dreamwork in groups, and that it will become widely used by Gestalt therapists.

Theoretical Overview

Although the widely held Gestalt view of dreams (Perls, 1971, 1973; Downing and Marmostein, 1973; Yontef, 1993) understands dreaming as the self's attempt to integrate those alienated aspects of itself that are projected into the elements of the dream, my experiences of working with dreams—especially those that recur—have led me to a somewhat broader and more existential understanding of the nature of dreams and dreaming. This is a position that *includes* but is *not limited to* the traditional Gestalt theory of dreams. I now think of dreaming as the means by which the person attempts to integrate and assimilate the results of her waking experiences into her ongoing living. Some dreams are "janitorial," simply "tidying up" the remains of the day and are rarely remembered. Others are attempts to assimilate those more complex and difficult experiences (or aspects of the self) that have remained unresolved and either poorly assimilated or unassimilated entirely, yet continue on in the person's living as unfinished business.

As the work unfolds I find that recurrent dreams are most often about issues of guilt, shame, regret, remorse, unresolved conflicts, and/or incompletely mourned loss. In Kurt Lewin's terminology (1936), when the person cannot integrate some element of experience he frequently accommodates it by attempting to "wall it off." The result is that these unresolved issues make claims on the person's energies and variously distort many of his natural processes.

Theoretically I came to this position by reflecting on what Goodman calls Post Contact, the fourth moment of a contact episode (Perls, Hefferline, and Goodman, pp. 411-12) — the process of assimilation of a contact process that goes on largely out of awareness. [Note: This view is supported by recent research in the nature and purpose of dreaming. Barrett & McNamara, Vol. 3, 2007] From this perspective, then, dreaming, is a manifestation of the organism's capacity for self-regulation and of its *compulsion to integrate everything in its experience into a functional whole*. The goal of Gestalt dreamwork is to enable the person to have *contact* with the dream's narrative and it imagery in ways that bring about a multi-level grasp of the existential issues embodied in the dream, and/or a broadened understanding of the self. The work thus sets off a process by which those issues that have not been fully integrated can be assimilated into an existential and functional whole; the self can become more whole; and the person's energies can be freed for living more fully in the present.

The Method of Gestaltdrama Dreamwork

Use of space

As stated earlier, Gestaltdrama borrows from Psychodrama, but transforms it into a method that is peculiarly Gestalt in theory and in practice. Gestaltdrama and Psychodrama both employ actual people in the therapeutic process, which heightens the sense of reality in the process itself. Both use space in ways that go beyond ordinary psychotherapeutic methods. This use of space shown in the dreams that follow gives the whole process a more realistic "feel" than if they were sitting down and describing the situation in purely verbal terms.

Involvement of the body

Another similarity between these two methods has to do with the involvement of the body. In both processes the therapist most often takes the dreamer by the hand or the arm and walks around the room while the person retells the dream as though it is happening in the present. This gives the dreamer a sense of being supported and accompanied by the therapist. Moreover, because of our holistic stance, we know that people store unfinished business and a variety of psychological issues in their bodies, and that the body helps keep these issues out of awareness by tightening/immobilizing the musculature in various ways. The walking helps to warm up the body and make it looser and more relaxed. This often has the effect of making more accessible those issues that are stored in the body, especially those issues that are related to the meaning of the dream. Further, the walking involves a series of quasi-involuntary movements of the person's whole body, especially the legs, as the person moves through space. This, coupled with the therapist's supportive presence, has the effect of somewhat lowering the person's resistance to letting certain issues come into awareness.

Role of group members

Like Psychodrama Gestaltdrama has the person whose work it is, the dreamer or protagonist, choose members of the group to play the significant parts—both human and non-human—of the dream. As the work unfolds the therapist/director facilitates contact between the protagonist/dreamer and each of the important persons/things in the dream. Unlike Psychodrama in Gestaltdrama *the dreamer plays all of the parts*, reversing roles with group members who were chosen to represent "mother," "trousers," the dreamer's "alter ego," and so on. When the dreamer addresses, say, her mother, at some point the therapist asks her to reverse roles and play her mother. The group member who is now playing the dreamer speaks the last line of what was said, in the same tone of voice, body language, and overall manner as the dreamer. Thus the dreamer is able to get some insight into how she presents herself in contact with her mother. This is a major contrast to Psychodrama, where the group members attempt to improvise the parts they play, thus unavoidably mixing their own psychological "stuff" with that of the dreamer. In Gestaltdrama all of the psychological material that is presented belongs to the dreamer, and that is why this method is, as Richard Kitzler has said, "pure Gestalt."] [Note: Zinker's (1977) use of drama in dreamwork has more in common with Psychodrama than with Gestaltdrama, since the group members are encouraged to bring their own psychological material into the process.]

Therapist's role

The therapist facilitates the dialogical contact between the dreamer and every significant element of the dream, in each case through the use of role reversal. As the dreamer reverses roles with each element in the dream, he is able to gain access to a variety of perspectives on the situation that the dream portrays. By means of such a rich and realistic portrayal and exploration of the context of the dream this method facilitates the emergence of the dream's meaning. I never really know what a given dream is about until we go through the dramatic process, even though I may think something like, "Oh yes, this must be about some sort of shame." But the very richness of the emergent meaning always leaves me with the sense that I was really almost clueless at the outset with respect to what the meaning actually was.

A counterpoint that runs throughout the process is the therapist's inquiry as to how the dreamer *feels* as he says certain things. It is also important in many instances to ask the dreamer—as he has become himself after playing, say, his father—how he feels about the statements he made *as the other person* to himself, the dreamer. For example, the therapist might ask the dreamer "How do you feel saying that to your father?" or ." . . hearing that from your father?" and then, after the person answers, may say to the client, "Tell that to your father." Often something significant emerges from the ensuing dialogue between then. It is not enough to stay with just the words or the actions that actually appeared in the dream. A holistic approach involves prompting the person to become aware of and to make explicit those affective responses that are not only of enormous importance in the person's internal dynamics but, as part of the dreamer's inner phenomenology, are powerful realities in the present field, prompting, sometimes even driving, many of the person's behaviors. Sometimes what is not explicitly present in the content of the dream but is importantly implied, for example, the missing father or missing clothing, may also be assigned to a group member and may be invoked as the dreamwork proceeds.

Processing the dramatic work

At the end of the enactment of the dream everyone involved sits down as the therapist first asks the dreamer how he is *like* each of the elements of the dream. As this part of the process goes on the meaning of the dream stands out in greater relief. The dreamer begins to identify how certain elements and certain movements within the dream pertain to his life. The therapist then asks each person who played a part how it was for him or her to play that part.

In the next part of the process, all of the group members are given an opportunity to share with the dreamer how his work has affected them personally.

The last moment in the dreamwork process is a group discussion of the work itself.

The process, like dreams themselves, has a surreal quality and is often filled with laughter, especially in the early stages. There is something slightly hilarious about asking group members to play the part of a toilet, or shit, or a man's trousers and underwear, and then placing them in the dream space. The hilarity and playfulness that occur at the beginning of many pieces of dreamwork seem to have the effect of loosening the protagonist's inhibitions, and thus preparing the way for the work to take place at a deepening level.

The dreams that are described in this section were recurrent dreams. The protagonists were therapists, although not all were Gestalt therapists. The method, practiced with appropriate support from the therapist, helps the dreamer move quickly to a depth where the meaning of the dream readily emerges. My assumption is that therapists who begin to use this method will do so in group situations where support is already part of the situation.

Finally, although the accounts of the dreamwork that follow have been telescoped to emphasize the dramatic unfolding of the dream's meaning, the actual work took upwards of an hour of time.

Part Two

George's Dream

George is a hypnotherapist in his mid-60's. He worked on this recurrent dream in a Gestalt dreamwork presentation I gave at a Gestalt conference.

"I leave my house and when I get outside I find that I do not have any clothes on from the waist down. In one version I go down the street and meet a women; I am surprised that she doesn't seem to notice that I am naked from the waist down. In another version I go into a restaurant and, again, no one notices that I am partially naked. This surprises me. In all versions of the dream I worry that my wife and my mother will yell at me."

After choosing group members to play the roles of a woman on the street, a person in a restaurant, his mother, wife, and the missing trousers and underwear, George and I begin walking as he tells the dream again, once again in the present tense.

SC *[to G]*: How do you feel about being out in public naked from the waist down?

G: I'm embarrassed. And scared too, because I think my wife and my mother will yell at me.

[We meet a lady on the street and immediately G tried to hide his nakedness by leaning over slightly, thus bowing his head a little, and shielding his genitals with his hands.]

SC *[to G]*: Do you have anything to say to the woman?

G:*(continues hanging his head, leans against the wall, almost in an attempt to go through it, continues to cover his genitals.)* No, nothing.

SC *(to both)*: Reverse roles. *(I ask the person now playing G to cue him with his last line, in the same body posture and tone of voice.)*

SC *(to G as woman):* What do you think about meeting G on the street. Do you notice anything strange about him.

G-*as-the-woman*: No he's just an ordinary looking guy. I don't know him.

222

SC (to *G-as-himself*): What's your reaction to meeting this woman?

G: I'm surprised, and I don't understand how she doesn't see that I'm naked from the waist down.

SC: Tell *her* that. Tell her you're surprised she doesn't notice.

[*G does so, then reverses roles and responds.*]

G-as-the-woman *[still not registering surprise at his nakedness]*: I still don't see the problem, but I can go get you some pants if you want me to.

SC: Reverse.

G-as-himself: No thanks.

[*We enter the restaurant, again without anyone's appearing to notice G's nakedness. He quickly moves to a booth in the corner.*]

SC: What are you experiencing now?

B: I'm scared, and my body feels tight. I'm afraid people are looking at me. And I think my mother's going to yell at me.

SC: Does she do that a lot?

B: Well, no. She's not that kind of person: she wouldn't actually do that. Now I feel that I'm in the presence of my mother. *And I feel really bad.*

SC: Do you have something unfinished with your mother?

G: I just woke up!

SC: You can't get out of dealing with your mother that easily! (*laughter*)

G: I feel bad because I think I failed my mother. When she died I felt bad that I had taken advantage of her.

SC: How did you do that?

G: My parents came over here from Russia. They couldn't even read or write and we were very poor. They made a living with a little store. When I was a boy I used to steal money and candy from my parents' store. I never had any good clothes, so when I was older I made a lot of money, but I always spent more than I made and I acquired a lot of debt. She never said "no" when I borrowed money from her, but I never paid her back.

SC: Talk to her about this.

G (*to the person playing "Mother")*: I feel so bad that I stole from you, and that I "borrowed" so much money from you and never paid you back.

G-as-his-mother: I knew all along that when you borrowed money that you wouldn't pay it back. I didn't say anything because I knew you needed the money, and didn't want to embarrass you.

G-as-himself: You always loved me and helped me whenever I needed it. I couldn't have had a better mother—and I still took advantage of you. I don't *deserve* your love. *I feel so ashamed.*

SC: Are you naked when you tell your mother this?

G: Yes. I hate to face her this way. *(to "Mother")* I can't *stand* for you to see me the way I *really* am!

SC: Reverse and speak to "George" as your mother.

G-as-his-mother: George, I *do* see you the way you *really* are, and I'm *proud* of what you've made of your life. You've done a lot of good, and you're a *good* person. I'm proud of you, son.

[*By this time I see clearly that this dream is about George's shame, and I begin to think that the symbolism of the missing pants and underwear is that he feels ashamed in some pervasive — existential — sense, yet no one else is aware of his shame or knows what he feels shame about. I begin to think that at this point George can be "reconciled" with his missing pants and underwear, so I ask the persons playing these roles to come over to where George is. But just as I am about suggest this George says:*]

G: No, wait. Something else is coming up.

[*He tells about selling aluminum siding when he was a young man. The night after his most successful day — he made some $6700 — he spent the night in a motel room burning candles and crying. Selling the siding involved a scam in which he manipulated his customers into believing that if they bought the siding and convinced their friends to buy it too, they could get a reduction in the price they would pay.*]

G: It helped me sell the siding, but very few people ever got a significant reduction in the price they paid for their siding.

SC: What's happening in your body as you tell about this?

G: I don't know.

SC: Close your eyes, take a deep breath, and notice where you have the most sensation in your body.

G: I'm a little bit aware of my hands, which I notice I have in my pockets. Sort of hidden.

[*I note that he seems quite comfortable standing there with his hands in his pocket. I feel curious about what would happen if he removed them, so I suggest an experiment.*]

SC: Take them out of your pockets, and notice how you feel doing it.

[*George hesitates, clearly wanting to keep his hands in his pockets. I wait, and soon he removes them and turns to the whole group and says with strong affect:*]

G: *I stand naked before you!*

[*I suggest that the remainder of those in the group who had not already played parts line up and become people to whom George had sold siding. I ask George to tell them what he had done and how he feels about it. But before he could say anything one of the "customers" began telling George how much his family had enjoyed their siding.*]

Customer One: We wondered why we hadn't gotten it years before, because it kept the house cool in the summer and warm in the winter. We knew "the deal" was part of your sales pitch and was just a come-on, that we wouldn't really save any money, but we still believed we were making a good buy. That's what it turned out to be—a good buy.

[*The person playing Customer One told us:* "This is a true story."]

[*Next I had George reverse with several of the other "customers" and, speaking from the point of view of less satisfied customers, telling him how they felt about being scammed.*

Customer Two: *(shouting)* We almost lost our house, you son of a bitch!

Customer Three: I never thought I'd have a chance to tell you this: you LIED to us!

George: *(to his "customers")* The day I made the most money I ever made — some $6700 — I stayed up all night burning candles and crying. I was so ashamed I decided to quit my job and spend the rest of my life making up for all the bad things I had done. I went to college, then to a Jewish seminary, and I've done a great deal of work in the Jewish communities wherever I've lived. I also became a therapist so that I could devote my life to helping people whose lives are stuck and unhappy.

G: *(turning to the group) I want you all to know that I've lived a changed life!* [*It is at this point that George is willing to be reunited with his trousers and underwear, symbolically moving beyond decades of accumulated shame.*]

Commentary

The pivotal moment in this process was when George and I entered the restaurant and he immediately went to sit way off in a corner booth where he would be less exposed. At that point he begins to feel dread that his mother will "yell" at him, which he immediately says would be out of character for her. At that point he feels he is in the presence of his mother.

The second pivot in the process occurred when, after George had dialogued with his mother, I suggested he might be able to be reconciled with his pants and underwear. He refuses because he senses that "something else is coming up." This introduces the unresolved issues with his work selling siding, his reaction to which had propelled him into a life of service to others. And yet all that had flowed from the fact that his changed life had not erased the remorse and the shame he had lived with for four decades.

George's work with the dream gave him the opportunity to give voice to several layers of shame that had colored much of his adult life, to face what he had done, to apologize, and to "show" important others that he had "lived a changed life." As sometimes happens in this approach to dreamwork, something serendipitous happens: the family of one of George's "customers" had actually been a customer of some siding salesman years before. This person assured George that the siding his family had bought had been a great value in all sorts of weather, and that they had not been taken in by the scam. Apparently George had focused so much on his dishonesty that he been blind to the likelihood that many of his customers were quite satisfied.

As a result of the dialogue with his "mother" and the interactions with his "customers," in which he confessed his remorse and shame and apologized, George was finally able to digest the fact that he had indeed led a "changed life," and that he could take some genuine pride in what he had done with his life.

When the scene shifts to the issues around the work as a siding salesman I ask him what he is feeling. He apparently becomes affectively blank as he stands there with his hands in his pockets. Given Gestalt therapy's holistic approach to the organism, when someone goes blank in a context that normally would involve strong feelings, I assume that some kind of excitement is registering somewhere in the person's body even though it is being "censored" in his conscious awareness. He says he is slightly aware of his hands, and that they feel "hidden" in his pockets. I suggest an experiment, anticipating that he will probably have stronger feelings if he removes his hands from their "hidden" position in his pockets. He later said that the experiment had been "grounding," and that apparently enabled him to turn to the group and say with strong emotion: *"I stand naked before you!"* At last he has faced the terrible old truth about his life—and in an illustration of the paradoxical principle of human change, his relation to that earlier life begins to shift and become reorganized.

George, a hypnotherapist, talks about walking. He says we don't consciously direct our legs; when the therapist walks and holds hands with the client, the latter is likely to access a deep level of suggestibility. A client's willingness to cooperate with the process sets the stage for the work. He adds that he could always feel my presence and support throughout, and that that had enabled him to do the work .

At the end of the session I tell George that I don't believe he has ever given himself enough credit for having changed his life so profoundly. He says he was so intent on totally transforming how he was living that he even changed his name.

Finally, one of the group members affectionately points out to George,

"Yet you still have the charm of the salesman."

George called me months later to thank me again for the work and to say that he had not had the dream again, adding, "And I don't think I ever will."

Angela's Dream

Angela is an African American woman in her mid-20's who had been working on a master's in counseling. Her major professor told me that she seemed depressed that her affect was "flat" no matter what she was involved in. She had been considering dropping out of school. I asked the members of the workshop to talk about recurrent dreams they had had, and she related the following dream.

I wake up in the middle of the night and need to go to the bathroom. When I get out of bed I see that the floor is covered with snakes, so I jump back in bed. A little later I try again, and this time there are no snakes on the floor. So I go down

the short hallway toward the bathroom, and just as I am about to go into the bathroom a big black snake jumps out at me. It scares me half to death and I run back and jump in bed. A little later, since I have my keys in bed with me (this is a dream!), and even though I live on the third floor, I decide to climb out the window and go in the front door to the elevator. When I get to my floor and open my apartment door, I'm just about to step into the bathroom when the big black snake jumps out at me again. I always wake up at that point in the dream.

After choosing group members to play the roles of the big black snake, the bed, the keys, the bathroom, and the hallway, and asking the other group members to lie on the floor and play the snakes, Angela and I begin walking around the room as she retells the dream in the present tense.

We begin the dreamwork with Angela's waking up and encountering the snakes. After she climbs out the window, re-enters the building, and opens her apartment door, she moves toward the bathroom and the big black snake jumps out at her again.

SC: (to Angela) What do you want to say to the snake?

A: I wish you'd stop scaring me! Why do you keep scaring like this?

SC: Reverse and play the snake. [*I decide to "warm" her up to the scene, so I ask her (as*
the snake): "Who are you, anyway?"

A-as-the-snake: (*gasps, and asks:*) "Should I say the first thing that comes to my mind."

S: Yes.

A-as-the-snake: I know who this is. It's Fareed.

Angela-as-herself: Fareed and I had been friends since childhood and had been boyfriend-girlfriend off and on. But I broke off relations with because he insisted on being friends with another guy we had grown up with, but who had gotten into drugs and crime. Fareed and I had gone to college but this person had gone to prison, and when he was released he wanted to hang around with us. Fareed wanted to befriend him and help him get on a better road in his life, but I believed he was no good and would only bring trouble. No matter what I said, Fareed insisted on trying to help the guy, but when he agreed to share an apartment with him, I broke up with him. After that he had called me repeatedly, especially during one week, but I hadn't taken his calls. But one Saturday I tried to call him but couldn't reach him.

SC: (*to Angela-as-herself*) Say whatever you want to say to Fareed. A: "Why did you keep calling me that week!?" Reversing and playing the role of

SC: Reverse and answer as Fareed.

A-as-Fareed: If you'd answered my calls, *you'd know who killed me!*

A-as-herself: (*turning to the group*) on the Saturday of the week when I got so many

227

calls from Fareed, I decided to try to get in touch with to see what he wanted. But I couldn't reach him. The next morning my cousin came into our apartment and said Fareed had been shot and was dead.

[*I think everyone in the room was utterly shocked at this revelation, especially since we had hardly begun to work on the dream when its meaning became crystal clear. I facilitated a dialogue between Angela and Fareed, with her playing both parts. She was able to express her anger at him for insisting on the unhealthy friendship, as well as the guilt she felt for not answering his calls*].

A: (*to Fareed*) You called me so many times that week, but I was so mad at you I didn't want to talk to you. But if only I'd taken your calls everything would probably be different. *But now you're dead, and it's all my fault!*

S: Reverse.

A-as-Fareed: No, you were right from the beginning. It's not your fault, it's mine! If I'd listened to you in the first place I'd be alive today. You've got to stop blaming yourself and you've got to go on with your life.

[*In the remainder of the dialogue Angela told him how much she had missed him and the sorrow she felt because of his death. She said she knew she'd have to get on with her life.*]

As we finished the dramatic part of the dreamwork and sat down to share and to process the work itself, Angela looked like a different person: her posture was no longer slumped, her facial expression was animated, and her voice quality was no long a monotone. I was struck by how different she was as she responded to what the group members told her about how her work had affected her, and then as we talked about the process of the work. Angela said she had had no idea what the dream meant, just that it had always frightened her and left her feeling upset and confused. She said she felt relieved to have had the talk with Fareed and to be able to express the feelings that had haunted her. Later her professor told me that from then on Angela was like a different person, clearly engaged with whatever she was involved with, and she no longer considered leaving school.

Yolanda's dream

I am giving a dreamwork presentation at a conference. After asking the participants to pair up and tell each other about a dream they've had, I ask for a volunteer to work on a dream. Yolanda raises her hand and comes forward. She tells me the following dream, which she has had many times over the years:

"I'm in a school I attended when I was about 15. I need to go to the rest room, so I go into the rest room where there are about six stalls. I open the door to the first one and see that the toilet is covered with shit—there's shit all over the place. I'm disgusted, so I go to the next stall, and find that it is also full of shit. It turns out that all six toilets are just covered in shit and I can't use any of them. So I'm just stuck. And I wake up."

I ask Yolanda to choose people to play each of the six toilets and six more to play the shit that covers each one. Next, suspecting that I might need to have Yolanda have a dialogue with herself, I ask her to choose someone to play her double. Looking back on this piece of dream work, I find it interesting that Yolanda chose a man to play her double.

I ask the people playing the six toilets and their shit to take their places, which Yolanda describes as a straight line of booths. Then we proceed to walk around the room while she, once again, tells her dream. While we are still walking and are about to begin working through the dream dramatically, I ask her a logical and apparently innocuous question:

SC: How do we get into the restroom?

Y: There are two heavy doors over there (*points to an area beyond the location of the toilets*).

SC: Choose two people to play the doors.

[*She does so, then places them opposite each other with their arms outstretched and overlapping. Yolanda pushes through the doors and we enter the restroom. We stop at the first booth and she opens the door.*]

SC: Describe what you see.

Y: There's shit everywhere, all over the toilet, on the floor, the wall, it's just a mess!

(*As we move on to the second booth she says:*) It's the same kind of mess — shit all over the place. (*The situation is the same in all six of the booths. We return to the first booth.*)

SC: Speak to the shit. Tell it how you feel seeing it all over the place in there.

Y: Ooooh, you're just *disgusting*! It makes me sick to look at you!

SC: Reverse and be the shit. (*The person who played the shit reverses roles and repeats Yolanda's words with the same inflexion and body language.*)

SC (*to Y, now as the shit*): Shit, respond to what Yolanda has just said.

Y-as-shit: I'm just here and I'm a complete mess! (*Tears begin to well up in her eyes*) I don't *want* to be this way.

SC (*to Y-as-shit*): Isn't someone, like a janitor, supposed to come in and clean up messes like this?

Y-as-Shit: No, there's no one. No one cares. (*Tears begin spilling down her face.*)

SC: Reverse and be Yolanda again. (*Then to Yolanda-as-herself*)The shit says there's no janitor, and that no one cares enough to clean up this mess.

Y-as-herself: That's right. No one cares.

SC (*I signal to the man Yolanda chose to play her double to come over, then I say to Yolanda*): Tell this person how you feel in this situation.

Y: I feel helpless to deal with this mess.

SC: Reverse with this person. (*I ask the double to mirror what Y has said in the way in which she said it; he does so.*)

SC *(to Y, now as her double)*: Give "Yolanda" some advice.

Y-as-double: You need to get some help!

SC: Reverse roles. *(double repeats words Y spoke as double)*

Y: Yes, I *do* need some help.

SC: How about choosing six persons from the audience to be the janitors. *(After she does this I suggest:)* Have a conference with these six "janitors" and instruct them about cleaning up the mess in the six booths.

[*Yolanda gets them in a huddle and tells them what to do. They get to work vigorously cleaning the toilet booths and getting rid of all the shit. She inspects their work with great approval, and thanks them for their help.*]

Y *(to SC)*: Now I can finally use one of these toilets. *(Pretends to do so.)* I finally feel relief!

[*We leave the rest room through the heavy doors, which Yolanda pushes through with an air of authority.*]

The dramatic part of the dreamwork ends here. I suggest that everyone now sit on the floor. I am a little surprised when, as Yolanda and I were in the act of sitting down, she says to me, "*You know, those doors weren't actually in any of the dreams. I put them there only when you asked me how I got into the restroom.*" I say, "That's interesting, but I'm not sure yet just how." I didn't understand its significance until the meaning of the dream began to emerge as we processed the work.

I begin the process discussion by asking Yolanda how she is like the shit. She replies with "I feel like I get shit on a lot." I ask how that happens. "Well," she answers, "I always try to be helpful to people, to be there for them, but a lot of the time I just get shit on. No one seems to be there for me." I ask, "How do you feel when that happens to you?" "Like shit. I feel like *shit.*"

Then I ask, "How are you like the toilet?" "Well, I feel like the place that people use to just dump stuff on. I get used a lot." I ask her to look at one of the recently cleaned up toilets and to describe how it looks now. She says, "Now that it isn't covered with shit it just *sparkles.* I see it now as something that is very useful in an important way, now that it's not covered with shit." I ask, "How is that like you." She answers, "I'm very helpful in some important way s— when I'm not being shit on. I can sparkle and I can be someone who is very useful."

I'm beginning to see why the doors not being in the actual dreams is not just an interesting fact but the key to the dream's meaning. How are you like the doors?" She replies that "the doors can let people in and can keep them out." "How are you like that?" I ask. "I can let people in or I can keep them out." I tell her, "Yes, you can have a choice about whom you let in and whom you don't let it. It sounds like you've been letting in a lot of people that wind up using you, *shitting* on you. And clearly you don't like the way that feels." "*No!*" she says, emphatically.

I notice that her eyes are very clear and shiny, as if they've been washed. I think she looked younger than she had at the beginning of the work. I ask her how she is like her double, to which she replies, "She's strong and level-headed." "And you're like that too, are you?" I ask. "Yes, but I'm not usually in touch with that part of myself." I suggest that it would be helpful for her to keep reminding herself that she can also be strong and level-headed, not someone's dumping ground. She says, "Yes, sometimes I need help too, but I don't like to admit that." I add, "And I hope you keep in mind you're not *merely* useful. There's a lot more to you than that."

I ask her to look at the people she asked to be janitors and to tell me how many of them she knows. She says she knows some of them but not all. I suggest that all of these people were willing to help her when she asked, and that in her life she'll find that lots of people will be willing to help, some of whom she will know and others she won't know. The main thing is that she must let herself be aware of when she needs help, and then reach out to others for it. She agreed.

Finally, I asked the various persons who played parts in Yolanda's dream how it was for them to play these parts. There were a variety of responses, most feeling that it had brought to mind some of their own issues.

We thanked everyone who participated and then opened up the discussion to the audience at large. There were some technical questions, and many expressions of enthusiastic appreciation for both the dramatic method and for Yolanda's courage to work on her dream in a room full of people, many of whom she did not know.

Commentary

The meaning that emerged from Yolanda's dreamwork was that she had continuing problems with her boundaries. Clearly she was a caring person, yet the fact that she essentially understood herself in this one-dimensional way led her (1) not to refuse other people's attempts to use (i.e. to shit on) her, and (2) not to ask for help, or even to admit to herself or others that she actually needed help. She was out of touch with both the fact that she needed help from others, AND that she was also a "strong and level-headed person" who knew how to take control of problematic situations and resolve them. The dreamwork made clear the ongoing issues she had been wrestling with for years and those aspects of her own personality that she had been ignoring.

These were vital existential issues that had a crippling effect on Yolanda's life and distorted her own personal growth. Her work also demonstrates the process by which alienated parts of the self begin to be integrated as she has contact with the neglected stronger, take-charge part of herself through the work itself. The dream was her own organismic effort to help her break through to a richer and more satisfying life. But, as is so often the case, until a person can face, come into contact with, the ways in which they block and impoverish their own life, they remain stuck. The dreamwork, in effect, "flew under her radar" and allowed that contact to happen. I believe the dreamwork helped her begin to move on, and that it brought to the surface several issues she could productively work on with a therapist.

Kara's dream

Kara is a woman in her mid 50's who is counselor at a mental health agency.

Both of her parents were deaf, as were her three stepfathers. Two of her siblings had died, one in an auto accident with her infant son, and the other who was lost in a winter storm; and her own 3 year old son was killed in a traffic accident 30 years ago. She worked on this recurrent dream during a Gestalt training workshop.

I'm in a nondescript room where I'm attempting — unsuccessfully — to make a phone call. In some dreams I can't remember the number; in other dreams I forget the number as I'm dialing it; sometimes I succeed in dialing the number but can't get a connection. In all of them I'm struggling to remember the phone number so that I can connect with some unknown persons.

As Kara tells her dream to the group she suddenly realizes "I think I want to talk to some dead people." The significance of this realization becomes clear as we begin to work on the dream. I have her choose people to play the "dead people" as they emerge in the dreamwork. I ask her also to choose someone to play the part of the telephone number, someone else to play the telephone, and another person to play the "nondescript room."

After we set up the dream space, Kara and I walk around the room as she re-tells the dream in the present tense. As we move into the dream space I ask the person playing the phone number to come over and stand near, and I ask the "telephone" to stand with his back facing Kara.

SC (*to Kara*): Dial the number on the telephone, noticing how you feel as you do it..

[*Kara begins making circular motions (as on a rotary phone) on the back of the person playing the telephone. The circular motion turns into a patting motion; Kara later says that in the deaf community making such a motion on a deaf person's back is a way to get that person's attention. This triggered her feeling herself to be in the presence of her dead father.*]

K (*exclaims with strong emotion*) I can't remember you! (*to the group*) I just now realize I'm saying this to my father.

[*Kara explains that her father died when she was 3 years old, shortly after undergoing open-heart surgery to repair a congenital defect. All of her memories of her father come from what her older sister told her about their father; she herself has no memory of him. I ask her choose someone to play the part of her father.*]

SC (*to Kara*): Talk to your father. Tell him about how his dying affected your childhood.

B *(to "father")*: I was angry you had abandoned the family when you died, but I also blamed myself for your death. When I was a child I was always told to behave myself, which meant I could not make noise or call attention to myself. But as a child I couldn't help making noise and wanting attention. I think you died because I broke your heart. They told me you had a broken heart, and that's why you died. I knew I caused it.

SC: Reverse with your "father." *(I ask the person playing her father to repeat Kara's statement "I think you died because I broke your heart," using the same affect.)*

Kara-as-father *(to "Kara")*: Oh, Kara honey, you didn't have anything to do with my death. I was just born with a bad heart and they couldn't fix it. It wasn't your fault.

SC *(to Kara-as-father)*: Reverse roles and respond as Kara.

K-as-herself: I feel so relieved hearing that I didn't cause you to die. I've carried that guilt my whole life!

[This dialogue with her father prompts Kara to think of her maternal Mormon grandmother, a person who was angry, cold, and rigidly religious, and who believed that "bad things happen to bad people." I have Kara to choose someone to play her grandmother.]

SC *(to Kara)*: Play your grandmother and speak to Kara.

K-as-grandmother *(to "Kara")*: Your mother's deafness was punishment for *sin, my sin!*

SC: Reverse and tell her your reaction to what she is saying.

K-as-herself *(to "grandmother")*: You constantly beat all of us kids over the head with that horrible belief. You caused my life to be wracked with guilt! *(Now feeling permission to be angry, Kara unleashes her anger toward her grandmother.)* You're absolutely wrong. Our mother wasn't deaf because of anything *you* did. That kind of thinking practically ruined our lives because it made me think something was wrong in our family and that something had to be *me!* All these years I believed my father died because of something *I did!* Now I realize *all of it* was just a tragedy, not a punishment for sin. *(then with passion and conviction)* LEAVE ME ALONE! FUCK YOU — AND THE HORSE YOU RODE IN ON!! *(then, as an aside to the group)* I don't know where *that* came from. *(laughter)* *(Later Kara said the "horse" was her grandmother's "high-horse" from which she judged people. She also reported that she felt herself "grow taller" in this encounter with her grandmother.)*

[Then she moves immediately into a dialogue with Earl, the most difficult of the string of stepfathers. He was a cruel man who apparently didn't want to be bothered by the mother's four children, and who constantly held Kara up to ridicule.]

SC *(to Kara)*: Choose someone to play Earl. Then reverse roles and play Earl.

Kara-as-Earl *(to "Kara")*: You've got a big head; you think you know everything — Four Eyes! You kids are just a nuisance, a pain. I don't want you here!

SC: Reverse.

Kara-as-herself: You made my life, and the lives of my siblings, totally miserable. You were so hateful to us, made fun of us, tried to break our spirits. You've been a pain in my ass from the time my mother brought you into our home! I could never *stand* you! It was a great day when my mother divorced your ass!

SC: How do you feel saying that to him?

K: I feel relieved to finally have the opportunity to tell him off, to tell him about the misery I experienced at his hands, and what an awful person he was to us.

[Kara becomes quiet and looks sad.]

Kara *(to "Earl")*: Now I'm remembering how you died, how you had a brain tumor and were paralyzed after they remove it surgically. You spent the last years of your life in a nursing home in a fetal position. I'm sorry you suffered so much and died like that. I feel compassion for you, even though you were mean to us. *(Kara becomes quiet again)}*

SC: Kara, what you are you experiencing now?

K: Feeling compassion for Earl brings to mind the compassion I felt for my grandmother after her death. I read some of the papers she'd written that showed how harsh and guilt-ridden her life had been. She blamed herself for every bad thing that ever happened, and saw herself as a sinner who had to be punished. She had so little joy in her life, maybe none at all. That makes me feel sad.

SC: Tell *her* that.

K *(speaking to the person playing her grandmother)*: I'm sorry your life was so hard and so unhappy. I'm sorry you tried to make everyone around you unhappy too, but your life was probably the unhappiest of all. I feel sorry for you. *(then to the group)*. I think I took in on a deep level the belief my grandmother held that all bad things that happened were punishment for sin. In a way I thought I'd broken the hearts of *all these people*, and had some responsibility for their suffering and, maybe, their death. *(to "grandmother")* I am not responsible for your suffering and your death. I did NOT "break your heart!"

SC: Reverse and respond.

K-as-grandmother: No, Kara, you did not break my heart or cause my suffering and death. I never meant for you to think that about me, though I did think your behavior contributed to some extent to your father's death. And now I see that that belief was never true.

K-as-herself: But I still have the feeling that I break hearts of the people I love, and they die. My husband had open-heart surgery almost three years ago, and you can imagine what I went through with that! Thank God he survived it.

234

[I knew from past experience with Kara that her 3 year old son had been killed in a car crash while spending some time with his father, from whom Kara was divorced.

Because she and her second husband were having some marital problems, her former husband offered to take care of their son until the couple could work through some problems. I had a hunch Kara's belief that she breaks the heart of those with whom she has important relationships, especially those she loves, extended to her son as well. I ventured the following question:]

SC: And do you believe that somehow you broke your son Shawn's heart and he died; that by loving him you caused Shawn's death?

K: On some level I blame myself. If I hadn't gotten married again, if we hadn't had marriage problems, if I hadn't let my ex-husband take him for a little while — then he'd probably be alive today. On some level I think I have believed since childhood that I kill all the people I love by breaking their hearts.

SC (*I ask Kara to choose someone to play Shawn, then*): Talk to Shawn about this.

K: I think I failed you as a mother. I should have protected you, I shouldn't ever have let you ride in a car with your father! I so sorry! I've missed you so much — I've missed you *every day* of my life.

SC: Reverse roles.

K-as-Shawn: It's ok, Mommy. It's not your fault. You were a wonderful mommy. Please don't be sad.

[For the next few minutes Kara and "Shawn" have a dialogue in which they express their love for each other, and Kara has an opportunity to give voice to her pain at the loss of Shawn and her deep love for him. She ends with the following statement:]

Kara *(to Shawn)*: *I will never forget you!* I want you to know that I've made sure your life *meant* something. I've dedicated my life to helping others *because* of you. *Your life*, Shawn, lives on through me as a therapist, a grandmother, and as a person. Thank you for the *great gift* you have been to me. I love you, Shawn.

The dramatic part of the dreamwork ends here. All who have participated in the process now sit down to begin the discussion phase of the work.]

Commentary

Throughout the dream work I noticed that Kara was either holding her breath or breathing in a very shallow way, to which I responded by reminding her to breathe. Controlling her breath was her way of controlling her feelings and her behavior as a young child, and became a lifelong habit of self-control. Part of the value of the experience of the dreamwork involved Kara's feeling that she "had permission" to feel her feelings and to express them. Even though I had to continue to remind her to breathe, she progressively "let herself go." The breathiness and disembodied quality of her voice gradually became stronger and more fully involved her body. During part of the work I noticed that Kara was gripping one of her thumbs with the other fingers on one of her hands. She explained that in sign-language this is the word for "shit." Clearly, she had been holding onto a lot of shit for most of her life, and the dreamwork "gave her permission" to respond to it by giving voice to her anger, hurt, and grief toward a number of important others in her life.

Kara said that the sense she had of the therapist's presence somehow removed the "social guard" she had against feeling her feelings and expressing them to important others. The dialing motion turned into the stroking motion, which in turn led to her remembering her father and the anger she felt toward him for abandoning the family. This released her to say, at last, to important others how she really felt. The presence of the therapist also kept her grounded, especially when she was talking to her son Shawn. The dreamwork left Kara feeling taller and lighter, relieved of much of the burden of guilt she had lived with, and a sense that she had turned the loss of her son into a commitment to make her life and his mean something, to transform the tragedy of his death into a life of service to others.

Kara later told me that a few nights after the dreamwork she had another dream that was a fitting end to a dream that had begun with her struggle with *forgetting* but had ended with her commitment *never to forget* Shawn. In the later dream all of the people who had appeared in the dreamwork were picking up suitcases and leaving!

Natalie's Dream

Natalie is a young woman in her middle 30's. She had a successful career as an business executive prior to starting her family. Her work involved personnel matters and mediation between conflicting factions in her corporation. When she became pregnant she resigned to devote her energies to motherhood. Later, as she was in the process of obtaining a master's in counseling, she had the following dream.

"I am a crew member on a cruise ship that has broken down while out at sea. The captain and officers plan to abandon the ship rather than trying to repair it, thus leaving some 530 passengers to die. Several crew members and I go to the captain and confront him about what he is about to do. I insist that they make an effort to repair the ship, but the captain refuses. Three crew members and I go down into the hole to try to repair the engines, but as we go down the stairs we can see through a window that a speedboat is circling the ship, manned by several Rambo-type men armed with guns. Two of my companions are killed by them and a third is wounded in the leg. I duck down out of sight, determined that they're not going to get me. I wait until the speedboat heads toward the other side of the ship and run up the stairs."

SC: We need someone to play the captain, then several officers, three crew members, a Rambo guy, and the rest of the group members can be the passengers.

[I realize later, to my chagrin that I neglect to have her choose someone to play the ship, although we come to that later during the last part of the dreamwork. After I take Natalie's hand and we walk as she tells the dream again in the present tense, we move into the scene with Natalie and crew members confronting the captain and officers about not making an effort to repair the ship.]

N: How can you just leave these people out here to die?! Can't you make some attempt to get the ship running again?!

SC *(to N)*: Reverse roles and play the captain. *[to person playing Cap]*: Cue her with her last line, in the same tone of voice and posture.

N-as-Cap: It makes me very, very sad, but nothing can be done.

SC *(to N, now as herself)*: Do you believe he's sad?

N: No, it's just lip service.

[She begs him to send some people below to try to repair the engines, but she can tell by his expression that he is unwilling to do anything. She and three crew members leave to go below to the engine room to see if they can repair the engines.]

N: When we start down the stairs I see these Rambo guys patrolling in a speedboat and they have guns. They kill two of my companions and wound the other in the leg, but I stoop down so they can't see me. I realize they are in cahoots with the captain and officers. They're like pirates and they intend to rob the passengers.

SC *(to N)*: Be the main Rambo guy. *[to N as Rambo]* What are you doing?

N-as-Rambo: I'm in with the captain. I have orders not to let any passengers leave the ship, to shoot anyone who tries. The captain tells me some people are trying to repair the ship and he orders me to shoot them.

SC: (to N-as-Rambo) Reverse roles.

SC (to N-as-herself): What's your reaction to what Rambo said?

N: I'm determined not to give up! *I'm determined not to let him kill me!* He's circling the ship so I wait 'til he's headed toward the other side and I run up the stairs. Actually I pretend I'm invisible — I often do that in dreams. *(laughter)* Then I wake up.

SC: *(to Natalie):* What are you feeling now?

N: I'm excited, especially since I have the feeling of refusing to give up.

SC: Does any of this resemble anything in your life?

N: Yes, in working in corporate America I often facilitated resolutions of conflicts and discontents. I'd go up to upper management — I liked working as a team — and we'd move to Plan B and go from there.

SC: Are you, or is anyone in your life, like the captain?

N: I'm comfortable being a leader and in charge. I like problem-solving. But I'm *not* like him in that he refuses to face the problem and do something about it. And I would *never* save myself and let other people perish.

237

SC: How are you like Rambo?

N: My first thought is that I'm not like him — I would never inhibit a process of getting things repaired. But I guess I am like him in the sense that I like to circle around things and use my power.

SC: Your leadership qualities?

N: Yes, those qualities. But I mostly identify with the people on the ship — I feel connected with the masses. And I'm not willing to give up without a fight.

SC: Is there a "captain" in your life?

N: I've thought about what might be keeping me from doing the right thing.

SC: Anyone who stands in your way? *[No response from N]* How do you stop *yourself* from doing that?

N: I don't engage in things I would normally like to. My husband and daughter stand in my way, *naturally.* I don't mind this.

SC: What else hinders you, especially dangerous things?

N: My being in academic settings where there are more highly educated people. They have power, and I *used* to have power and people would come to *me.* Now I have to go to *them.*

SC: Now you're more like the people than the officers, right? So now you have to work "down below."

N *(begins to cry)*: I want to do more, but being a mother takes a lot of energy, and I can't yet do as much as I want to. I quit my job when I got pregnant, and I lost power. I had to take a backseat to a little baby. I feel sorrow over all the losses I've had.

SC: Losses of prestige, power, money?

N: Because I chose to leave that life and pursue another life I never actually grieved the real losses.

SC *(asks members of the group to play "money," prestige," "power," then to N:)* Speak to each of these things you've lost, telling each how you feel about the loss.

N: I don't think money is very important. But I didn't realize how important prestige — which to me is leadership — is to me. And power —the ability to choose what's going to happen in my everyday life. *[to "prestige" and "power"]* I didn't recognize that I would *miss* you. Especially as being *seen* as competent and able in intellectual ways.

SC: I imagine that's taken a toll on you, how you feel about yourself.

N: Yes. I have a lot of inner turmoil. I see this as part of my journey. Feeling the loss teaches me so much — to experience life in a different way, not having power and prestige. Having a life with little power and control is neat in itself.

Colleague Ansel Woldt *(to Natalie)*: The way you're talking about your recent life and the transition to motherhood sounds like what's happening to the ship. Can you identify with the ship?

SC: Do you feel stalled?

N: Stalled, *yes*! I hadn't thought about it that way before. I *do* feel stalled because I can't yet do the things I want to do. I think my engine needs to be repaired, a tune-up. I'm stalled, but lots is going on inside.

SC: And you have a very powerful mechanic working inside getting the repairs done!*[laughter]*

N: My husband is like Rambo: he hinders my process. Or I *perceive* that he does. I'm working on that. I'm trying to see what part of the gunk is his and what is mine.

SC: And you've said, "He's not going to get me!"

N: *No! He's not going to get me!*

[Natalie, clearly touched by the work and suddenly pensive, nods her acknowledgement of the truth of the statement.]

Commentary

Although there are several issues Natalie is dealing with by means of this dream, what appears to be central is the fact that she has not grieved the important losses her entrance into motherhood and the change of career path have entailed. Working through the dream leads her to face the importance of these losses, and to focus on those factors that currently hold her back from doing the things she wants to do ("the right thing").

The dream also brings into clear relief certain strengths Natalie has, and which she brings to any endeavor to which she commits herself: she is a competent problem-solver, who knows how to work well as a leader/member of a team; she is committed to "doing the right thing," which often involves her in serving the welfare of those with less power ("little baby, "the masses"). Even though she has temporarily lost prestige and power, Natalie still has the strength of character and the power of commitment that allow her to be successful in any project she undertakes, whether that be in "Corporate America," counseling, or the roles of wife and mother.

Several years later Natalie told Ansel and me how important this dreamwork had been to her. In her graduate work she was preparing to "doing the right thing" in new venues, and in the process redeeming what she had lost when she quit her job.

Part Three

Conclusion

As I have worked with dreams with Gestaltdrama I have become convinced in a new way of the holism of the human organism. I have been able to see more clearly than ever that the whole person — body-emotions-awareness-thinking-knowing-and being-with-others — lives *as a whole* through time and circumstances, and that the distinctions we make about facets of the whole are nothing more than *distinctions of reason, not of fact.* I have often been surprised, even stunned, at how the unfinished business of a person's past is "just under the surface," just a little out of awareness. An apparently trivial question such as "how do we get into the restroom?" can bring "to center stage" a huge swath of the dreamer's painful past and its effects on his present functioning.

I also have come to a deeper understanding of human beings' capacity for self-regulation, as well as a broader appreciation for the ineluctable whole-making propensity that exists in the human organism (no doubt in all organisms). I believe that dreaming enables the person to digest the events in his life, assimilating some elements and discarding what is not useful. Recurring dreams repeatedly prompt the person to address and deal with issues he has not sufficiently resolved, so that they can then be more functionally assimilated into his ongoing life.

Like other forms of Gestalt therapy, the dramatic method of Gestaltdrama is both dialogic and experimental, but it is through its use of space and real people representing the various elements of the dream that this method raises the work to a higher level of intensity and increases its liveliness and its realistic "feel." The dreamer's dialogic contact with the "others" who emerge into the dream space as the work unfolds induces important aspects of the internal organization of a person's living to begin to stand out relief. Moreover, the dramatic process effectively connects the dream with the dreamer's waking experience —and thus with those issues in the client's history that have remained unresolved — providing the person with the opportunity to work through what has persistently remained incapable of healthy integration. All of this contributes to the heightened impact of the dreamwork.

This approach to dreamwork clearly exemplifies Gestalt therapy's use of the clinical phenomenological method. This method requires that (1) the clinician put aside any and all preconceptions she may have about the client. (2) The clinical exploration of the client and his concerns must begin with immediate experience with the client, and further, all hunches, hypotheses, or thought *about* the client must be verified by a return to immediate experience with the client. (3) Finally, no gesture, posture, verbal mannerism, or any other verbal or nonverbal detail in how the client reveals himself in the clinical situation can be set aside as unimportant *a priori*, since anything may prove to be significant.

In working with a client's dream the therapist attends closely to the narrative story, asking questions that bring forth greater experiential detail throughout the process. She also has the client engage in a dialogue with each element of the dream, playing not only himself but also identifies with the other as he plays the part of a given element of the dream. The therapist is not only interested in the content of the dialogue, but asks how the dreamer feels bodily and emotionally as the dialogues proceed. Some detail that emerges in any of the dialogues may pique the therapist's curiosity, prompting her to ask questions or suggest an experiment. As the dreamwork unfolds, connections with other persons or situations emerge and these can then become the subject of exploration and/or experimentation. At the end of the dramatic part of the work the therapist asks the dreamer to say how he is like each of the dream's elements.

In this process we are discovering and then tracking the *intentionalities* or relationships that emergent phenomena have with other persons and/or situations in the dreamer's life. The process of the dreamwork enables the client to *refract* and *expand* the dream's content, thereby *accessing* its intentionalities, its connections with these existential factors. It is by means of this dramatic process that the dream's *meaning* — its connections with other aspects of the dreamer's personality and/or his existential situation — emerges and begins to stand out in relief from its ground in the person's ongoing living.

As Gestalt therapists we are frequent witnesses to the truth of *the paradoxical principle of change*: when what-is is allowed to stand-out in relief, is confronted and acknowledged, it then begins to shift and change. In contrast to other approaches that attempt to place human behavior into categories, the Gestalt therapist "has sought ever *more* intimate contact with the activities of the human organism as *lived* by the human organism." (PHG p.21) In working with dreams by means of Gestaltdrama it is possible to have such contact with how the person has organized his ongoing life, and in so doing to open up that internal organization itself to the possibility of change. The past cannot, of course, be made *never to have happened*, but in so many ways we, as Gestalt therapists, are able to help our clients change the *outcome, the impact* of the past. Indeed, their very living begins to become reorganized in more functional ways.

In my experience, Gestaltdramatic dreamwork is the most powerful and awe-inspiring method by which this happens. While it is in some ways a simple process, working step by step with whatever emerges in the work, it often *seems* like *magic!* I invite other Gestalt therapists to discover this for themselves.

Bibliography

Barrett, D. & McNamara, P. (2007). *The New Science of Dreaming, Vol. 3.* Westport, Conn.: Praeger.

Crocker, S.F. (1999). *A Well-Lived Life: Essays in Gestalt Therapy.* Cambridge, MA.: GIC Press.

Downing, J., Marmorstein, R. (1973). *Dreams and Nightmares.* New York: Harper&Row

Fantz, R.E. & Roberts, A. (1998). *The Dreamer and the Dream.* GIC Press, Cambridge.

Lewin, K. (1936). *Principles of Topological Psychology.* McGraw-Hill, New York.

Perls, F, Hefferline, R., & Goodman, P. (1951). *Gestalt Therapy: Excitement   and Growth in the Human Personality.* New York: Dell.

Perls, F. (1969). *Ego, Hunger, and Aggression.* New York: Vintage Books.

Perls, F. (1971). *Gestalt Therapy Verbatim.* New York: Bantam Books.

Perls, F (1974). *The Gestalt Approach* and *Eyewitness to Therapy.*

Yontef, G. (1993). *Awareness, Process, and Dialogue.* Highland, N.Y.: Gestalt Journal Press.

Zinker, J. (1977). *Creative Process in Gestalt Therapy.* New York: Brunner/Mazel.

Chapter 12. Being Present to the Emergent Creation of the Field: Wordsworth, Buber and Gestalt Therapy
Brian O'Neill

Chapter Introduction

There was a recent discussion on the genesis of the "self" in a recent lively, even heated, and scholarly discussion on the email list for the New York Institute of Gestalt Therapy (NYIGT). Our conversations went to which came first, organism or self and is the self a property of the field or of the individual. True to form the discussion went from this 'either/or' position to one of "both/and" and Bud Feder (also true to form) came in with a pithy quote:

> *I have heard talk of the beginning and the end, but I do not talk of the beginning or the end.*
> *There has never been more inception than there is now"*
>
> Walt Whitman

This stimulating discourse from the Institute email list inspired me to choose this article — *Being Present to the Emergent Creation of the Field: Wordsworth, Buber and Gestalt Therapy.* I have found a continuing inspiration in my writing and sense of self throughbeing in contact with friends and colleagues at the Institute. I have felt their wider influence with their support for the *Association for Advancement of Gestalt Therapy: an International Community* and through the writing of those at the Institute, beginning with the seminal text of Perls, Hefferline and Goodman.

For me much of what Goodman brought to the seminal text was about the nature of the child, and this finds a deep accord for me with other spiritual writing — especially that of Taoism. As Lao Tzu states in the writing of the Tao Te Ching:

> *There are those who want to control the world by action.*
> *But I see they cannot succeed.*
> *The world is a sacred vessel*
> *It should be not interfered with*
> *To interfere is to spoilt it*
> *To grasp it is to lose it.*
>
> Tao Te Ching
> *The Way of Nature and its Powers*
> Lao Tzu

These Taoist teachings are similar to Perls, Hefferline and Goodman description of a way of being in the world which counters the anxious and controlling mode of many adults and organizations in the modern world. There is a richness in connecting Lao Tzu with a modern psychotherapy, where each have similar language in striving to describe states of being which provide a sense of hope, joy and excitement.

In particular it is Goodman's emphasis on the recovery of childhood (as he rescues it from the psychoanalytical restrictions of Freud) that the emergent figure of *Gestalt Therapy: Excitement and Growth in the Human Personality* shines for me:

> *A child leaves off capriciously, but while he is engaged he gives himself. The adult, partly because he is so preoccupied with being so responsible for himself, gives himself less earnestly. Again, it is only the gifted person who retains this ability of childhood...* (Perls, Hefferline and Goodman, 1951, *pg. 304)*

And it is perhaps surprising (or not to some) that these existential statements by PHG on how to live with suffering aided by the 'middle mode' of the child and poet are found in the writings of current Christian mysticism:

> *. . . the rediscovery of childhood and consequently the perceptive appreciation of the secret surprise of customary objects is a very rare and precious kind of experience, enjoyed almost exclusively these days by unspoiled children.*

> (William McNamara,
> 1979, pgs. 57-58)

So this chapter is a gift of hope for the child in us all and a thank you to the New York Institute for Gestalt Therapy for all it continues to offer to the world at large.

References

McNamara, W., (1979). *Mystical Passion — The Art of Christian Loving* San Francisco: Harper & Row.

Miles. T. (1992) *Tao Te Ching: About the Way of Nature and Its Powers by Lao Tzu.* Avery Publishing, New York.

Perls, F., Hefferline, R., and Goodman, P. (1951) *Gestalt Therapy: Excitement and Growth in the Human Personality.* Souvenir Press edition (1984) London

Being Present to the Emergent Creation of the Field: Wordsworth, Buber and Gestalt Therapy.

Abstract: The field perspective in gestalt therapy remains a rich source of controversy and challenge in outlining and articulating a theory of practice. In teaching gestalt therapy, particularly the field perspective, it is useful to find examples of the principles that direct and support practice, as well as enhance and expand theory. Latner offers the field as an inspiring, evocative idea and suggests that when a term such as this has a connotative richness, we can best define it by searching for examples that "speak to us" (Latner, 2008). He offers how he is inspired by the writing of Dogen, a Zen Buddhist teacher writing a thousand years ago, and how he intuitively understands a field universe through his writing. In a similar fashion, Martin Buber and William Wordsworth speak with a connotative richness of *emergent creation* and *paradoxical agency*, two principles of the field perspective recently described in the literature (O'Neill & Gaffney, 2008). This article is an experiment in reaching out for just such connotative richness - an intuitive understanding of these two principles of field theory, *emergent creation* and *paradoxical agency*, to find an articulation of these principles in ways that speak to gestalt practitioners.

> *While with an eye made quiet by the power*
> *Of harmony, and with deep power of joy,*
> *We see into the life of things."*

(Wordsworth, *Lines Composed a Few Miles Above Tintern Abbey, On Re-visiting the Banks of the Wye During a Tour, June 13, 1798*, pgs 104-105)

There are blessed moments in the life of every gestalt therapist where they experience in their work a sense of ease, of fluidity, of being attuned to the moment and the context of existence. At such moments the more directive, goal oriented aspects of the self are "made quiet" and out of the chaos of our work with individuals, couples, families, groups, organizations and even communities, a world of harmony becomes apparent. Such moments are manifest and manifold in the arts. We are no longer playing violin solo but are part of the orchestra and music; as a painter we sense that the painting is painting us; and we are so well rehearsed in the play that something more than the words come through and we surf the wave of this new creation. Such experiences are frequently joyful, and bring an expanded sense of self and other, so that "we see into the life of things".

As all students of gestalt therapy would know, the journey to these blessed states of being take many years and it is with furtive longing that we view the work of experienced practitioners and trainers, and with painful, at times shameful, exasperation that we struggle to emulate the apparent effortless wisdom of these masters. As all trainers and supervisors know, such apparent skill only comes through years of ardent work and of learning from our mistakes, and it is with an eventual humble surrender to principles of life greater than those our ego would prefer, that allows us to reap the rewards of practice, practice, practice.

The work of a trainer, supervisor or mentor, while guided by similar principles to that of the practitioner, is also importantly different. While both the practice and teaching of gestalt rests in gestalt therapy as a philosophy of being, the way in which these principles are lived in teaching is important to distinguish from practice. For example, Tiger Woods may be a great golfer but he goes to a golf coach to help him improve his game, as there are different skills and attitudes required in the "preparing for doing" compared to the "doing". Each of course is a form of "doing" yet the work of preparation, of training, supervising and mentoring is a learning process which may impart knowledge and even understanding, but cannot, as again trainers and supervisors know, impart the "lived wisdom" where practitioners allows the efforts of their ego to "go quiet" and surrender to the "power of Harmony" and thus "see into the life of things".

As described elsewhere (Levine BarYoseph et al, 2008) the training of gestalt therapists has received little attention in the literature. .In part this may be due to the challenge in imparting more than the basic skills of counseling and psychotherapy (to which less holistic approaches are amenable) and that the gestalt approach requires a more complex articulation of that which is a "lived wisdom.

Added to this challenge is the complexity of the initial text itself (Perls et al, 1951) and the controversy of the field perspective in gestalt therapy, which has been described as difficult and demanding (Yontef, 1993) and which has tended to divide into two camps of those who prefer the work of Levine and those who eschew this for the foundational "organism/environment field" of Perls et al. This initial conceptualization of the organism/environment field of Perls, Hefferline and Goodman (1951) is complex in its simplicity. It presents as an amalgam of esoteric writing, social critique, psychoanalytical terminology and practical exercises on awareness and contact. Since it was written there have been notable developments in gestalt therapy literature to refine or better describe field theory and link theory to practice (Latner, 1983;Yontef,1993; Parlett, 1993,1997, 2005; Staemmler, 2006;O'Neill, 2008).

More recently O'Neill and Gaffney (2008) present an integrative articulation of these two field theories in gestalt therapy and apply this conceptualization to therapy with a case study, describing the philosophy and principles of field theory in practice. In this previous work, rather than describing this as field *theory*, this is denoted as a field *perspective* and there is presented a heuristic list of principles which guide practice (common to all field theory approaches) and suitable for application in gestalt therapy research. They have termed this integrative view of field theory as the field perspective to denote it is wider than a single theory alone and that it includes the main elements and commonalities of these theories as applicable to our practice as therapists, as well as trainers.

The One Field in Practice

It is the intention of this current article to thus further explore two of these principles of a field perspective, both from an integrative view of field theory and more importantly to explore a creative way to support training and practice of gestalt therapy. Hence rather than being a further critique of field theory, the purpose will be simply to extend and expand upon this field perspective by attending in more detail to two of these principles.

The two principles which will be addressed are precisely those which attend to the struggle of trainees and trainers alike, as mentioned above, which require a degree of surrender of the ego to a wider process in the field while at the same time paradoxically and intentionally making use of this expanded awareness as a therapist. These two principles have been described as *Paradoxical Agency* and *Emergent Creation.* It is also the intention of this article to explore these field perspective principles by utilizing other creative sources and writings which "speak to" these principles and which more poetically articulate that which traditional theory cannot help but leave a little dry. The examples which most speak to the author are those of Wordsworth and Buber.

As a reader please note the shift as we move from theoretical articulation to the poetry and back, and how each informs you in its own way. I would suggest for its fuller impact, and to allow the poetry to be appreciated in its own form, that you might consider reading aloud with a pace that allows the grace of the work to speak to you. Hopefully this will support moving between the theory and the poetry, as one might in actual therapy when we find ourselves moving between being present in the moment and at times reflecting and thinking about the process. This thus also demonstrates an alternative teaching method, of using literature or music or art to "inspire" us and remind us of those experiences which do not dwell in the heady world of theory alone and which hopefully enhance and delight our theoretical musing and direct our choice as we practice theoretical principles, to the stage where practice becomes lived authentic being.

This approach of using wider sources than the traditional theory of therapy is discussed by Latner (2008) who described the field as an inspiring, evocative idea which is best thought of as an attitude. He critiques attempts to describe the field as a theory, a rigorous set of interlocking ideas, and prefers to define it as an "evocative field perspective" from which he derives a "constellation of ideas that come out of field thinking" (Latner, 2008, pg. 27).

Both Latner and O'Neill & Gaffney coalesce in their writing on the importance of creativity in describing the field in gestalt therapy. As Latner states:

The field is an encompassing pregnancy, a potentiality that becomes actual and takes a specific form from contact. Its nature is spontaneous and ephemeral; its form is fluid, continuously created and recreated." (Latner, 2008, pg. 24)

Emergent Creation

O'Neill and Gaffney note that while creativity has been given attention in Gestalt therapy it has not been well defined from a field perspective. They describe creativity from a field perspective as "emergent creation", a figure/ground formation in the field as a whole, in comparison to an experience of creation from an individualistic paradigm, (which includes the co-creation of both individuals together). They propose that emergent creation is a process whereby a figure emerges from the greater whole and, as such, is different and more than the sum of the creations of each part. This is a creation from the field without individual agency or intention – a holistic paradigm of creation as compared to an individualistic one.

In essence, this equates to the agency of the whole towards the parts as aptly defined by Wertheimer when describing the field perspective in Gestalt psychology, when he states –

*There are wholes, the behavior of which is not determined by that of their individual elements, but where the part-processes are themselves determined by the intrinsic nature of the whole (*Wertheimer, 1925 in Ellis 1938, p. 2)

This principle wherein a whole determines the behavior of the individual parts is more common place than it might at first seem. It is particularly prevalent in everyday life, where individuals are part of a team and they become swept into the synergy of the functioning of the team – such as with a sporting team, an orchestra or band, a choir, a emergency team in a hospital, a family and community. Even with individual pursuits in arts, theatre, sports, and drama, the combined experience of the performer and the audience can come together to create an experience (or figure) that emerges creatively from the whole and is not dependent on the performer.

In therapy the authors describe this creative process as a figure which emerged from the field of the implicit reality (or implicate order) of the client/therapist field (O'Neill & Gaffney, 2008) and so in order to discriminate this from other creations which are more explicitly individually co-created, they chose the term emergent creation in that it is created and emerges from the implicate order of the field.

In the previous work Gaffney describes working with a client involved with three men. He notices that when he mentions one she has a pattern of mentioning the others as well. He notes this as a figural pattern in *her* field or life space. He later notices how she looks at him at times and this reminds him of his father when he was angry. Eventually he risks sharing this and she tells him this does not apply to her. This figure has emerged from *his* field or life space. Later in another session he keeps getting images of gloves and sees no pattern of sense to this in either his or her field. As the image is repetitive he trusts this might have meaning and shares it with her, tentatively. She becomes emotional and relates how when she was young her parents bought her woolen gloves that itched and no matter how often she would lose them they were replaced. She had no choice. Now she was an adult she could afford as many pairs of gloves as she wanted and had a rich collection at home to choose from. This connects with her current difficulty in choice of the men. The figure though has somehow emerged from the wider field of the therapist client dyad and as such is more than just the field or life space of one or the other. It is a figure that connects both in some way and arises beyond the simple individualistic logic of the separate egos and life spaces. As we stated previously, the process whereby an event of the client's past emerged as an image in the therapist and returned to the client is the magic and the mystery of a field approach. While there is no doubt that the process of the gloves image can be, or soon will be, open to a generally acceptable "scientific" explanation, our interest is not in such an explanation as we are more concerned with the experience of this process and its value in a therapeutic setting.

Surrendering to Paradoxical Agency

Such notions of reality as emergent creation are challenging to students and practitioners of gestalt therapy. To accept and work as a therapist from this principle of emergent creation requires a degree of surrender on the part of the student or therapist. O'Neill and Gaffney title this "surrender to paradoxical agency" and describe how in Gestalt therapy, as opposed to other schools, we do not try to measure or "control" the individual as a separate phenomenon.

The field perspective consists of being aware and attuned to the operation of the contact boundary in the organism/environment field, rather than satisfying the need for the therapist to exercise control of the therapeutic situation as in some approaches. That is easier said than done of course, particularly for a student or beginning therapist who is doing their best to apply the theory to practice, and therefore "trying" to exert some form of control over what is happening.

In part, the challenge of allowing and working with emergent creation is a paradoxical process of searching for balance between willful choice and acceptance of what "is" for both the therapist and client. This is described in the original text of Perls et al (1951) as the middle mode - the space between active and passive functioning, where the person is accepting, attending and growing into the solution, with the substitution of readiness (or faith) for the security of apparent control (Perls, Hefferline and Goodman, 1951).

The original text of Perls et al (1951) asks therapists, from a field perspective, to have faith in something more than their individual agency, to let go of their need for security and control and instead to be present in the moment – to be present to the emergent creation of the field.

This *readiness* of middle mode described by Perls et al (1951) offers a paradoxical agency to the therapist - an ability to sense and chose being "in control" by relinquishing control. They equate this state to one which is more familiar to children and artists, and indeed examples of such paradoxical agency are found aplenty in the arts, music and poetry, such as in the work of William Wordsworth. It is also a state frequently referred to by people who describe spiritual experiences, such a Martin Buber.

In teaching gestalt therapy, particularly the field perspective, it is useful to find examples of the principles that direct and support practice, as well as enhance and expand theory. Latner states that when a term has a connotative richness, we define it by searching for examples that "speak to us" (Latner, 2008). He gives the example of how he is inspired by the writing of Dogen, a Zen Buddhist teacher writing a thousand years ago, an how he intuitively "understands how to think about a field-universe in which each being construes his/her reality as universal" (Latner, 2008, pg. 25). In a similar fashion, Martin Buber and William Wordsworth speak with a *connotative richness* about creative emergence and paradoxical agency. So it is in reaching out for an intuitive understanding and enrichment of emergent creation and paradoxical agency that we now turn to Wordsworth and Buber for articulation of these principles of a field perspective.

Wordsworth's poetry is popular with many, and in particular he speaks to those who have loosened the bonds of what Charles Tart refers to as Ordinary Waking Consciousness (Tart, 1975), allowing perception and awareness to expand beyond normal everyday affairs. In his poem *Lines Composed a Few Miles Above Tintern Abbey, On Re-visiting the Banks of the Wye During a Tour, June 13, 1798*, Wordsworth describes a state of awareness neither totally directive nor passive –

> *"That blessed mood,*
> *In which the burden of the mystery,*
> *In which the heavy and the weary weight*
> *Of all this unintelligible world,*
> *Is lightened: - that serene and blessed mood,*
> *In which the affection gently lead us on, -*
> *Until the breath of this corporeal frame*
> *And even the motion of our human blood*
> *Almost suspended, we are laid asleep*

In body and become a living soul;
While with an eye made quiet by the power
Of harmony, and with deep power of joy,
We see into the life of things."

(Wordsworth, 1798, (1950), pgs. 104-105)

Some may at first draw back and wonder at the relevance of this esoteric and mystical language in relation to the practice of gestalt therapy, yet consider the struggles of Goodman in Perls et al (1951) in finding ways to describe similar states of being such as middle mode. This is particularly so when describing the Id state, which reads in a similar fashion, in part, to that described by Wordsworth. Perls et al (1951) used poetic language similar to Wordsworth at times, several times mentioning the "soul" and discuss the nature of poetry and its importance as a language for reality.

Martin Buber, in a similar fashion, is not shy to leap into script which might leave the uninitiated reader behind -

> The fiery stuff of all my ability to will seethes tremendously, all that I might do circles around me, still without actuality in the world, flung together and seemingly inseparable, alluring glimpses of powers flicker from all the uttermost bonds; the universe is my temptation, and I achieve being in an instant, with both hands plunged deep into the fire, where the single deed is hidden, the deed which aims at me – now is the moment!
> (Buber, 1958, pg. 51-52)

With these words Buber describes the shift from a reign of causality in the world of It, where every event and experience is either caused or causing, to the world of relation, where the I and Thou "freely confront one another in mutual effect, that is neither connected with, nor colored by, causality."

He defines the nature and stance of the paradoxical agency of the therapist poetically, when he avows that destiny and freedom are "promised to each other." By this he means there is a choiceful acceptance of "what is" rather than pursuing control of the situation, as promised by the perspective of causality. He describes this poetically and paradoxically as the "deed which aims at me". He goes on to describe how such a state is only available to those who have the freedom given by knowing relationship and the presence of Thou.

Poetic Practice

It is the task of the trainer and supervisor to envisage ways to create a setting which, though structured, provides the safety and stage wherein the trainee can justifiable let go a little of the need for control and allow themselves to be in the moment. One such exercise developed in training at the Illawarra Gestalt Centre has been borrowed from work with Frank Farrelly and Steve Brigham. It has three steps or stages. Trainees begin by sitting in dyads and we explore first how each person prepares themselves so as to be less distracted and more present. The first experience then involves one person taking the time to be in a state where they feel ready and then at this point they signal the other person to begin talking. As the second person talks the "job" of the first person is to sit silently attuned to the other.

This first part is usually very challenging as students who are being silent and centered want to indicate in all variety of ways that they are, indeed, attending and so some vigorously nod and gesticulate in order to do so. The result, as they discuss afterwards, is that paradoxically such concerns reduce their sense of being present, both for them and the other person. Yet this now offers the student and practitioner a choiceful awareness of being as doing, and not needing to do for the sake of doing.

The next step in the experience is for the silent person to now talk when they want to and to allow this to emerge from whatever takes their own fancy, irrelevant to the person opposite them. Hence as an example the trainer may demonstrate how to talk gobblygook and speak in word salad.

This experience is tremendously freeing for some and alternatively excruciating for others who hold a need to be the "good attentive" therapist and once again, when discussed afterwards, brings fruitful discussions around the balance of overly attending versus relaxing into a spontaneous space.

The final phase of the experience involves the person now being centered and present, as well as sensing their ability to be spontaneous, and using this therapeutically. In this instance the spontaneous responses which are invited are the various images which arise for the therapist. They are thus able to practice being spontaneous therapeutically by sharing whatever images come into their head while the other person talks. They are encouraged to trust in the image and share it (and not further explain it) for the other person. The result is that they experience these images arising spontaneously and outside their ego control, and the person talking begins to make meaning from the images. As with reflective listening, the images may be altered or changed by the person talking and that is also encouraged as a co-created field. One might say "as you talk about your work, I get the sudden image of a cage" and the person may say "well it is but I am aware the door of the cage is open."

This experience also brings both therapist and client outside of the world of "talking about" the issues and more actively accessing a richer language of experience of imagery, similar to that of poetry. In such moments the barrier of talk can dissolve into a mutuality that is evident in the case study above with the image of the gloves and which is described by both Buber and Wordsworth.

Wordsworth, like Buber, had a knowing relationship with the presence of Thou, and this appears time and time again in his poetry –

> "And I have felt
> A presence that disturbs me with the joy
> Of elevated thoughts; a sense sublime
> Of something far more deeply interfused,
> Whose dwelling is the light of setting suns,
> And the round ocean and the living air,
> And the blue sky, and in the mind of man:
> A motion and a spirit, that impels
> All thinking things, all objects of all thought,
> And rolls through all things."

(Wordsworth, W. *"Lines composed a few miles above Tintern Abbey"* lines 93-103, 1950, pg. 106)

In the Womb we know the Universe, In Birth we forget it.

This state of being they each describe, a state open to emergent creation and accepting paradoxical agency, is seen by both Wordsworth and Buber to be a faculty that already exists and is found by un-learning as much as by new learning. Both are clear that such states of being are available but have been "lost" by a process of psychological "development".

Buber presents developmental stages that signify the transition from the life in the womb, which is cosmic in nature, to life in the world of It. The first stage of this development is also a loss, as described in the mystical Jewish saying "in the mother's body man knows the universe, in birth he forgets it", and so is this initial experience of birth a loss as well as a gain.

This change that is happening, unlike the physical birth itself, is not a sudden one but gradual – "time is granted to the child to exchange a spiritual connexion, *relation,* for the natural connection with the world that he gradually loses." (Buber, 1958, pg., 25)

In a strikingly similar manner to Buber's developmental devolution, Wordsworth describes this evolution and paradoxical devolution of the child into the adult in his poem *Intimations of Immortality From Recollections of Early Childhood* -

> "Our birth is but a sleep and a forgetting;
> The Soul that rises with us, our life's Star,
> Hath had elsewhere it's setting,
> And cometh from afar:
> Not in entire forgetfulness,

And not in utter nakedness,
But trailing clouds of glory do we come
From God, who is our home:
Heaven lies about us in our infancy!
Shades of the prison house begin to close
Upon the growing Boy
But he beholds the light, and whence it flows,
He sees it in his joy;
The Youth, who daily further from the east
Must travel, still is Nature's Priest
And by the vision splendid
Is on his way attended;
At length the Man perceives it die away
And fade into the light of common day.

Intimations of Immortality From Recollections of Early Childhood,
(William Wordsworth, 1950, pgs. 542 -543)

In this poem, similar to Buber, he provides a model of human development which portrays the early years of childhood through to adulthood as one of spiritual devolution or un-development. The child begins "trailing clouds of glory" as with Buber's description of the cosmic nature and awareness in the womb. Wordsworth almost shouts the next developmental stage – "Heaven lies about us in our infancy!" and Buber describes this as the infant's instinct is to make everything into a Thou (Buber, 1958, pg. 27).

The stages into adulthood are irrevocably contained in the metaphor of light, or its loss, for the next stage of being a boy is to experience "Shades of the prison house" while still beholding the light and by the stage of being a Youth is still attended by "the vision splendid". It is the man to whom this cosmic inscape dies, as this initial expanded awareness fades "into the light of common day" – the common light of Buber's world of I-It and Causality.

Buber is more paradoxical and apposite in his use of light as a metaphor, yet conveys the same meaning when he states "He (the child) has stepped out of the glowing darkness of chaos into the cool light of creation." (Buber, 1958, pg. 25)

How sad if that was the end of our developmental process. Yet it is at this point when we reach our mature state as physical and psychological beings that Buber tells how there is a call to return to the initial experiences of the states of awareness and for childhood to re-emerge for the adult.

Buber speaks of this developmental process as a movement, like a tidal force, in which the relation of Thou, which the child is born from, gives birth, as it were, to the experience of I. This is a movement, not linear, back and forward, between a sense of relation and a return to the cool light of creation. In this tidal process of back and forth the "I" grows stronger and becomes conscious of "I". As this happens the discrimination of "not I" also develops, so that "The man who has become conscious of I, that is I-It, stands before things but not over against them in the flow of mutual action" (Buber,1958, pg. 29).

From this stance of I-It the person takes possession of all It and objectifies things with the magnifying glass of observation and the field glasses of remote inspection. In such existential isolation lies the aloneness of the modern world – the person detached from universality and uniqueness. This allows for the co-ordination and causal control of these objects, and the desired security of the illusion of control.

A World that is ordered is not the World Order.

Yet this cool light of creation, this age of Causality, is not the end point. As Buber states in iconoclastic brevity – " a world that is ordered, is not the world order." (Buber, pg. 31) The world of relation, the world of Thou, calls out with a note as the individual stands fully present in the world order.

"These moments are immortal, and most transitory of all; no content may be secured from them, but their power invades creation and the knowledge of man, beams of their power stream into the ordered world and dissolve it again and again." (Buber, pg. 31)

All are affected by this call, this note, in one way or another. It may be through illness or death, through a gentle change in life, through marriage or child rearing, or in the pursuit of what one loves doing best. Whatever way it happens the note is sounded and the world of I-It begins to dissolve in deference for the experience of the world of relation. This is the emergent creation of the field. Such experiences challenge and deconstruct the world of Causality and the illusion of control, and demand an acceptance of the paradoxical nature of the agency of the field – of which all are a part.

Some, like Wordsworth, hear this note relatively early, are ready and respond. Most struggle and move back and forward between the coordinated world of order and the relational world order of Thou that surrounds us. Some fight the experience and the stronger the note and the stronger the fight, the greater the illness or dis-order that results.

Today many people cling to the world order, get lost in the appearance of job success, of financial security or any of the treasures which attach so easily. Others turn the call into a battle with their demons, or the demons of other people, and miss the "clouds of glory" in the battle. Many try to sedate the call with drugs or alcohol or food - feeding the physical self until it weights down the I-Thou with its gravity of biological processes.

These experiences, these struggles, this sense of loss of order, control and Causality are experienced as a dis-order. The rise of the professional mental health worker and counselor have created a work force which in many cases is a part of the institutions of order and seek to help the individual reduce the experience of dis-order and restore order once more. Like religion in the past, psychotherapy has developed as a social endeavor to assist in finding order for those who are experiencing these struggles of disorder.

Already the potential trap of therapy becomes evident. If it does not have the ability to transcend the institutionalised world of Causality, therapy itself becomes part of the problem. It is as an alternative to this trap that gestalt therapy and other approaches developed, and it is the field perspective principles such as emergent creation and paradoxical agency which articulate principles to guide this work.

Initially people enter the therapy process due to struggling with the lack of order and to try to gain control again. Many therapies have been developed to support this aim. Yet the nature of gestalt therapy, instead of offering control per se over the experienced symptoms, is to heighten awareness, contact and dialogue with the faith that through being present to "what is", change happens. This change is a developmental change, not a cure for an ill, and from Buber's perspective we enter again, more and more, into the world of relation, of I-Thou.

As both therapists and clients learn, or un-learn, to open to and be present to emergent creation with a sense of paradoxical agency, then a change happens in how they view the world and others. Wordsworth and Buber both note the significant impact this has on relationships in the world – not only with people but also with nature, such as trees and daffodils.

Buber talks of how a tree can be looked at - as a picture, perceived as a movement, classified as a species, subdued in actual presence so it is viewed as an expression of a biological law, and even dissipated in number, by counting it as one of many. In all these contacts the tree remains an object. Yet if he becomes "bound up in relationship to it" the tree is no longer an "It" and he becomes seized by the power of its exclusiveness - a mutuality of I-Thou, the tree itself. (Buber, pg. 7-8). The tree is no longer only an It to be numbered, classified or viewed (like clients can be also) and is experienced more fully and mutually *in relationship*. This attitude and experience instructs and hopefully inspires us to remember such mutuality in mental health care and therapy. While assessment and diagnosis have an important role to play, they become full as we also maintain and live the relationship with the "other".

Like Buber, this wealth of relationship with nature is abundant in the poetry of Wordsworth. His most famous poem is perhaps that which begins with "I wandered lonely as a cloud" which tells of this I-Thou relationship with a hill of daffodils He extends this relation with nature and his environment even more so to the city of London. The poem, "Composed Upon Westminster Bridge, Sept, 3rd, 1802", offers a view of the city early in the morning where Wordsworth senses the very life of the city itself, at a time when the air was still clean and the city flowed easily into the surrounding countryside, long before the congestion, smog and pollution of today.

"Composed Upon Westminster Bridge, Sept, 3ʳᵈ, 1802"

Earth has not anything to show more fair:
Dull would he be of soul who could pass by
A sight so touching in its majesty:
This City doth, like a garment, wear
The beauty of the morning, silent, bare,
Ships, towers, domes, theatres, and temple lie
Open unto the fields, and to the sky;
All bright and glittering in the smokeless air.
Never did sun more beautifully steep
In his first splendour, valley, rock or hill;
Ne'er saw I, never felt, a calm so deep!
The river glideth at his own sweet will;
Dear God! The very houses seem asleep;
And all that mighty heart is lying still!
(Wordsworth, 1950, pg. 474)

It is this very relation to our environment, this movement to I-Thou with nature and animals, that has inspired the work of organisations such as Greenpeace and the politics of ecology which seek to avert the impact of a world used from an I-It stance - to more readily embrace a relationship with our environment, with the greater whole of which all are part. Our world today is, perhaps more than any other time, impacted by our ability to control so many processes through technology and science. This approach to making use of technologies has also carried over into health care and therapy, so that the application of techniques and modalities is valued, at times rightly so. However it is in balance to this technological ability that an appreciation of emergent creation and paradoxical agency stands out as being so necessary and important. Like the poetry of Wordsworth and the writing of Buber, gestalt therapy stands out as a field perspective which accommodates and enlarges to include the wider environment, "A sight so touching in it majesty."

To Conclude

This wider connection with the greater whole is in part the intention of this article – to inspire therapists and trainers to reach for writing and experiences outside of the traditional therapeutic writing – to find poetry and prose which speak to them with beauty and embolden therapists to surrender to the paradoxical agency of the emergent creation of the field. There is nothing as useful as a good theory, and as teachers aspire to encourage a theory of practice, then ethically what happens is training and practice is guided by principles, which in turn based on coherent theory.

At the same time, there is learning beyond traditional theory that comes from experience and a way of being in the world. This requires a different approach to learning, both are valid, and the more intuitive learning is often found in creative pursuits and in poetry, music, drama, and the visual arts. This article attempts to offer a path of learning in the field perspective by reaching out for an intuitive understanding in the work of Wordsworth and Buber, who provide an articulation of these principles of emergent creation and paradoxical agency.

This brief article has been written as an experiment in finding other sources of to encourage the reader, as trainer and therapist, to consider the potential for examining their relationship with the greater whole, as described in the theoretical statement of Wertheimer. To find examples of the principles which direct and support training and practice with a connotative richness by searching for examples that "speak to us" and support how we intuitively understands how to live such principles as emergent creation and paradoxical agency. To inspire them to move with Buber's tidal wash between the world of Causality and the world of relation, between a world that is ordered and the World Order, and as such experience the risk of occasionally surrendering to the determination of the intrinsic nature of the whole, of which all are a part.

References

Buber, M., (1958) *I-Thou*, Scribner Books, New York
Latner, J. (1983) This is the speed of light: Field and systems theory in Gestalt therapy. *The Gestalt Journal*, 6,2 (Fall 1983), 71-90
Latner, (2008) Commentary I: relativistic Quantum Field Theory: Implications for Gestalt Therapy, (or The Speed of Light Revisited). *Gestalt Review* Vol 12, 1, pgs. 24-32.
O'Neill, B. (2008) Post Relativistic Quantum Field Theory and Gestalt Therapy, *Gestalt Review*, Vol 12, no 1, 2008, pgs.7-24.
O'Neill, B., & Gaffney, S. (2008) The Application of a Field Perspective Methodology, in Brownell, P., *Handbook for Theory, Research and Practice in Gestalt Therapy*, Cambridge Press Scholars Publishing, Cambridge.
Parlett, M.(1993) Towards a More Lewian Gestalt Therapy, *British Gestalt Journal*,2,2 p. 115-121Parlett, M.(1997) The Unified Field in Practice. *Gestalt Review*, 1,1 p.16-33

Parlett, M. (2005) Contemporary Gestalt Therapy: Field Theory in Woldt, A. & Toman, S. *Gestalt Therapy: History, Theory and Practice.* SagePublications, Thousand Oaks.

Perls, F., Hefferline, R., and Goodman, P. (1951) *Gestalt Therapy: Excitement and Growth in the Human Personality.* Souvenir Press edition (1984) London.

Staemmler Frank-M., (2006) A Babylonian Confusion? – The Term 'Field' *British Gestalt Journal,* Vol 15, No 1.Tart, C., (1975) States of Consciousness. E P Dutton and Co, New York.

Wordsworth, W. in Van Doren, M. (1950) *William Wordsworth Selected Poetry*, Random House, New York.

Yontef, G. (1993) *Awareness, Dialogue and Process: Essays of Gestalt Therapy.* The Gestalt Journal Press, New York,

Chapter 13
Power of the Immediate Moment in Gestalt Therapy
Gary Yontef

Chapter introduction

The NYIGT represents a most rigorous dedication to recognizing, discussing, debating, practicing, and embodying the fundamentals of gestalt therapy. New horizons are understood in light of these fundamentals. This article represents my thoughts about fundamental philosophic, methodological, and practice principles that are essential to an encompassing framework and often assumed rather than made explicit. The paradoxical theory of change, a relational perspective, dialogue, and active phenomenological focusing and experimenting are core ideas that guide me in understanding gestalt therapy theory and practice.

The Power of the Immediate Moment in Gestalt Therapy: *A Gestalt Therapy Paradigm*[89]

Therapists are usually trained to think about how to get patients to be different than they are. Some might say: "Of course. Why else do patients come to us?" From this viewpoint, patients come to be "fixed" and the therapy aims toward that fix. In such a model the therapist is expected to know how to fix and to do so. Current pressures in health care delivery and attempts at scientific validation have strengthened this tendency.

Humanistic/existential approaches stress something quite different. They emphasize the importance of an existential meeting in the here-and-now whereby shared understanding of a patient's life situation emerges from the interaction between therapist and patient. This existential meeting is the vehicle for improving patient functioning and satisfaction. Gestalt therapists aim to meet and understand the patient rather than to move the patient in any particular direction. The gestalt therapy version focuses more on the immediacy of how the patient functions moment-to-moment and on what is happening in each moment between therapist and patient and less on content (story, history, reinforcement schedules, etc.).

People Do Not Change by Trying To Be Who They Are Not

This is called the Paradoxical Theory of Change (Beisser, 1970). Trying to be who one is not is a disowning of oneself or denial of aspects of the self and leads to internal conflict and prevents wholeness and organismic change. The paradox is that the more people try to be who they are not, the more they stay the same. For example, self-loathing patients who spotlight being overweight often try to change their entire life, who they are, by dieting without really exploring why they are self-loathing, the function of overeating, the choices made, and so forth. This usually fails.

But what is the alternative? Of course people come to us for change. So how can people grow out of a dysfunctional, stuck position without trying to be what they are not? How can people move toward their goals and wishes without rejecting who they are?

Efforts to change based on self-recognition and acceptance of the self-as-a-person differ from efforts to change based on a pejorative attitude about the

---

[89] This first appeared in 2007 as "The power of the immediate moment in gestalt therapy." *Journal of Contemporary Psychotherapy*, 37(1), Special Issue: "Contributions of Humanistic Psychotherapies to the Field of Psychotherapy." pp 17–23

self-as-a-person. Change occurs with self-recognition, self-acceptance, owning, and healthy interpersonal contact. If a person identifies with how he/she actually is, including internal conflicts and dysfunctional behavior, in an attitude of self-love and self-respect, a fundamental change is much more likely to happen. The Paradoxical Theory of Change makes the therapeutic relationship central because the therapist's acceptance of the patient's moment-by-moment experiencing — including the patient's struggles and conflicts — is a primary support for the patient's self-recognition and self-acceptance.

People Learn From Experience

Ordinarily people change their thoughts and behavior by learning what works and what does not work. Spontaneous reinforcement and insight guide this natural growth. This is not a disowning of self-as-a-whole but an expansion of self. When a person does not learn from experience, therapy is indicated.

Learning How to Learn

Usually the pattern of not learning from experience will also manifest itself directly in therapy. For example, a patient complaining of worry and anxiety reacted at each moment by speculating on "why" and "what if" and did not gain grounding or new insight by noticing what he felt and wanted, his body sensations, a more detailed description of his experience, etc. Each obsessive question in the session was a doubting or denying of himself that blocked learning, and increased worry and anxiety. This was his pattern in life and it happened in sessions. He did not need me to ask "why" but needed questions such as: "What do you experience right now?" What do you sense right now in your body?" "What do you need right at this moment?" "What were you thinking or feeling the second before you started to doubt yourself?" From this kind of focusing, he learned more about his actual experience and learned to recognize when he was interrupting some important awareness — and then learned to interrupt that interruption. This helped him learn how he interfered with reaching his own goals.

Another example is a patient who did not use her power and her "response-ability" to set boundaries at work and in her personal life. The resultant turmoil and difficulty in her life was also present in therapy. From moment-to-moment this patient felt helpless to do anything for herself and she pulled on me to be the provider of both truth and also basic comfort. She believed I was a source of omnipotent knowledge and infinite provisions. In a variety of ways I communicated to her that although I cared about her, I did not wish to — nor could I — take care of her. I held firm to the position that the best I could do was support her to find her own way in life. By refusing to try to meet such elevated expectations, two things happened. First, the patient learned that she had more resources for self-care and support than she had known before, and second, she did not fall into a rage that would likely have followed from her disappointment had I tried and failed to support her idealizations of me. (Yontef, 1993).

It is important to respect the necessity of the patient's self-interruption process, even though it subverts the learning how to learn that is a natural process of living. The interruption serves, or served, a function. What is the function of the self-interruption? What drives the self-interruption? It is definitely not helpful if the therapist gets frustrated, confronts, asks "why" questions that the patient experiences as judgmental. Some confrontive versions of gestalt therapy publicized by Fritz Perls in the 1960s erred in this direction. This is not true of contemporary gestalt therapy.

When patients identify with what is interrupted and also with the interrupting process itself, stalled growth is reactivated. When people fully identify with what they think, feel, desire, choose, and how they behave, the stuckness of self-rejection and denial are replaced by a new felt sense (Gendlin, 1981) of responsibility, possibility, expanded awareness and greater capacity for learning from their experience. They can be who they are – and who they are becoming – by increased awareness and by increased honest and respectful contact with the therapist and others in their lives.

In the following example the patient was helped to identify her actual experience.

P: What if he does not come back? What if. ...(P. escalated her pitch and pace in a series of 'what if' questions about her husband in Iraq).

T: What are you feeling emotionally right now at this moment?

P: (Pause). I don't know.

T: Try an experiment. Take several long, slow breathes, and on the exhale let your jaw drop.

P: (Does the experiment, tension decreases, and the patient cries deeply). God how I miss him. I was getting so wound up in my worries that I did not realize that I miss him so much that it is painful – and that worrying does not lessen my fear or increase his safety.

The Phenomenological Attitude and Method in Therapy

The soil that makes restoration of learning-by-living possible in the gestalt model is composed of: (1) phenomenological focusing and experimentation to increase awareness, and: (2) a relationship based on dialogic contact. This combination (both discussed below) fosters self-recognition skills, self-respect, the patient's experience of being guided by working with a person who understands him/her and treats him/her her with love and kindness, and the use of active techniques (experiments). The therapist's attitude toward the patient and the quality of the contact between them, especially when there are ruptures in the relationship, and the kind of interventions that the therapist uses, largely determine the outcome of the therapeutic process.

The chief tools in a phenomenological approach are description rather than theory-driven interpretations or strategies aimed at preset goals such as symptom removal. In the phenomenological method the therapist puts aside ("brackets") assumptions, preconceived ideas, and fixed attitudes about what is real, about self and the world, in order to sense, describe, and clarify what is actually experienced in this very moment. Using a phenomenological method gets to a deeper, more textured understanding by focusing, by experience-near clarifications, and by experimenting rather than explaining. The phenomenological therapist is curious and wants to understand what the other person experiences and does not take the role of a change agent, judge, or arbiter of truth. Such a stance seems to enable patients to become less-critical and more interested in their experiential world. One result is that so-called "symptoms" come to be understood as integral dimensions of their self-functioning, for example as signals to them about what is vital to them (e.g. a symptom of profound isolation might protect one's sensed fragility from becoming overburdened). At the point when symptoms are appreciated for the function they serve, new learning may take place that expands a patient's range of responding to life's challenges.

The patient who is frightened in the session might be asked questions such as "How do you experience this moment?" "What am I doing that frightens you?" "What do you experience in your body?" "What do you want and not want?" The answer might be something like "I am afraid that you will think I am stupid," "I don't know what I experience and that leaves me feeling chaotic and ashamed," "I am afraid you will tell me I have to...," or "I feel hopeless and desperate," or "You look so stern," or a number of other responses that can be followed by the therapist accepting the patient's experience as valid and continuing the exploration and dialogue.

In years past, many gestalt therapists tended to see such patient fear as something that resided within and emerged from the patient's self-organization. In the now outdated version of gestalt therapy publicized by Fritz Perls in the 1960s, the intervention to these traits of the person was often theatrical, abrasive, confrontational, and/or organized around cathartic experiments. Contemporary gestalt therapists lean more on our grounding in Buber's philosophy of dialogue and on phenomenological field theory to stress — as in the example questions above — that this patient's fear is an emergent property of the immediate situation, which includes the therapist's participation.

In the example below with a new patient, the therapist begins as follows:

T: What are you experiencing right now?

P: I am afraid to speak.

T: Are you afraid of something right here in the room with me?

P: You will think I am crazy and put me in a hospital.

T: Do you feel crazy or think you are crazy?

P: No. I am confused and angry. But when I get emotional, my husband thinks I am crazy.

T: And you don't know yet how I will react to you when you show your emotions.

P: That's right. Maybe I should trust you – you are a therapist.

T: I think you have to find out if I can be trusted and it makes sense not to assume that I am trustworthy until you know me better.

Experiments

Experiential focusing can be extended by using active techniques — such as experiments. Experimenting can be as simple as suggesting that the patient take a few slow, deep diaphragmatic breathes with a long exhale. Possibilities are only limited by imagination and creativity. The experiment might involve an expanded dialogue in which the therapist gives voice to what he actually experiences with the patient, e.g., "I don't think you are stupid. In fact, you make a lot of sense." That dialogue would be an experiment for both the patient and the therapist.

Experiments in gestalt therapy are cooperative efforts of the therapist and patient to understand more deeply and to explore alternate possibilities. Experiments are an attempt to explore and understand and not attempts to move toward pre-established goals. It is assumed that both the patient's and therapist's experience are valid data. The data from the experiments might be that regardless of what the therapist believes and affirms, that the patient's affective reality continues to be that he is stupid. This might open the door to exploring how the patient learned that he is stupid (or silly, or absurd, or undesirable, etc.). Or the experiments might involve homework, role-playing, sensory experiments, journaling, use of art, music, or movement, fantasy experiments, and so forth.

The exploration brings into focal awareness aspects of the patient's experience that had been kept in the background, e.g., longing or disgust. When these shameful aspects are brought into vivid, visceral awareness in the context of an accepting relationship with the therapist, spontaneous change often results. The patient "gets better." This is the paradoxical theory of change. Embracing your current existence, including your conflicts and shame, reinstates the learning that is a natural aspect of living and makes growth possible. Patients' resilience in the face of anxiety becomes enhanced by their more nuanced awareness of their self-process, and their decreased shame and isolation as they come to trust in the therapist's genuine respect for their life choices on a moment-by-moment basis.

The new awareness also points to avenues of exploration. For example, a patient with an impoverished romantic life discovered a previously denied longing for connection. This led to an awareness of an even more intense terror at the prospect of either success or failure with women. He became aware that his lack of a romantic life came from his isolating defenses and not from women rejecting him. This also put his emotionally isolating behavior in the therapy sessions into a meaningful context.

P: I am aware now that my life is without romance mostly because I isolate myself.

T: Sometimes I experience that happening right here between us.

P: Really? How?

T: Sometimes you seem in your own world and when I try to connect, I feel a barrier, like I am shut out.

There are moments in which patients become sharply aware, with great emotion, of the value of their self-interruptions. One isolating patient had such a moment: "I won't be vulnerable and let someone hurt me again!" As he became aware that this defense keeps him from a new connection, he also became aware that this attitude was a healthy response to adverse conditions in his past, but now doomed him to reliving the trauma. He then started experimenting with contacting rather than isolating. The therapist facilitated this by identifying the thoughts and feelings as they emerged moment-to-moment, by formulating the theme emerging from these moments, and respecting the patient's core emotions and his defenses.

Example: Tom was a 45 year old man proud of his self sufficiency and unaware of unmet dependency needs (Yontef & Jacobs, 2005, p. 328).

P: [With pride.] When I was a little kid my mom was so busy I just had to learn to rely on myself.

T: I appreciate your strength, but when I think of you as such a self reliant kid, I want to stroke you and give you some parenting.

P: [Tearing a little]. No one ever did that for me.

T: You seem sad.

P: I'm remembering when I was a kid.

These interactions created new satisfactions, a new sense of hope, and also new material for exploration, e.g., reexamining core belief system. If the same experiments are suggested by the therapist as a way to get the patient to behave better, the spirit of the venture is very different. Often patients then will experience that they must succeed and please the therapist or fail and disappoint the therapist. The experiments then become something to pass or fail rather than to learn something. Pleasing or frustrating the therapist can then become the organizing principle rather than a felt sense of curiosity, excitement, spontaneity, and self-expansion. This can occur even if the therapist is not at all aware that he or she is triggering this reaction.

The phenomenological attitude, focusing and experimenting can contribute to any therapy, behavior therapy, psychoanalytic therapy, or an existential experiential therapy such as gestalt therapy. Our interest in, and methodology for, accentuating and expanding here-and-now awareness can vivify and increase the specificity of the therapeutic process whether one is focused on a particular symptom or on the broader questions of enduring life themes. The other central aspect of this approach is the dialogic relationship.

The Dialogic Relationship

Psychotherapy in the gestalt therapy model is "healing through meeting" (Jacobs, 1995). In a dialogic relationship the therapist "meets" or contacts the patient rather than aiming to get the patient to be different. The therapist wants to experience what the patient experiences; the therapist is authentically present and willing to be emotionally affect by the patient.."

Therapeutic effectiveness is largely determined by the nature and quality of the therapeutic relationship. If the therapist tries to effect a specific the outcome, the patient is encouraged to conform rather than grow through engagement. The emergence of spontaneous and self-directed change is inhibited as the expectation of cure by the therapist is reinforced. This issue is relevant to any kind of therapy. This does not mean that the therapist ignores the urgency of a patient's suffering. But our acceptance of the meaningfulness of their difficulties seems to help patients move from a position of shame and self-loathing for having problems, to one of compassion and interest about what their problems say about important life themes and what they can do about it. This also becomes the foundation for new learning, experimenting with alternate coping tools, and exploration of avenues for solving the problems that are now accepted without shame and self-loathing.

When the therapist attempts to organize or change patients, or has an attitude of "knowing how the patient ought to be," the patients get a message that they are not OK as they are and that the therapist knows better than they what is true, how they should be, and what they should do. If the therapist takes charge, the client would not be encouraged to clarify and trust his or her own felt sense of reality and would instead defer to the superiority of the therapist. This is relevant to both behavioral approaches and also to insight and experiential explorations. In a dialogic relationship change is an emergent phenomenon of the shared wisdom of the patient and the therapist.

Characteristics of Dialogic Contact in Psychotherapy

Martin Buber suggested there were a few essential elements of dialogue. Using his language, they are: presence, inclusion, confirmation and commitment to "the between."

Presence

In a dialogic relationship the therapist reveals him/herself truthfully rather than seeming or pretending in order to be seen as he/she would like to be seen. Congruence comprises one aspect of presence, but it is more than congruence with what is visible; it is a commitment to *be* as visible to the patients the therapeutic task and conditions warrant.

In gestalt therapy the therapist engages in a full range of behaviors and emotions. This presence is manifest verbally and/or nonverbally; it is revealed by word, gesture or movement; it is demonstrated in all of the ways that a person's emotions and sentiments are revealed to others. When the therapist feels powerless in the face of the patient's pain or powerless in the face of the patient's needs and desires, presence might include sharing the therapist's affective reaction. requirement of dialogic contact is the therapist's willingness to be "genuine and unreserved" by honestly revealing anything that the therapist believes will enable the ongoing dialogue. Presence is shaped and limited by the needs of the clinical situation and by the creativity of the therapist. The style of the therapist in this approach can be as varied as the personalities of the therapists. Zinker refers to gestalt therapy as "permission to be creative (Zinker, 1977)."

Ideally there is congruence between what the therapist shows and what the therapist actually feels. Presence requires the therapist to recognize, feel, understand, accept, and take responsibility for his/her feelings in the therapeutic contact. However, it is of crucial importance that therapists be able to make discerning judgments about whether or not they are speaking in order to further the therapeutic dialogue, or whether they are reacting impulsively to their own emotional impulses or urgencies. This suggests the need for psychotherapy and supervision for the therapist in training and periodically over the lifetime?

Inclusion

Inclusion is the process of the therapist putting him/herself so thoroughly into the patient's perspective — as if the therapist could feel it in his/her own body — while simultaneously maintaining a separate sense of self. By practicing inclusion, often referred to as empathy, the therapist imagines the reality of the patient, thereby clarifying the patient's reality and confirming the existence of the patient as experienced by the patient. When the therapist shows this kind of grasp of the patient's reality, the patient usually feels understood and cared for but also understands him/herself better. Patients have a sense that they are not alone in the world, that at least one person recognizes, cares, respects them, and can feel something like what they feel.

Inclusion as practiced in gestalt therapy focuses not only on what the patient is experiencing, but also on the experiencing process (Jacobs, 1995).

Although presence and inclusion are necessary for optimal therapy practice, explicating the experiencing process itself also requires skill at directing phenomenological experimentation and the guidance of a good professional background.

Confirmation

An existential meeting in which the therapist experiences the actuality of the patient's existence confirms the patient's being and becoming. Whereas "affirmation" might refer to validating the patient's current experience, confirmation includes both the present reality and what the patient can become. Confirmation is an inherent aspect of inclusion.

Commitment to "the between."

The therapist trusts and surrenders to what emerges in the interaction. The therapist's "truth" is not privileged, is not considered objective, and is subject to change in the interaction. What the therapist believes to be fact, real, including his or her self-beliefs are "put in brackets" — subject to modification in the dialogue. Interpretations are tentative and held lightly. The therapist learns from the phenomenological exploration and dialogic interactions.

Suggestions for Practice

Consider your primary task to contact the patient

Enlarge your own awareness to include the patient's experience rather than trying to find a causal explanation or to change the patient. "Start where the patient is." Consider the patient's "reality" as valid. What does the patient experience and how does he or she experience it? Try to understand patients from their own frame of reference. Instead of asking "why," ask questions like "how do you experience that?"

Use discrimination

Too often patients experience the message, with or without full awareness, that their experience, existence, feelings, longings, despair are too painful, disgusting, frightening or shameful to be shared. Usually patients hunger to be met by a therapist who does not recoil. But for some patients their fear, shame, and self-loathing, threaten to engulf them when the therapist engages with their feelings.

While ordinarily inclusion is a healing balm, with certain patients, practicing inclusion with their despair and self-loathing will be taken as a confirmation of the accuracy of the patient's self-picture, i.e., that indeed they are unworthy of being in human contact and that there is no hope. For at risk patients, such as borderline patients, this can exacerbate suicidal urges or trigger suicidal attempts (Yontef, 1993). With these patients it is very important to hold and express the polarity of the therapist's experience and the patient's. The therapist can say, "I feel very differently about you and your future than you do – but I want to sit with you and share your experience."

Be Curious about the Patient's Actual Experience

Be curious. What is it about the patient's life circumstances and way of thinking that makes sense out of the fixed and recurrent pattern in which the patient is stuck? How can we understand the patient's incongruence? What is it like to be this patient at this time?

The initial disclosure by patients is limited by how skillful they are at sensing deeply held affect and beliefs. Self-acceptance is only as meaningful as the depth of that self-reflection. The fog of denial and the learned storm of self-loathing obscure an accurate sense of self. While we start with what the patient reports experiencing, the therapist needs to be curious about the awareness that may emerge from the therapeutic work. Use your curiosity and your knowledge of how to focus to guide the patient to discover more about self, to go beyond the fixed beliefs constructed to cope with experiences in earlier times but not freely adjusting to the immediate field. By doing so, you find out more about the patient and the patient finds out more about him/herself and also how to be more aware. The accuracy and fullness of the awareness is judged by the patient's grasp of the experience– not by the therapist's analysis.

Therapists' curiosity about patients' actual experience is a wonderful asset; but fixed notions about the patient are not. Curiosity can guide the therapist and patient to inquire and acquire a deeper understanding. Fixed notions, whether driven by theory, premature conclusion, or outright bias, are a hindrance to an accurate understanding, the therapeutic relationship, the development of autonomy and self-awareness by the patient, and growth based on self-recognition and self-acceptance. The therapist's curiosity and open attitude can also help stimulate patients' curiosity and open attitude about themselves and the people in their lives.

Inner conflicts

Most patients come to therapy with conflicts that are soon revealed. Often they want something but there is a conflict between what they want and feelings fear, guilt, or shame that oppose the basic desire. Or, they want things that are mutually inconsistent. Or, they want things to be different and do not want to give up what they are doing that is part of the undesired outcome. Be curious about and open to the validity of all sides of conflicts. Be curious about the function of any "resistance," e.g. self-interruption.

Choice of Intervention
Of course the therapist does something besides just "relate." The therapist can experiment in a variety of ways: construct reinforcement schedules, construct step-by-step behavioral sequences, can offer guesses about the patient's experiential process, or can use phenomenological focusing and phenomenological experimentation. Phenomenological methods have decided advantages. Patients not only gain more knowledge through focusing, experimenting, and homework, but also learn tools they can use on their own.

When you have a choice, use a method that the patient can fruitfully adopt. Theory-driven interpretations, interpretations that are not close to actual experience, only lead the patient to speculate about themselves rather than sense and feel. This is not useful. If you make interpretations, make interpretations that are close to the patient's experience that you consider tentative and subject to the patient's sense of things, and that emerge from inclusion and dialogue. This kind of interpretation can aid the patient's focusing skills and experienced sense of self whereas theory-driven interpretations leave the therapist as the expert with access to truth and the patient to speculate or believe the expert rather than deciding for him/herself.

Focus on Actual Experience

When the therapist uses focusing or experience-near interpretations, patients can learn to differentiate observation from inference, thought from feeling, and what could be from what is. Using methods of focusing enables patients to get clearer about their situation and experience. From an emotional morass, a patient might distinguish a longing and despair, or uncover a desire long hidden in a mode of self-protection. If a therapist focuses experientially on the unfolding of directly felt sense and emotion rather than theory-driven interpretation, patients can learn to observe and feel rather than speculate on why they do what they do. This observational focusing approach strengthens patients' ability to know and accept themselves and experiment to find out what is possible for them.

Give attention to interruptions and resistance.

Notice how energy (interest, excitement, animation, affect) emerges and develops. What is the pattern? Does the energy flow from initial awareness, through a building of excitement, into action or expression, and then resolution? Are there signs of anger, joy, sexuality, sadness, or other feelings that start to show and then are stopped? Or if allowed into expression, does it transform into action? How does the patient prevent resolution?

The forces of interruption are as real and functional as the forces of the primary affect. We may call them resistances, which means resisting affect, as opposed to resisting the therapist or the therapy, but this resistance is not unhealthy. It is best explicated, understood, respected, and directly expressed.

The Time Dimension

Pay careful attention to each moment. As patients talk about their present or past life, give special attention to what is present in the room at the very moment. What does the patient feel while telling of his or her story? What is the quality of contact between therapist and patient while the story is being told? Does the demonstrated affect match the story? How are you affected emotionally? The here-and-now in the therapy session often mirrors or exemplifies a general characterological pattern and presents an opportunity to work on the general theme first hand.

The task and the situation

How the therapist contacts the patient and the choice of intervention must be in service to the context and task. The context includes the setting (agency) and the limitations of the service provided. The figure organizing the therapist's interventions must be related to the specific patterns of the patient's personality organization, life context, and level of awareness. The therapist has to recognize not only what the patient is doing and experiencing contemporaneously, but how specific moments represent larger patterns. The task requires the therapist to recognize openings and learn the sequence of what must come before what.

Example

P: (Reports a story of a man being hostile to her)
T: It sounds like he was being a jerk and this time it made you angry.
P: Yes. I did not feel embarrassed or afraid, as in the past, but angry.
T: That is an improvement, isn't it? Are you interested in seeing what part you may have played in that interaction?
P: Of course, that could be useful.
T: OK. Let's go over the interaction from the beginning. How did it start? (Patient goes over the story in detail and the therapist helps clarify).
T: Let's role play the moment when he said he was attracted to you. I'll play him. I want to feel how I am affected by your response. (Role plays what she reported the man saying).
P: (Role playing, looks disgusted, rolls her eyes toward the ceiling, and frowns. She does not say anything.
T: What did you experience at that moment? In the role play I experienced being exposed and ashamed.

P: I thought: "What is wrong with him that he finds me attractive, but he is probably is lying. I felt disgust and shut him down."
T: You had a strong impact. Did it get you what you want?
P: No.
T: OK. Let's explore what else you could have done.

The Marriage of Dialogic Relating and Active Interventions

The most effective therapy can only happen when the therapist uses both discrimination and creativity in making contact with the patient by directing the focusing, and by devising experiments that carry the work into new dimensions of awareness and action.

Techniques and experiments are also relational events. They can emerge as reactions to the therapist's frustrations, or in a spirit of cooperative exploration that is very helpful for the patient and actually builds the relationship. When they emerge as a creative response to the temper of the moment, the results are usually a surprising enrichment of the therapeutic dialogue and the patient's awareness of possibilities. Without empathic contact, therapeutic effectiveness is very limited; but empathic contact without creativity in actively engaging in the learning process is also limited.

References

Beisser, A. (1970). The paradoxical theory of change. In J. Fagan and I. Shepherd (Eds.). *Gestalt Therapy Now*. New York: Harper. (pp. 77- 80). Download at: *http://www.gestalttherapy.org*.

Gendlin, E. (1981). *Focusing*. New York: Bantam Books. "Six Steps," a very http://www.focusing.org/sixsteps.html

Jacobs, L (1995). Dialogue in Gestalt Theory & Therapy. In R. Hycner & L. Jacobs (eds.). *The Healing Relationship in Gestalt Therapy*. The Gestalt Journal Press: Highland, NY. pp. 51-84.

Yontef, G. (1993). *Awareness, Dialogue and Process: Essay in Gestalt Therapy*. Highland, NY: The Gestalt Journal Press.

Yontef, G. (1995). Gestalt Therapy. in A. Gurman and S. Messer (Eds.), *Essential Psychotherapies: Theory and Practice*. pp. 261-303 at pp. 268-269. New York: Guilford Publications.

Yontef, G. & Jacobs, (2005). L. Gestalt Therapy. In Corsini, R. and Wedding, D. (Eds.). *Current Psychotherapies*, 7th Edition, Chapter 10, pp. 299-336. Belmont, CA: Brooks/Cole – Thompson Learning.

Zinker, J. (1977). *Creative Process in Gestalt Therapy*. New York: Brunner/Mazel.

Chapter 14. "Undoing the Shame Spiral: Working with a Narcissistic Client Trapped in a Self-Hating Depression"

Elinor Greenberg

Chapter introduction

I have found most of the literature on what are commonly called personality disorders rather daunting. Much of it is difficult to read, written in rather obscure and specialized language, and lacking in clear and practical advice on how to deal with commonly encountered therapeutic problems. In recent years, I have set myself the challenge of doing something about this situation. I am writing a series of papers that are grounded in basic Gestalt therapy theory that address specific difficulties that all therapists encounter in the treatment of clients who have made Borderline, Narcissistic, or Schizoid adaptations. My goal in each paper is to clearly and simply describe the theory and the details of the intervention, using many clinical examples, so that most therapists can understand and apply the method immediately without years of specialized training. In this paper I address how to deal with one of the most difficult problems in the treatment of narcissistic clients: how to help them when they start to spiral down into a shame-based self-hating depression.

I am eager for this paper to reach the widest possible audience because I believe that the simple method that I describe can rather quickly alleviate a great deal of suffering. I introduced this method at the 2010 AAGT conference in Philadelphia and a year later, to my great pleasure, I had a Gestalt therapist come up to me and say that he had successfully given my workshop from my handouts at the community mental health center at which he worked. And, even better, the therapists who attended his workshop were able to immediately apply its principles successfully!

This paper is also important to me because it uses the Gestalt therapy theory of Figure/Ground as the basis of the primary intervention. This is the culmination of a very long process that started for me in the late 1970's when I was unable to find a Gestalt therapist in the New York area who could teach me about personality "disorders." I began to study with anyone who taught the topic: psychoanalysts, self-psychologists, ego psychologists, and object relations theorists. My goal always was to return to the Gestalt therapy community and teach others what I was learning so that they could find ways to apply it in their practice.

My very first presentation of this material was in 1983 at the New York Institute for Gestalt Therapy, a paper called: "Psychotherapy with the Borderline Client." Naturally, I was very nervous, even though I was already a full member of the NYIGT and a student of Isadore From's. Isadore very kindly offered to read my paper before I gave it at the meeting. However, those who knew Isadore will remember how precise and exacting he could be, especially about language and theory. I thanked him and said that I was grateful for his offer, but that I was too intimidated by him to accept it. Laura Perls was present when I gave my paper and afterwards said something that continues to influence my work today: "I think your ideas are useful. However, I hope that you will not simply introject what the psychoanalytically-oriented theorists have to say. I would like to see you eventually assimilate the material and express your thoughts and interventions in terms of Gestalt therapy theory and practice." That became my goal, but it has taken me over thirty years to achieve it. However, I still have a little voice in my head that sometimes looks over my shoulder as I write and says: "And how is this Gestalt therapy?"

Undoing the Shame Spiral: Working with a Narcissistic Client Trapped in a Self-Hating Depression[90]

Abstract: Narcissistic clients are easily shamed and can rapidly spiral down into a "self-hating" depression in which they see themselves as totally worthless. Unlike most other types of depressions, a self-hating depression can come and go rapidly in response to external criticism or praise. This article describes how to use the Gestalt therapy concept of figure/ground formation in order to facilitate a quick shift in the client's awareness away from what is perceived as shameful about the self to what is authentically positive.

Key words: shame, figure/ground formation, narcissism, self-hating depression

Introduction

One of the challenges of working with highly narcissistic clients is that they are extremely vulnerable to threats to their self-esteem.[1] When their thin veneer of confidence is pierced, they can rapidly spiral down into a self-hating depression. I call it a "self-hating depression" because narcissistic depression has a very distinct character. Although the person feels terrible, the key feature is not sadness or grief; it is shame about the self. And unlike most other types of depressions, it can come and go rapidly in response to external criticism or praise.

This is because narcissistic clients lack a stable, realistic, and integrated view of themselves. Instead, because they have not yet achieved the developmental milestone of whole object relations (the capacity to see themselves and others as mixtures of good and bad traits that exist simultaneously), they tend to shuttle back and forth between two equally unrealistic extremes: either they are perfect, special, and unique or they are inferior, worthless, garbage (Masterson, 1983). For example, Clare came into therapy and said the following:

> *I am so depressed. I feel like such a total loser. I made a mistake at work today that my boss noticed and pointed out to me and since then I have felt terrible. Everyone else has it so together and I don't. I can't do anything right. I feel like a fraud. Maybe I should just quit my job before everyone finds out how incompetent I really am.*

---

[90] Originally published in *Continuity and Change: Gestalt therapy now,* (Bloom D, Browell, P, Eds),p.p. 185 - 196 Cambridge Scholars Pub: Newcastle on Tyne, UK

The more Clare talked, the worst she felt, and her statements became more and more extreme.

Figure/Ground Formation and Narcissistic Depression

After working with dozens of clients like Clare (and trying every intervention that I could think of), I realized that a very basic Gestalt therapy theory that of figure/ground formation, held an important key that could help them (Greenberg, 2005). Figure/ground formation refers to the idea that because there is so much data in the world around us (and coming from within us), we are designed to only attend to that which is most relevant to us at the moment (Perls, Hefferline and Goodman, 1951). What is most relevant becomes the visible "figure" and all else becomes part of the unseen ground of experience, the background. This is an ongoing process in which figure follows figure as our attention shifts. It became clear to me that narcissistic clients like Clare, in the face of unavoidable evidence that they are not perfect and have flaws, begin to form a figure that contains **only** their failures and flaws. Moreover, as they do this, adding flaw to flaw, they begin to feel worse and worse and rapidly lose any sense of objectivity about themselves.

How to Shift Awareness and Change the Figure

We know from Gestalt therapy theory that in order to make a change, sometimes all we have to do is facilitate a shift in awareness (Perls, Hefferline and Goodman, 1951). This is particularly easy in the case of narcissistic clients because their sense of self is so fluid and easily influenced by environmental factors. This is in accord with what Kurt Lewin (1935), the Gestalt psychologist and field theorist, observed when studying children and environmental forces. He noted that individuals vary in the "functional firmness of the wall between the self and the environment..." and that various environmental factors may interact with certain psychological factors to relatively rapidly increase or decrease an individual's sense of security (p. 108-109). I discovered while working with narcissistic clients that I could use their lack of a stable sense of self and their vulnerability to environmental influences to relatively quickly shift their attention to aspects of the self and the field that were outside of their current awareness.

When I asked myself the key question: "What is out of Clare's awareness?" I realized that her picture of herself and her situation when she was in a self-hating depression focused so narrowly on her flaws that she was oblivious to the larger context. Such things as: (1) her past successes; (2) her strengths, talents, and positive qualities; (3) her future opportunities; and (4) other possible ways to understand and organize her organism/environment field were out of her awareness. All of these were part of the unseen background for Clare, but clearly visible to me and, thus, available to be used in interventions.

The larger context is particularly important because the nature of a shame-based self-hating depression is to spiral inward and become more and more narrowly focused on the individual's perceived flaws. Putting the insult to Clare's self-esteem in a larger, less threatening context redirects her attention to the larger picture that includes realistic and supportive information that is currently invisible to her. As a wise psychoanalyst once said, "Telling the truth about the patient to the patient is the analyst's major task..." (Dorpat, 1990).

All of the above gives the therapist at least four different ways to intervene that can help shift the client's attention to the larger context in which the current situation is imbedded. This can help the client form a new, realistic, more supportive figure that contains more than their failures and flaws. In addition, these four (focusing on past successes, current strengths, future opportunities, and other possible ways of understanding the situation) can be combined in various ways and utilized together for additional power. Not every client will benefit from all of them. It is important to keep an open mind, experiment, and see what works with the individual client in that moment. In the following section I give examples of how I actually use this method during sessions.

(1) Clare: Using Past Successes and the Larger Context

I decided to help Clare see herself in a more realistic and balanced way by using examples of her past competency to remind her of successes that she is forgetting. I began by empathizing with how she is currently feeling (always a good policy when dealing with narcissistic injuries), made a transitional statement that points in a more positive direction, and then started turning her attention to her past successes and the larger context of her work life as a whole, while being as detailed and specific as possible. I continued until I got feedback from Clare that she was fully attending to this new and more positive figure. I said something like the following:

Clare, I know you are feeling bad about yourself right now and certainly I don't know anyone who likes to have their boss point out mistakes that they have made." (**Empathic statement that normalizes her bad feeling**) *I can understand why you are feeling down.* (**Another empathic statement**)

However, I do feel that you are being a little unfair to yourself. (**Transitional statement that begins to shift the topic from negatives to unseen positives**)

You bring a lot to the firm. Just last week, I remember, you were telling me how your boss praised your work in a group meeting in front of all your colleagues and how proud you felt. (**Shifting her attention to a past success and past**

feelings of pride and accomplishment) *And afterwards, he took you aside and thanked you for all your hard work on the project.* (**Reinforcement of the positive figure that I want her to focus on instead of the negative one**)

Now I pause and wait to see if I have her attention. She shifts her gaze from the floor and looks at my face, so I continue with more positives that she can recognize as true.

If I am remembering the details correctly, your work brought in a lot of new revenue to the firm. (**Positive detail**) She nods her head and is now listening intently with a rather more hopeful look on her face. *Isn't this the same boss that gave you the good performance review last month?* (**Positive detail**) *I got the impression that he likes your work and that a small mistake isn't likely to change his mind.* (**Reminding her of the bigger picture**)

I am taking a chance here to see if she will allow me to put her mistake in the larger context of her overall excellent job performance and good relationship with her boss or whether mentioning the mistake will shift her back into her wholly negative perspective. (**I wait for her to reply**) Clare then says something that shows me that her attention has shifted back to a less self-critical picture of herself:

Yes, you're right. I guess I had forgotten all about that. I get so upset when anyone I respect finds fault with me. I wish I wasn't so sensitive, but I can't help it. It feels good to be reminded about the positives. I'm glad that you can remember them, because sometimes I sure can't.

(2) Bob: Using the Client's Unseen Strengths

Bob, one of my severely exhibitionistic narcissistic clients, initially presented with extreme grandiosity. When he was narcissistically wounded, his first reaction was to attack and devalue whomever or whatever had caused the wound. He was loud, insulting, and he screamed at people, including me. Often this was not sufficient to protect his fragile self-esteem and he would descend into a self-hating depression that could last for weeks. After one of these episodes, Bob confided that he secretly thought of himself as stupid because he had experienced academic difficulties in high school. He had paid other students to do his homework. When Bob was not being defensively grandiose, he often compared himself negatively with others. However, after working with him for a while, I could see that he really "got" psychotherapy. That was something about which he was clearly not stupid. In group therapy, he could quickly and easily tell the difference between when a group member was really working on an issue, or just complaining about it. He also delighted in the "Aha!" experience, that sudden burst of clarity that a good therapy session can produce.

One day when he was feeling depressed and starting to call himself "stupid" again, I said something like the following:

Bob, I know that you are feeling like you're stupid again. (**Empathic statement**) *And that once you start down that path, you start feeling really worthless.* (**Empathic statement**)
However, I've noticed some ways in which you are really quick and smart.

Transitional statement:

For example, you have a real knack for psychotherapy. In group therapy you find it easy to spot who is really working and who is just telling stories. In the last group session you were the first person to notice that Sarah (another group member) was describing her new boyfriend in exactly the same words that she described her last two boyfriends. I remember you saying: "Sarah, how can they all be exactly the same? You always tell us that each one is sweet and cute and not much else. It's hard to tell them apart from your descriptions. How are they different?" (**Detailed example of his ability**) *Sarah said that she found your questions really helpful and the group agreed that you were on to something.* (**More positive detail**) *In fact, you do this so quickly and easily that you sometimes feel impatient with the others in the group who cannot do this as well as you.* (**Realistic detail**) Bob nods his head in recognition.

I continue: *And in private therapy, even when you are in a terrible mood and come in ranting and raving; if I make a valid therapeutic point, you get an "Aha!" experience really easily. You get the point of Gestalt therapy experiments and are able to spontaneously go with them.* (**Focus on another ability**) *Remember the time when you were so mad at me for making some mistake that you wouldn't stop bawling me out? Finally, in desperation I asked you to stand on a chair and I knelt in front of you begging and saying: "What do I have to do so that you will forgive me? You paused, cracked up laughing and said, "Nothing will work, I guess."* (**Vivid and specific example**) *Then, you went on to have a really productive session in which you explored what it felt like to be looking down on me while I begged for forgiveness. Thank God you have a great sense of humor or I wouldn't have dared try that.* (**Casual mention of another positive attribute**)

By the end of this, I could see that I had Bob's full attention and his mood had switched. He recognized that what I was saying about him was true, laughed at some of the details, and was able to feel genuine pride about his accomplishments (as opposed to defensive grandiosity). Through interventions such as this, I gradually helped him develop an increasingly stable and realistic sense of his own self worth.

Summary: How to Change the Figure from Negative to Positive

Basically what I did in the above two examples can be broken down into three basic steps:

1. Empathize: Make a couple of empathic statements that show you understand what the client is feeling and why.
2. Transition: After you have the client's attention, make one or two transitional statements that reflect reality and lead in a positive direction.
3. Shift Focus to Successes: From your notes or memory, start describing in vivid and realistic detail one or more past success that is out of the person's current awareness. Use as many of the person's own words as you can.

Naturally, it is important to do this as artfully as possible. Pause periodically, look at your client and give him or her a chance to respond where appropriate. Pay attention to your client's nonverbal cues. Do you have your client's full attention? Does your client look more relaxed after hearing what you have said?

Use Positive, Detailed, and Realistic Examples

When using this technique, it is important to paint a vivid and realistic picture that rings true and is not just idle flattery. As the client listens to the positive and detailed examples that you give, the client's attention automatically shifts from the wholly negative picture that he or she has painted to the more realistically positive one that you are describing. In many cases, this can be enough to shift the person out of the self-hating depression and restore the person's availability for further productive psychotherapy work.

Keep a Record of Clients' Strengths and Successes

As you can see from these examples, in order to use this technique you need to keep a mental list of the client's strengths in mind and also the details of their successes. One of the ways that I do this is by highlighting these in my session notes and periodically reviewing them so that they are always foreground for me. Every time a client reports something that he or she considers a success, I put a check next to it in my notes so that I can easily find it later.

Use the Client's Own Words When Possible

I also try and write down the incident using the client's own words as much as I can. Later, when I bring up the incident in order to shift what is figure for the client, I again try and use the client's own words and descriptions. This makes it more compelling for the client because hearing it that way makes it harder to deny. This fact has long been recognized by psychoanalysts. As far back as 1952, Theodor Reik said:

It is an astonishing and hardly noticed psychological fact that one's own words once spoken are differently evaluated than those which we only think in our representations of words. (Reik, 1990).

Mirror Strengths

I have also gotten in the habit of noticing my clients' strengths, talents, and competencies and mirroring them back to them in session when appropriate. This helps them construct a more accurate and balanced self-image and also fosters a very positive and trusting relationship between us. For many clients this is an intensely reparative process. It is somewhat analogous to a mother bird chewing the food first in order to give it to the baby bird in a form it can digest.

Mirroring back a client's strengths is useful with all clients, not just narcissistic ones. It contributes to a feeling of safety during sessions. Everyone feels more secure when they know that the person they are with thinks well of them.

Ask Questions

It is also useful to ask questions that get clients to expand on their stories of their successes. Get as many vivid details as possible. This tends to make these incidents more memorable to clients and gives the therapist more to work with later. It also gives the events an enhanced sense of reality (Basch, 1980).

For example, you might ask such basic questions as: *What did it feel like? Who else was there?* If you work with the body, you can incorporate body-oriented questions, such as: *Where in your body did you feel this?*

Challenge Overly Negative Self-Assessments

I also gently challenge clients when they begin to present an overly negative assessment of themselves. "You **never** succeed at anything? Not once?" I remind them that the emotional centers of the brain cannot judge the truth or falsity of what we say to ourselves; they just react according to the statement. I might have them experiment with noting how they feel after saying, "I never succeed at anything" versus "I don't always succeed" or "I sometimes succeed."

Defensive Grandiosity Is Replaced by True Self-Esteem

The method that I am describing carefully focuses narcissistic clients' attention on their real accomplishments and real strengths over and over again. As narcissistic clients begin to recognize and internalize a sense of their real accomplishments, they have less need to fall back on defensive grandiosity to shore up their sense of self-worth. In this way, true self-esteem is built up over time. Because this self-esteem is based on real accomplishments, it is much more stable and less easily disrupted than defensive grandiosity. As this happens, clients experience fewer and less severe narcissistic self-hating depressions and their defensive grandiosity and their exaggerated assertions of omnipotence and specialness diminish. They begin to talk in a more realistic and nuanced way about themselves and their experiences. The following clinical example illustrates this process.

The 5 Stages of Undoing Self-Hating Depressions

Bob's therapeutic progress followed a fairly typical pattern, so I will use his therapy to illustrate the stages that the unraveling of self-hating depressions typically progress through. For the sake of clarity, I have divided the stages into five discrete steps. In reality, progress is always characterized by a few steps forward and then a regression; more steps forward and another regression. Eventually, something gets internalized and there are fewer and less extreme regressions. Sometime during this process, clients begin to develop a more stable and realistic sense of themselves. As a result, they become less vulnerable to having their self-esteem destabilized by external events and less reliant on other people's praise and opinions.

From the point of view of Object Relations theory, the client has integrated their two part-self object relations units (the unrealistically all-good or all-bad views of the self) and has achieved whole object relations: a more realistic, integrated and stable self-image (Hamilton, 1988, Greenberg and Mitchell, 1983). In Gestalt therapy terms, the client has gone from relying on environmental support to self-support.

Step 1: Self-Hating and Hopeless

Bob would come into the session in a self-hating depression and would report feeling angry, helpless, hopeless, and worthless. Sometimes he would scream at me. He would complain that his therapy wasn't helping him. His sense of depression was like a dark, heavy weight in the room and I had to do all of the therapy work. It felt like I was trying to swim upstream against a strong current with a sack of potatoes in my arms. I had to work hard even to get his attention. After many tries, I would finally be able to engage his attention, shift his focus to his strengths (or another aspect of the unseen ground of his experience), get an "Aha!" insight and, as a result, move his sense of himself and his mood in a more positive direction. By the time he left the session, he would be feeling more optimistic and better about himself. After doing this in many, many sessions; we progressed to Step 2.

Step 2: Self-Hating, but also Hopeful

Bob still would come into the session in a self-hating depression, feeling worthless, but he was no longer without hope. He now expected that sometime in the session, I would intervene in a way that would help him get out of his dark mood.

In Steps 1 and 2 the client is still totally dependent on the psychotherapist's ability to shift the figure to a more positive one.

Step 3: Working Alliance

After many more sessions, Bob gradually began to find ways to help me help him. Bob had begun to internalize the idea that he could be helped and that it was just a matter of finding the right words or intervention and then he would feel better. At this point, we now had a true therapeutic alliance in which we were both working hard to help him. Bob decided to make himself a set of index cards that he could carry with him to remind himself of the kinds of things that helped him in session. One of them said, "Just because it "feels" real to me, doesn't make it real."

Step 4: Introjection of Support

Bob comes into session and reports that he had started to go into a self-hating depression, but had heard my voice in his head reminding him to look at the situation more realistically. He feels pleased and proud that he did this on his own. We both celebrate his progress.

Step 5: Self-Support

Bob begins to feel a sense of control over his moods and his self-esteem. For example, when a colleague gets praised at a meeting, instead of feeling like a failure and berating himself; he is more able to stop and remind himself of his strengths and past successes. As a result, he spends less and less time depressed.

Conclusion

As you can see from the above, finding a way to undo your client's self-hating depression may be only the first step in a long process. It is a tool to use in a psychotherapy that will require many other types of therapeutic interventions as well. And, as is true with all Gestalt therapy experiments and interventions, some clients are able to fairly quickly make use of what the therapist is offering, while others refuse to even try. However, the first time that it does work with a client and you manage to stop the emotional train wreck that is happening in front of you, it feels wonderful!

One of the things that I like best about this method is that it takes a psychological flaw (the inability of narcissistic clients to maintain a stable sense of their self-worth) and utilizes it to help them. Because they are so easily flipped from feeling good about themselves to feeling bad, they can easily be flipped back by an artful and practiced psychotherapist. One can think of this as the practice of emotional Judo.

Notes

[1] In this paper I am using the terms "narcissism" and "narcissistic" to refer to those clients that habitually organize the interpersonal field at the contact boundary in such a way that cues relating to the potential for the enhancement or diminishment of the individual's self-esteem are repeatedly made figure (Greenberg, 1999, 2005).

References

Abraham, K. (1921). Contributions to the Theory of the Anal Character. *Selected Papers on Psychoanalysis.* Hogarth Books, London, 1927.

Basch, M. (1980). *Doing Psychotherapy.* Basic Books, New York.

Dorpat, T. (1990). In Bauer, G. P. (Ed.) *Wit and Wisdom in Dynamic Psychotherapy.* Jason Aronson, Inc., New Jersey.

Greenberg, E. (1999). Love, Admiration or Safety: A System of Gestalt Diagnosis of Borderline, Narcissistic and Schizoid Adaptations that Focuses on What is Figure for the Client. *Studies in Gestalt Therapy: Dialogical Bridges*, 8:52-64.

Greenberg, E. (2005). The Narcissistic Tightrope Walk: Using Gestalt Therapy Field Theory to Stabilize the Narcissistic Client. *Gestalt Review*, 9 (1): 58-68.

Greenberg, J. R., and Mitchell, S. A. (1983). *Object Relations in Psychoanalytic Theory.* Harvard University Press, Cambridge, Massachusetts.

Hamilton, N. G. (1988). *Self and Others: Object Relations Theory in Practice.* Jason Aronson Inc., New Jersey.

Lewin, K. (1935). *A Dynamic Theory of Personality: Selected Papers.* Magraw- Hill Book Company, Inc., New York.

Masterson, J. F. (1983). *The Narcissistic and Borderline Disorders: An Integrated Developmental Approach.* Brunner-Mazel, New York.

Perls, F., Hefferline, R. F. and Goodman, P. (1951). *Gestalt Therapy: Excitement and Growth in the Human Personality.* Julian Press, New York.

Reik, T. (1990). In Bauer, G. P. (Ed.) *Wit and Wisdom in Dynamic Psychotherapy.* Jason Aronson, Inc., New Jersey.

Chapter 15. Developing Mutuality: Techniques of Relational Gestalt Therapy

Kenneth Meyer, Ph.D.

Chapter introduction

I became a member of the NYIGT in the mid-90's, when the Institute was re-envisioning itself as an umbrella for all Gestalt therapists, opening the possibility of Full Membership to those of us who has not been trained by Fellows of the Institute. While I had studied some with Magda Denes, Isadore From and Richard Kitzler, my practicum training had been entirely with Marilyn Rosanes-Berret, who taught the more psychodramatic version of Gestalt psychotherapy. During the period of my training there existed quite a chasm between what was (somewhat inaccurately) labeled the "East Coast" and "West Coast" schools of Gestalt therapy, a difference great enough that one knowledgeable observer questioned whether these were two different therapies having the same name only because of their historical roots (Latner, 1985).

Marilyn, while based in New York, had maintained ties with Fritz while he was developing the "West Coast" techniques: the hot-seat group, the empty-chair dialog, dream-work, etc. At the time it was not merely a difference, but mutual distain; Fritz and Marilyn declaring PHG as "obsolete" and From bemoaning, in his "requiem for Gestalt (From, 1984)," the sloganeering and showmanship of the psychodramatic methods. Having grown up with parents who spent 28 years divorcing, I went about, in my quiet way, learning from both camps while staying out of the fray.

So it was with palpable relief that I found my own cohort group moving past the very real possibility of a split, and for many of us it was the NYIGT that provided a home for this rapprochement.   As much as I appreciate, even revel in, the depth and prescience of PHG, I was not about to abandon the creative, and dare I say — *effective* — methods that Marilyn practiced. So this paper was my modest effort to contribute to this melding of what could have become two different therapies called "Gestalt."

Developing Mutuality: Techniques of Relational Gestalt Therapy[91]

"Must every case be mutual – and to what extent?"
Sandor Ferenczi, 1932

Abstract: While "techniques" might seem an oxymoron in regard to relational psychotherapy, there are gestalt methods that serve to set the ground for relational work, and others that make less likely, or even preclude, developing mutuality in the work. The point is that mutuality has to be developed; it cannot simply be declared. This workshop is designed to provide an historical perspective, experiential understandings and practical tools for making visible the unique and unfolding bi-personal field of therapist/client. It will be a practical, hands-on workshop that will include demonstration, discussion and experiential exercises.

While "techniques" might seem an oxymoron in regard to relational psychotherapy, there are gestalt methods that serve to set the ground for relational work, and others that make less likely, or even preclude, developing mutuality in the work. In this workshop I hope to provide some historical perspective, theoretical understandings and practical tools for co-creating a unique and mutually defined endeavor with each client.

While much has been written in both psychoanalysis (Aron, 1996) and gestalt therapy (Hychner and Jacobs, 1995) about the change from a one-person to two-person psychology, the specific discussion of how this may require changes in our methods has not been much addressed. Whether originally trained in the "directed attention" methods of PHG (Perls, Hefferline and Goodman, 1951) or the psychodramatic methods of Fritz's later work (Perls, 1969), many of our habits, techniques and, in particular, our languaging have embedded in them assumptions left over from single person, expert-oriented approaches that do not quite fit with the relational orientation that many of us, at least in our theoretical views, have adopted.

So in keeping with our theme of "Continuity and Change," I am going to emphasize today that it is not at all necessary to throw away the more directive or psychodramatic methods of our earlier training, and show you how a transition can be made to using them in a context of mutually developed exploration.

---

[91] Originally published in *Continuity and Change: Gestalt therapy now,* (Bloom D, Browell, P, Eds), Cambridge Scholars Pub: Newcastle on Tyne, UK, pp. 304 – 333.

However such mutuality must be *achieved*; it cannot be *produced*. As Margherita Spagnuolo Lobb expresses it,

> It is not the technique used by an expert on another person ...but two people who together find possibilities of fulfilling interrupted intentionalities. It is the dance that the therapist with all her/his knowledge and humanity, and the patient with all his/her pain and desire to get well, create in order to rebuild the ground on which the life of the relationship rests (Spagnuolo-Lobb, 2009).

Much can be done to prepare the setting for this dance — to establish from the start an interactive, relational and non-hierarchical atmosphere. What we will be looking at today is how to change our language and habitual ways of responding in a way that *consistently* communicates that this is to be a mutual endeavor, and to do this without throwing away any of our expertise, or our experience with a range of techniques. Later in the workshop you will have an opportunity to practice some of the suggestions.

MUTUALITY

Gestalt psychotherapy has always had a humanistic, "we're just two people engaged in a dialogue," bent. But one cannot simply *declare* equality, nor signal it by wearing love-beads. Nor does it suffice to join the relational perspective by claiming, "Of course I'm relational — I've always related to my clients."

As Lynne Jacobs has written,

> Every utterance, every thought, feeling, sensation, every movement that happens in our consulting rooms is variably mutually influenced (and influencing). Nothing happens that arises pristinely from "within" the therapist or "within" the patient (Jacobs, 2009).

This understanding of "co-implication" leads us to the view that mutuality is not developed through the therapist's mere recognition that this is the case, but by the therapist giving assiduous and mutual *attention* to this as the dialogue unfolds. The skills involved are the same one's that gestalt therapists have always used — attention to breath, choice of words, posture, flashes of fantasy, etc.— but now the therapist's impact on the client, and the client's impact on the therapist, become a major and mutual focus of curiosity.

But this cannot be foisted on clients out of the blue — that in itself would be starting the building of mutuality in a non-mutual way! Nor am I referring to those magical "moment's of mutuality" that arise spontaneously in the course of a relationship (Schack, 2008) What I mean here by "mutuality" begins with close attention, as the session proceeds, as to whether we are on the same page regarding what we are doing, why we are doing it and how we are going about it. Very often this process of coming to a mutual figure of interest is itself quite a healing interpersonal event, not only breaking unaware confluence, but engendering the client's optimism about taking initiative, being heard and being responded to.

HISTORY

Stawman has given us a historical review of the successive "waves" of the relational point of view coming into Gestalt theory and practice (Stawman, 2009). And Lynne Jacobs has recounted her journey into, out of, and then back into Gestalt practice with a relational perspective (Jacobs, 1992). Let me tell how I made that transition in order to help you understand the changes in technique that I am advocating.

Despite being in New York, my initial training was in what Joel Latner labeled the "West Coast" style of Gestalt Therapy, with an emphasis on intrapsychic phenomenological inquiry combined psychodramatic enactment (Latner, 1985). I sometimes call this "side-ways" Gestalt therapy because the therapist acts in a facilitative role, guiding the client's investigations but avoiding becoming figural in it. I had one supervisor who advised that the therapist should be a "ghost-like" voice, facilitating the client's explorations while staying outside of it as much as possible.

Meanwhile, my partner at the Gestalt Center of Long Island began studying with Isadore From and bringing his approach, which was referred to as "contact-boundary work," into our trainings. From made a point of eschewing psychodramatic techniques and the use of the "empty chair," in favor of working at the client's contact-boundary with him (From, 1984). As I learned myself while attending some of his trainings, even From's approach to dreams emphasized the interpersonal rather than the intrapsychic (Rosenfeld and Wysong, 1988). Because of the consistent focus on direct contact rather than facilitation, I began referring to this as "front-ways" gestalt therapy.

So we now had two kinds of Gestalt therapy that we were teaching, the "side-ways" style popularized by Fritz in his films and the "front-ways" style of Isadore, who followed PHG. Or as I sometimes said, *Gestalt Therapy: the Movie* vs. *Gestalt Therapy: the Book*. And as is often the case, the Book and the Movie seemed to bear little relation to each other. So our students began asking us the obvious question: when do we use psychodramatic work and when contact-boundary work? For which, at least initially, we had no answer.

I want to emphasize that neither of these approaches are what we today would call "relational." The facilitative style gave lip-service to an equal relationship — we were "facilitators," not "therapists" on whom one might become dependent — but in fact was quite directive and often shaming. And the contact-boundary approach had no interest in the therapist's contact with the client, only the client's contact-making with the therapist (Mueller, 1996). To me, it had a strangely psychoanalytic flavor, including the assumption that the therapist is the most interesting contact-making opportunity in the client's life, even when asleep. From's work focused on transference, if such a term were allowed, and he rarely acknowledgement the therapist's contribution to these projections (Weaver, 1990).

But these partial and contrasting approaches — and our students' questions about when each is appropriate — did prod me toward a more relational view. What occurred to me is that there exists a basic Gestalt principle that answers our students' question: *context* is what gives meaning to the figure.

So the interaction between the client and myself — the asking of a question, the giving of an experiment — is the context that gives shape to what follows. The client's response to *being questioned* takes precedence over the answer to the question; the client's response to *being offered an opportunity for experimentation* take precedence over the experiment itself, even when these reactions are quite subtle.

Let me give an example that will be familiar to any of you who use the empty-chair technique. You know how the client will say something to the person in the chair, and then sneak a glance at you? And how you ignore this and try to get them to stay with the empty-chair dialog? This is what I am talking about: *that glance takes precedence over anything that can happen in the psychodrama.* There is a whole story there*: Am I doing this chair thing right?* Or *Am I saying what you want?* Or *This is the silliest thing he has had me do yet!*

My point is that *whatever* that glance may mean, clients cannot wholly enter a psychodrama, or any other experiment that requires letting the setting recede to background, as long as they have concern about what is happening with you. As both a client and as a therapist, I have been privy to extremely valuable psychodramatic work — intense, multi-sensory, hallucinatory experiences — but only when the contextual situation holds no major unfinished business or distracting concerns for the client.

Psychodramatic methods, empty-chair dialogs, guided fantasy and physical experimenting do not have to be jettisoned from our repertoire in order to work relationally. What we *do* have to do is to be quite ready and willing to abandon a path we have started on the very moment it is clear that the client is not wholly entering into it, or obviously just complying. It is not simply that we are not "respecting resistance" when we ignore things such as slight hesitations or furtive glances; when we ignore these we are encouraging clients to split their attention, the opposite of what we mean to do in Gestalt therapy.

I have offered as an example the client who gives you little glances when doing an empty-chair dialog because it is one that most of you will recognize. But let me give another example of what I mean by paying *assiduous* attention to our impact on the client. This took place at a conference with about 50 therapists present. The volunteer client began in a loud, undirected voice, but after some time suddenly spoke in a more focused, direct way to the therapist. At this point the therapist said, "Wow, I feel like I've been listening to a radio broadcast, and the radio has suddenly spoken just to me." Now this metaphor was certainly an evocative and memorable description of the client's manner of contact-making, and it also brought a laugh from the audience.

My point in telling this anecdote is that the session demonstrated what *appeared* to be a relational, interpersonal focus — the client's style of making contact or not with the therapist. What was missing was the therapist's immediate attention to the impact of his joke had on the client: did he feel upstaged, or used by the therapist to get a laugh, or shamed by the remark, or any of the other things one might have felt?

I want to be clear that I am not suggesting you tip-toe around or becoming stilted in your feedback to a client because of fear of your impact. I am talking about staying hyper-alert, about using your eyes and ears to check out what impact we may have had other than what you intended.

My image of this is that anything we do— making a remark, asking a question, directing the client's attention — is like tossing a stone into a pond. What we are used to doing is relaxing at this point, simply following the stone to see where it lands: does it have the intended effect? But it is just as important, at least in the first few moments, to notice the ripples: what are the unintended effects on the client? And to ask yourself if any of these seem worth making figural instead? Or is the client about to make this figural if you do not cut him or her off by keeping them on the track of where you intended to focus?

SETTING THE GROUND

As I have said, such mutual engagement cannot be guaranteed by philosophical fiat or explicit declaration. But a great deal can be done, from the beginning of therapy, to set the ground for assuring agreement of what we are doing as we do it, encouraging open questioning and promoting increased initiative from the client as to the direction of the work. That is what the specific ideas and exercises we are going to do are about.

Let me take a common method — a particularly "gestalt" one — as a paradigm. I am sure that all of us at one time or another have asked a client who reports feeling anxious some version of the following: "Where in your body do you feel that?" So let me suggest — as a model for how to change our languaging

— another way to make the same inquiry: "If you can tell me how in your body you feel that, then I will have a better sense of what mean when you say 'anxiety.'"

I am offering this as a paradigm, not as a script. Notice several things about this:

- It references both of us, not only the client.
- It signals that this is not an ordinary question, nor to be answered quickly.
- It signals that I do not have a preconception about what is meant.
- It includes my wish to understand rather than convince or direct.
- It follows our own requirement that questions not be hidden statements.

Let me take each one of these individually, and use these to give you more indications as how changing our habits and language can support a more mutual engagement.

Reference both, not only the client

From the beginning, I try to use language that refers to us as a dyad. I hardly ever say "you" or "me" without referring to the other. Concomitantly, I never use the parental "we" when I mean "I" or "you." And I never use "therapy" as a substitute for "our sessions," "our meetings" or "our work together. "Except when I slip, of course. This *is* what we are talking about here: changing long-ingrained habits!

Later in the workshop we will have some practice doing this.

Signal that this is not an ordinary question

The "if" in my paradigmatic statement is sincere, and important. I try to convey, through language, posture, pace and, very often, by saying explicitly that this is not an ordinary social conversation, and that they often will need time for something to emerge in response to a question or statement from me. The model that many clients come in with is that the doctor asks questions and a cooperative patient answers, even if unsure. I try to make clear that I know that I am asking things that they have no *ready* answer for — or sometimes do not even have the words for — and will be as patient as necessary. "If you can tell me. . ." is one way of conveying that.

Signal that you do not have preconceptions

How many times have you seen a movie or television therapist use a Socratic method of leading the patient to an answer that the therapist already has in mind? Well, your clients have seen that many more times than you have, since you probably can't stand watching such travesties! And that is where many get their impression of how therapy works.

So I find it really important to convey that my questions or means of inquiry are not based on preconceptions. I am not referring to the kinds of protestations of humility that therapists of various persuasions will use to avoid revealing what they are thinking. I am talking about you expressing a genuine curiosity based on the realization that you can always refine what you know, guess or intuit about a client's state. And when I do have a preconception I grade it to the client: I have a "hunch," or am "putting something together," or have a "strong sense," etc.

Convey a wish to understand

Answering a question is compliance; making oneself more understood is engagement. Lynne Jacobs (personal communication) talks about how we under-estimate the degree to the therapist's visible and palpable *efforts* to understand the client contribute to the healing that takes place. That is why Rogerian psychotherapy is not memorable: the understanding that the client-centered counselor shows is too immediate, and too facile, to have a lasting effect.

But a thoroughly relational psychotherapy has to take into account a basic reality of the situation: the major influence we have on our clients is to direct their attention during sessions. The questions we ask, the way we listen and, in Gestalt therapy, the experiments we propose are all explicitly meant not simply to guide the discussion, but to guide what the clients pays attention to at key junctures. Junctures that are chosen by the therapist. The problem is how to make this more mutual — how to be sure the client is engaged in the same way and for the same reasons that we have invited engagement.

This is particularly important when it comes to introducing experiments. By their very nature, the setting up of an experiment requires structuring and giving directions. So it becomes particularly important to agree upon the purpose of an experiment as a way to find out something that cannot be discovered by speculation or ratiocination, only through co-creating a situation that may bring something into greater clarity.

I am not saying that the possible outcomes of a specific experiment should be discussed; this would of course only preordain the experiment to be useless. But this preliminary introduction, whatever form it takes, marks off the experiment as a distinct instance in which I am being directive, and during which the client has agreed to this. And while I hate the word "experiment," it well describes my attitude, both my willingness to suggest something based on my experience and expertise, and my readiness to let go of my anticipation in the face of whatever the client discovers.

How often do we tell our clients what prompts our questions? Doesn't their knowing this increase the probability of filling us in more completely and accurately on what we are asking about? Or telling us when we are completely off track? If nothing else, revealing what thoughts, hunches and, to be frank, forgetfulness prompts our questions keeps us from being too glued to our experts' perch.

I have always explained our methods to clients. I do this not in the abstract, but as they are relevant, and in whatever language and metaphors would communicate this to a particular client. For example, I may explain that the body is a valuable source of information, experimentation is a way finding things out or that dreams often show things that are easily ignored during the distractions of the daytime.

But while I used to think of this as "psycho-education," or perhaps "orientation," I now view it as an integral to the therapy itself. I am not about to deny my expertise or deprive myself of my tools, but I can be more open about what they are. And in a subtle but effective and meaningful way, demystifying our methods is modeling self-revelation.

I learned something about this when I was doing demonstrations of therapy as part of training others. I became aware that my questions were often based on subtle cues that were only observable to me, but not very visible to the students who were watching from more of a distance. So I began including statements about what prompted my questions or statements for the benefit of the students, and found that it had a profound effect on my interaction with the client. I noticed immediately that including more of my observations and thought process ramped up the working relationship tremendously. I attribute this partly to my transparency engendering greater trust, but also to this allowing the client to enter into, and correct, the direction of our inquiry.

One of my first realizations of this came when I asked a client, "What would you want from me right now?" I then added, for the benefit of the students watching, "I am asking because your eyes seem to be asking something from me." She responded that what I was seeing in her eyes was actually nostalgia, a reaction to a memory that had just occurred. She then went on to describe this meaningful memory. Without my adding what I had about what prompted my question, she probably would have complied in the way most clients do — by half making something up. Something meaningful perhaps, but not organically emerging from what was actually happening for her.

EXERCISES

Let me say something in general about how I structure practice exercises when people are learning a new way of doing something. We will be working in triads — groups of three — with one person as Therapist, another as Client and the third as Observer. But in most cases it is the Observer who will actually be doing the practice exercise.

The reason I do it this way is because it is hard to be in the role of 'therapist" and at the same time change ingrained habits. As Observer you can develop an ear for habitual language and silently consider some alternatives, without having to interact in an immediate or ongoing way. Also, the Observer should write down some examples that the triad can discuss later. Don't be concerned about writing down everyone, just a few for discussion.

So the role of Therapist is very simple: to generate material for the Observer. So be at your absolute worst! Do NOT try to apply anything that I have talked about; that is the job of the Observer and the group during discussion. Do therapy as you would after a very long day, operating completely by habit and on remote.

The person who is Client can be himself, or it is sometimes fun to be one of your own clients. Remember, in this case the Therapist has no need to come off well. So you can have fun being your most difficult client and do your worst!

By the way, you can practice each of these skills on your own by listening to recordings of your sessions. Even short snippets will do. For here, I have three exercises in mind, so you each should have a chance to be in each role.

Exercise I: We

The Observer is to listen for instances where either the Therapist or the Client is referred to, but not both. Or where an abstraction, like "the therapy," is used. Or when a parental, insincere "we" is used. You won't need to do this long to generate examples!

After about five minutes, stop the role-play and discuss the statements or questions that the Observer noticed, brainstorming how it might have been said differently. Part of the discussion can be letting the Client imagine how he or she might have felt if the alternative language had been used.

Exercise II: Directives

The Observer is to listen for instances where the Therapist's language is directive when not necessary, or when directives are appropriate but not acknowledged as such.

After about five minutes, stop the role-play and discuss the examples that the Observer has noted, brainstorming how it might have been said differently. Part of the discussion can be letting the Client imagine how he or she might have felt if the alternative language had been used.

Exercise III: Demystification

The Observer is to listen for instances were the Therapist might have said more that would clarify what about the Client or the interaction prompts a question or remark. Note those that puzzle you, but also try to note those that would not be clear to you if you were not a trained therapist.

The Therapist can try, if s/he wishes, to practice adding one simple sentence to each question or thought expressed, making clearer what the intervention is based on in his/her experience of the client. But do NOT change anything you might say, but after saying it add one short sentence making it clearer. Simply imagine that the Observer is your "student" watching from the side, and add an additional clue for his or her benefit.

After about five minutes, stop the role-play and discuss the examples that the Observer has noted, brainstorming how it might have been said differently. Part of the discussion can be letting the Client imagine how he or she might have felt if the additional information had been given.

CONCLUSION

I would like to end with another anecdote, this time told to me by a colleague, who is a very short woman. She was standing at her doorway, saying "goodbye" to a client, when the client, a very tall woman, asked, "Would you like me to change this light-bulb here? It has been out for a month."

As my friend tells it, a million thoughts raced through her mind: *"Would I be taking advantage of her? Would she try to take advantage of me? Is it ethical? How would this affect the transference? Would I be like her mother or unlike her mother if I were to say 'Yes?' If I were to say 'No?' "*

Finally, realizing how she was almost stammering, she blurted out: *"Yes, I would love that. But let's be sure to talk about what just happened with us the next time we meet."* She realized in that moment that she was placing an impossible burden on herself by making these kinds of decisions in the isolation of her own head —"behind the curtain," so to speak.

I have no idea if the subsequent discussion ever took place, but also have little doubt that if it had practicing the things we have been talking about today would have prepared them for the a productive interchange. Maybe she would have found out that she did make a 'mistake. Or maybe that her decision had had a positive effect on the client. Or maybe both. I tell the story, though, to illustrate how *freeing* this way of working can become — that dancing on the ground of mutuality relieves us of a tremendous and arrogant burden, and makes most "mistakes" recoverable.

References

Aron, L. (1996*) A meeting of minds: mutuality in psychoanalysis.* Hillsdale, NJ: The Analytic Press.

From, I. (1984) Reflections on Gestalt therapy after thirty-two years of practice: A requiem for Gestalt. *The Gestalt Journal,* 7(1) pp. 4-12.

Hycner, R.A. & Jacobs, L. (1995) The *healing relationship in Gestalt therapy.* Highland, NY: Gestalt Journal Press.

Jacobs, L. (1992) Insights from psychoanalytic self-psychology and intersubjectivity theory for Gestalt therapists. *The Gestalt Journal,* 15(2) pp. 25-60

Jacobs, L. (2009) Relationality; Foundational assumptions. In Co-*creating the field: Intention and practice in the age of complexity* (pp. 42-72). D. Ullman, & G. Wheeler, (Eds.). Orleans, MA: GestaltPress

Latner, J. (1985) What kind of figure does gestalt therapy cut? *The Gestalt Journal* 8(1) pp. 55-60.

Mueller, B. (1996) Isadore From's contribution to the theory and practice of Gestalt therapy. The Gestalt Journal, 19(1) pp. 57-82.

Perls, F., Hefferline, R. & Goodman, P. (1951) Gestalt *therapy: Excitement and growth in the human personality.* New York, NY: Julian Press.

Perls, F. (1969) *Gestalt therapy verbatim.* Moab, UT: Real People Press.

Rosenfeld, E. & Wysong (1988) An *oral history of Gestalt therapy.* Highland, N.Y.: Gestalt Journal Press.

Schack, M. (2008) *Moments of mutuality* (unpublished manuscript).

Spagnuolo-Lobb, M. (2009) Co-creation of the contact boundary in the therapeutic situation. In Co-*creating the field: Intention and practice in the age of complexity* (pp. 103-134). D. Ullman & G. Wheeler (Eds.). Orleans, MA: GestaltPress.

Stawman, S. (2009) Relational gestalt: Four waves. In *Relational approaches in Gestalt therapy* (pp. 11-36). Orleans, MA: GestaltPress.

Weaver, J. (1990) *Creating Gestalt therapy with Isadore From.* Portland, ME: Expanded Vid

Chapter 16. If You Could Change Your Parents, You Could Change Yourself: A Workshop on the Psychogenetic System, A Transgenerational Approach to Re-imprinting Couple and Parenting Introjects.
Ann Teachworth (1938 – 2012)

Chapter introduction

A chapter introduction written on behalf of a long time and much loved member of the NYIGT who died before being able to write this for herself is a sad task. Anne was more than a member of the institute. From her home base at the institute she founded, The New Orleans Gestalt Institute (that was also the New Orleans/New York Gestalt Institute in her life), she maintained close personal and professional relationships with us. Anne studied with Laura Perls and Richard Kitzler. The Gestalt Institute press that founded and directed published the works of Bud Feder, Ruth Ronal, Renate Perls, Richard Kitzler, and others.

Her dedication to us perhaps achieved its high water mark when labored over Richard Kitzler's unpublished manuscripts so they could become his only book, *Eccentric Genius: An anthology of the works of Master Gestalt Therapist Richard Kitzler* (2009), published shortly before he died.

And she was a friend. – a friend with a sense of whimsy, fancy, and play mixed with a serious understanding of gestalt therapy. One of us, Dan, was her "Rhett Butler," to her "Scarlett O'Hara" and our email exchanges were parodies of how those two separated lovers might have handled Reconstruction. We will all miss her Anne's Southern charm and the sparkle dust of enchantment she seemed to throw over our world. This published essay is her final essay. We are proud to include it here.

If You Could Change Your Parents, You Could Change Yourself: A Workshop on the Psychogenetic System, A Transgenerational Approach to Re-imprinting Couple and Parenting Introjects[92]

Abstract: This workshop describes the Psychogenetic System™, my new transgenerational approach to couple and parenting therapy which deactivates negative introjects and re-imprints positive new patterns into clients' current relationships. The Psychogenetic System™, focuses instead on the unresolved adult-adult and parent-parent issues between the client's parents in childhood, uncovering amazing repetitions in introjected family interactional patterns that have previously been overlooked.

Corrective re-imprinting occurs as clients role-play their childhood parents "in couple therapy" resolving their own relationship issues with each other which had been introjected by example into the clients in childhood. If left untreated, these unconscious Inner Couple and Inner Parent Imprints, as I identify them, will remain dormant in the clients' unconscious in childhood, only to automatically resurface as the primary Introjected Interactional Patterns (IIPs) for the clients' own couple relationships in adulthood.

Presentation to the Workshop Participants

Without any prior explanation, I will begin this workshop by asking all of you to fill in this Psychogenetic Profile, an assessment form I developed in 1991 and originally called the Selection Test in my book, Why We Pick the Mates We Do (1997). Even though this form was initially designed for couples, because it is so effective at uncovering unconscious patterns, I now use it as an intake form for all my individual clients, too. So let me begin by asking you to complete a Psychogenetic Profile.

These are the same questions that I ask every client who comes into my office. Your answers are completely private and confidential. There will be no turning to Partner A or B and sharing your family history. You will not have to show them to anyone, in fact, I can tell you how to interpret the Psychogenetic Profile yourself without ever seeing your answers myself. So let's begin.

The Psychogenetic Profile
1. Describe yourself as a child in the first ten years of your life.
2. Describe your mother as the adult she was when you were a child.

---

[92] This chapter was originally published in *Continuity and Change: gestalt therapy now.* (2011) pp 253 – 370 (Bloom D, Brownell, Eds) Cambridge Scholars Publications, Newcastle in Tune: UK

3. Describe your father as the adult he was when you were a child.
4. Describe your mother as the parent she was to you when you were a child.
5. Describe your father as the parent he was to you when you were a child.
6. Describe your relationship with your mother when you were a child.
7. Describe your relationship with your father when you were a child.
8. Describe your mother and father's relationship with each other when you were a child.

These eight questions are inquiries into the first ten years of your life, not how things were in your teen-age years, not how your relationship with your parents is now, not how your parents' relationship with each other is now, but how it was in the first ten years of your life. I'm not primarily interested in chronological accuracy or facts here. I'm more interested in the first memory or emotional response that is spontaneously elicited as you read my requests for descriptions of your genetic parents' personalities and their relationships with each other and you in your childhood.

I encourage you as I do my clients to write the first five or six words, phrases or events that come to mind with each request, even if you don't understand why that particular word or phrase comes to mind, and particularly if you don't understand why. Your very first emotional or right brain responses are important because this is an inquiry into your unconscious stress imprint. So take out your pens and begin your descriptions. Thank you.

Most often, when I ask people to complete the Psychogenetic Profile, I continue to talk out loud like I am doing now while they are trying to think of the answers. Sometimes people will say, "Please be quiet," or "I can't think while you're talking." Then I reply, "Hurry, you only have five minutes to finish the test." "Hurry" and "test" induce more stress. Often, I caution people, "Do it right," and then, "You'll be graded on it," which adds even more stress.

Now that you are finished, let me apologize and explain that I kept talking because it's important to access your automatic stress reactions, regressed memories, childhood feelings and imprinted reactions from childhood without editing out what you write down. Auditory overload of the left-brain is one way to accomplish that.

History of the Psychogenetic System™

I developed my Psychogenetic approach after years of working with thousands of broken-hearted single or divorced clients who had gotten themselves involved in relationships that didn't work out well for them. Over and over, these clients had said to me, "Why do I pick the mates I do? And why the same type over and over and over again?" I couldn't explain it either. No matter if these clients had tried to select a new partner unlike the one they had selected last time, their couple relationships still hadn't worked out. My clinical observations after years of working with unhappy couples had already convinced me that most of their mistakes began at the attraction stage and that mate "chemistry" was not under control of the left brain.

A lot of my divorced clients had given up on finding another partner and decided to remain single because they were afraid to make another bad decision. They no longer trusted their own mating instincts. And rightly so! In fact, I began to tell clients who had had one bad relationship after another, not to dare trust their immediate "chemistry" attractions. Furthermore, I would warn them to run the other way if they met someone and fell madly in love at first sight. The key word here was "madly," and my advice grew especially strong if their parents had been mad for or at each other, too.

In search of the answer, I began studying my clients' attraction, selection, rejection and couple interactional patterns. Growing up with parents who were a "set of opposites" or who had fought a lot as a couple was one of the first big clues to trouble ahead for a client. For years, I felt I had wasted a lot of time doing parent-child work with couples. Typically, I'd facilitate a parent-child resolution using a two-chair dialogue. The problem, of course, was that the more I explored the client's childhood relationship with Mom and Dad, the more unwittingly I accessed the client's child's unmet needs, coping skills and childish behaviors. In retrospect, I finally realized the last thing I needed to do with a troubled couple relationship was to focus on the client's unfinished business as a child with a parent.

Over the years, I had become increasingly dissatisfied with the results I was getting, especially in the 1980's, when the divorce rate spiked to a new high even though more couples were coming into therapy. I often joked there should be a sign above therapists' office doors warning clients, "Beware. One out of every three couples who enter here will divorce." However, back then, I still assumed the source of their couple difficulty was an interaction with one or both parents. It was an expensive and ineffective process for couples. Unfortunately, at that time, couple therapy was a rather new aspect of therapy and we were all learning by trial and error. Now with the Psychogenetic Profile, we can go right to the source of the problem. So let's take a look at yours.

Rating Your Psychogenetic Profile

Each client who comes into my office fills out this same family-of-origin inquiry as an initial intake form just like you did at the beginning of this workshop. Your next step is to review each of the eight categories on your profile and put a plus (+) or a minus (-) in each section to rate the person or relationship therein. This is not a rating for each individual word, but an overall rating for each of the eight categories. I say a plus (+) or minus (-) but you can use any combination of pluses and minuses you want.

Typically, if describing #2. Your mother as an adult, you might put one plus (+) to indicate she was a good adult or one minus (-) if she was a bad adult or if she was absent from the home in your first ten years. If either one of these two adult role models was not present in your childhood home, i.e., divorced, died, or disappeared, put a minus (-) in either the #2 Mother or #3 Father category to identify which of your two genetic parents was absent, and at what ages you and that parent(s) were when it happened. Anne Schutzenberger, who wrote The Ancestor Syndrome, (1999) gives case studies of similar events reoccurring at the same ages or points in time generation after generation and you may also notice repetitive family patterns in yours, too.

If your personal experience in any category was "very bad," put two or three minuses (--) in that numbered category. Put two or three pluses (++) if it was "very good." One client put two pluses in #5 for her father as a parent, even though she listed him as an alcoholic, because her memories of him were as a "happy drunk" and a fun parent. It's the child's emotional experience that counts in this inquiry. You can put both a plus and a minus (+-) if any category was both good and bad. If you liked your experience as a child, certainly put a plus (+) in #1. If your childhood was great, put two pluses (++).

Like I have done here with you, I always ask clients to fill out the Psychogenetic Profile before I give information about my new approach. Most people assume taking a family-of-origin inquiry means I will focus on parent-child relationships. I don't. A lot of therapists believe their child-self picked a mate like the parent with whom they had the most unmet needs. I don't. Most couples that come for couple therapy are expecting me to focus on their own relationship difficulties. I don't do that either. Assessing the introjected adult role models and interactional examples learned from the parents' relationship with each other in childhood is the goal here.

Interpreting your Psychogenetic Profile

Now that you have already filled in your own Psychogenetic Profile, I'm going to show you how to interpret it and re-imprint your own ineffective introjected patterns so you can use this same process with your couple clients. The first request on the Profile asks you to describe yourself as a child. #1 describes your Inner Child. However, as I said, we are not going to focus on you as a child (#1) or on your parent-child relationship (#6 or #7) with either of your parents (#4 or #5). Instead I will focus on your couple relationships and you will learn a new transgenerational approach to working with your couple clients.

If you're in a relationship now, keep your current partner in your mind's eye. If you're not in a relationship, remember the very first couple relationship you ever had. It has to be a romantic or a long-term sexual adult-adult relationship that you've had. Or recall the relationship with your most recent ex-mate. Now spend a minute visiting with that mate in your mind's eye. Spend a little time re-experiencing that relationship with that person, whether current or past, and pay attention to how the two of you interacted with each other. Review the relationship between the two of you. What were the pluses (+) and the minuses (-)? How do you feel about yourself and your partner in this relationship? Were you two a set of "Opposites" or "Likes?"

Inner Mate

Now, I'm going to ask you a question and I want you to write down the first answer that comes to mind. Reviewing how you described your mother (#2) as an adult woman then, and your father as an adult man in #3, which of those two personality and behavioral descriptions is more similar to this current or ex-mate that you have in your mind's eye? Don't let gender get in the way. Your girlfriend could actually be more similar to your father's personality, or your husband could interact more like your mother did with your father. It is not a gender-bound question. And remember, I am asking how your mother and father were with each other then, not with you.

Which one of these two descriptions is this mate (or ex-mate) more like? Particularly, how does (or did) this mate of yours interact in the couple relationship with you? Write this mate's name on at the top of either #2 or #3 to denote which of your two couple adult role models (i.e., your genetic parents) your mate is most like with you. That particular adult/parent your mate is/was most like in a relationship with you now is called your Inner Mate model.

If you wrote your mate's name on #2, this signifies your mate (or ex-mate) is more like your mother was as a mate to your father when you were a child. So in that case, your mother would be called your Inner Mate model. If your current mate (or ex-mate) is more like your father was as a mate to your mother back then, write your mate's name on #3, thereby identifying your father as your Inner Mate model.

Inner Adult

The Inner Adult and the Inner Mate are two terms I created to identify your introjected role models for your own adult/parent relationships. Whichever adult/parent your current mate acts more like as a mate to you is your Inner Mate, your secondary adult role model, and the other adult/parent is your Inner Adult, your primary adult role model. Your Inner Adult role model is the adult/parent you act the most like in your couple relationships. So write your name on that other adult's description (either #2 or #3). For example, if you identified your mate (or ex-mate) as reminding you more of your mother's adult personality (#2), then put your name on #3. If you put your mate's name on #3 as reminding you more of your father as an adult partner to your mother, then put your name on #2.

This identification process is a pleasant experience only if you have described the adult/parent (either #2 or #3) you act most like with a plus, but if you have described your Inner Adult role model with a minus, you may not like the idea of putting your name on that adult's portion of the questionnaire. Some of you may even feel tricked into putting your name on the minus (-) side. Nevertheless, your Inner Adult is the adult/parent you act most like now in your own couple relationship, the adult partner whose feelings and behavior you have introjected for your own adult relationships.

Notice whether you put a plus (+) or minus (-) to describe this Inner Adult role model in your childhood. If you have used a plus or pluses for this adult role model, then you consider yourself to be a positive mate, too. If you put a minus (-) to describe your Inner Adult, then your self-esteem as an adult and a mate is as low as it was for that adult/parent back then. If you put a minus (-) on your description of the adult/parent who was your Inner Mate model, do you rate your own mate's personality and behavior traits as a minus, too? If you put a plus (+) to describe your Inner Mate model, you probably admire that own mate as much you did that adult/parent back then. However, if you have a minus (-) on your own Inner Adult and a plus (+) on your Inner Mate, then you probably respect your partner more than you do yourself. The minuses on the Profile identify the areas that need to be re-imprinted in therapy.

Identifying Your Inner Adult Role Model

Often, it is not easy to identify which of your parents your own mate is most like so I ask you to remember how your mother or father interacted as a mate with the other one. It's very likely that most of us didn't really know our parents as people. We knew them mainly as parents. We certainly didn't know them as well as the adult mates they were to each other. So, indeed, if you or your mate has some of the traits and qualities of either couple role model, it's possible that there are even more hidden adult personality similarities to them than you were consciously aware of in your childhood. If one of your parents was absent, divorced or deceased, (-) be aware that you are likely to repeat that in your own relationship later on unless the introjected pattern is re-imprinted.

Now, why did I ask you first which one of these two adults your mate is most like instead of asking which of your two birth parents you are most like as an adult now? Because most of us would rush to put our own name on the adult/parent that had the most pluses. None of us see ourselves objectively, yet we all think we see our mate clearly. However, mates are viewed on the screen of projection while our self is hidden on the screen of introjection. In that way, love is blind. Each of us thinks we are experts on our partner's behavior. We all recognize behavior traits and personalities in our partner quicker than in ourselves. It is ourselves we can't see clearly. Often others recognize traits in us that we ourselves don't realize. Consistently, most of us don't recognize the similarity to our parents' relationship (#8) until we see it written in our own handwriting on the Psychogenetic Profile. It is the universal AHA moment when we realize history has repeated itself in our own couple relationships.

Some of you may also find that you have switched Inner Adult and Inner Mate role models back and forth from one relationship to another, first being one than the other, while others of you consistently picked the same type of partner. Often clients tell me, "I didn't want to make that same mistake again. So last time I picked someone completely opposite from my last partner, but it still didn't work." That's because the Inner Couple Imprint (#8) is the main behavioral introject that rules every relationship.

Inner Couple Imprint

How you described your parents' relationship when you were a child (#8), describes your Inner Couple imprint. Does their description in any way also describe your relationship with the current or ex-mate you have in your mind's eye now? For nine out of ten people, the precedent is obvious. The chances are that you have recreated a similar plus (+) or minus (-) relationship in your own life now. Most of you will find #8 is 80 to 90% accurate, especially for your first marriage. In effect, what you wrote in #8 was what you learned in your relationship school, the home where you studied day in and day out with your parents as your only couple teachers. Their relationship formed your unconscious model of a couple relationship.

Your Inner Couple Imprint is your adult-adult and parent-parent relationship precedent, and although the introjected imperative controls your selection, it doesn't show up in full force until you are parents, simply because none of us knew our parents before they were parents. Your Introjected Interactional Patterns (IIPs) are absorbed from observing them as a couple and parents. Their ineffective stress patterns from the past are the introjected problem in most adult-adult and co-parenting relationships. For some reason, only the second child in the family escapes because they often rebel against the family pattern. More about that in my next book, *How History Repeats Itself.*

Your genetic mother and father were not only your couple relationship teachers. They were the first and often only live-in example of how to be parents (together or apart) when you grew up. At the same time you were learning their native language, you were also learning their couple and co-parenting language. It's an introjection, not a choice. Even though you may have sworn to never be like them, we all have experienced the very words they once said jumping out of our own mouths particularly under stress. Are their same behaviors being acted out, too?

Inner Parent Imprint

#4 and #5 describe each of these adults as the parents they were to you and your siblings at the point in their life when you were born to them. Your Inner Parent Imprints are formed in your first ten years. (#2 and #4 go together as do #3 and #5.) For example, if #2, (your mother) is your Inner Mate, then #4, how your mother was as a parent, predicts how your mate will parent your children. If #2, (your mother) is your Inner Adult role model, then, #4, how she was as a parent, is your Inner Parent Imprint. If #3 (your father), is your Inner Mate model, then #5 predicts how your own mate will parent your children. Conversely, if #3, (your father) is your Inner Adult model, then, #5, how he was as a parent, predicts how you will parent your children.

The Cycle of Abuse is introjected into your couple and parenting relationships.

Participant: "My wife's anger didn't show up in our dating relationships. Her temper didn't show up in our relationship either before my son was born, so it's shocking to me that she's short-tempered now and hits my son. My father hit me and I never wanted a repeat of that. I knew she was physically abused as a child herself but she swore she wouldn't ever treat her own child that way. But she does. Now she's impatient with me like her father was with her and her mother. Oh my God, her father is her Inner Adult and her Inner Parent role model, isn't he?"

Anne: Unfortunately, yes!! Take a look at your Psychogenetic Profile description of your father's (your Inner Mate's) abusive parenting style. This explains why you unconsciously picked her as a mate. And her abusive impatient Inner Parent imprint surfaced at the birth of your first child and overwhelmed your wife's patient Inner Adult personality. Often, under stress, new mothers will shift personalities to becoming "mothers' to their husbands, too.

A lot of couple difficulties occur at this same point in relationships, either when a pregnancy occurs or a child is born. In fact, in my clinical observations, the biggest stress in a couple relationship is the transition from being a couple to being parents or stepparents. Wouldn't it have been great if you could have predicted how your couple relationship would change after you two had a child? Or how you two would parent together?

Because if you knew, you could have deactivated the troublesome Inner Mate and Inner Parent "landmines" beforehand and your marriage wouldn't be in such a crisis when the "ghosts of parents past" appeared as they will. Parenting from the Inside Out (2003) describes the emotional transference that happens with parenting. Psychogenetics identifies why, how and "from whom" you each learned your particular set of parenting interactional cues and responses.

Your Relationship Teachers

Without a doubt, you and everyone of us learned how to interact in a couple and parenting relationship from our parents. "'One like this" and 'one like that.'" Transactional analysis calls it a "script." Neurolinguistic Programming (NLP) calls it "programming. Gestalt calls it 'introjection.' In Psychogenetics, I call it 'imprinting.' The Inner Couple and Inner Parent Imprints are a repeat of the experiences you had of them. Your parents were your relationship teachers and the behavioral shift you automatically make to interacting like them when you marry and/or become parents is often quite dramatic.

I asked a client of mine, "When did you first notice your husband had changed? How soon after you married?" She said, "What do you mean, how soon after we married? How about during? We were at the altar and all of a sudden, this glaze came over his face, like he was someone else. I was trying to figure out what had happened to him. If we hadn't been standing in front of five hundred people, I would have waved my hand in front of his face to bring him out of trance. I still don't know where my boyfriend went. He's never been the same since."

I have another set of clients right now that had a wonderful live-in relationship for two years, until she wanted to get married. I knew he had been married twice before and was a terrible husband both times. I could see from his Inner Adult (#3) how he had repeated his father's abusive example with his mother. I warned my client, "Take my advice. Don't marry him." She absolutely insisted anyhow, got mad and stopped seeing me. However, six months later, she was back in my office crying. "I should have called you three months ago, because it's been miserable ever since we came back from our honeymoon. He's turned into some mean person I didn't even know or like." (His father, of course!) I always warn clients to take a good look at their future in-laws because they might turn into one of them!

Likes or Opposites

Now, those are the negative cases. In pre-marital assessment, I often see people who have good Inner Couple and Inner Parent Imprinting (#8) and I can safely predict that their relationships will improve after they marry. They typically come from good parents who were a Love Match, usually a set of "Likes," similar in personality, needs, values, and backgrounds. Their children are not only attracted to a mate of similar personality, they are also imprinted to marry "Likes" and get along well. The Cycle of Affection repeats itself, too, particularly in families who had parents who knew how to teach "happy couple" skills.

If your parents were "Opposites," your "chemistry" has attracted you to Inner Mates unlike your personality. Couples who are opposite from each other in personality, backgrounds, values and so on, have more difficulty resolving everyday issues because they have different needs or methods of dealing with difficulties. It is not a coincidence that most troubled couples I see are a set of personality "Opposites" whose parents were also "Opposites." Most report having fallen "madly in love" and had Passion Matches that deteriorated when their relationship shifted to becoming parents. Fighting over parenting the kids is the biggest source of couple stress I see.

Couples who are "Likes" handle parenting problems easier because they don't disagree about how to solve them. "Likes" don't fight over who's going to be in charge. It's usually more of a shared decision making, and so they get along better and can resolve problems easier, rarely coming to a therapist. When people ask me if "Opposites attract, I usually say, "Yes, they attract marriage therapists and divorce attorneys."

A New Transgenerational Approach

For years, I regressed clients into childhood hoping to free them from reacting in the present as they did with their parents in childhood. Now I am regressing clients to free them from reacting like their parents did with each other in the clients' childhood. Gradually, I have realized parent-child difficulties from the past are NOT the primary influence in the clients' couple difficulties. It has become more and more "A-Parent" to me that we as therapists need to explore our clients' "parents" couple relationship—and focus on their unmet needs and unfinished business with each other, not their child's with them. Your clients' troubled parents have set the example for your clients' troubled adult-adult relationships.

Simply put, I am now thoroughly convinced it is the adult-adult and parent-parent relationships between the clients' parents in childhood that formed the client's couple introjects, not their early relationship between parent and child. These two early relationship examples demonstrated by the clients' parents in childhood had formed an unconscious couple precedent that we need to re-imprint through role play.

Role Playing Your Parents' Relationship

Little children playing "Mommies and Daddies'" are already practicing how to be when they grow up, because Inner Couple and Inner Parent precedents are already introjected inside of them. Latent until puberty, their Inner Adult personality will initially surface as "chemistry" and produce an attraction to someone like the other adult/parent (Inner Mate). As I always say, "While your conscious mind is searching for the perfect mate, your unconscious imprint is searching for the perfect match." (The perfect match, of course, is someone who can help you recreate your parents' early relationship, whether you liked the way they were or not.)

If you or your clients have had unhappy relationships, it's important to identify the Inner Couple imprint as the source and change it on an unconscious level by repetitively role playing parents changing theirs. It is not enough to just read about it, because under stress, you will unconsciously regress back to the same ineffective, inappropriate or abusive behaviors your Inner Adult role model exhibited under stress in their own relationship, either as a husband, wife or as a parent. People often say, "Oh, I'm trying to be better, but something just happens, something just comes over me." It's actually your Inner Adult and Inner Couple imprints emerging from inside of you automatically, and before you can stop it, you'll act it out. Psychogenetics re-imprints these unconscious adult-adult and parent-parent introjects before they show up.

To accomplish this, I have both clients role play their parents in the first person, present tense, at the age they were when the client was a child with them. Using three chairs, one for the child self, and one each for the mother and father, over and over in separate individual sessions, clients reenact their parents' early couple relationships as each other, "once as they were" and then "once as they wanted them to be," and then as them, practice effective couple behaviors until the original introjects (-) are interrupted. Do I have a volunteer to demonstrate the process?

It's important to note before we begin the demonstration that the positive change in the current interactional behavior must start with role playing your own Inner Adult role model being positive first, rather than your Inner Mate model. Your own introjected feelings, cues and responses, and couple behaviors from your Inner Adult of the past are the introjects that need to be changed inside you to produce a corrective emotional experience in your current adult relationship. Otherwise, under stress in your current relationship, your original Inner Adult, Inner Parent, and Inner Couple imprints will continue to produce an automatic unconscious repetition of that role model parent's dysfunctional couple and parenting patterns from one generation to another in your family.

Since I believe the mother and father to be the primary bond in the family, not the parent-child bond, I will consistently work on resolving your introjected adult-adult relationship issues first, and co-parenting issues afterwards. Often, re-imprinting a peaceful resolution to the fights a young child experienced between parents resolves the unmet parenting needs in itself once you can re-enact and then remember a 'new experience' as the child of a happy couple. Often, corrective Inner Couple and Inner Parent re-imprinting reduces the need for parent-child work. As one client told me, "Now that they are finally getting along, I can go outside and play."

Demonstration of Re-imprinting Process

Participant #3: Ok, I'll volunteer. (Anne sets up three chairs in a triangle.)
Anne: Thank you. Please sit in this chair and go back into a time in your life when you were a child somewhere before ten years of age...a time when you were with your mother and father. Take the first time that comes to mind. Tell me what you are seeing and hearing and how you feel.
Participant #3 (as child) : I'm five. Mom and Dad are in the kitchen fighting about not having enough money. I'm scared. Maybe I won't have enough to eat. Or maybe I cost too much.

Anne: Where in your body do you feel scared?

Participant #3 (as child): In my stomach.

Anne: Put you hand on your stomach for self-support and shiver out the fear.

Participant #3 (as child): Brrrrrrrr….(shivering)

Anne: Now move to your father's chair because he is identified as your Inner Adult. Introduce yourself by first name and tell us the age he is when you are five years old. Tell us about yourself and what is going on here in the kitchen.

Participant #3: (as Father) Hello, my name is George. I'm thirty and I work hard and my wife spends money at the grocery like it is water. She makes me so mad.

Anne: What are you feeling (as your father) and where in your body are you feeling it?

Participant #3: (as Father) I'm burning up and my stomach hurts.

Anne: Put your hand on your stomach and make the sound of the hurt.

Participant #3: (as Father) GRRRRRRRR……(shaking his fist in the air).

Anne: Thank you. Now move to the other chair and be your mother. Tell us your name and how old you are and what is going on here.

Participant #3: (as Mother) I'm Mary and I'm just sitting here listening because if I say anything George will leave and go out drinking.

Anne: What are you feeling?

Participant #3: (as Mother) I'm mad but I'm not saying anything. It doesn't do any good. My mother raved and ranted like this and my father just waited it out and did nothing. She finally left him when I went to first grade and that's what I'm going to do when little George goes to school and I can go to work.

Anne: Can you two talk about this with me in a therapy session?

Participant #3 (as Father): If you can get her to appreciate how hard I work for the family. She never seems to care how tired I am.

Anne: (to Mother): Can you tell him you appreciate how hard he works?

Participant #3 (as Mother): I do care but he doesn't.

Anne: (to Father): Can you tell her you care about her, too?

Participant #3 (as Father): Sure, if I thought it would do any good.

Anne: (to Participant #3) Ok, return to the child chair and tell me what it is like to be a child of these parents? And if you had a wish for how they could be happy together, tell me what you would have wished each of them would have done?

Participant #3 (as child): I feel sad for them. Maybe I cost them too much money. Maybe it is my fault they are fighting. I wish my father would stop hollering and smile at my mother sometime and maybe hug her when she cries. I wish my mother would stop buying me stuff and tell my father she is going to save money. I wish she would smile at him, too.

Anne (to child):Ok, I want you to imagine them smiling at each other. Imagine them telling each other that they really do care and they can work this out. Imagine them telling each other they need to solve this problem. Imagine them telling you that it is not your fault. And then get over into your father's chair and begin this new attitude with your mother.

Participant #3 (as father): Honey, I'm sorry. I have to stop wasting money in the bar. It's a bad and expensive habit. We'll have enough money for some nights out together as a family if I do that. I didn't like it when my mother drank when I was a kid and I am going to stop (smiling at Mother's chair).

Participant #3 (as mother): I've waited so long to hear that. Thank you so much. I loved it when we used to go out together. We had so much fun. (smiling at Father's chair)

Anne: (to Participant #3) Ok, return to your child chair. What is it like to be the child of these parents?

Participant #3 (as child): My stomach doesn't hurt anymore. I can eat my cereal. They are hugging each other. I like seeing them smiling at each other. (Smiling)

Anne: Ok, I want you to close your eyes and review what just happened between your parents. Remember how they just changed and what they said and imagine that they actually accomplish them and their relationship evolves to where they are a happy couple from this moment on. In fact, write down this new Inner Couple Imprint and for the next twelve nights, read it to yourself at night before you go to sleep so it will slip into your unconscious mind.

Participant #3: You know, I'm surprised. This really feels good to remember my parents being this way. It is much different to role play them interacting in a happy way...I could really feel it happening inside me. Funny how I want to go home now and try that new Father approach with my wife. I'm not so mad at her anymore for some strange reason. Maybe I have been out of line. I didn't like it when my own father hollered. Neither did my mother.

The Psychogenetic System™

A Three Chair Approach

Like we just did here, I now set up three chairs instead of two, and invite clients to re-enact their childhood parents' interaction with each other as they witnessed it in childhood. I suggest each client imagine their parents coming into couple therapy with me and I facilitate clients' role playing them improving their communication with each other. In addition to the amazing insights I get interviewing their parents, I have consistently noticed simultaneous improvements in my clients' communication in their current relationships, too. I suggest you use this Psychogenetic process with your clients, too.

Once your clients are no longer focused on resolving their own arguments with each other, they can focus on remembering how they wished their parents would resolved their arguments long ago. Re-imprinting occurs as they role-play their parents meeting their own unmet needs with each other in the here and now of your office. As their parents, your clients will be less defensive and more able to practice better conflict resolution skills than these same parents had taught them by example back in the there and then of their childhood. By role play repetition, re-imprinting of positive Inner Couple and Inner Parenting introjects occurs on the unconscious level.

Conclusion

I quote Laura Perls on introjects, "What is transferred is not father-mother-child relationships, but what is transferred are certain fixed behavior patterns which at the time when they were acquired, were acquired not as resistance but as assistance for something. It's part of the development and then it becomes automatic. This implies a gestalt of which one is not consciously aware. What we do in gestalt therapy is to de-automatize these fixed gestalten and thus make the patient aware of them as sources of energy which form a new basis of activity."

The Psychogenetic System tm utilizes the wish of the client's child-self as a redecision (2010) to deactivate the negative behavior patterns originally introjected into the client's Inner Couple and Inner Parent Imprints, and re-solve their fixed behavior patterns. Using three chairs instead of two, each client re-enacts their childhood parents into the here and now of the therapist's office and role plays them practicing this new activity, namely, a corrective interactional couple example for the client to repeat. By re-imprinting this wish as a positive precedent, the client de-automatizes the fixed gestalten previously introjected from the parents' ineffective relationship examples.

In the spirit of this conference's theme, "Continuity and Change," couples are now able to continue with their same partners and change their fixed behavior patterns... instead of changing partners and continuing their fixed behavior patterns. I often call this approach, "The Star Trek Approach to Couple and Parenting Therapy" because with this Psychogenetic System, clients can "boldly take their parents further than they have ever gone before" and create a new adult world for their own new adult worlds.

References

Schutzenberger, A. A. (1998). *The ancestor syndrome: Transgenerational psychotherapy and the hidden links in the family tree.* London: Routledge.

Siegel, D. & Hartzell, M. (2003). *Parenting from the inside out.* New York: Penguin Group.

Smith, E. (1992), *Gestalt Voices*, A Trialogue between Laura Perls, Richard Kitzler and Mark E. Stern. Westport, CT: Ablex Publishing

Teachworth, A. (1996). Three couples transformed. In Feder, B. & Ronall, R. (Eds.), *A living legacy to Fritz and Laura Perls: Contemporary case studies* (pp.185–202). NJ: Walden Printing.

Teachworth, Anne (1997). *Why we pick the mates we do.* Metairie, LA: Gestalt Institute Press.

—   (2000). Response to Ted Schwartz's article, The landmines of marriage: Intergenerational causes of marital conflict. *Gestalt Review*, 4(1), 66–70.

Teachworth, A. & Jenkins, P. (2010). Psychogenetics with redecision, *Transactional Analysis Journal*, 40(2), 121–129.

Chapter 17. Theater as Field: Implications for Gestalt Therapy
Karen Humphrey

Chapter Introduction

The NYIGT in the 20th Century maintained a somewhat defensive and rigid position in the world of gestalt therapy. Organizationally we embraced our role as the originator of gestalt therapy as a serious practice backed by a legitimate theory. Like many long-time members of the New York Institute for Gestalt Therapy, I felt a responsibility to advance gestalt therapy as an experiential practice firmly grounded by its theoretical roots. Formally, knowledge of the theory expressed in the theory volume of *Gestalt Therapy* by Perls, Hefferline, and Goodman was built into requirements for Full Membership in the Institute. Informally, allegiance, even affection, for our theory has been an important organizing norm of the Institute culture.

Just in time for the Millennium, shifts within the culture of the New York Institute, reflecting changes in our contacting of the wider world, allowed for expansion and flexibility in an ongoing analysis of our beloved theory. My paper, Theater as Field, arose from work in a study group devoted to reading hermeneutics, postmodern philosophy, and significantly for me, critical performance theory. My paper was an attempt to illustrate or "picture" primary gestalt therapy concepts. For several years the Institute monthly presentation meetings were devoted to a re-examination of core theoretical concepts. We invited "outsiders"— artists, scientists, and academics — to come speak to us about how our core concepts manifested in other arenas. We actively sought to engage with others in examining what exactly do we mean by experience, and what does co-creation of meaning look like. In common with most dialogic psychotherapy modalities we hastened to qualify as relational psychotherapy.

In re-reading my paper I was reminded of the challenge of depicting embodied experience using only written description. How much more efficient and fun it would be to link to a YouTube clip. The struggle to represent and describe contact, traditionally understood as embodied face-to-face contact, within the confines of linear text has been with us since the beginning of gestalt therapy. In the 21st Century the NYIGT is far more welcoming of collaboration with others engaged in this intellectual enterprise. Organizationally, the challenge of reconciling embodied contacting with linear text has expanded to include decision making in a membership organization where members are dispersed around the world. It will be interesting to see what progress has been made at mid-century.

Theater as Field: Implications for Gestalt Therapy[93]

During the 1996-97-program year, members of the New York Institute for Gestalt Therapy developed a series of papers revisiting core concepts of Gestalt therapy theory. That same autumn, after several years of ensemble building and performing our stories for each other, the improvisational theater group of which I am a member performed in front of an audience for the first time. In the latter instance the same performer's abstract sound and movement organized itself into a coherent narrative when joined with one performer's words and gestures and a completely 0ther narrative when joined with those of another performer. Meanwhile, in an Institute presentation, Carl Hodges placing a rock in the middle of the floor said, "This is a rock. In the field theory of the Gestalt Psychologists, we would say...that at this time, in this space, at this temperature, and, at this pressure and gravity...this is a rock...Given these particular conditions in the field, given this equilibrium there is an event called this rock." (Hodges, 1997,p.1). As he went on to describe, for example, race and gender as events and processes not things; I had the playful and dramatic notion of myself becoming figural in the group as an adolescent boy, dissolving and reaching another equilibrium as an old black woman, and so on, depending on the particular conditions of the field.

In the improvisational theater workshops, these sorts of imaginings were the raw material of our work. We were weaving our stories. My stories sometimes figure, and sometimes the background out of which another's story emerged. I began to see how the theatrical event dramatized field dynamics. When our director announced that something worked she was recognizing the law of *pregnänz*: organization in the field tends toward maximal simplicity and balance, or the formation of as good a form as the prevailing field conditions allow. Or put the other way around, field theory helps explain aesthetically satisfying theater.

It is satisfying to be now addressing the convergence of these two areas of interest because it echoes another convergence thirty-five years ago. My first experience of Gestalt therapy corresponded to a time when I generated a series of student papers on aspects of theater and it was Paul Goodman who introduced me to both Gestalt therapy and a broader understanding of theater imbedded in culture.

While studying literature at Columbia University in New York City, my friendship circle included students and ex-officio students attracted to Paul Goodman. Goodman, enjoying a modest fame as a social philosopher, was particularly interesting to young people attempting to form a synthesis of community activism and intellectual pursuit. He was a frequent visitor to my shared apartment, which had become a locus of political activity. We benefited

---

[93] Originally published in *Studies in Gestalt Therapy,* (1999), No 8, 99 172 – 181.

from the access to a larger world that he provided and he seemed comfortable exercising the natural authority that comes with maturity. The time was 1961, just prior to the nation-wide student uprising and the anti-war movement, but many of us were already active in organizations opposed to nuclear testing and the arms race. Paul Goodman recruited me to participate in the General Strike for Peace, an idea conceived by Judith Malina and Julian Beck, founders of The Living Theatre [94].

It was a week at the end of January 1962 when in Paul's words there would not be business as usual. Participants spent the week picketing their usual places of employment, and demonstrating against the nuclear arms race at the United Nations, the New York Stock Exchange, the Atomic Energy Commission, etc. It was my first "up close" look at the Living Theatre. While walking the picket line we talked politics, but we also talked theater. Malina and Beck saw the General Strike as a theatrical activity, and it was certainly an experience of stage fright for me as I marched all by myself, with my placard, before the statue of Alma Mater on the great steps of the Loeb Library of Columbia University.

Paul Goodman's interest in writing for the theater was of longstanding, as was his connection with the Living Theatre. He first met Julian Beck in 1944 in Provincetown where Tennessee Williams introduced them (Tytell, 1995, p.20). All during the 1950's he was involved with the Living Theatre, not only in the production of several of his plays but in the "communitas" as well, an accord in seeing art as a means of creating community value. According to Goodman, "To me, writing for the theatre is the only kind of writing that is not lonely, and if I had my choice I would write mainly for the theatre." (Goodman, 1977, p.140). His collaboration with Julian Beck and Judith Malina overlapped and commingled his collaboration with Laura and Frederick Perls. 1951 marked not only the publication of *Gestalt therapy: Excitement and Growth in the Human Personality* by Perls, Hefferline, and Goodman, but the Living Theatre productions of his plays

---

[94] The Living Theatre was known as the most radically uncompromising and experimental group in American theatrical history. Its story paralleled the formation of the advance guard in New York in the 1950's and the consequent counterculture in the 1960's. When Beck and Malina were doing Goodman's plays they were using fairly straightforward conventional theatrical forms. Over time, from the belief that there could be no separation between art and life, they evolved a communal lifestyle within the ensemble, developed plays collectively, performed on the streets as well as in theaters and involved the audience in the action of the performance. Their commitment to a theater that would challenge the moral complacency of its audience, as well as the unconventional lifestyle of the ensemble, often put them in conflict with authority, sometimes even in jail. In later years they found a warmer welcome in Europe than in their home country, and as recently as 1992, in Italy, Judith Malina had a successful two-month run in The Zero Method. (Tytell,1995, p. 347). The Living Theatre is most often remembered for productions of Jack Gelber's The Connection, Kenneth Brown's The Brig, Jean Genet's The Maids, Bertolt Brecht's Man is Man, as well as the collaboratively developed Frankenstein, Seven Meditations, Paradise Now, and Prometheus at the Winter Palace.

Crying Backstage, and Faustina, and the start of Judith Malina's therapy with Goodman. (Tytell, 1995, p. 73).

In the early years of the New York Institute for Gestalt Therapy, founded in 1952, there was more diversity in membership; visual and performing artists, educators, composers, writers, were interested in Gestalt therapy theory as it applied to their work. The notion of patients being trainees in therapy was taken seriously and patient/trainees brought their own perspective to monthly meetings. By the early 1960's when I was first patient and then student of Laura Perls, there was a whole new "second generation" of art and theater people in both her therapy and professional groups, many of them, like me referred by Paul Goodman. Some of us found a vocation in the group, discovering a talent for doing therapy. Others saw the therapy group as an opportunity for serious play and experiment. Certainly, my first understanding of the method of Gestalt therapy came in the focused awareness and body sensing exercises arising from Laura Perls' background in movement and dance, as well as the interactive therapy experiments developed by group members who were part of the Judson Poets Theatre Company. Frederick Perls, apparently, was informed by Max Reinhardt of Berlin's Grosses Schauspielhaus. (Roberts, 1998, p 19). Dr. Perls' method, at least as it has survived in student demonstration films, was inherently dramatic. He was the inspired director leading the volunteer in the "hot seat," step by step, toward a better understanding of the part in which he had been cast. A patient's dream becomes a play in which he reads for every part. Many of the experiments Perls devised for the method volume of Gestalt Therapy involve listening in on the dialogues in our mind, making them bigger as in the theater.

As a student I was thinking not about theater, but about Drama as literature. Through exposure to advance guard theater and the use of theatrical events for consciousness raising I began thinking about the effect of drama and the cultural function of putting on plays. Paul Goodman with admirable restraint suggested Aristotle would be useful here. I tried an Aristotelian analysis of Bertolt Brecht, (Goodman proof-read that one), worked at understanding what Samuel Beckett was doing with the audience, worked very hard on a paper on ritual in the theater of Jean Genet, but I never completely satisfied myself that I knew how theater worked. At the same time I was just beginning a first reading of the theory volume of *Gestalt Therapy* and was really sure that I did not know how therapy worked.

Now all these many years later I feel ready to advance a bit on both fronts. What has filled in the gap, aside from the passing of many years, has been a seminar with Richard Kitzler on the "Philosophical Bases of Gestalt Therapy," that had also the adjunctive result of emboldening me to tackle post-modern critical theory, the hard work of members of my institute honing core concepts, and the new of experience of being involved in theater as a performer. In my work in a women's improvisational theater group, I have had the opportunity, over and over again, to see how gestalt formation looks when it is slowed down and/or made large.

Obviously, I have been speaking not of a specific production or dramatic text, but of theater as theatrical event or the process of theater. Paul Goodman refers to theater as the art form in which ..."some do and others watch." (Goodman, 1977, p. 132). It is the relationship of "doing" and "watching" that I am noticing, a very everyday experience that in a theatrical event is concentrated and projected, rendering it easier to capture as process. I am interested in the watching done by actors of each other as they develop a non-naturalistic play, as well as the watching done by the audience. I am interested in the effect being watched has on the doing. And, of course, I am interested in watching and doing as they relate to therapy.

It is essential that, in the language of phenomenology, theatrical events are embodied events.

> On one hand, the field of performance is scenic space, given as spectacle to be processed and consumed by the perceiving eye, objectified as field of vision for the spectator who aspires to the detachment inherent in the perceptual act. On the other hand, this field is environmental space, "subjectified" (and intersubjectified) by the physical actors who body forth the space they inhabit. From this perspective, theatrical space is phenomenalspace, governed by the body and its spatial concerns, a non-Cartesian field of habitation which undermines the stance of objectivity and in which the categories of subject and object give way to a relationship of mutual implication.... This implication includes the audience, which is situated in the phenomenological continuum of space through physical proximity, linguistic inclusions, and the uniquely theatrical mirroring that links audience with performer in a kind of corporeal mimetic identification. (Garner, 1994, p.3).

Thus the watching that goes on in a theatrical event has a "charge." As a spectator there is the possibility that the object of my gaze could look at me; something that would not happen with a film or a painting on the wall. As a performer I feel the here and now gaze of this audience. This "relationship of mutual implication" is the element of theatrical experience that sets it apart from other art forms. Not only is it an embodied text, but also as the audience is embodied, the theatrical experience is subject to the dynamics of the human/organism field. Therefore, some of the ways we look at groups from a gestalt field perspective are also useful ways to look at the special "group" which organizes around a theatrical event.

Even much so-called post modern theorizing when applied to performance rests on a model in which "...the theater plays its meanings before the gaze of a privileged spectator who stands (or sits, as it were) outside the conditions of spectacle." (Garner, 1994, p. 45). Phenomenological theorizing moves to include the perspective of the spectator in "...the uniquely theatrical mirroring that links audience with performer in a kind of mimetic identification." Gestalt therapy field theory, of course, has ready to hand in the unifying concept of contact an explanation of what goes on in the field of performance. Contact, especially as thickened by Richard Kitzler's inclusion of philosopher/social psychologist George Herbert Mead's work in the bases of Gestalt therapy theory provides an adequate description of how creation of meaning comes to be shared by those who do and those who watch.

"We speak of the organism contacting the environment, but it is the contact that is the simplest and first reality." (Perls, Hefferline, Goodman, 1951, p. 227). Contacting may be described as figure/background formation and destruction. As Joe Lay summarized in his long paper for the New York Institute, "It has been the brilliant insight of many people from Aristotle to Goethe to the Gestalt psychologists that 'in act' there is unity not only of the organismic function, but also unity of organism/environment. This unity 'in act' is figure/background formation and destruction." (Lay, 1997). Thus the unity in act is contacting; our familiar fore contact, contact, final-contact, post-contact. Or in George Herbert Mead's formulation, the four stages of the act, which are impulse, perception, manipulation, and consummation. It is Mead's social analysis of the act that thickens our understanding of contact. It is not necessary for one individual to complete the whole complex act in order to participate in the consummatory stage. Because of the social nature of our experience (the social formation of our selves) we have the capacity to take the attitude of other selves as they complete the act. "A social act may be defined as one in ...the class of acts which involve the co-operation of more than one individual, and whose object as defined by the act...is a social object. I mean by a social object one that answers to all the parts of the complex act, though these parts are found in the conduct of different individuals." (Mead, 1934, p.7) As spectator I can "answer" to the impulse and perception parts of the act, while an actor, continuing on, "answers" to the manipulation and consummation parts. "Meaning is that which can be indicated to others while it is by the same process indicated to the indicating individual." (Mead quoted in Kitzler, 1996, p.27) This, of course, is another way of understanding the hermeneutics of performance; the performer's interpretation is given in the moment.[95]

---

[95] Letting the ripples form, performance is often seen as the hermeneutics of culture. "'By their performances ye shall know them wrote Victor Turner, in the belief that cultures express themselves most fluently by means of performance. (7) A key Turnerian concept in support of this belief is liminality, the state or process of living on the margins, of crossing the boundaries, of literally being at the 'threshold' of culture's inside/outside, which he associated particularly with performance and performers."(Roach, 1992, p.13).

In the field of performance the figure of interest is the dramatic event, structured or loose, and the usual emphasis is on how effectively the performance moves the audience. While it is a commonplace to praise the artistry of the artist who helps us discover what we have known all along, it is less usual to recognize when it is in contact with her audience that the artist discovers her meaning. A patient who is a performer reported watching videotape of her performances of the same piece on two consecutive evenings. In the tape of the first evening she watched herself discover and expand the humor in the piece in response to the laughter of the audience. The second evening, her former lover, (still beloved), was in the audience. On this night the piece was sensual, its humor less playful, colored by longing. Meaning arises, as Mead has shown us, in part because of our human capacity to put ourselves simultaneously on the moving train and in the passing scene. The actor working in the moving train of the performance piece puts herself in the passing scene of the audience, while in the passing scene the audience member puts herself on the moving train of the theatrical event. Jean Genet, in the play within the play in The Blacks, includes a stage direction that there be a white audience member at every performance, and if no white person will come, then a black person in whiteface is to sit in the audience (Genet, 1960, p. 13).

By staying close to our understanding of contacting, we usefully broaden the evolving development of meaning. "The process of figure/background formation is a dynamic one in which the urgencies and resources of the field progressively lend their powers to the interest, brightness and force of the dominant figure." (Perls, Hefferline, Goodman, 1951, p.231).

In the theatrical productions that are most familiar, of course, the degree of presence of the audience's urgency is limited. In conventional fourth wall theater, actual interaction between performers and audience is negligible; certainly everything mediates against direct contact. The audience is supposed to experience only what it was designed to experience and the performers are not supposed to indicate that they know they are being watched. Paul Goodman observes that the shape of the stage where the scene is the center of attention not the whole field of vision restricts the audience to psychological participation. The persistent sense of spatial discontinuity is one of the things that keep the audience in its seats in "...the psychological conditions of projection, as in day dreams." (Goodman, 1977, p. 90) Of course, the fourth wall is an illusion and there is contact. If night after night a funny line doesn't produce laughter the performers make a change. If the audience is seen to be responsive and "with" the actors, the performance goes better, everyone's experience deepens. Nevertheless, fourth-wall plays are examples of fields in which there are many constraints, not quite like machines where what comes out is rigidly determined by what goes in, but similar to the field of systems theory in which sub-groups are clearly identified and managed. The product is a result of an original notion that has guided and formed the process. (Which is not to say the product can't be wonderful.)

In non-naturalistic theater the presence of the audience is not denied. The possibility of contact becomes part of the ground. This is not to say that the audience is expected to join or interfere with the actors (although sometimes they can), but that there is an understanding that the story on the stage emerges from a field that includes the stories of the witnesses[96]. A non-naturalistic play or theater piece is formed from elements that grow organically, perhaps assuming a finished shape one would not have predicted in the early stages of the creative process. The audience is represented in the final piece as a sort of skeleton in so far as the actors first watch each other and flesh out the piece by inventing out of the watching as they go along. This is more like the field of Gestalt group therapy where it is understood that each person "speaks" for some part of the field and no part is fixed except in momentary present structures that reflect prevailing conditions.

I would like to give you some examples from my theater group. In our group we watch each other as we build a performance piece from elements improvised in workshop. The examples are of exercises out of which some of the elements of the piece come into being. In these exercises I became aware that we were performing an almost textbook representation of figure formation. Further, I was seeing an embodiment of Mikhail Bakhtin's description of the chemical union as opposed to a mechanical bond that forms when one person's discourse enters the speech context of another (Bakhtin, 1998, p. 531).

In my first example, one person starting from a story or current concern is directed to pay close attention to her impulses toward movement. An impulse is allowed to grow until the actor yields to it and produces a movement (perhaps accompanied by sound or words.) The other actors as witnesses are directed to watch this repeatable movement kinesthetically as well as visually. Optimally we will experience our own impulses based on our experience as witness. We are then instructed to, one at a time, using this witness-based impulse toward movement enter the actor's world and space, adding to the formed figure in ways that amplify, underscore, or in some way edit the meaning. As each person enters, the emblem changes and each joining person must respond to the new figure. In one exercise the original actor is asked to maintain her sound and movement without alteration. Even without a change of form, actors almost always experience new emotion and understanding connected to what they are doing. The potential then exists for new impulses to emerge authentically in the original

---

[96] Paul Goodman, referring to Artaud's wish that the play come out and do something to the audience wrote: "But I'd rather have the watchers moved by what they are doing – watching – I guess I'm not confident enough in myself to wish to act on other people, no less to do it. I want accomplices." (Goodman, 1977, p. 132).

actor in relation to the gestalt formed by the ensemble. We call this a transformation[97] (4).

In another exercise an actor is again instructed to begin a repeatable movement and sound. The remainder of the ensemble is instructed to closely witness this sound and movement and yield to the first impulse toward giving it a verbal "title." The actor is again asked to maintain the original movement as each "title" is given. Witnesses experience dramatic changes in what they see based on how the same sound and movement is named. The actor, also, although maintaining the same form throughout experiences kinesthetic and emotional transformations upon hearing her movement variously named.

In a third exercise, an actor again begins an abstract sound and movement. From the ensemble witnesses, a second actor joins the original actor with a sound and movement that is in relation to the original figure. Together the two actors are now performing their movements. The original actor allows herself to be informed by the joiner and to yield to an authentic transformation. This transformation that grew kinesthetically from the experience of being joined, gives new meaning to both the original abstract sound and movement and to the scene that was created by the joiner.

These three examples of theater exercises illustrate how meaning first emerges in the contact of doing and watching and being watched. As I hope is becoming evident, there is a parallel between the sort of watching and doing that goes on in building a non-naturalistic play, and what happens in a therapy group, or for that matter a therapy session with an individual. The meaning in both organizes and emerges in the meeting of all participating elements of the field. As therapist or group member witnessing another's struggle, our task is to pay close attention to our own witness-based impulse to join, trusting that as I am of the field, if it is in me it is in the field, and yielding to the impulse so as to add to the figure in ways that amplify meaning. And too, as "actor/patient" in the therapy, our task is to pay close attention to the new emotion and understanding that occurs as our action is witnessed, joined and variously named.

It is important, of course, to be aware of the impact of witnessing and naming. My theater group uses Authentic Movement, a form of movement meditation, as a warm-up exercise. In Authentic Movement one person with eyes

---

[97] Coming full circle, these exercises, developed by our director Stephanie Glickman, evolved out of the "sound-and-movement procedures devised by one of her teachers, Joseph Chaikin of the Open Theatre. Chaikin, as a member of The Living Theatre had appeared in plays of Pirandello, Jack Gelber, Paul Goodman, and William Carlos Williams. He reported being transformed into a political being by his role in their production of Brecht's Man Is Man. (Pasolli, 1970, p.2).

closed follows her movement impulses while another person witnesses, paying attention to her responses to the mover. On one occasion I was following movement impulses arising from tight back muscles. I was standing against a wall, using the wall to smooth out the tightness. My witness reported "seeing" a person tossing and turning bed. The experience was so strong that she kept checking to confirm that my feet were on the floor. As she reported this, my movement experience recollected became as she witnessed it. I can no longer remember/recall (including kinesthetically) the event except as including someone tossing in bed. Now, it is possible that this is diagnostic, (I can hear Isadore From clearing his throat and beginning in on Introjection), but it is also an example of the irrevocable shift in gestalt that occurs when the observer's view is added.

In theater and therapy, particularly Gestalt therapy, share many structural similarities.

> Taken together, theatre and psychotherapy form a fold of that continuum of human endeavor which seeks to explore our place in the universe – and they do so in highly ritualized fashion. The underlying structure of both is essentially the same: the participants-by virtue of a social arrangement – agree to meet at predetermined time and place in order to tell emotionally charged stories about what it means to be human….Theatre is a communal event in which two parties (audience and actor) can experience a kind of salubrious emotional release through partaking in the live, immediate experience of an unfolding story. Similarly, modern psychotherapy is the ritual evocation of a transformational space in which a living story is enacted and experienced. It was psychotherapy's intrinsic similarity to the ritual space of theatre which Freud, Perls and others recognized. (Roberts, 1998, p. 18)

Roberts observes that both theater and therapy are fundamentally defiant acts. Both give rise to uneasy concern for their effect. His point is that stories told in the theater and in therapy consulting rooms are enacted stories. "This unavoidable unpredictability of live storytelling is threatening to the pervasive hegemony of social rules and conditioning." (Roberts, 1998, p. 20). Paul Goodman in his essay Censorship and Pornography on the Stage also reasons that the stage is heavily censored because "…the offensive thing is not only spoken, it is acted out in the flesh….But most important of all, I think, is that the stage plays to a public audience not isolated readers; the audience shares the risk, the excitement, and the guilt…." (Goodman, 1977, p. 103) We are here in the realm of the "charged" watching that goes on in the making of theater as well as in the process of therapy. The audience in contacting, partaking of the consummatory phase of the act, is implicated in the outcome of the drama, just as the therapist in contacting, in act, is implicated in the outcome of the therapy session. Goodman understands some of the power of such watching psycho-dynamically.

> In the very notion of theatre there is a peculiar tension, a kind of ambivalence. The fundamental theatrical relation is that A watches B and is moved by watching him, but he must not get up and do something on his own. We are here drawing psychologically on survivals of very early experience...but certainly and basically on the child curious about and imitating any behavior of his grown-ups, his heroes. In general, and even in the theatre of naturalism, the actors are "bigger" than life-size'."(Goodman, 1997 p. 103).

Certainly, aided by Mead's construction of the social nature of the act, one may also speculate that what Goodman calls the fundamental theatrical relation also echoes even earlier experience, the social formation of the self through the acquisition of the vocal gesture. The infant, not yet able to get up and do something on her own, indicates to herself what the grown-ups indicate to her, and responds to herself as she responds to them, thereby becoming aware of herself in the awareness of them. The primary drama: A in watching B discovers both A and B in the watching, and is moved.

In the process of making theater pieces and beginning to hypothesize about therapy as improvisation, I developed a renewed respect for the delicacy required in joining another person's story. How different does the narrative become when I contribute what I see? In doing therapy I am sustained by a faith that I act as part of a dynamically equilibrated field. If I proceed from my witness-based impulse in a spirit of improvisation, and what happens next has grace and form, then I trust that the meaning thus discovered creates ground for the next step. Likewise, just as in gestalt formation where the clearest most vivid gestalt forms against a ground from which everything relevant is drawn to form the figure, so the most powerful and moving theatrical experiences are those in which the novel action of the stage, the figure, creatively organizes every relevant background element of the performer/spectator field. Both "those who do" and "those who watch" end knowing that all that needed to be was said and done.

References

Bakhtin, M. (1998). Discourse in the Novel, trans. Caryl Emerson & Michael Halquist. In: "The Critical Tradition," (Ed.) David H. Richter, Boston: Bedford Books.

Garner, S.B., Jr. (1994). *Bodied Spaces*. Ithaca, NY: Cornell University Press.

Genet, J. (1960). *The Blacks: A Clown Show*. New York: Grove Press.

Goodman, P. (1977). *Creator Spirit Come!* New York: Free Life Editions.

Hodges, C. (1997). Field Theory. Unpublished Paper.

Kitzler, R. (1996). The Bases of Gestalt Therapy: An Evolutionary Restatement. Unpublished Paper.

Lay, J. (1997). On the Nature of Gestalt Therapy. Unpublished Paper.

Mead, G. H. (1934). *Mind, Self, & Society.* Chicago: University of Chicago Press.

Perls, F.S., Hefferline, R.F., Goodman, P. (1951). *Gestalt Therapy.* New York: Julian Press.

Posolli, R. (1972). *A Book on the Open Theatre.* New York: Discus Books.

Reinelt, J.G., Roach, J.R., (1992) (Eds.). *Critical Theory and Performance.* Ann Arbor: University of Michigan Press.

Roberts, A. (1998). *Theatre & Therapy, introduction to: Rainette Eden Fantz, "The Dreamer and the Dream."* Cambridge, MA: Gestalt Institute of Cleveland Press.

Tytell, J. (1995). *The Living Theatre.* New York: Grove Press.

Chapter 18. Elsa Gindler: Lost Gestalt Ancestor
Susan Gregory

Chapter introduction

Arbeit am Menschen – Working with People

For me, growing up in Brooklyn in the 1950s was like being in the suburbs, only with the school and candy store right around the corner. We kids walked wherever we needed to go. There were trees, birds, flowers all around. The ocean was a short distance away. I bicycled to it every weekend.

While I lived in the city, I was not truly part of New York as it was understood by those living in Manhattan. These early years in Brooklyn were a rich time for me. I sang, wrote poetry, played kid-organized sports, went to dance and acting lessons on the Lower East Side - "another country," important to me because my dad had grown up there.

In high school, my world began to expand. I chose a specialized music school located in Harlem. The subway trip each way was one hour and twenty minutes. I began to meet a wide variety of people - my classmates, their relatives, my teachers, the riders on the subway. The world of the intellect began to become apparent to me.

In particular, I encountered a group of European émigrés, who fascinated me, whose accents sounded musical, whose conversation seemed more profound than any I had come across before, who had skills and specialties that I wanted to learn. I began to study singing technique, repertoire, acting, and languages with members of this group. They all seemed to know one another and could often be found together in the now-defunct cafeteria below Lincoln Center, sipping coffee, gesticulating and conversing in German.

The person among them whom I most revered was Carola Speads (Spitz before she Americanized it), a woman who taught a method of bodywork - did we have that expression in those days? - which she had brought with her from Berlin. In her classes, I found myself changing physically and emotionally in ways I had longed for and had had no language to describe.

When my singing teacher was preparing to move to California, she sent me to study "breathing" with Carola. I took my first class before summer break; and that single class changed how I experienced myself and the world. I can say now that what we students were doing in Carola's classes was encountering id functioning in ways which were utterly accepting and which brought about unsought and felicitous change.

It is from my love and appreciation for Carola Speads that I offer this article, written 13 years ago for publication in the British Gestalt Journal, for inclusion in this anthology.

I consider it important that we Gestalt therapists know the crucial if little acknowledged part, which the work of Elsa Gindler plays in our theory and practice. Yet, more personally significant to me is that her teaching assistant Carola Speads, fleeing Hitler in 1940, brought Gindler's work to New York, where I was fortunate enough to find it. I believe that this work saved my life, and that training in Gestalt therapy subsequently helped me process what I had learned from *Arbeit am Menschen*, as Gindler called her approach and her intention.

Elsa Gindler: Lost Gestalt Ancestor [98]

Abstract: Attending to body experiences has been integral to the practice and theory of Gestalt therapy since its inception. This is so because of the influence of Elsa Gindler's work on both Laura and Fritz Perls. This paper explores their historical connections.

Key words: somatics, Gestalt therapy, Elsa Gindler, body awareness.

Introduction

When I began my studies in Gestalt therapy eleven years ago, my familiarity with terms such as organismic self regulation, interrupting contact, here and now, experimenting, and awareness surprised me. I had explored these ideas experientially in a different context, with my mentor in breathwork, Carola Speads. Curious to find the connections between her somatic approach and Gestalt therapy, I began an historical inquiry and discovered that the common root for both was the work of Elsa Gindler.

Elsa Gindler's Work

Elsa Gindler lived in Berlin from 1885-1961. During that time she developed and taught a method of working with people which she called exactly that: *'Arbeit am Menschen'*. Although influenced by some exercise and breathing specialists of her day, including Stebbins, Kallmeyer and Kofler, she surpassed them, creating a fresh approach which eschewed rote repetition and predetermined outcomes.

In Gindler's ground-breaking work, students were guided to be curious about their own functioning, and to experiment, both in class and throughout their daily lives, with new ways of moving, breathing, speaking, and perceiving. In 1926, she wrote, 'Suddenly each student is working in his own fashion... and begins to feel that he is in charge of himself... his consciousness of self is heightened' (Johnson, (Ed.), p 8).

Gindler was the first to use the word 'experiment' in relation to people's working with their own awareness of body sensation in interaction with their environment. She encouraged her students to notice and talk about the details of their movement and breathing. She stated, "I always advise my students to replace my words with their own... in order to avoid getting a knot in their psyche" (Johnson, (Ed.), p 6). She had (hem speak up during class experiments and also write reports of those experiments which they did at home, much as the

---

[98] Originally appeared in the *British Gestalt Journal,* 2001, Volume 10, No. 2, Pages 114-117

students at Columbia University did with the experiments found in Part I of *Gestalt Therapy: Excitement and Growth in the Human Personality* (1951), by Perls, Hefferline and Goodman.

People from all walks of life studied with Gindler. Over the course of her long career, 1917-1960, she taught teachers, musicians, artists, psychologists, scientists, physicians, social workers, factory workers, soldiers. As her teaching assistant, Carola Speads (Spitz), has stated, "In whatever field they were, they were affected in that field. They were different; and they saw things differently" (Roche, p 22).

Gindler kept careful records of her work, including hundreds of before-and-after photos, recordings of voices, films of people moving, anecdotal records, and her students' journals. These all were destroyed in 1945 when, one week before the liberation of Berlin, her studio went up in flames. All her papers, with the exception of one essay published in 1926, were destroyed. And, more tragically, a group of Jewish students whom she was hiding in her cellar, were forced to flee from the flames, were captured and murdered. Gindler found it hard to go on working after this, but was eventually convinced to do so by her surviving students.

Many teachers trained with Gindler, helping to establish the field we call bodywork today. Among the teachers who carried on and extended her work were Clare Nathansohn Fenichel in California, Sophie Ludwig in Berlin, Lotte Kristeller in Israel, Lily Ehrenfried in Paris, Elfriede Hengstenberg in Switzerland, Emi Pinkler in Budapest, Charlotte Selver in California, and Carola Speads in New York. These, in turn, have taught and inspired further generations of bodyworkers and helping professionals. Among those who studied with Gindler were both the first and second wives of Wilhelm Reich. Historian, David Boadella, has referred to the influence of Gindler's work on Reich's ideas about body armoring being a key element in character assessment. Boadella states that Reich only began to articulate these ideas after marrying his second wife, Elsa Lundberg, who energetically advocated Gindler's approach to him (Boadella, p 11).

Fritz Perls had been a patient of Reich and refers to Reich's ideas in *Ego, Hunger and Aggression*, the book he wrote with his wife Laura Perls in Capetown, South Africa in 1941. Ego, Hunger and Aggression was the first exploration of the theory that was later to be named Gestalt therapy. Part of the book was entitled 'Concentration Therapy', which recalls Gindler. 'The aim of my work is... the achievement of concentration' (Johnson, (Ed.), p 5). The new technique developed in Perls' book '... is theoretically simple: its aim is to regain the "feel of ourselves."... to awaken the organism to a fuller life' (1947, p 220).

Laura Perls Reflecting Gindler's Work

Central to our Gestalt heritage is the fact that Laura Perls was a student of Gindler's in Berlin in the early 1930s. It was at that time that Laura nursed and weaned her daughter, paying attention to and keeping notes on the physical and emotional details of the process, as Gindler urged her students to do.

The understandings Laura gained through her experiential study of nursing and weaning became core concepts in *Ego, Hunger and Aggression.* Laura wrote two complete chapters of that work, collaborating with Fritz on the rest of the text. The chapter "Concentrating on Eating," for example, bears comparison to Gindler's work with her students, as reported by Johanna Kulbach: "We worked on tasting and eating. We had zweibach. We took a very small bite and had it in our mouths and tried to feel what happened... I felt the texture and tasted the sweetness. A lot of sensations come through if you allow yourself time to really taste..." (Roche, p 17)

Once leaving Germany for South Africa in 1934, Laura changed her way of doing therapy, "I started to use face-to-face dialogue and body awareness..." (Rosenfeld, p 8). At that time, Fritz was still sitting behind patients who were lying on a couch. In Laura's book *Living at the Boundary*, there is a workshop transcript, sixty-one pages in length, containing twenty-seven examples of her work with body and breath awareness. This is not a "Gestalt and Bodywork" approach, but is a fully integrated, ongoing attention to body experience as part of the Gestalt therapy dialogue. As Laura says, "It's not use of the body... the point is to be a body" (1995, p 210). Laura's style was an integrated way of working where participants were encouraged to attend to their body experiences, to be 'somebody'.

In one exchange, Laura explains that in working this way, she "observes and deals with small things or what is usually taken for granted, what is called obvious, because it is in the obvious that resistances and difficulties are embedded" (1995, p 180). Laura said that "Resistance was assistance," reminding us that interruptions in contact had practical, self-preservative origins. These interruptions include muscular retroflexions and disruption of breathing patterns.

Similarly, Gindler "I have tried to show to what a great extent constriction is bound up with disturbances in breathing and these, once again, with disturbances in the psychic realm" (Johnson, (Ed.), p 12). Laura did not suggest that clients in her workshop "improve' their breathing, but rather be more aware of it." She continued, ".. any strong manipulation I would reject, because it tends to break through, to hit through a resistance without seeing that there is sufficient support when it is done" (1995, p 172). Again, Gindler: "Any correction made from without is of little value..."(Johnson, (Ed.), p 14).

Both Gindler and Laura Perls helped clients become aware of how they were interrupting themselves, with Laura taking the work further by helping clients discover what meaning interrupting had for them. Laura pointed out that support must be present for contact to take place. Here is Gindler on support: "For real standing, we must feel how we give our weight pound for pound, onto the earth..." (Johnson, (Ed.), p 13).

Language In Common

In reading the workshop transcript, I noticed that many of Laura's expressions echoed ones I had heard from Carola Speads when I studied the Gindler approach with her in New York from 1963 to 1995. Carola had been Gindler's teaching assistant from 1925 until 1938. In a published interview, Carola describes attending a workshop given by Gindler in 1955, after they had not seen each other for seventeen years: "I got there, and it was as if I had never left... After all those years, I found that she used the same comparisons and examples that I had come to use in my work in New York" (Johnson, (Ed-),p33).

Here is a list of some expressions Carola used in class in New York when teaching the Gindler approach:

- What are you aware of right now?
- Be curious about the details of what you are feeling.
- Be interested not only in what you do, but in how you are doing it.
- Let change occur on its own.
- Simply notice what is.
- How are you doing that right now? (In response to a student reporting muscle cramping.)
- It's an experiment; be open-minded.
- Accept what is available.
- No expectations.

Here are some expressions of Laura's from *Living at the Boundary*.

- No expectations.
- Are you breathing right now?
- Awareness of what is.
- What are you in touch with now?
- Take it as it comes, start with that.
- You experience yourself as a body... When you don't have that, you easily experience yourself as nobody.
- Paying attention....
- I work with the obvious.
- We can experiment

Fritz Perls' Awareness of Gindler's Approach

In 1947, Fritz Perls, having recently arrived in New York from South Africa, was trying to start a practice while at the same time taking lessons with Charlotte Selver, a former student of Gindler's. Selver is quoted in Jack Gaines' book, *Fritz Peris: Here and Now*: "He started to take private lessons with me... he asked me to work with him. He wanted me to take his patients before him and kind of open them up for what he wanted to work on with them later... a collaboration... I did not want to work his way"(1979, p 34).

In that same year, Fritz addressed the William Alanson White Institute in a talk entitled Planned Psychotherapy. In this speech, he said, "I recommend as necessary complementary aspects of the study of the human personality at least three subjects: Gestalt psychology, semantics,, and last but not least, the approach of the Gindler School" (1947/1979, p 22).

This remark was made four years before the publication of Gestalt Therapy. Laura states that Fritz already had part of the manuscript with him when he came to the United States. Here are the names of some of the experiments from Book 1 which strongly recall the work of Elsa Gindler: Attending and Concentrating; Sharpening the Body Sense; Contacting the Environment; Technique of Awareness.

Richard Kitzler described the process of group experimenting and discussion that led to the writing of die final manuscript of Gestalt Therapy during the early days of the New York Institute for Gestalt Therapy. Although Laura Perls' name does not appear as co-author on that book, he states that she was significantly involved in the discourse which led to its writing.

Here is a quotation from Paul Goodman's writing in Book 2 of *Gestalt Therapy*: "The complex system of contacts necessary for adjustment in the difficult held, we call ëselfí" (p 373). This sentence implies that self is ongoingly created by contact between organism and environment, and that self is experienced as activity. Not too different from that is Gindler's sentence written twenty---five years earlier. ."..by that I mean consciousness that is centered, reacts to the environment, and can think and feel... For me, the small word ëlí summarizes all this" (Johnson, (Ed.), p 6). Gindler's 1926 statement was unusual for its rime because it included environment as an essential part of experiencing "I" or self. To put it in contemporary words, both writers describe self as co-creation of organism and environment.

Conclusion

Work in somatic awareness, specifically that which was developed and taught by Elsa Gindler in Berlin in the 1920s and '30s, is an important part of the ground from which Fritz and Laura Perls developed Gestalt therapy. I have endeavored to illustrate how Gindler's method of guiding people to experience themselves and to speak about their experiences, revolutionary in its day, was fundamental to the way Gestalt therapy emerged. It is my hope that, along with phenomenology, Gestalt psychology and existentialism, "Arbeit am Menschen" will now be understood to be an essential part of Gestalt therapy's historical ground.

References

Boadella, D. (1997). Energy and Character. *The Journal of Biosynthesis*, 28,1, pp. 9-12.

Gaines, J. (1979). Fritz Perls: Here and Now. Integrated Press, Tiburon, CA, USA.

Gindler, E. (1927). Gymnastik for Busy People. *Sensory Awareness Foundation Bulletin*, 10,1, pp. 36-40.

Kitzler, R. (2001). Personal communication.

Johnson, D. H. (Ed.) (1995). *Bone, Breath and Gesture.* North Atlantic Books, Berkeley, CA, USA.

Joyner, P. (1993). Interview with Carola Speads. *Carola Speads: A Glimpse of Paradise*. Published privately, New York.

Perls, F. (1947/1992). Ego, Hunger and Aggression. Gestalt Journal Press, Highland, New York.

Perls, F. (1969/1993). A Life Chronology. *The Gestalt Journal*, 16,2, p 6.

Perls, F. (1947/Ed. 1979) Planned Psychotherapy. *The Gestalt Journal, 2,*2, pp. 4-23.

Peris, F., Hefferline, R., and Goodman, P. (1951). *Gestalt Therapy: Excitement and Growth in the Human Personality*. Souvenir Press, London.

Perls, L (1992). *Living at the Boundary*. Gestalt Journal Press, Highland, New York.

Roche, M. A. Interviews with Two Gindler Students. *Sensory Awareness Foundation Bulletin.* 10, 1, pp. 14 -24.

Rosenfeld, E. (1982). A Conversation with Laura Perls. An Oral History of Gestalt Therapy. Gestalt Journal Press, Highland, New York.

Speads, C. (1981). Interview. *Somatics*, Spring/Summer 1981, pp. 10-13.

Speads, C. (1977). Physical Re-education: What it Is and What it is Not. *Somatics*. Spring 1977, pp. 21-23.

Speads, C. (1978). *Ways to Better Breathing*. Healing Arts Press. Rochester, VT, USA.

Chapter 19. Lesbian Tomboys and "Evolutionary Butch"
Lee Zevy

Chapter introduction

From the beginning Gestalt therapy has always treated sexuality as an organic creative process that was often interrupted by the constraints and forces of societal definitions and repression. In keeping with this philosophy homosexuality by and large, was considered as just another form of sexual experience. Although there was little focus on understanding developmental process, therapy, particularly by the lesbian and gay practitioners who flocked to join this welcoming community, modeled new relational and environmental possibilities for deeply wounded, fearful clients. Gestalt therapy and other new humanistic/experiential therapies with their focus on an experiential phenomenological field considered sexuality within a more fluid human context. These new modalities co-committently arising out of the social/academic changes of the seventies and eighties helped to reconfigure the entire discussion and process of sexual and gender identity development.

In the early days of this new revision of sexual identity labels were fairly binary in nature; straight/gay and gay (male)/lesbian were the predominant definitions delineating the larger categories with butch/femme seen as a further refinement of the sexual roles women were thought to play. Bisexuals were thought to be inhibited homosexuals who had not yet come out and sexual reassignment in the form of transsexuals who had actually changed their gender was a poorly understood feared phenomenon and considered pathological. Understanding psycho/sexual development on any level vis-a-vis homosexuality was usually through a traditionally psychoanalytic lens that was grounded in various misogynistic concepts.

The explosion of writing by feminists, LGBT authors, scientists and others in mental health from the 1970's through today coupled with the individual freedom to reinvent and live according to internal representations previously unheard of not only changed the entire view of sexuality but supported the permeability of human boundaries on all levels. For decades now, gender and sexual creativity has been occurring very rapidly within certain communities and very slowly in others. Within this reality, theoretical writing often captures the ground of only a moment in time and place before there are additional permutations and combinations.

This article, "Lesbian Tomboys: Evolutionary Butch," braided personal experience, Gestalt therapy theory and practice with lesbian psychological development. It was written to shift previously held views on the rigidity of sexuality and role formation for lesbians and to move the thinking to include a lifetime trajectory that is fluid and changing in response to relational and environmental possibilities and constraints. Although the boundaries relating to transgression are no longer viable for many lesbians who grow up in accepting environments society at large has a long ways to go and many in the LGBT community still face unique stressors. Lesbians seek psychotherapy in the hope of finding a relational mirror that will move them on a path toward understanding and integration. Hopefully this article will help.

Lesbian Tomboys and "Evolutionary Butch"[99]

Summary. Lesbian tomboy development occurs within a psychosexual experiential field on a continuum from childhood gender dissonance to "evolutionary butch" in adulthood. Through the process of integrating gender development, sexual orientation, and identity development, tomboy lesbians learn how to maintain a sense of self and organize desire within a complicated familial/socio/cultural/context. Traversing these complications usually brings adolescent and adult lesbians into therapy where they need clinicians who under this unique course of development.

Keywords. Lesbians, tomboys, sexuality, gender, gender identity, therapy

Introduction

Lesbian tomboy development occurs within a psychosexual experiential field from childhood gender dissonance to "evolutionary butch" in adulthood. Unlike heterosexual tomboys whose tomboy qualities diminish or refocus at puberty, the lesbian tomboy journal to adulthood is a complicated pathway, one having few or no role models to assist in integrating gender and identity with sexual orientation into a whole organization of self and desire. Without adequate mirroring of role models, lesbian tomboys maintain desire, capability, and power sub Rosa through fantasy, heroic imitation, and inchoate longing. In adolescence and adulthood as lesbian tomboys come out, these early forms of desire can be externalized and shift from fantasy and inchoate longing into conscious sexual awareness and experience. This process of integration occurs through the experiencing of various fluid forms of being, a process I call "evolutionary butch."

Although much of this process may be manifest through the assumption of various roles as performance play, they are tried and examined in the service of the development of a more defined integrated sense of a lesbian self. Since lesbian psychological development can be so traumatic because of a social, cultural and familial homophobia (in addition to the confusions of sorting out gender, identity and sexuality), many lesbians turn to psychotherapy at some point in their lives in an effort to find ways to understand these complicated processes and untangle the healthy creative aspects from those that are rigid and may be a response to the lack of choice or a sign of early trauma. Yet because of the unique quality of this experience, clinical understanding is often too narrowly defined to accommodate the fluid creative adjustment necessary to evolve from lesbian tomboy to "evolutionary butch." Understanding this experience will not only

---

[99] This was originanlly published n Lesbians, Feminism, and Psychoanalysis: The Second Wave; Judith M. Glassgold and Suzanne Iasenza (Eds.)The Haworth Press; 2004, co-published simultaneously as Journal of Lesbian Studies, Volume 8, Numbers 1/2 2004.

expand the potential for treating this population, but will go a long way toward opening up a clinical perspective that views all forms of sexuality in a more creative fashion.

Tomboys and Social Construction

As a rule, tomboys occupy an imagined space created by diverse cultural and familial definitions of gender. The term according to the *Compact Oxford English Dictionary* (1994), which became defined in the late 16th century, originally meant a rude, boisterous boy, and then evolved into a "ramping, frolicsome, rude girl." As "cultural rebels" resisting social restriction, Secrist (1996) maintains that tomboys are able to manipulate this more fluid space existing between the gender determinations for both girls and boys. In this way, they create new possibilities containing excitement and risk for the girl who dares being the ongoing creator.

In societies or families where assertive attitudes and behavior are seen as a factor in success at sports or business, the acquisition of male attributes in young girls merits praise and encouragement and the space between male and female is extended. Yamaguchi and Barber (1995) contend that because tomboyism is often patronized and devalued, it has often been overlooked as a valuable place for learning for girls. Girls not only learn the nurturing and social skills that will gain them acceptance into a female world. Girls, also by imitating boys, learn about adventure, activity, irreverence, fighting, competition, and bonding. These tools acquired from this period of their life will translate into power, mobility and visibility, and adult forms of achievement and satisfaction.

Although, the space can be very limited or quite open as determined by cultural norms for behavior, dress, role and function, as long as the tomboy exists in play and imagination she is relegated to a place of little significance because it is usually regarded as a "phase, a condition that girls pass through on their way to growing up and becoming women" (Yamaguchi & Barber, 1995, p. 13). The difference, between those tomboys who will grow up to be heterosexual, or even femme lesbian, and tomboy lesbians, is a difference in intensity of the need to use and manipulate space to match the boys and men who are being used as models. These models are used not only in terms of the eventual attainment of relationships with woman, but also as examples of power, capability, and agency, which will support organic need. Contrary to what Harris (2000) maintains, that genders are constructed and exist only in terms of social matrix, almost all societies as they are currently constituted, are constructed as binary male-femaie systems and lesbian tomboyism is not a "soft assembly." Underlying all the external imitation and activity; sexual/emotional desire for women fuels this process providing the energy behind the unconscious longings that become manifest in a different form from those tomboys for whom tomboy life is not as intensely goal" driven.

For example, one client reported anonymously that as a child, she would wheel her doll carriage to the ball field, then play games, and run with the boys, and when she was finished, she would wheel her doll carriage home and play dolls with the girls. For another woman, a tomboy lesbian, playing with dolls was unthinkable. She would, against family prohibition, sneak out a pair of high top sneakers, run without a shirt with a gang of boys who were her buddies and steal her father's fencing swords to play pirate capturing the princess as a reward.

Tomboys are allowed by adults and boys to exist. In a previous article, Zevy (1999) notes that being a tomboy means that a girl has left the safety and security of socially expected behavior and entered a creative but potentially dangerous play space, a "warning zone" whereby she can create herself as long as she is wary of approaching the dangerous boundaries designated as "all male territory." The degree to which a tomboy will be tolerated or disliked is the degree to which she attends to and keeps a distance from the boundary of all male behavior that is always bound up in sexuality and the male ownership of sexual difference.

Creed (1995) has pointed out that historically, the penalty for role transgression has ranged from admonition to death, and is tied to genital differences between men and women. Up until the 1700s, only a one-sex model was thought to exist, with the ovaries and vagina being thought of as undescended testicles and penis. "Given the concentualization of a woman's body as thwarted male body and the clitoris and labia as penis and foreskin, it is no wonder that desire was also thought of as masculine" (Creed, 1995, p. 91). Once it was discovered that two sexes did in fact exist, Freudian theory (1931/61), based on the principal that biology is destiny, determined that women were psychologically castrated males and, by defining the point by moving the site of pleasure for the "mature" woman from the clitoris to the vagina, preserved once more, through the differences in physiology, the boundaries of gender. It was only in the 1970s that, in Western thought, these ideas gradually changed to include physiological difference and sexual parity for both men and women.

In keeping with this shift in understanding in Western thought the role of tomboy-for girls who become heterosexual at least-has broadened considerably. In many places gender role rigidity has been reduced, and has been replaced by mutual success and independence for both sexes in many areas of significance. In contrast, Desquitado (1992) offers quite a different perspective, one that dominates in many parts of the world, when she writes of the Philippines where the word tomboy means lesbian, and girls are subject to the harshest limitations of gender role with dangerous consequences for minor transgressions. Regardless of the changes, paradigms for power continue to pervade human existence even where there is great laxity. For example, if one examines children's television with particular attention to action shows, even though women are now allowed to fight and join forces with men to best the enemy, they are only in rare exceptions allowed to be in the top power role. The alpha position is always accorded to a man. Although the play space may have changed, the boundaries now require more vigilance because they are now so variable.

Lesbian Tomboy Development

Although positive changes have meant greater equality for heterosexual tomboys, for lesbian tomboys who by definition transgress the boundaries of sexual difference the situation is still quite different. Although it is usually a given for heterosexual women who wish to attract men and marry that they relinquish or refocus many tomboy freedoms in adolescence, for tomboy lesbians it is precisely these traits that will guide their sexuality. Even though the boundaries of lesbian tomboy life are defined by sexuality, a word that always conjures up transgressive play and potential sexual transgression, that period of childhood is still regarded as an asexual time. Tomboy as a constructed category signifies a presexual time, demarcating nonthreatening masculine behavior before it signifies a change to lesbianism, a warning space perhaps that designates an approach to "Biblical abomination."

However, although the term tomboy is socially constructed, theories of lesbian development that focus on social constructionism are insufficient. For example, the difficulty with using Kitzinger's (1987) ideas of the social construction of lesbianism is that like the construction of tomboy, as a category, it is too limiting to explain a lesbian childhood where lesbian sexuality is a continuum from childhood to adulthood. Although it is quite clear that labels are socially constructed, the notion-that lesbianism is only constructed by cultural definitions leaves out the genetic, biological and psychological aspects of sexuality that are specific to lesbian development.

All sexual development, including lesbian, begins in infancy, continues throughout the lifespan, and is bound up within a matrix of emotional reciprocity containing desire, admiration, adoration, specialness, pleasure, understanding, reflection, and excitement. A theory of lesbian sexual desire that begins around adolescence and object choice is inadequate to explain lesbian sexual development. Such a theory excludes those lesbians who evolved defined as lesbians with a recognized masturbatory sexual object choice from their first memories; those whose early lesbian sexuality, also sometimes masturbatory, was expressed through heroic fantasy; those whose sexual `Orientation developed within intense exclusively girlhood friendships and inchoate yearnings; or those women who retained pleasurable memories of infant female connection that led to lesbian relationships later in life. Many tomboy lesbians report quite early that they were aware of their own sexuality through masturbation and childhood sexual games and that it was directed toward girls and women (often baby sitters, neighbors, and teachers). During these games, they were always the male counterparts of a female role having limiting heterosexual choices to imitate. Later on, at latency, sexual experimentation with girls was not a pathway toward relationships with men, but was usually a painful experience of being outside and feeling that something was wrong with them.

The desire to be desired by someone who one desires is a need originating at birth when reciprocated desire between maternal figures and children begins. Wrye and Wells (1994) illustrate how maternal erotic desire forms the foundation of the experience of sexual desire and is always embedded within nurturing and caretaking.

> The beginning of relating is evident in babies as young as three days: they show distinct preferences for their mothers and select by smell the breast pads of their own mothers ... Much attention has been given to the sensual bonding of feeding, bathing, cooing and holding the first year of life ... this sensual, erotic attachment proceeds developmentally and included reciprocal visual, tactile, olfactory, taste, and auditory behaviors, cues and fantasies." (Wyre and Wells 1994, p.34)

Wells and Wrye further elaborate upon the eroticism involved with daily care through the exchange of fluids and bodily contact and further stipulate that. "the early sensual bond between mother and baby ... becomes the basis for all loving relations and all eroticism ... " (1994, p. 34).

Although most psychological theory insists that in normal development girls must relinquish the maternal figure as an erotic object and transfer these needs to fathers and eventually other men, some feminist analytic work, namely Benjamin (1988) and Chodorow (1918) argue that theory should be more inclusive of the maintenance of maternal erotic love throughout life. However, even these current positive developments to not take this idea far enough, beyond heterosexuality, into what seems to be another logical theoretical extension, that of lesbian development. While the relinquishing of the mother is often an inadequate substitute for heterosexual women, for the lesbian child it is confusing and harmful as she tries to integrate an erotic representation of self and other into the physical/emotional experience of daily life.

The requirement that children relinquish the maternal erotic object is reinforced repeatedly as most children are predominantly exposed to media images of a one-dimensional heterosexuality and taught a similar brand of gender appropriate social/sexual behavior. The recognition of lesbian identity for girls who felt "different" from early childhood does not always occur, as is usually thought, at the point where object choice is consciously identified. This felt "difference" is actually a continuous and changing process from early childhood onward, as recognition of how one is like or not like others within a kaleidoscope of changing images brings into focus new realities of self and other. Each time a fragment of mirror is twisted a new pattern of recognition occurs as multiple representations in turn are experienced and then dissolve into new possibilities of identity. For girls who will become lesbian, tomboy is simply part of the evolutionary process of establishing that within a gendered world sexual/emotional excitement will be directed toward women and that one's active relationship to the world, embedded in a concept of self and identity reflecting this reality, will be altered in both subtle and profound ways to accommodate this desire. As Harris aptly points out, "both agency and masculinity still come from the father" (2000, p. 243) and if these qualities are prized by women then imitation and appropriation of these qualities will begin much earlier in life than has been acknowledged.

Tomboy is an adult appellation for that prepubescent period where tomboy lesbians can learn to negotiate the shifting spaces between excitement' activity, and danger before they become sexually active as adults. Within this period lesbians try on all sorts of male/female combinations trying to arrive at workable images that are acceptable to those significant adults while preserving the integrity of self. Some lesbians, like Feinberg (1993), incorporated masculinity in all aspects suffering great hardship, while others wore their hair and dressed in feminine attire, but ran with the boys for games, activity and fun, fitting in externally and resisting internally. In actuality, tomboy life is never simple, stories of early lesbian development vary considerably from woman to woman as the contingencies of cultural location, familial identity, and individual need intersect. Julie Penelope makes this point when she writes,

> I decided that something I'd done in a past life (my karma) had dictated that I would spend my life as a male soul "trapped" in a female body, as punishment for some transgression ... I was uncomfortable with my femaleness (at least what I was told I was supposed to be as a "female") because I couldn't accept the weakness, passivity' and powerlessness that such "femaleness" required. Since I refused to be "female," as I understood it, I concluded I had to be male." (1992, p. 6).

Penelope clearly points out a child's understanding of the internal and external meaning of transgression, clearly illustrating how the creative adjustment to such a closed system can recreate again other bounded systems that at the time seem freer hut ultimately imprison. Since boundaries can be both defined and amorphous, a developing skill in lesbian tomboy life is to develop, most often through painful trial and error, sensitivity to approaching transgression. However, an intrinsic problem for lesbian tomboys is that because they can only perceive and imitate boy behavior from an external vantage point they are caught unawares when that behavior reveals the internal physical/emotional/sexual male experience that dictates male behavior.

One client reported that as a young girl, she would hang out only with the boys and they would roam around the neighborhood and into the woods and fields. She was accepted into the group, and looked, acted and played as they did. One day they were heading through a field to a creek when they encountered an older group of boys. One of the boys made a sexual reference to her and suddenly her group was laughing and shifting loyalties. She was suddenly alone in a recombined larger group of jostling, sexually bonded boys. She ran home alone; recognizing that what she thought was acceptance was only skin-deep.

Stories abound in Mullins (1995) book of lesbian tomboys who trespassed and were punished with violence and actual or threatened sexual domination. Yet, learning to negotiate these sexual systems early in life is a skill that paves the way for adult lesbian who will have an easier time maintaining their adventuresome spirit as the ground of safety and danger in lesbian life shifts. In keeping with cultural prohibitions toward lesbian sexuality, Zevy (1999) describes how lesbian tomboys secretly develop other skills that help them maintain their erotic/emotional desire through childhood into adolescence and adulthood when they can officially "come out."

Living within a heterosexual matrix, they must negotiate an "outsider position," while at the same time holding on to identity and desire, and maintaining often competing relationships with enough flexibility to meet ongoing needs. Then these lesbian tomboys must find adults or images to model where freedom of desire is expressed and realized. These models in childhood used to require the acquisition of behavior of heroic male figures whose attributes would be transposed into female role, but now a sufficient number of female role models exist, although because of the paucity of examples of lesbian desire the search continues. In addition to the search for models, lesbian tomboys need to develop emblems, scripts, and symbols of a future fantasy life that will help project them out of a heterosexually embedded childhood into a future where desire and longing (conscious or unconscious) of being sexually desired by a woman can be realized. All of these skills are braided into the creation of an internal gendered representation of maleness/femaleness that will evolve over the period from childhood through adolescence and eventually in adulthood transform the lesbian tomboy into some form of "Butch."

"Evolutionary Butch"

For lesbians, "Evolutionary Butch" like sexuality in general, is a complicated multidimensional creation that continually reinvents itself over the lifespan. Unlike most of the literature, such as Vance (1992) and Stein (1993), that portrays butch as a unitary entity or as submerged within the Butch/Femme dyad, butch evolves not only within culture but also internally and externally within the individual. Since cultural constructs change as society changes in its flexibility toward sexuality in general, the understanding of butch has split many times in language, meaning, and activity. In the 50s, for example, when lesbian social existence dictated that one had to be butch or femme, the range for butch was limited to hutch, bulldyke, bull dagger, diesel dyke, dyke, stone butch, truck driver, etc., all close approximations of certain limited types of maleness. Today, there are as many names, incorporating both masculine and feminine aspects, as there are combinations, each one designating a variation of the theme. Although these new images of Butch are more narrowly focused, they can be traversed more easily as individuals change and grow. These new names range from babybutch, bois (gender identity leaning toward male), guppies (designated by Materialistic acquisition, dykes, queers, and the even newer labels of psychobutch, powerbutch or blazerdyke. Then there are the many categories signifying trans (transgender) and the possibilities of transexual so that the variations have become endless. Contrast these multiple categories with the concept of femme, which up until very recently was a single entity to which power femme and `barracuda have now been included. It is clear how these inventive names, as performance, mirror cultural constructs, but do not truly signify the intensity of organic drive beneath. Butch, as an internal representation of the continuum of masculinity, is not an appropriation of maleness, but a transformation of maleness into female form incorporating aspects of both in highly inventive and changing ways. Schwartz makes the point that "A `butch' woman, a man in drag, calls into the question the very nature of the binary gender system and destabilizes phallic privilege" (1998, p. 30).

In doing so, Schwartz challenges butler's (1990) notion that the gendered body is largely performative existing on the surface of the body. Halberstam (1994) also limits the conception of butch to a superficial reading, "Butch is a belief, a performance, a swagger in the walk; butch is an attitude, a tough line, a fiction, a way of dressing" (1994, p. 226). She further fragments lesbian development when she writes, "The postmodern lesbian body is a body fragmented by representation and theory, overexposed and yet inarticulate, finding a voice finally in the underground culture of zines and sex clubs" (Halberstam, 1994, p. 226). The notion that "gender is created as fiction" (Butler, 1990) is too insubstantial to explain the layered facets of "evolutionary butch" development leading to an internal sense of self from which performance, as play, leads fun and excitement to a committed way of life. In a female form and separated from femme; butch takes on its own new meanings. In its external form butch can be a style of dress; attitude, sexual stance, activity, action, and means of relating to the world. Internally, as part of self and core identity, butch can bind the shaded meanings of male/female into other forms until an integration of internal/external experiences of power, capability, and sexual entitlement provide a substantive ground that will support life experience. During this process these creative forms can vary widely ranging from designating various body parts as male or female; inventing new names for what one is. One client disclosed creating a completely new image; she declared that she was a third sex because the male/female categories did not fit.

Although many of these forms are temporary in nature dissolving and reforming as the need arises, others are more enduring having been established in childhood and arising out of biological predisposition and personality in

344

combination with familial and social learning. The categories and labels of butch individuals apply to themselves are ways of externalizing internal desires, so that a means is created whereby internal representations of self can be brought into a social/relational field and tweaked through exploration and experimentation. Tomboy lesbians grow up being defined by externally determined boundaries so that until adulthood they are in a process of resistance to what does not fit. It is only after "coming out" in adult life that the freedom exists to create their own definitions of self, and it is often a complicated process to untangle the healthy creative aspects of these combinations from those that are rigid and developed because of the lack of choice or in response to trauma.

Because lesbians tend to be hidden or restricted during adolescence they often learn about dating and relationships after coming out through serial relationships. This process, in combination with role experimentation, new friendships, and community paves the way for awareness to develop in regards to psychological inhibitions and anxieties that may be a part of a fear of being gay or an indication of early trauma that block greater fulfillment. For this reason at some point in the search of psychological meaning and the need for a witness, most lesbians turn to therapy.

Therapy

Therapy has been a route many lesbians have sought to untangle the confusions derived from such a complicated path. Although the psychiatric nomenclature changed in the 1970s to remove homosexuality as a diagnostic category, the current Diagnostic and Statistical Manual's (4th Edition, 1996) diagnosis of Gender Identity Disorder equates the evolution of "Butch" with pathological process. Although most non-lesbian therapists no longer see homosexuality per se as pathological, they are not yet familiar with the evolutionary process of sexual identity formation in all its shadings, nor are they familiar with the language and action of female-to-female sexuality as a multifaceted experience. Schwartz describes a common experience. "One particular identification that surfaces often but not exclusively among lesbians is the feeling that they are "not female like (their) mothers." Then these "Identities based on being not female like (their) mothers often coincided with negative body images, as their bodies are perceived to be out of synchrony with gender stereotypic icons" (1998, p. 11).

Initially, many lesbians enter therapy to reconcile this dilemma and supported by the weight of psychotherapeutic theory, believe that if they reconcile their "feminine" side the problem will be solved, but this approach does not go far enough nor deep enough toward the formation of new individual representations. The process of separating from gender stereotypes is the work of becoming lesbian, but after separation when adult sexuality and relationship occur new needs arise, those that are often unfamiliar to the therapeutic community.

Two experiences reported anonymously by a "butch" lesbian, who had been in a successful long-term therapy with a male analyst, offer examples of the kinds of therapeutic ruptures that emanate from a lack of knowledge and a more traditionally distant stance. In the first example, she reported a dream she brought into therapy one day describing that she is seeing a soft cloth striped in many soft colors lying in a cart with other fabric; the fabric is bunched and raised in the center. The therapist interpreted the image as phallic, but the client said she laughed and pointed out, it was clitoral, and the cloth was about women. At that point, she needed him to mirror the softer feelings, emerging out of the toughness she usually expressed, and which were reserved for her relationships with women.

Although the dream had multiple meanings embedded within a variety of affectual responses, the client restricted her discussion of them because the therapist could not move away from traditional theory. More importantly, he could not accept the softness she was trying to give him as a way of deepening the intimacy of the therapeutic relationship. Many approaches would have opened the discussion to include the meaning of softness of both the cloth, and its colors; the many colors might have represented gender, role, and identity possibilities that she was experimenting with at that time. A helpful response might have been for him to say, "That's a wonderful dream, so soft and colorful it must have a lot of meaning for you about your feelings for women."

In the second example, she reported that the therapist came in with two fingers bandaged and the client said, laughing, "that would be my form of castration." The therapist did not respond but sat and waited. At that time, she was trying to open a dialogue about her sexuality. Although she already had a successful ongoing relationship, she felt fearful that he would be angry and shaming at any overt attempt at bonding with him over a commonly held desire. Kaufman and Raphael note, "To proclaim oneself openly as gay is, above else, to come out of shame-profoundly, to break the silence. This is why the term 'coming out' is a shame metaphor" (1996, p. 11). In both of these situations the therapist was not aware of the subtleties of shame and discomfort in regards to her relationship with him that were the foundation of these disclosures. It was not that she was questioning her sexuality, which had been laid to rest before she came into therapy, but she was trying to find a way to bring her intense pleasurable feelings about women out of hiding, and she needed him to understand and help her.

Without a warm inclusive response, the sexual meaning along with its concomitant affect and potential symbolic representation was not encouraged to emerge using mirroring and attunement, and the opportunity was lost. In addition, the therapist could have just moved beyond what he thought he already knew and simply joined her in her fun of the moment. What the therapist was not aware of was the way in which in both of these situations, the client was approaching what was for her a boundary of potential transgression, testing the limits of safety and danger and looking for a way to discuss deeper meaning with someone, whom she already knew from previous allusions loved women as she did. Many areas of lesbian life relate to the holding on to desire and sexuality within a foreign system and most lesbians initially feel therapists to be part of that foreignness. They come to therapy with a hope that this time they will find a person who can help them heal the split between their outsider" position and the "foreign" culture.

Significant issues like that of the "closet," or "coming-out-of-the closet" are poorly understood by non-gay/lesbian/bisexual therapists. These issues are very meaningful parts of everyday lesbian and gay life where clothing and attitude play important roles in the creation of agency and competency. Thus, therapists often fail to examine the meaning of creating an image that supports identity. Falco (1991) addresses the differentiation that must be made between lesbian identity (who am I as a gay person), lesbian sexual activity (who do I sleep with), lesbian erotic interests (where are my sexual fantasies, day-dreams and `excitements directed), and lesbian attachments (who do I actually have relationships with). Understanding these differences would offer a deeper knowledge of lesbian life as well as the interplay between these important issues. Because so much of the theory about homosexuality is based on pathological functioning, as evidenced by works like McDougall (1980), therapists, who have not read the more recent lesbian affirmative work (O'Connor & Ryan, 1993; Glassgold & Iasenza, 1995; Mageec Miller, 1991; Schwartz, 1998), often mistake the interweaving of fear and desire and the ways that these are overcome through fantasy and sexual play as problem signs. They often fail to see the ways in which altered states of consciousness using costuming, fantasy, and sexual games are creative tools that help lesbians and gay men overcome fear and anxiety and propel them forward into the realization of sexual contact and relationships. For lesbian and gay therapists, a problem can occur if the specific individual meanings are missed because of the use of shared terms and culture.

Even where clients are able to discuss their lesbianism it is often accompanied by diminished emotion and limited relatedness (poor eye-contact, uncomfortable body movements, avoidance of contact) because of the level of fear and/or a first time experience of bringing themselves into dialogue with another person. The fear and shame cannot be underestimated. A lesbian acquaintance, who had recently gone into therapy, described how as late at the 1980s and 1990s she would lie on the floor with her ear to the radio and play the gay station very softly so her family could not hear.

In another example, a butch lesbian colleague reported a dream to a male analyst in which she is eating a melted tuxedo cat with a spoon. He sagely asks, "What does eating pussy mean to you?" She is delighted he is giving her permission to enter into dangerous territory, but cannot reveal this to him because she would be in open competition with him (she knows he is heterosexual) and becomes flustered with excitement and fear. He is unaware of how thrilled yet endangered she feels as she backs away. Erring again on the side of traditional analytic unintrusiveness, he does not create a safe foundation for her to continue to explore the dream. Instead, he could have asked how she feels about his comment or the dream elements; how she feels about oral sex with a woman; what the meaning of "cats" and "pussies" is to her; and how oral sex fits into lesbian life. However, the most important absence is that he does not offer to explore the nature of competition with him or men. In addition, she needed him to explore the transferential aspects of the dream where she felt she was melting because she was changing and was afraid she would be eaten up by him. She definitely felt that he offered her a supportive opening, but she needed him to enter the space between them with more active interest and to provide reassurance that he would not be angry, rejecting, or need to assert power over her.

Buloff and Osterman offer an explanation for the way in which a lesbian client might interpret silence by writing of lesbian childhood experience "Mirrored back are grotesque and distorted images reflecting back in words like perverse, sinful, immoral, infantile, arrested, inadequate or she --- no reflection at all silence invisibility (1995, p. 95). This is particularly meaningful for lesbian tomboys, and in particular, those whose mirrors became increasingly distorted the further out from convention they traveled.

Lesbians seek therapy to find new mirrors within safe environments in the form of therapists who not only encourage them to re-live the excitement of risk taking and the adventure of creating themselves, but who reflect back excitement, admiration, and approval. Bollas writes that, "Generative mutuality in human relations depends amongst other things on an assumption that the elements of psychic life and their different functions are held in common." If A talks to B about grief over the loss of a parent then he should be able to assume that B knows what grief is and will share A's problem with him." (Bollas, 1987, p. 157). Lesbians need to know that a therapist understands the elements of their psychic life, not simply as it is constituted emotionally in common human terms, but as it revolves around an erotic foundation existing from childhood that gives centrality to relationships with women. It is only within this kind of context, that the complexities of their experience will be revealed to them and the processes of self-creation will open and continue in new ways.

References

American Psychiatric Association. (1996). *Diagnostic and Statistical Manual of Mental Disorders* (4th ed.). Washington, DC.

Benjamin, J. (1988) *The bonds of love*. New York: Pantheon.

Bollas, C. (1987). *The shadow of the object: Psychoanalysis of unthought known*. New York: Columbia University.

Buloff, B. & Osterman, M. (1995). Queer retlections: Mirroring and the lesbian experience of self. In J. M. Glassgold & S. Iasenza (Eds.), *Lesbians and Psychoanalysis: Revolutions in Theory and Practice* (pp. 93-106). NY: Free Press.

Butler, J. (1990). *Gender trouble: Feminism and the subversion of identity*. New York: Routledge .

Chodorow, N. (1978). *The reproduction of mothering: Psychoanalysis and the sociology of gender*. Berkeley: Univ. of Caliifornia Press.
Compact Oxford English Dictionary (ZniJeiJ.). (1994). Oxford: Clarendon.

Creed, B. (1995). Lesbian bodies: Tribades, tomboys and tarts. In E. Groz & E. Probyn (Eds.), *Sexy Bodies: The Strange Carnalities of Feminism*. NY: Routledge.

Desquitado, R.M. (1992). A letter from the Philippines. In J. Nestle, (Ed.),

Falco, K.: L. (1991). New York: Brunner Mazel,.

Feinberg, L, (1993) *Stone butch blues*, Ithaca, NY: Firebrand Books.

Freud, S. (1961). Female sexuality. In J. Strachey (Ed. & Trans.), *The Standard Edition of the Complete Psychological Works of Sigmund Freud* (Vol. 21, pp. 223-243). London: Hogarth Press. (Original work published 1931).

Glassgold, J.M. & Iasenza, S. (1995). *Lesbians and psychoanalysis: Revolutions in theory and practice.* New York: Free Press.

Halberstam J. (1994). F2M: The making of female masculinity. In L. Doan (Ed.), *The Lesbian Postmodem* (pp. 210-228). New York: Columbia University Press.

Harris, A. (2000). Gender as soft assembly: Tomboy's stories. *Journal of Gender and Sexuality*, 1, 223-250.

Kaufman, G. & Raphael, L. (1996). *Coming out of shame: Transforming gay and lesbian lives*. New York: Doubleday.

Kitzinger, C. (1987). *The social construction of lesbianism*. London: Sage Publication

Magee, M. & Miller, D. (1997). *Lesbian lives: Psychoanalytic narratives old & new*. Hillsdale, NJ: The Analytic Press.

McDougall, I. (1980). *Plea for a measure of abnormality.* New York: International Universities Press.

Mullins, H. (1995). Evolution of a tomboy. In Y.L. Yamaguchi and K. Barbara (Eds.), *Tomboys: Tales of Dyke Derring-Do* (pp. 40-49). Los Angeles: Alyson.

O'Connor, N. & Ryan, J. (1993) *Wild desires and mistaken identities: Lesbianism and psychoanalysis.* New York: Columbia University   Press.

Penelope, I. (1992). *Call me lesbian: Lesbian lives, lesbian theory.* Freedom, CA: Crossing Press.

Schwartz, A. (1998). *Sexual subjects: Lesbians, gender and psychoanalysis.* NY: Routledge.

Secrist, J. H. (1996). Choices of midlife tomboys: A narrative study (girls, adolescents, and women). (Doctoral dissertation, University of California, San Diego, 1996). *Dissertation Abstracts International, Section A*, 57-04, 1881.

Stein, A. (Ed.). (1993). *Sisters, sexperts, queers: Beyond the lesbian nation.* New York: Penguin.

Vance, C.S. (Ed.). Pleasure & danger: Exploring female sexuality. London: Pandora Press.

Wrye, H.K. & Welles, J.K. (1994). *The narration of desire: Erotic transferences and countertransference.* Hillsdale, NJ: The Analytic Press.

Yamaguchi, L. and Barber, K. (Eds.). (1995). Tomboys: Tales of dyke derring-do. Los Angeles: Alyson.

Zevy, L. (1999). Sexing the tomboy. In M. Rottnek (Ed.), Sissies & Tomboys: Gender Nonconformity & Homosexual Childhood (pp. 180-198). New York: New York University Press.

Chapter 20: Exploring Intimacy-A Gestalt Therapy Approach
Perry Klepner

This chapter is special to me because it deals with the subject of intimacy, or as I like to express it, "in-to-me-see". This experience has been at the heart of the most important moments and decisions of my life. Discovering and developing my intimacy as an adult, an in-to-me-see with my self, enabled my loving relationships with others as well as my finding Gestalt Therapy and utilizing it in my life's work. Intimacy has been a fundamentally transforming, empowering experience in my life.

I also believe the subject of intimacy is integral to the growth and development of the NYIGT in the 21st century. The institute has been evolving from its 20nth Century founding with a charismatic authoritative leadership with a Council of Fellows. In the 21st century there is a changing local and world-wide membership of new members with their own ideas living in a new time and culture of this new century.

This has importantly involved contacting the novelty of these differences and questioning our needs, goals and mission. Who am I/we with this membership and our mutual membership together? These considerations and challenges are involved with intimacy. The Institute's members require new initiatives in communication; self/other understanding; and organizational identification as we, the membership, change and grow individually and are similar/different together, i.e., the "in-to-me-see" of an I and a you, organizing a we.

Exploring Intimacy — A Gestalt Therapy Approach[*]

Abstract: This article highlights intimacy as an essential aspect of human experience and in the context of the theory of Gestalt Therapy as a function of human self-regulation. Issues of practice are clarified by focusing on the sequence of contact making and withdrawal and boundary disturbances. Diagnostic and practice approaches are discussed along with case studies.

I became interested in the subject of intimacy as an issue for many clients in my practice. Sometimes clients had insight into their relationship issues and often they did not. They wouldn't be able to meet someone or an ongoing relationship would mysteriously fall apart. They were bright, intelligent, attractive and the "normal," "natural" process of meeting and getting to know someone and developing a relationship eluded them. I observed people feeling inhibited or unable to talk about sadness, joy, anger, fear and love; feelings of inadequacy and neediness; and issues of sexuality, wealth, poverty, aging, AIDs, illness, death and dying. I noticed how intimacy could be problematic for couples, friends, colleagues, children and parents.

In a broader cultural context, I began to see the roots of intimacy in the philosophic and cultural values and attitudes of our society. The Socratic ethos "Know thyself" and in Polonius's instructions to Laertes in Shakespeare's Hamlet, "This above all to thine own self be true and then it must follow as night the day that thou can'st not be false to any man." — themes valuing honesty, disclosure and self-awareness, a personal intimacy of knowing one's own personality or individuality, i.e. feelings, motivations, behaviors and values, comprising the personal, cultural background for being intimate. In contrast, the Puritan Ethic, rugged individualism and the attitude of "keep a stiff upper lip" foster inhibiting disclosure, physical touch, vulnerability, spontaneity and the expression of tender and loving feelings. I also observed how expectations and beliefs about intimacy were shaped by the romantic visions produced by the movie and television industries and still larger western economic, political, social and religious institutions which have economic, political and ideological agendas. These create idealized images of personal conduct, work, relationships, marriage and family which contribute to a culture comparison, self-consciousness and competitiveness which undermine personal spontaneity and self-esteem, discourage trust, sharing and cooperation, and foster personal frustration and feelings of inadequacy which inhibit people being intimate. In addition, I perceived intimacy issues in sexism, racism, class distinctions and homophobia

---

[*] I am indebted to Tema Fishbein, Herb Rosenzweig and my clients who inspired this article with their wisdom and courage being intimate. I am also grateful to my colleagues for their encouragement and thoughtful insights

which pit one group against another, are dehumanizing and alienating, and do not recognize human relatedness and interdependence. It was my hope that by better understanding what intimacy was I would be better able to work with individuals and couples with intimacy concerns.

The Meaning of Intimacy

Intimacy derives from the Latin word *intimus* meaning innermost. It's a common notion in the western languages: Spanish — *intimo*, Italian — *intimo*, French — *intime*, German — *innig*, refers to sharing one's innermost reality with another, a special knowledge that is personal, private, sincere, from the heart. *Webster's* defines intimacy as "Close confidential friendship. An intimate act; especially, illicit sexual connection: a euphemistic use." And Intimate as "Closely connected by friendship or association; personal; confidential. Pertaining to inmost being; innermost; in dwelling; intimate knowledge. Adhering closely. Proceeding from within; inward: internal: An intimate impulse. A close or confidential friend." (*New Illustrated Webster's Dictionary of the English Language*, p. 513, 1992) Another definition of the meaning of intimacy is one which derives its meaning from the components of the word itself as in: "in to me see." I like this since it identifies the self revealing nature of being intimate, its co-creation by a person disclosing and another perceiving.

Working to identify the particulars of intimacy further and allowing for uniqueness and variation between persons and cultures, I formulated some thoughts about intimacy:

The social nature of humankind involves intimacy as an essential ingredient. When infants are not touched intimately enough they don't develop but become ill and possibly die. When not touched enough and not made "intimate with" infants, children and adults are prone to be ill, withdrawn and cold. Indeed, persons who do not have qualities or capacity for intimacy present as somewhat less than human.

As social creatures humans act cooperatively utilizing capacities for communication, disclosure and trust to develop intimacy that avoids loneliness and isolation and fosters acceptance, companionship, mutual reliance and forgiveness that support survival and growth. Intimacy is learned and practiced throughout our lives as children, adolescents and adults and within family, cultural and national communities.

It's a different experience depending on context. Who is being intimate with whom, father and daughter, husband and wife, sister and brother, etc. People who are just getting to know one another are intimate and yet differently intimate than longtime acquaintances, family members and lovers. Also, intimacy is a different experience and means different things at different ages. Adult intimacy may exist in a variety of forms and settings such as love, friendship, family, and within collegial-professional, social, ethnic, religious, intellectual, economic, and political communities. People find a variety of contexts and activities promote intimacy such as talking, watching T.V., fishing and dinning together.

Intimacy does not only involve trust, caring and loving feelings. Intimate contact can include the full spectrum of emotional expressions including anger, fear, sadness, dissatisfaction and appreciation of differences with another. Intimate relations can have a context of mutuality, understanding, relatedness, respect and appreciation of other's unique qualities and life experiences, differences which support connection. Sharing one's personal knowledge with another and feeling understood and valued with similarities as well as differences is a basis for intimate connection and, ultimately, loving and being loved.

Intimacy can be narrowly defined as a heartfelt or innermost disclosure of one person to another or broadly defined to include nonverbal disclosures and indirect or distant connections. People have intimate experiences with pets, food, communities of people living in distant places, a national entity, the earth, the universe and God.

Intimacy is not part of all loving, caring and committed relationships. This is the case with parents, children, relatives or lifelong friends with whom many people feel strong caring, loving feelings and attachment but do not share their innermost thoughts and feelings. They do not consider these relationships to be intimate and often don't need or want them to be. Not all intimacy is desirable. Most people prefer to be intimate with a few people and some people are incompatible which precludes the desirability of intimacy.

Intimacy also has creative, artistic, social, and political implications. Having a value of introspective self-awareness, heartfelt authenticity and emotional experience, i.e., being "in touch," and disclosure to others, intimacy involves independent thinking, feeling and behavior. By exploring and developing one's personal aesthetic people develop increasingly sophisticated creative and individualistic identities. This breeds self confidence and supports freedom of thought and feelings of entitlement to individual rights for self-expression.

Intimacy in Gestalt Therapy

Gestalt Therapy, by Perls, Hefferline and Goodman, (1951) and the subsequent writings of Fritz Perls have been criticized for not emphasizing the interpersonal dynamic and issues of couples, long term relationships, families, children and group work. The often quoted poem by Fritz: "I do my thing and you do your thing . . . And if by chance, we find each other, it's beautiful. If not, it can't be helped." (Perls, 1969, p.1) is sometimes perceived as expressing unconcern for the interpersonal. Indeed, *Gestalt Therapy* emphasizes individual therapy and the achievement of an authentic and autonomous individual with capacities for differentiated feelings, thoughts and behavior. This reflects the emphasis of Perls and Goodman who, in 1950-51, were primarily concerned with the theory of contact and individual psychological change. They were attempting to get their ideas across in a largely hostile psychoanalytically dominant environment and the expression of angry aggressive feelings, rather than relational, intimate concerns, were better suited in work done by Fritz in demonstration workshops.

However, Gestalt Therapy was always part of the important reaction to pseudo intimacy. Its emphasis has always been authentic human experience, communication and relationship and these themes that are integral to intimacy are woven into the fabric of Gestalt Therapy. Contact, a central and unifying concept in Gestalt Therapy, has qualities essential for intimacy. Contact involves "being in touch" including approaching, understanding, manipulating in order to assimilate and make one's own. Self-awareness, the locus of Gestalt Therapy, is the recognition of one's innermost feelings, a personal "in to me see," and a necessary ingredient for interpersonal intimacy. References to humanity's social-cultural, biological and physical field, community, mutual dependency and social need for interpersonal disclosure, trust and love emphasize the social and dynamic components of intimacy. Indeed, the text is organized to integrate false splits which alienate persons from themselves and each other. (Perls et al., *1951, pp. 240-243, Vol. II, Ch. II, 5)* It makes a case for family and group therapy: "The disturbances are in the field . . . their essence in the felt-relation is irreducible to the parts. Thus, child and parents must be treated together. Or again, the lapse of community in political societies . . . is a disease of the field, and only a kind of group-therapy would help.. .all individual personality and all organized society develop from functions of coherence that are essential to both person and society (love, learning, communication, identification, etc.) . . . "(Perls et al., p. 354, Vol. II, Ch.IX, 2) Speaking of the hierarchy of values the text underscores the importance of intimate connection:." when actually is pressing, certain values oust other values, furnishing a hierarchy of what does in fact marshal brightness and vigor in its execution . . . Sickness and somatic deficiencies and excesses rate high in the dominance hierarchy . . . But so also do the need for love, someone to go out to, the avoidance of isolation and loneliness,." (Perls et al., p. 278, Vol. II, Ch.IV, 5)

Defining Intimacy in Gestalt Therapy

Intimacy can be seen, similar to other contact functions, as a self-regulating capacity of the individual that is the work of the self facilitating survival and growth. Intimacy is an integrative awareness of the relationship of the person and environment that provides essential information of the conditions of the field. Intimacy avoids loneliness and isolation, and supports forgiveness and acceptance that facilitate living in close proximity for safety and being nurtured. Similar to other human emotional experiences which orient and motivate us, such as anger which provides energy to understand and work through a frustrating obstacle or sadness which supports accepting the loss of something valued, intimacy promotes revealing oneself to another for social connection, companionship, mutual support and dependency, caring and potentially loving and being loved.

In terms of figure/background and contact intimacy involves an experience of closeness derived from understanding, valuation and trust, a whole of awareness, motor response and feeling forming a shared figure/ground. All intimacy requires contact. However, not all contact is intimate. Intimate contact involves the destruction of an existing figure and the creation of a new shared figure, an "I" and a "you" forming a "we." Intimate contact has observable properties providing autonomous criterion for its evaluation: clarity, brightness, unity, grace, fascination, completion, force of movement. As a boundary phenomenon it is a softening or melting of the contact boundary, a temporary, healthy confluence "as if" no boundary. (From, 1982) As figure/ground intimacy defines the parameters of a relationship with an understanding of what is acceptable closeness, sharing, trust and behavior.

Intimate contact is experienced differently depending on the complexity of figure/ground activity and longevity of the relationship. An "intimate moment" is one where knowing the other, being close, and experiencing a common or shared figure occur. This is a moment of intimate personal contact — "being in touch." An "intimate experience" involves a number of moments, comprising more complex implications for one's life in terms of meaningfulness and importance. Here the ground of the intimacy is more developed, involving more than a momentary experience. Lastly, an "intimate relationship" made up of many intimate experiences, involves even more mutual dependence, understanding and importance. The ground of shared experiences provides strength, durability and reliability enabling the relationship to withstand stressful events involving differences, disappointments and dissatisfied feelings. The relationship contributes to how people experience themselves and others, know who they are, what they need and how they will conduct themselves.

Relationship Phases and Their Interruptions

In analyzing people relating to others I have identified a series of phases people experience in developing intimate relationships. With each phase there are a number of challenges requiring capacity for experiencing feelings, understanding, responding, reaching out and adapting. I have found identifying where a person's intimacy with others is interrupted helpful for directing therapeutic work.

1. Meeting

In this phase a person approaches and interacts with others identifying areas of common and diverse interests accompanied by feelings of attraction, concern and compatibility or lack thereof. When there is an interruption in this phase a person doesn't meet people or has difficulty interacting with them. If there is an introductory conversation it wont involve an exchange of authentic and meaningful ideas or feelings. The interaction, if there is one, may involve a perception or feeling that the other is not really caring, listening and seeing them. The compulsively verbal person may come away with no lasting impression of the other or a temporary feeling of being enlivened by the conversation that quickly fades. There will not be an exchange of addresses or telephone numbers that would allow a follow-up contact.

2. Getting to Know the Other Person

In this phase people meet and become involved in learning about each other. They exchange feelings and ideas about themselves. They go on consecutive dates that involve a "getting to know the other," such as interests, histories, habits, preferences, styles of living. In this process they expand the boundaries of their self-disclosure and personal interest as they reveal themselves and learn about one another. As their ground of relatedness develops, they form understandings of one another identifying more detailed thoughts and feelings of their suitability. Interruptions in this phase commonly involve some perception that the other is not appropriate or compatible in some way.

3. Committing

In committing to an intimate relationship an individual vests him, her self by word, action or personal decision to be available through disclosure to another person, accepting feelings of caring and limitations of behavior such as to communicate one's innermost thoughts and feelings. Commitment involves sufficient involvement that the individual identifies himself inclusive of another. His, her "I" includes a "we" and within this integration his functioning proceeds. Laura Perls in her opening address at *The Gestalt Journal's Annual Conference* given May 17, 1985, referred to "The Woman in The Dunes." This is a parable about commitment. She states: "When you are really committed, it is for better or worse, for whatever may occur within the confinement of a situation; not only in marriage and family, but any relationship in which you have assumed responsibility, a profession, an art, a vocation, there is no way out. As long as our man in the story cannot accept the limitations of the situation, he feels trapped. When he accepts his confinement, possibilities within its boundaries become realities: the desert becomes fertile; the women a mother." In this parable Laura identifies the importance of commitment and with commitment the quality of "acceptance." That is, accepting one's personal identification inclusive of another, an "I" with a "we."

Interruptions in the committing phase sometimes occur as a last minute hesitation or panic. For example, the "final" commitment of getting married which has been popularized in novels and movies when the bride or groom panics and flees. Another interruption in this phase is pseudo commitment where the authentic commitment is avoided by a hasty or premature commitment that later is reconsidered.

4. Changing and Growing Together

Change and growth[100] is a complex process for an individual and even more so between people in intimate relationships whether lovers, family members, friends or colleagues. People develop continuously including interests, preferences, values and goals. Change and growth varies by environmental circumstances, genetic, physical, emotional, esthetic and intellectual capacities, sensitivities, learning experiences, life stage, the aging process, etc. As a result there are multiple opportunities for persons, especially young persons, to develop in different directions, in varying ways and rates from people they are intimate with. Both similarities and differences can make compatibility and intimacy more difficult or can be enlivening and nourishing as shared experiences that provide stimulating novelty, challenge, and opportunities for companionship and shared accomplishment. During this phase routines for communicating and resolving differences are identified and practiced and intimacy is developed as participants integrate their changing circumstances and personal growth with one another.

Interruptions in intimacy during this phase depend on individual preferences and capacities to assimilate personal and shared changing life experiences in a way that contributes toward a satisfying "mutual experience." In the "changing and growing together" phase personal capacities for independent functioning, creativity, insight, communication and intimacy enable people to change and grow similarly, differently and together. The capacity for mutuality derived from shared common and diverse experiences creates interest and excitement that can make growing and changing together vital and fulfilling.

The changing and growing phase involves individual change and growth in a context in which the participants are committed to being with one another. This involves the individual integrating individual needs and preferences, their "I," and the preferences and requirements of another, their "we." This integration is not always possible or accurate resulting in misunderstandings, confusion, being wrong, feeling hurt, resentful, angry and conflicted. Here the qualities of intimacy involving trust, understanding, valuation, forgiveness and acceptance function to support contact while differences are considered, evaluated and worked through.

---

[100] I am indebted to Tema Fishbein, Herb Rosenzweig and my clients who inspired this article with their wisdom and courage being intimate. I am also grateful to my colleagues for their encouragement and thoughtful insights

5. Intimacy with Differentiation and Renewal

In this last phase the emphasis shifts from establishing and maintaining an intimate relationship, a "we," with commitment and experience assimilating change and growth, to intimacy emphasizing the individual's evolving personal identity, their "I," and that of their intimate other. Where contact in prior phases emphasized organizing a shared experience, a "we," now involves reconstituting with one's emerging "I," along with new intimate contact. Now the individuals' become committed to intimacy as a process of individual and mutual growth and learn about themselves and one another in new ways. Their achieved intimacy strengthens and provides a more comprehensive supportive ground for the relationship while intimate contact in the present, including positive, negative and differing perceptions and feelings, makes the relationship vital, new and renewing. There is enjoyment of similarities as well as acceptance and appreciation of differences. This is "intimacy with differentiation" in which each person values their emerging experience as well as each others'. There is also "renewal" during this phase, i.e., the ability to find novelty, interest and involvement in shared interests and concerns. These attributes contribute to the participants' having feelings of confidence, satisfaction, and, at times, contentment in their achieved mutuality.

There are a number of ways interruptions in this phase occur. Without renewal of intimacy in shared satisfying experiences intimacy can become narrowly focused, static and dissatisfying with concomitant loss of interest and relevance. In the beginning of a relationship intimacy is energized by the excitement of the novelty and attractive caring, social, sensual and sexual appetites that motivate people to explore and know more about one another. However, over time the history, habits and interests of persons in relationship become known to one another and there is less novelty available from these sources. As a result, they can experience a decline in interest, involvement and satisfaction from "the same old intimacy," although there may be other feelings of connection, need, caring and love. However, in instances where intimacy is desired but not achieved, continued contact can cause painful feelings of "no contact." Ultimately, couples, friends or family members will a) discover how to renew their intimacy; b) will stay involved with satisfying, loving feelings but limited or no intimacy; c) will stay involved without enough intimacy and bear painful feelings such as anger, frustration, sadness, despair, resignation, stagnation and numbness; or, d) will separate.

People can also "lose touch" being intimate when day-to-day work and home routines and pressures overshadow and crowd-out being intimate. Also, emergencies may prompt people to limit intimacy as a defense against the anxiety of facing or discussing fears and concerns.

In addition, during this phase personal change and growth will continue. These changes may result in differences that are not compatible despite the participants accomplished intimacy, learned and practiced approaches for integrating change and their best intentioned efforts at resolution. Personal change and growth may require they redefine the basis of the relationship including limiting or circumscribing their intimacy, separating and, or ending the relationship. Here intimacy with differentiation emphasizes the individuality and authenticity of the participants as well as valuing the authenticity and intimacy of the relationship. Thus, recognizing the need to distance and agreeing to limit intimacy is also a way of being intimate, i.e., by recognizing and valuing differences, even incompatibility.

6. Closure

Closure occurs with completion of an experience. It is necessary for experiences to be finished so one can go on to new emerging interests and concerns. The ability to achieve closure involves all the phases as a potential difficulty or interruption in developing intimate relationships. For example, by suffering the loss of an intimate relationship and coming to accept the rejection, a person becomes available for meeting someone new. Lack of closure due to unfinished feelings, e.g., loss from death or hurtful rejection, can detract from being able to be fully present, disclose, trust, and commit in a new relationship.

Closure is also essential for people to assimilate their ongoing personal changes such as aging; mental, emotional, physical adjustments; circumstances of living; work and their partner's changes. Additionally, the relationship in which they originally fell in love, committed to and have been growing and changing from requires closure. If this does not occur the past achieved "we" can take the place of current contact, "living in the past," so to speak, versus a memory of shared experiences and accomplished growth that supports contact. Thus, closure enables participants to see and experience each other with a fresh, current perspective evoking interest and involvement.

Intimacy Issues for Couples

Difficulties relating intimately for long-term couples can present themselves in many ways. In addition to those mentioned above, there are the following:

1. As couples become familiar over time each partner gets to know the others private preferences and habits that are not shared with others. Although their is significant safety and support in the relationship, tolerances change and partners can become a source of injury to each others sense of adequacy and self-esteem from negative reactions and judgments to their private and, or public behaviors. These criticisms can result in partners' feeling deficient or "no good."

360

2. Long-term couples have an expectation of intimacy. When the expectation for intimacy is there and momentary intimate contact is not, there can be confusion and disorientation. Intimacy requires contact and needs to be distinguished from the state of a relationship which has a "ground" or "background" of intimacy but which at any particular moment does not involve intimate contact. This divergence can be experienced as a loss of intimacy. Also, in the midst of conflict involving hurt feelings, frustration, anger and even rage, these feelings may dominate the couple's consciousness so they are not conscious of the ground of intimacy in their relationship. They also do not perceive their conflict as a function of their accomplished intimacy which they are finely attuned to. They immediately sense its absence or jeopardy and are quick to fight for it. Instances of conflict may also involve confusing present experience with past experiences involving rejection, abandonment, betrayal and accompanying feelings of sadness, anger, fear and rage.

3. Over time couples may grow confluent assuming they know what the other feels and thinks. They lose a contact-boundary derived from awareness of their differences. This can mean they are "out of touch" and not really seeing and knowing their partner who has been changing. As a result there is a misperception, i.e., thinking they "know" the other and, therefore, not paying attention to them since what is "known" is normally of little or no concern. The result is taking the other for granted and a loss of intimacy. This can be startling, frightening and estranging when it is recognized in behaviors or statements in which partners perceive they are not understood and are having different experiences or perceptions about events and each other.

4. Over time the qualities that first attracted a couple to each other can become a source of conflict. Thus, an assertive strong-willed quality that is appreciated early in a relationship can become a characteristic that is criticized for being controlling and inflexible. This is sometimes difficult to identify but worthwhile examining when it reveals unfinished business, i.e., being controlling out of a fear of failure by one partner and the wish to be controlled so as to gain environmental support that is not available internally by the other partner. When ambivalent reactions are understood, they can be explored and responded to differently by both partners.

5. Growth over time is often not equal or synchronous. By synchronous I mean how a couple's work and life style preferences coincide or diverge. People change over time at their own rates and in unique ways. As a result, people may find their preferences, interests, styles and needs for living quite different over time. For instance, differing work routines and interests in politics, the arts or travel may mean quite different preferences or personal availability. These differences can cause difficulties in getting needs met, a lack of mutual interest and time for involvement.

I don't have a cookbook approach or prescribed standards of intimacy. Because people have personal styles and preferences as well as protect their vulnerable selves by limiting intimacy I don't try to make people different such as softer, warmer, social or more intimate. My approach will vary with the particular person, their available support and concerns. I rely on experimentation emphasizing moment-to-moment awareness, the phenomenology and quality of their experience, the clarity, brightness, sharpness, force and grace of their figure/ground formation, so as to facilitate their inventing and discovering new ways of experiencing strong feelings, clear perceptions and acting forcefully in their own behalf. I do not rush to judgment concerning a client's interpersonal manner or quality or suitability of their relationships. I am mindful that there is great variety in how people form and conduct intimate relationships. Each involves the unique personal composition of the individual's genetic/biological make-up, history and social-cultural field. These are the unique, creative, self-actualizing creative adjustments of the person.

My knowledge of intimacy, similar to all knowledge I bring to the therapeutic meeting of me and another, details the ground of my experience and helps me to perceive opportunities to respond in contact. I work with intimacy as much as the interest and support of the client makes intimacy appropriate as fertile ground for therapeutic progress. I will utilize my own capacity for intimacy to support my being at the contact boundary with the client. To be available and to meet the client where the client is. Being vulnerable myself, sharing personal and ongoing experience in the session I will practice being intimate, providing the client opportunity to explore closeness by experiencing the intimacy we have together. Further, my experience of the client's intimacy with me provides immediate feedback concerning the qualities of our contact and informs me of possible ways the client interrupts his, her experiences with others. I take growing intimacy with myself and others as a sign of the client's increased self support, capacity for contact and assimilation of the therapeutic experience.

Exploring an individual's experience of intimacy I emphasize moment-to-moment awareness in which we may discuss:

1. Past experiences of intimacy with families and influential events.

2. Present attitudes and reactions in their current experience of intimacy. Is it okay? What's missing?

3. Life story or script involving attitudes that influence behavior towards themselves and others. For example, how thinking of one's self as smart and attractive influences behavior and attitudes, planning a career, and how and with whom one is or isn't available or intimate.

4. Understanding other people's perspectives, motivations and reactions regarding intimacy in group and social encounters. This can help people recognize and understand differences as well as similarities between themselves

and others. Sharing experiences and understanding others is learning about and being intimate.

5. Engaging their spontaneous creative process using poetry, art, writing, fantasy, and visualization exercises that facilitate thoughts and feelings, i.e., "in to me see."

Exploring intimacy in interpersonal relations involves examination of inhibitions to intimacy, interruptions to contact making and withdrawal and mobilizing the individual's aggressive capacities. The healthy role of conflict and aggression has always been primary in Gestalt Therapy that works to undo fixed gestalts by integrating disowned capacities. Self-assertion to deconstruct the differences between individuals so as to acquire understanding and appreciation of differences is essential for intimacy. In Gestalt Therapy aggression is utilized to destroy barriers to intimacy, this is how an "I" and a "you" becomes a "we." Thus, love is revitalized by aggression that leads to a new synthesis between persons. Perls states: ". . . if the association of two persons will in fact be deeply profitable to them, then the destruction of the incompatible existing forms they have come with is a motion toward their more intrinsic selves, which will be actualized in the coming new figure; in this release of the more intrinsic, bound energy is liberated and this will transfer to the liberating agent as love. The process of mutual destruction is probably the chief proving ground for profound compatibility." (Perls et al., 1951, p. 342, Vol. II, Ch. VIII, 5) All the capacities of the self contribute to achieving intimacy, e.g., seeing, hearing, analyzing, evaluating, questioning, asking, telling, feeling and responding to needs and appetites for closeness, sex, love, soothing, melting into tender caring feelings, identifying with personal preferences for living and relating to others.

I may present concepts which help explain and focus the client's concerns. I may talk about phases of developing intimacy as "stuck points" or identify prominent feelings and attitudes as "invisible walls" to help clients think about and practice paying attention to their experience. I may explain that sometimes we are aware of them, often they are only partially or not known to us. While we can feel our anger or loneliness, we may not see how our anger or loneliness cause others to distance themselves or how others perceive we are distancing from them. They block ability to reach out, share and be emotionally and intellectually available to ourselves and others. I may refer to making "bridging statements" as expressions which convey a thought or feeling which help one feel closer and more intimate to another. I may pose an experiment of "speaking from the heart" to explore what that may feel like.

Examples of feelings, behaviors and attitudes which can limit intimacy include:

a. Feelings of shame, guilt, anger, depression, humiliation, emptiness, being burdened, sadness, self-pity; compelling feelings for love and sex, moodiness, hatred; loneliness.

b. Dreaded Events such as fear of abandonment, being engulfed, betrayal, being judged, hurting someone, impoverishment, saying the wrong thing, making a mistake;

c. Behaviors including being impulsive, provocative, seductive, tolerating others, withdrawing, silence, being confused, forgetting, being sick, keeping secrets, helplessness, being controlling, exaggerating, manipulative.

d. Attitudes, for example, having expectations which cannot be fulfilled, cynicism, belief in romantic myths, perfectionism, hopelessness, self-involvement.

These feelings, behaviors and attitudes present themselves in a variety of ways and are overlapping. For example, a person with standards of perfection and fear of personal adequacy experiences anxiety when being disclosing or learning about others. This person experiences chronic low-grade tensions which restrict emotional availability in, for example, the "meeting" and "getting to know you" phases. These tensions are achieved "creative adjustments" which serve to interrupt emotional pain, anger, fear, etc., from becoming aware. Over time such an individual is likely to grow wary and anxious about the disappointing experiences they've had and grow to avoid trying to meet someone altogether. In this case there is dread as well as perfectionism. This person may get stuck in the meeting phase in order to avoid the growing anxiety of further contact bringing rejection or failure. Here both perfectionism and habituated fear and anxiety of the past defeats the person's present appetites for social connection and love. Often these needs can be sublimated to another activity such as work or play, thereby avoiding the real conflict but giving some satisfaction and outlet for the frustration of unsatisfied needs.

I may work with language/communication limitations using experiments, modeling and explanation. The most common language people use in our Western culture is one which is descriptive. This involves describing something and is appropriate and well suited to a mechanistic and work oriented culture. However, descriptive language doesn't promote understanding and communicating feelings or having emotional needs understood and appreciated by others. Many people have learned to be uncomfortable with their feelings and experience stress when trying to know and express their needs. They have not had the communication of feelings adequately modeled and taught at school and home. To have a language of feelings one must be able to "feel" oneself, know what one's feelings are, know words which identify these feelings and be able to communicate them. Not using a language of feelings regularly, it is likely to become less familiar, feelings themselves become more alien and then they are more difficult to know and express.

There are other non-verbal communicative languages such as touch, movement, and art which express intimacy. For example, touch is also used in intimate relationships to communicate many subtle feelings of togetherness, separateness, caring, sadness, support, happiness, affection, sensuality, comfort, sexuality, anger, fear. Often touch is taken to be a sexual communication or is seen as too personal. Similarly, expressions of dissatisfaction are perceived as a basis for rejection and the reassuring holding of a friend's hand while communicating a dissatisfaction isn't considered. As with verbal communication, people's subtle sensitivities and capacities for touch, movement, play and art don't develop or atrophy if not utilized. As a result, they are less and less competent to know their feelings, words and physical actions to communicate them.

Intimacy and Interruptions to Contact

I have also found it helpful to consider the point at which contact is interrupted. (From, 1983) In examining interruptions to intimate contact I will consider:

a. Where in the contact sequence the interruption or loss of ego-function is occurring: at fore-contact, contact, final-contact or post-contact.

b. How the interruption is made — the mechanisms of retroflecting, projecting, demands for confluence, introjecting, egotism and their characteristic patterns.

c. The nature of the disturbance, i.e., a loss of ego-function caused by an id function or personality function disturbance.

By identifying characteristic patterns of where in the contact sequence a person loses contact I gain important direction as to when to be especially alert for suggesting an experiment or not. Secondly, by identifying how the interruption is made I gain direction as to how to intervene[3]:

A. When in the stages of the contact sequence the interruption occurs pattern a person's experience at any particular time. Interruptions in "fore-contact" result in vagueness to a person's perception and feelings. For example, fore-contact disturbances may include the person making scanning eye contact that avoids seeing or physically pulling back to avoiding possible touching. Persons with disturbed fore-contact may present as vague, fearful, confused, sullen or angry without apparent reason and, or awareness. They will fill the vagueness in their experience with repressed feelings thus limiting their capacity for intimate contact. Thus, the hypochondriac mistakes in fore-contact his body tension for illness rather than, for example, the excitement and anxiety of being with an attractive other person. Similarly, the hysteric experiences "love" or fear instead of feeling her, his interest upon being introduced to another person.

In the contact stage thoughts and feelings will be discussed, clarified, defined, differentiated, modified and evaluated. Interruptions in this stage may involve a subtle rationalization, a loss of hearing, vision, feeling or judgment expressed in feeling anxious, confused, or overwhelmed. Also, physical tensions may manifest as tightening of the scalp or chest that constricts and limits the diaphragm resulting in pain and shortness of breath. For example, a thought may arise that he, she desires, dislikes, loves or hates a quality in another person. Interruptions in this stage of contact may be noticed in a vagueness in the person's understanding of their experience in relationships, how or why they behave or make interpersonal decisions and their personal history. They may identify intimacy difficulties in general terms or may be unaware or unclear of how their difficulties occur and how they contribute to their difficulties.

In final-contact disturbances a last minute anxiety will arise involving distancing and avoidance of an "intimate" conclusion to a social evening. For example, during a dinner date an individual arrives on time, enjoys the initial period of conversing about the day's events as well as the dinner itself where a lively conversation is maintained. However, as the evening is drawing to a close the person with a final-contact disturbance may think to him, herself: "I really find her, his features unattractive, I better say good night now, I don't want her, his telephone number." Part of spontaneous closure of final-contact is "withdrawal" from contact. Interruption here prevents final-contact as in the lover who won't separate, but insists on not ending the date. He, she, thereby undoes the pleasure of the evening, unaware. This interruption is not felt but rather is projected and heard in the rationalization: "I was emotionally available it was he, she that couldn't be intimate."

Post-contact occurs after final-contact and involves a process of digestion or assimilation. In this stage something new has been taken in from the environment, as in a good meal or a pleasing date. A post-contact disturbance will occur after having a good date, the next day perhaps, when a person will have doubts and criticisms which undo the pleasure and satisfaction of the encounter and inhibit the person initiating further contact.

B. Intimate contact can be interrupted by mechanisms of introjection — an identification, attitude or belief which the individual has adopted; a projection — an emotion experienced as if it were in the environment; a retroflection — a holding back involving turning an outward going impulse toward oneself and containing it; confluence — being unaware of something one is in touch with or the experience of no difference between things, no-contact; and, egotism — a fixation that disrupts final commitment and action. These are healthy when performed with awareness or available to awareness and choice, e.g., available memory. (Perls et al., p. 450, Vol. II, Ch. XV, 3) In these instances they are learned adaptations serving purposes of security and gratification and can be modified if necessary or not purposeful. However, if unaware, i.e., not perceived or felt, these interruptions are lost ego-functions. They involve a loss of choice by the individual, result in bound, inhibited excitement and conflict with other impulses in a way that diminishes capacity to think clearly, feel strongly and act decisively.

Together unaware introjection, confluence, projection, retroflection and egotism comprise a neurotic mechanism. That is, if there is an introject, an adopted attitude; there is also a confluence, something unaware; a retroflection, something held back; a projection, some disowned emotion; and an egotism, a fixation; and together they comprise a neurosis. For example, with regard to intimacy we might postulate a person whose intimate contact is interrupted with the introject "I'm not attractive." There would also be a projection, perhaps the thought "Others see me as unattractive"; a retroflection involving a tight or tensed musculature reflected in pale skin, causing the person to appear as if expecting not to be welcomed by others, and uncut hair, as if "what's the use"; also, a confluence which results in the individual not experiencing feelings of anger and frustration in response to these self-critical, devaluing feelings and thoughts; and an egotism, as a conceit, "I'm my mother's daughter, just like she said I was."

C. I have found the structures of the self, presented in *Perls, Hefferline and Goodman,* (1951, pp. 371-383, Vol. II, Ch. X) to be helpful in providing direction for my therapeutic work. The ego identifies and alienates with the emerging needs and appetites, i.e., the id-function, and the person's learned preferences, i.e., personality-function, and a figure is perceived. The ego-functions can be lost by interrupting mechanisms of introjecting, projecting, confluence, retroflecting and egotism. Lost ego-functions include blanking out, not seeing, hearing, thinking, i.e., a loss of contact. The id-function consists of the person's needs, appetites, and feelings. The personality-function is the individual's assimilated learning about whom he, she is and what he, she wants to satisfy him, herself. By discerning whether an interruption derives from an id or personality-function disturbance I gain direction as to posing experiments to either explore feelings involved in id-function or the attitudes and acquired knowledge that shape personality development. This distinction supplements the when and how of the contact interruption identified in points a. and b. above. Of course, eventually both id and personality aspects require attention. For example, when working with a male client I may suspect a possible projection when he says: "When I arrived to pick her up I thought she was angry with me." With this client I may pose experiments which support contact with his unaware retroflecting which prevents his feeling his anger. This may be an id-function disturbance involving anger and associated loss of ego-function at the fore-contact stage. I may suggest he pay particular attention to his visual experience, what he specifically is seeing and his physical experience such as feelings of tension or tightness around his eyes and jaw, and his tense breathing as he now imagines the moment of meeting his date again. In contrast, I could pose an experiment to explore a personality-function disturbance if he made the statement "Even though she seems angry, I'm not an angry person, and therefore her anger doesn't bother me." In this instance I may direct his attention to what he knows about himself as a person who doesn't get angry. I may then pose an experiment that involves his exploring feelings about his father's rules about expressing anger.

I will be alert for vagueness in the person's understanding of their experience in relationships and personal history. Persons with relationship and intimacy difficulties are often vague and unaware of what their difficulties are. People with id and personality function disorders don't know what relationships require, what they prefer and appropriate behavior in a relationship. They have experienced an emotional deprivation or injury early in life and, as a result, learned to become anxious with interpersonal contact. Their anxiety is a loss of ego- function so they don't clearly see, hear or think when they are anxious, in place of feelings and thoughts they experience anxiety, blankness or a physical tension such as a headache. This disturbs their capacity for assimilating their experience from personal involvement with others. Instead of experiences which would develop their personality, that is, who they are, what they need and know of themselves and the world they live in, which would contribute to their sense of self and competence in the world, they present as somewhat immature, ignorant of what to do and have thoughts and feelings appropriate in much younger persons. They haven't developed the patience, judgment and repertoires of social skills such as sharing time speaking, showing interest and concern required for mutual ongoing relationships. They may be immature in their knowledge about sexual matters, making conversation, dating, and, or may not identify themselves as a father, or mother when dealing with their child, or as an equal partner in a relationship.

Confluence and Intimacy

The healthy interruptions to contact making and withdrawal, introjection, projection, retroflection, confluence, and egotism, contribute to individual functioning and present obstacles to intimacy when unaware restricting figure/ground formation, a fixed gestalt. Healthy confluence is part of absorption at final-contact when in intimate contact an "I" and a "you" form a "we," a shared figure. This is a temporary, healthy confluence as if a melting occurs at the contact boundary in which lovers or friends experience being together with a boundary temporarily softened and inclusive of the other. The contact boundary is as if dissolved, as if not there, when at final-contact the identification with the figure is total. (From, 1982) Too little healthy confluence early in life from inadequate nurturing such as empathic responding and holding, as well as forced confluence from too much parental control, intrusiveness, lack of freedom of expression, causes anxiety at healthy confluence. This is importantly disruptive to intimate final-contact where authenticity, understanding, agreement and disagreement is required.

Neurotic confluence involves a fixed response, which unaware interrupts contact and creates an apparent intimacy, sameness or agreement in an individual's experience or between persons when there is none. An individual may anxiously avoid recognizing differences so as to achieve a premature confluence, a "we," before there is an "I" and a "you" at fore-contact, contact or final-contact or may avoid healthy confluence at final-contact where an "I" and a "you" would dissolve into a "we." (From, 1983) Premature confluence leaves unfinished feelings, a vague sense of not being seen, heard, and involved with others. This is anxious making, confusing and undermines confidence in one's ability to be compatible and have satisfying, successful relationships with others.

Neurotic confluence in fore-contact prevents the emergence of a clear figure/ground involving impulses, emerging needs and appetites that would energize interest in and movement toward another. Some confluent persons have little to say because their confluence, i.e., a loss of ego-function, makes it difficult to identify meaningful details required to identify what to talk about. These discriminations are necessary for clear figure/ground formation, i.e., good contact. When such a loss of ego-function occurs there is a blankness which the individual can experience as a void or can fill with projections of idealized images or fears. Being out-of-contact but with idealizing projections in fore-contact, individuals can experience exhilarating feelings of love, romance - "being carried away," "breaking through to the stars," and a new lover as "perfect." Fearful fore-contact may evoke not seeing, hearing or panic with another.

Neurotic confluence in the contact stage can occur in long-term relationships when couples have an extensive ground of intimacy and assume intimacy in day-to-day encounters. They think that they know what their lover, friend, partner, spouse is experiencing. Neurotic confluence can also occur during the contact stage by the denial or avoidance of differences. For example, selecting a partner with whom one does not share a common boundary and with whom opportunities for contact are minimized such as a much older, younger, culturally different, withdrawn, depressed partner.

Neurotic confluence can occur at final or post-contact by endings that have "apparent" but not authentic agreement. The person will realize later in a sudden awareness: "I don't really want to agree to that." Healthy confluence at final-contact may also be avoided by changing the subject, bringing up a sensitive subject that provokes a fight, identifying differences which avoid agreement or not allowing "withdrawal," by not allowing the date or contact to end by persistent phone calls or not letting the other out of sight. Contact always involves withdrawal. Resisting withdrawal at final-contact results in the compartmentalization, a fixating, which attempts to maintain the achieved figure, the "we." This, holding on however, does not allow spontaneity, growth and change. The achieved excitement becomes numbness, no feeling and, or pain and undoes the achieved intimacy.

Gestalt Therapist-Client Intimacy

Gestalt Therapy has unique qualities relating to intimacy that arise in the client-therapist context. Gestalt therapeutic contact involves being "in touch," at the contact-boundary and open to the jointly created, novel experience of the moment with the client. This may evoke feelings of mutuality and connection as well as personal disclosures by the therapist. This "therapeutic intimacy," involves an "I," the therapist, and "you," the client, forming a share "we," an intimacy supportive of and compatible with the therapeutic context. This can be advantageous for the therapy because the Gestalt therapist, working at the contact-boundary, uses his, her emotional experience to inform his, her responses to facilitate the therapy. Therapeutic intimacy contributes to an intense and meaningful therapy experience. The therapist may experience interruptions to this intimate contact by him, herself in this process. This can result if the therapist-client contact evokes feelings for which the therapist does not have adequate self-support. Common defenses against therapeutic intimacy by the therapist are avoidance and withdrawal, overwhelming the client, identifying with the client as victim, "acting out" the therapist's personal issues, e.g., as a way to fuel the therapist's narcissism or advance his own therapeutic needs.

Case Studies

Three brief case discussions may serve to clarify work with contact disturbances involving issues of intimacy.

Herb

Herb, a 32-year-old white male, the second child of four from an intact family of American-Italian origin, grew up in Newark, New Jersey. He was physically attractive at six feet tall, broad shouldered, slim with a dark complexion. He presented as severely depressed with concerns of slipping into psychosis. He had been hospitalized eight months previously for depression with auditory hallucinations of "think gay, be gay." This psychotic episode was precipitated by the loss of a television acting job and cocaine and alcohol abuse. At the time of the consultation, he was sexually involved with four women. He was concerned that he was "falling apart" because he was hearing voices again "think gay, be gay." Over the course of his therapy Herb revealed a long history of multiple simultaneous female relationships. These relationships would usually last three to four months, although one or two lasted for a couple of years.

In the course of his therapy he realized that these relationships were a way to maintain self-esteem. When he would be with just one or two women he experienced a vague, chronic anxiety. He was able to associate this anxiety with physical and psychological abuse by his mother. During the course of his therapy the auditory voice and message "think gay, be gay" was identified by him as an expression of his fear and wish for support and comfort from a strong male figure. Herb's course of therapy was one which took many twists and turns. The content would change week to week including romantic, sexual, work and family experiences, conflicts with friends and business associates, critical paranoid concerns and the pressured need for information and clarification regarding his feelings, personal conduct, sexuality and morals.

I understood these shifts as resulting from rapidly manifesting id and personality-function disturbances occurring with concomitant losses of ego-function. Staying at the contact-boundary these interruptions were worked

370

through as they arose. Awareness of his feelings helped identify his desire for closeness with a secure and loving person and the introject — "if you show yourself you won't be loved and secure." His projected voice "think gay, be gay" transmuted and feelings of sadness, weakness and vulnerability emerged, were recognized, felt and expressed. In the course of his therapy Herb did what I call personality- function development work in which he raised questions about his preferences and choices and worked through learning about himself — choices he made, what satisfied him and why. This learning about himself filled in areas of self-knowledge his prior losses of ego-function didn't allow him to have. This seemed like basic education, for example that homosexual feelings were not inherently bad and were not, for example, contagious, and anal stimulation was one way of being sexually stimulated and feeling warm, sensuous and good, and did not mean he was gay. He also identified feelings of grief and powerful expressions of anger principally at his mother for her physical and emotional abuse. One challenge for me in my work with Herb was staying with the unknown and unknowable regarding the direction of his work.

Herb's therapy lasted four and a half years. During that period he was able to work through his rage at his mother's abuse and father's passivity and identify feelings and preferences and how to communicate them to others. Gradually, he was able to find a woman he was comfortable with whom he married and had a child with.

Leonard

Leonard, a 28-year-old gay male, the oldest of two sons, grew up in an intact family with a Jewish cultural background. He presented as severely depressed. He began therapy saying that he found himself walking the streets of Manhattan at 5:00AM thinking over whether to kill himself or try therapy. He experienced a deep and painful agony in his desire to love someone and have an intimate relationship. He could find temporary relief from his pain in all day and night sexual binges, and sporadic sexual encounters, or retreating to his home and bed and withdrawing from the world for three to five days. Leonard had one two month relationship six years prior to seeing me that was one-sided, idealized and painfully rejecting. Indeed, as he presented his history, he viewed his whole life as misguided and a failure. Instead of going to college he had run away to Europe. His work as a medical typist was dissatisfying and his past involvement in a communist organization was misdirected. Besides his friends he had no satisfying love relationships or work direction and felt a deep despair in living that made suicide an attractive alternative. Early in his therapy I reassured Leonard that I would not try to argue him out of suicide. This was importantly reassuring and made it possible for Leonard to come to therapy.

Leonard's therapy lasted approximately eight years with three breaks of three to ten months. Leonard made important changes in the conditions and experience of his life. He recognized and explored his neglected and abused childhood at the hands of two narcissistic parents. He learned to tolerate and carefully observe his anxiety regarding his mother. He learned to observe his loss of ego-function under the pressure of her subtle guilty making and self-referential manipulations. Leonard's interruptions in the contact sequence were importantly in the contact stage during which he could observe his changes in mood and capacity. He was also able to identify post-contact disturbances involving guilt and feelings of "nothingness." Work on these interruptions led to his developing his personality-function, i.e., sense of who he was. Concurrently, his anger and anguish at the loss of his childhood to parents who he was care provider to fueled his capacity and self-support to recognize his parents' limitations and how they hurt him. In time he was able to maintain his sense of self with his parents. He now relates without guilt and "craziness" with his mother. After seventeen years of not speaking to his father he contacted him and felt good about their monthly phone conversations. Although anxious, he is looking forward to seeing his father soon. During his therapy he went back to college and graduated with honors and was awarded a full scholarship to Yale in an economics doctoral program. Thoughts of suicide and sexual binges no longer occur. A satisfying ongoing sexual, love relationship has not yet occurred. Meanwhile he has a number of loving friendships from which he is getting deep satisfaction.

Miriam

Miriam, a 34-year-old editor at large at a newspaper, began therapy with concerns about her relationship with Gary. During the past ten years she had relationships with men generally lasting three to eighteen months but all had "failed." She saw herself as getting involved with men who were inappropriate for a long-term relationship. These men were either married or lived far away and when increased intimacy occurred something would then go wrong. She had been friendly with Gary for seventeen years and last year their friendship changed to dating and romance. Miriam decided to enter therapy because she was experiencing severe stomach cramps when she was with Gary and felt dissatisfied with their current arrangement. He lived in Maryland where he went to law school. She lived and worked in New York City.

Miriam's therapy lasted approximately three years. Her work covered many areas of her life. Two main topics stand out. Over the first two years Miriam worked importantly on feeling aggression that was retroflected in fore-contact and contact phases. For a long time she would punch a pillow in anger and frustration with her boyfriend. This evolved into identifying what she wanted and didn't want and expressing what she wanted, first to me and then to him.

In the second and third years of therapy her relationship with her mother and father which had been worked on throughout her first two years became clearer and her sexual feelings toward her father were examined. During this work she recognized that the men she was attracted to and with whom she could not successfully establish a relationship, were quite different from her father. In contrast, men she would find uninteresting had qualities resembling his. Appreciating these differences was a watershed in her therapy. Following this she was able to perceive men in general and Gary, in particular, in a clearer and less anxious making manner. In the third year of her therapy she became engaged and married Gary.

Summary

This article has been intended to highlight intimacy as an essential aspect of psychological experience, an important subject of client concern and as fertile ground for therapeutic experimentation, invention and discovery. Perls, Hefferline and Goodman speaking of the emotions state: "The animal must know immediately and truly what the relations of the field are, and he must be impelled by the knowledge." (Perls et al., p. 408, 1951, Vol.11, Ch.XII, 6) Intimacy is impelling knowledge involving mutual disclosure, trust, valuation, and dependence that goes to the heart of social relations, family and community. Its consideration in the course of therapy can meaningfully contribute to our clients' capacity to creatively adjust, to feel, perceive and act, and, thereby, self actualize their individual and social powers.

References:

From, I.,1982-1984. *Theory and Practice of Gestalt Therapy*, notes.
Perls, F., Hefferline, R . & Goodman, P. (1951). *Gestalt Therapy: Excitement and growth in the human personality*, New York: Julian Press.
Perls, F.(1969). *Gestalt Therapy Verbatim*, Bantam Publishing.
Perls, Laura, Opening address at The Gestalt Journal's Annual Conference, May 17, 1985.
New Illustrated Webster's Dictionary of the English Language, (1992). Pamco Publishing Co."

Chapter 21. Inclusive and Exclusive Aggression: Some (Gestalt) Reflections.

Phillip Lichtenberg

Chapter introduction

I wrote this piece because the topic of aggression, so basic to the origins of Gestalt therapy as begun by the original members of NYIGT, has come under criticism and has not been updated to emphasize the relational aspect of aggression. At the 2010 AAGT Conference, and in later works, Frank Staemmler downplayed the vitality of the approach that has characterized the Institute since its early days, and Erv Polster and I mumbled to each other our common defense of the aggression concept. When I proposed to Susan Fischer, the editor of *Gestalt Review* my interest in the topic, she encouraged me to write on it for that journal.

When I composed the article, I realized how varied was the subject in my previous writings, from the 1950s when I worked in the psychoanalytic field, which at that time also featured themes on aggression, into my later work as a Gestalt therapist and as a member of NYIGT. I had been impressed with the analysis in the founding text that failure to deal with aggression in daily life was basic to the social tolerance, if not enthusiasm, for wars and other violent ways of being. When I did anger workshops in the 1960s and 1970s, I relied on the view that being angry could be bonding in relationships because it was "admixed with desire" as the founding text put it. I had been working on responsibility, had found democratic forms of responsibility combined initiative (primacy) and accountability, so there too I found overlap with the concept of initiative as a form of aggression. I had been pitting aggression against the tamer idea of assertion. As well, I had earlier attended to aggression in parent-child relations. Thus, it all came together in this piece on inclusive versus exclusive aggression.

In the early days of Gestalt therapy, aggression, which is properly understood as forceful presentation of oneself, was enunciated without attention to the other in any relationship. Thus, persons when angry were encouraged to express that anger, without any regard to how the recipient of that anger was affected by it. This meant that aggression was conceptualized within an individualist framework. In recent years with a focus in Gestalt therapy as a dialogical therapy, attention centered on how the object of that aggression was influenced by it.

Two matters of concern came into view. Did the aggression promote or did it suppress dialogue? Similarly, did aggression serve to facilitate or did it interfere with the construction of a meeting of the persons in the relationship? To respond to these concerns, I introduced the qualifiers that made aggression *inclusive* of others or *exclusive* of others. I considered it insufficient to refer to aggression without invoking the qualifiers: when we refer to aggression, we need to specify its relational component, is it inclusive or is it exclusive? I consider this a useful updating of Gestalt therapy as a theory of human encounter.

Inclusive and Exclusive Aggression: Some (Gestalt) Reflections[101]

Abstract: Aggression – the energetic, forceful, protective quality of a person in relation – is differentiated into inclusive aggression and exclusive aggression following Angyal's (1965) conception of universal ambiguity. This paper compares these differently-based aggressions with respect to initiative, assertion, criticism and self-criticism, anger and parenting. It also refers to experiences in being the object of these varying aggressions from others, and being affected by the self-directed aggressions of the other. The aim is to promote inclusive aggression more generally so that citizens are less prone to support wars and engage in violence.[102]

Background

Wars and violence are all too common in the modern world, and any ideas we can contribute to lessen their tolerance by citizens of the world may be worth attention. In 1951, Paul Goodman (Perls, Hefferline, and Goodman, 1951, pp. 339 ff.) suggested that because we do not live out aggression well in everyday life, we lay the psychological basis for acceptance without adequate countervailing struggle concerning the many wars about us, and the massacres of children in schools in the USA, Norway, Russia, etc. With the decline of capitalism as a basis for organizing society, a system based on aggression, the need for countervailing effort is even enhanced. If we can learn to deal with aggression in everyday life, to promote those ways of being aggressive that build community, and to manage well those ways that are destructive of common welfare, we can possibly change how the world works; and we can contribute to a more peaceful future.

Within the fields of Gestalt therapy, psychoanalysis, and social psychology, there are competing conceptions of aggression; the purpose of this essay is to note these alternatives and to attempt to support the provocative perspective introduced by the founding text of Gestalt therapy. One goal of this paper is to update the relational view of aggression implicit in the original text but inadequately explicated. Providing a sampling of topics in which I have been personally involved over the years carries this aim forward. It does not intend to encompass the multitude of other topics that can readily be related to aggression.

In recent years two seminal thinkers have taken up this subject: Frank-M. Staemmler (2009) in Gestalt therapy, and Jessica Benjamin (1999) in relational

---

[101] Originally appeared in the *Gestalt Review* (2012) 13(2), pp 145-161 and reprinted with their kind permission.

[102] Many have contributed to this work, but three individuals have made concrete suggestions that are incorporated into the text – Catherine B. Gray, Susan Gregory, and Lisa Pozzi – for which I am grateful.

psychoanalysis. Their inclusion of the relevant literature can serve as background for this essay. Staemmler adopts the common sense, colloquial view of aggression as always describing efforts that harm another who is the object of that aggression. His scholarship is extensive and well worth examining, and it contains an extended critique of the founders of Gestalt therapy. Benjamin, who stays within the realm of psychoanalysis, presents the alternative view in "Recognition and Destruction: An Outline of Intersubjectivity," one that is coherent with the original statement of the founders of Gestalt therapy. Rather than recapitulate their arguments, I alert the reader to their function as background to this essay, and I shall reference some relevant points from them in my analysis. Both writers importantly go beyond the individualism that is the underpinning of capitalist society.

I believe that aggression is much misunderstood in our common sense usage, because it is used only in reference to wars between nations and between citizens within nations. Yet, in my view, there is no human relation without aggression since there is no relationship without persons energetically presenting themselves to others. To bond with another, to converse with another, to work alongside another, to love another, one must exert oneself in reference to that other, and such exertion is the essence of aggression. Even the subduing of oneself in relation to another involves aggression; in this matter, self-aggression. As we regulate ourselves in relationship, we are also exerting ourselves in that relationship.

The various topics in this paper are not meant to be organized by any systematic orientation other than that they are matters I have personally attended to. A different author would choose a significantly different group. They all have pertinence to the everydayness of life, and they aim to promote a culture that is an alternative to what dominates at the present time.

After defining aggression and locating it within the conceptualization of Gestalt therapy, I take up initiative as aggression, a major part of a capitalist world; assertion as an alternative notion to aggression; criticism and self-criticism as aggression; anger as aggression in both its divisive and bonding forms; parenting as aggression, where each of us learns positive and negative forms of aggression; what happens when one is an object of aggression in both its bonding and destructive forms; and aggression against the self as an undergirding of oppression.

Defining Aggression

I want to explore the matter of aggression in its inclusive and exclusive aspects. In distinguishing such positive and negative aggression, I rely heavily on Andras Angyal's (1965) conception of "universal ambiguity":

One outlook, while not indiscriminate optimism, reflects the confidence that the "supplies" for one's basic needs exist in the world and that one is both adequate and worthy of obtaining these supplies. The neurotic belief is that these conditions are not available or that they can be made available by extremely complicated and indirect methods. Thus, in one way of life, the two basic human properties [autonomy and homonomy] function in an atmosphere of hope, confidence, trust or faith. [...] In the other, the propelling forces [of autonomy and homonomy] are the same, but they function in an atmosphere of diffidence, mistrust, and lack of faith. (p. 100)

Autonomy refers here to the trend toward self-expansion. In the trend to homonomy, a person strives "to surrender himself [herself] and become an organic part of something that he conceives as greater than himself" (p. 15). In Gestalt therapy, homonomy is considered to be healthy confluence at final contact: a merging with the other, and a losing of self in this larger unit. Angyal labels these two orientations as a healthy Gestalt and a neurotic Gestalt, respectively, and the orientations give different meanings to the same subject; thus, aggression means one thing within an inclusive orientation and something quite different in an exclusive orientation

In relation to Angyal's "orientations," I have developed a continuum of what I call "dispositions" (Lichtenberg, 1988). At the ideal positive extreme is a disposition labeled "confident expectation"; at the negative extreme of this continuum is an "essential ambivalent anticipation." No real person has a disposition at either extreme because these are central tendencies, and all persons are sometimes very confident, full of hope and faith, and sometimes quite ambivalent, full of diffidence and mistrust, believing every gain is accompanied by serious costs. Persons can be placed on this continuum according to their typical way of being. Those nearest to a confident expectation fit into Angyal's healthy Gestalt when they are functioning with confidence, whereas those nearer to the ambivalent anticipation fit into his neurotic Gestalt when manifesting their ambivalence. I have located these dispositions within a psychoanalytic tradition.

So, here are some definitions of aggression in the two orientations or dispositions: an *inclusive aggression* based on confidence that one's needs will be met; and an *exclusive aggression* based on the anticipation that every gain is burdened by costs. In either case, aggression is an energetic, forceful, affirming, asserting or protecting self in human relationships. Aggression is the energy of action.

In its inclusive form, aggression appears in the process of engaging in a connecting way and keeping engaged with an other or others who are the object of one's attention, and who may partner in one's goal striving, or be a perceived obstacle to one's goals, or who are a felt challenge to one's integrity. Such aggression is attuned to the capacity of the other(s) to receive it and to keep engaging with the aggressive person. In its exclusive form, aggression appears as the energy in the processes that diminish or negate the other or others in the relationship, or alternatively diminish or negate self in the relationship. One may diminish others via domination, overpowering, or escalating forcefulness. One may diminish self by withdrawing emotionally or physically from the relationship, or by hiding or obscuring oneself from the other. The ambiguity of aggression, thus, is that it can be bonding or divisive, inclusive or exclusive, egalitarian or opposed to equality depending upon whether it is embedded in a healthy or neurotic Gestalt.

With respect to aggression, a person must be seen always as simultaneously dealing with self and other. In dominating an other, for example, a person is also controlling self as part of the process, obscuring vulnerability or felt weakness. In withdrawing, one is making one's absence known to the other. In meeting and bonding with an other one accounts to the other's needs and to one's own needs.

Aggression is an important component of the sequence of contacting and withdrawing. It most properly appears during the contact phase of that process. In its inclusive form, to be aggressive is energetically to promote a distinct "I" and a distinct "You" in the relationship (Lichtenberg, 2000). A person both defines self openly and clearly and urges the other to define self openly and clearly when being in the service of communion at final contact. In its exclusive form, aggression diminishes or negates both the "I" of the other and the "I" of the self in the relationship and thus promotes faulty confluence. The excess energy used in dominating or negating others is related to the degree of vulnerability, anxiety, helplessness arising within the person that is more than usual for that person. It is best seen as an indication of the person's unaccepted feelings of vulnerability.

Initiative as Aggression

We do not ordinarily think of initiative as aggression, although it is so announced in Perls et al. (1951, p. 342). In various dictionary definitions of "initiative," we do not see reference to aggression: "an introductory act or step;" "readiness or ability in initiating action;" "the power or opportunity to act or take charge before others do." The term initiative derives from a Latin word meaning "beginning." When we think of aggression as the energy of action, therefore, we can see initiative as a force bringing something into an interaction in a social context that was not there before that act of beginning. It is an energetic arousal.

Yet, what brings me to focus attention on initiative in my concern to modify tolerance of violence and war? I do not think it is self-evident, though we intuitively know that an entrepreneurial spirit is characteristic of modern industrial societies, and that spirit relies on initiatives taken. So, too, wars of aggression turn on how initiative is taken while blaming the object of that war for requiring such action. I think of Nazi Germany in the 1930s, and the United States of America in the 1990s and later in respect of Iraq and Afghanistan. Initiatives to go to war were taken after extensive projections upon others. What has brought me to this focus oddly enough has been an interest in responsibility, which I first studied in respect of applicants for public welfare (Lichtenberg and Pollock, 1967; Lichtenberg, 1988).

In our research, my colleague and I learned that these applicants for assistance were sometimes "irresponsible" and sometimes quite "responsible" depending upon how the authorities who worked with them handled the initiatives which their position afforded them. In our work with these caseworkers, we were able to transform disputatious and frustrating encounters into relationships that placed both applicants and authorities into friendly, homonomous experiences. We saw that initiative could be inclusive or exclusive, bonding or divisive, rewarding and effective or frustrating and ineffective, depending upon how it was connected to answerability or accountability to those affected by the initiative. We considered responsibility to be two-pronged: *responsibility for* (bearing initiative, primacy) and *responsibility to* (bearing answerability or accountability).

Some of these caseworkers utilized their power to level demands on the applicants and required those applicants to be answerable for carrying out these demands. For example, an applicant was told she must go to the District Attorney and set in motion a process in which her absent husband would be required to support her and her children. The caseworker was regularly frustrated and angry when the applicant for her own reasons or excuses did not carry out that requirement. The applicant was then criticized or turned down for assistance and left frustrated and angry as well. The caseworker then recorded the applicant as "irresponsible." Or a mother was to take her child to a dentist but reported she did not have the bus fare or the time or gave some other reason. She, too, was held blameworthy. The pattern was repeated many times, as we were able to record.

Others of these caseworkers had learned to share their power and leaned upon initiative developed by applicants. They balanced primacy (initiative) and accountability and found their work with applicants pleasant and productive. For example, one male caseworker dealt with a difficult male applicant who had previously been told he must actively seek employment or he would not receive assistance. The applicant provided many excuses for not doing so. This new caseworker took a different approach. He noted that he was required by law and by the agency to put the applicant in the way of employment, but he would rely upon the applicant's interest and creativity in how that effort would proceed. He offered to drive the applicant to places that the applicant chose and to help in other ways he could. The applicant was visibly moved by the offer and together they set out to look for appropriate jobs. Uniting primacy and answerability led to communion. The demand was still present, but it was embedded in a more egalitarian and inclusive social relation.

For many years now persons lower in hierarchies in modern society have been held accountable beyond the support given to them in doing the work they

381

are assigned to do. Teachers are made to be answerable for the performance of their students on tests created by outsiders. Speed-up is common in factory work and performance demands are put on workers in service jobs beyond their own decisions and creativity. These developments are seldom classified as aggression, but they are experienced as aggression by those being held to account. So, too, downsizing or closing of plants and organizations are aggressive actions not listed under the heading of aggression. It should not be surprising that these actions promote rage, frustration, resignation, and sometimes counter-aggression. That this type of action is a new normal does not mean that such aggression of exclusion should be acceptable and tolerated in a humane society. This pattern becomes doubly negative when such social safety nets as unemployment insurance are cut back; or when it is made ridiculous to talk of a minimum guaranteed income.

Business and politics in a capitalist society are built upon the separation of initiative and answerability to the detriment of all citizens. We have a paucity of warm and friendly encounters as a result, and I am not surprised by how much depression and alcoholism as well as other addictions characterize societies of today.

Assertion as Aggression

To "assert" is to state with assurance, confidence or force; to state strongly or positively; to put oneself forward boldly and insistently. To be assertive is also to be aggressive. In the 1970s, women's consciousness-raising groups encouraged women to be assertive and fostered assertiveness training groups.

More recently Frank-M. Staemmler (2009), in his critique of the approach to aggression by the founders of Gestalt therapy, considered their view of aggression as individualistic (pp. 27 ff.), centered on the side of the aggressor and avoiding the other as the object of that aggression (p. 31); and he adopted the colloquial view of aggression as always harming the other. He noted Laura Perls's two conceptions of aggression (the positive and negative variants) as belonging to two different motivational systems, as specified by the psychoanalyst Joseph Lichtenberg (pp. 38-39). He quoted Lichtenberg as positing the "need for exploration and assertion" and "the need to react aversively through antagonism or withdrawal (or both)." If I apply Angyal's (1965) idea of universal ambiguity in this context, the two motivational systems can be located within the healthy and neurotic Gestalts. Thus, Laura Perls's view of aggression contains both aggression within a healthy Gestalt and aggression within a neurotic Gestalt; whereas Staemmler's and Lichtenberg's view of two motivational systems simply divides the issue into aggression (neurotic Gestalt) and exploration-assertiveness (healthy Gestalt).

I think there is something right and something wrong with collapsing aggression into assertion. On the recommended side, assertion does not have the connotation of diminishing or negating the other, as aggression is often (falsely) assumed to mean; that is, aggression is typically conceived as what I have called exclusive aggression. Against this recommendation, assertion refers only to the "I" of contacting and omits any attention to the other. When I specify inclusive aggression, I am pointing to its function in contacting as leading toward a merging with the other in the relationship, as promoting homonomy. To be aggressive is to support the other becoming a distinct figure, as much as it suggests energetic presentation of self (Lichtenberg, 2000). Rather than diminishing the other, inclusive aggression promotes the individuation and clarity of the other. Assertiveness could do this too, but then it would have to be redefined as inclusive assertiveness and little would be gained over the use of "aggression."

Criticism and Self-Criticism as Aggression

I believe the same themes of inclusive aggression and exclusive aggression clarify alternate meanings of criticism and self-criticism. When we ask a person to look at something critically, we want that person to assess or judge the strengths and limitations of that which is being scrutinized; we are not inviting blanket rejection or wholesale acceptance. So, criticism can be a means to connection, or a means to diminishing the other.

Historically, the down side of criticism and self-criticism was illustrated in China during the Cultural Revolution there. What began as an effort to unite academics and intellectuals with peasants and workers degenerated into the domination of those academics and intellectuals by the "Red Guards," youths who came from the peasants and workers. Criticism was a put down rather than becoming a move toward equality. People were coerced to be self-critical. What Mao intended, I believe, was that persons in groups would become direct and frank with one another inside the group and refrain from criticism and gossip outside of the group (Mao, 1966, pp. 258-67). Criticism and self-criticism were meant to contribute to group solidarity with members as equals. The process degenerated into aggression as domination, because the oppressed changed places with the oppressors and became the oppressors themselves – an all too common process in revolutions.

When liberal arts education promotes critical thinking, it is attempting to enable the ability to weigh the strong and weak components of complex phenomena and to have students arrive at sound conclusions. Film and drama critics are charged with a similar responsibility. We rely on their judgments for a wise appraisal of a motion picture or a dramatic play. So, too, we expect reviewers of books to provide a sound judgment about the book, though I have personally experienced an unsound and condescending review, and it rankles to this day.

We train participants in the training program of the Gestalt Therapy Institute of Philadelphia to observe therapeutic work of fellow trainees and to give commentary to the therapist that is insightful, geared to what the therapist can assimilate, and challenging. We have come to call such commentary a "gift for growth." It is not useful if it is not aggressive commentary, but it is also not valuable if it diminishes or negates the therapist who is trying to grow as a Gestalt therapist.

Editors help authors by their criticism as well as by encouragement of self-criticism, as do teachers with their students.

In our time of exclusive aggressive talk radio shows, we see daily illustrations of negative criticism, which leads even to death threats against those criticized. Such programs have debased journalism, to the decline of our civilization.

Anger as Aggression

Anger is commonly viewed only as a negative emotion aimed at limiting or diminishing the other. Staemmler (2009) devotes a lengthy part of his book to describing anger in its negative form. He has no space for anger as a means to reach communion in final contact. Yet, in Gestalt therapy we see anger also in its positive light as containing passion with respect to the other and, when well done, leading to union with the other: "[I]n general, anger is a sympathetic passion; it unites persons because it is admixed with desire" (Perls et al., 1951, p. 343).

Over the years I have had occasions in groups that I have facilitated, when a member has become angry with me, and I have had positive resolutions such as Goodman suggests in the quotation above. In these encounters, I explore what I have done that was angry-making, what the offended person experienced internally, and what was going on inside me that brought me to do what I did. Every time each of us has explored all of these matters thoroughly, we have met in a friendly way. Indeed, some members of the group did not believe that anger was present at all, since there was no outburst in the scene. From these events, I wrote a little piece to share with colleagues which I called, "The Incomplete 'I': An Impediment to Reaching Mutual Understanding and Community." Here, with a slight modification, is what I wrote:

I am angry with Gabrielle. I have the feeling of anger. Gabrielle has done X, which arouses in me the feeling of anger.

There exists an I-Gabrielle, an I-You, in my experience, which seems to fulfill the requirement for awareness of the experience of the organism/environment field. In my awareness, I perceive in a complex way what Gabrielle did to arouse my feeling of anger. Her action is vivid for me as is my feeling of anger.

Yet, I now contend that beyond my feeling of anger is something in me, a memory, an association, a bodily process that has contributed to the arousal of my feeling with respect to Gabrielle. This is less vivid in my awareness than my perceptions of Gabrielle and her action. This limit to my awareness is what I am calling an Incomplete "I."

Example: Gabrielle says I am stealthily planning to do something she does not like. She is accusing me of being underhanded. As a result, I am angry with her. But why am I angry? There are many possibilities, including my not being angry but interested in what she is about. One reason I might be angry is that I believe she has attacked my integrity. Anger is a common response when one's integrity is threatened, yet we have not established why there would be a threat. We have transferred anger to the feeling of being threatened. Perhaps Gabrielle has power over me, could hurt me, and I become anxious about that possibility. But I have not had that anxiety in my awareness vividly. So, my awareness is more distinct about Gabrielle and her action than about what has been stimulated in me by that action.

Perhaps Gabrielle has accused me in a public setting and I feel exposed and somewhat shamed. But the feeling of shame, like that of anxiety referred to above, is not vivid in my awareness.

Perhaps there is some truth in Gabrielle's criticism. I do not want to experience that truth, and the shame or other feeling connected to my conniving, however innocent I consider myself to be. So, that is dimmer in my awareness than my perception of Gabrielle.

There may be many other inner memories and associations stirred up by Gabrielle's action: for example, she reminds me of others who have criticized me as my father was ready to do. The significant element in the Incomplete "I" is how the perception of the other is balanced by the interoceptions, which are registrations in awareness of one's interior. The feeling of anger is composed of both perceptions and interoceptions, but the clarity of the interocepts is often lesser than the clarity of the percepts. This is what I am calling an Incomplete "I."

Put in a relational context, my expressing anger at Gabrielle is quite different if 1) I emphasize only the perceptual origins of my anger, her action; and 2) I give equal weight to my own contribution to my angry feeling and to her contribution to that feeling. In the first instance, when I emphasize her action and obscure my inner part, I come across as blaming Gabrielle – and she will have to defend herself, either by aggressing in response or withdrawing from me. My anger can be seen as aimed at dominating Gabrielle. In the second instance, when I give equal weight to what she has done to me and what I have contributed to my feeling, I come across as being open to her as well as to me – and she is more likely to want to meet me on this plane of equality.

We tend to obscure our own contribution because it makes us vulnerable. We forget in such circumstances that we can be both vulnerable and substantial in the same interaction. And, after all, at bottom this is what life is: we are both vulnerable and will be controlled by others, and we will ultimately die; and we are substantial as we nonetheless go about living. A more complete "I" is thus life affirming.

Parenting as Aggression

Parenting children can be an egalitarian endeavor or an authoritarian enterprise, and whether it is egalitarian or authoritarian depends heavily upon whether the aggression is of an inclusive or an exclusive nature. The interplay of vulnerability and aggression assumes significance in parenting activities because infants and children represent the fullness of vulnerability in their innocence and receptivity; parents and other caretakers wield the most obvious aggression in the negotiations that ensue between the smaller and larger one.

In a psychoanalytic study that my colleagues and I carried out in a child psychiatry clinic in the 1950s, we did an analysis of parent-child relationships over many domains, ranging from feeding patterns, weaning and toilet training to friendships, schooling, household chores, religious indoctrinations to independence strivings (Lichtenberg, Kohrman, and Macgregor, 1960). We were interested in how parents and children came to mutually inclusive divisions of satisfactions; we were studying how they "met" each other in daily life. We believed that infants and children were moved by their own needs; they were originally oriented to cooperating with others and were sensitive to others, such that they monitored when others were available to them or too anxious to meet them, and so forth. We also believed that caretakers needed to find and deal positively with the needs of the infant and child as the child expressed these needs, but that in doing so they had also to attend to and take care of their own desires. This was a central lesson we derived from psychoanalysis and from progressive education. We defined permissiveness such that parents attended to their own desires while encouraging their children to find and express their needs and preferences.

Central to our assessment was how early in the child's acting upon his or her needs the parent saw conflict with their own desires and acted to curtail the child. Conversely, as would be expected in mutual adaptation, we analyzed how parents imposed their desires upon their children, or accommodated themselves to their children. For example, we looked at whether the parents allowed the children to participate and regulate their own weaning from the breast or the bottle; how children leaned upon developments within their bodies to toilet train themselves while watching their parents use the bathroom; how children were free to deal with playmates; how the little ones expressed interest in morals; how they chose to nurture themselves as well as others; how they dealt with cleanliness; and how they became independent. We developed a scale that would rate early and late interventions, took a central tendency to record how mutually inclusive children and their parents were in their ongoing daily lives, and correlated that tendency with family motivation for treatment in our clinic.

The scale we used was called "Stage of Earliest Application of Power." We rated the place at which parents *first* conceived that a child's need conflicted with their own need. It ranged from parents inducing needs in children (as in over-protecting parents) to seeing conflict only after the child had explored alternative ways of meeting his or her needs and settled upon one behavior that challenged the parent's needs. We were able from these ratings to see the constellations of problems shown by the children, not only by the central tendency of inclusiveness or exclusiveness over many areas, but also by which domain showed early intrusions by the parents and which were more mutual and led to meetings of parent and child.

For us, child-rearing was aimed at promoting a general confidence in the child, such that the child would have the faith that Goodman suggested (Perls et al. 1951 p. 415); the healthy Gestalt that Angyal (1965) referred to; and the confident expectation that I derived (Lichtenberg, 1988). To promote a child's growth was less to foster particular behaviors than to support the child's creativity and sense of self. Where behaviorists suggested that parents reward some behaviors to promote them, we focused on mutual adaptation of parents and child and the meetings that were created.

Parents use their influence in relation to their children, and this can be inclusive aggression or exclusive aggression. Parenting when viewed in the light of aggression is not only dominating a child, using anger as a control, spanking a wayward boy, or reacting to the temper tantrum of a frustrated little girl. It is using influence to find an infant's need when the infant is mysteriously crying; it is providing situations in which the child uses its creativity; it is dealing with one's own needs in ways that a child can understand and come to terms with. Because aggression has long been narrowed to mean exclusive aggression, we have handicapped ourselves from seeing the relevance and significance of aggression in child-rearing. When we see inclusive aggression as the energetic part of actions that lead to moments of communion between parents and children, we have a better view of democratic, progressive child-rearing. We can then normalize the anger that every parent and every child experience in relationships, since anger indicates influence gone astray and helplessness beginning to appear.

Benjamin (1999) has suggested that intersubjectivity develops in the child through mutual influence of mother and child. Drawing on the work of Winnicott, Stern and Beebe, and her own thinking about the need of both child and mother for recognition, Benjamin posed that conflict between mother and child as well as support is vital to healthy development:

How she responds to her child's and her own aggression depends on her ability to mitigate such fantasies [of omnipotence] with a sense of real agency and separate selfhood, on her confidence in her child's ability to survive conflict, loss, imperfection. The mother has to be able to both set clear boundaries for her child and recognize the child's will, to both insist on her own independence and respect that of the child – in short to balance assertion and recognition. If she cannot do this, the omnipotence continues. (p. 191)

Benjamin stated further:

> As Beebe and Lachmann [...] have proposed, one of the main principles of the early dyad is that relatedness is characterized not by continuous harmony but by continuous disruption and repair. [...] A relational psychoanalysis should leave room for the messy intrapsychic side of creativity and aggression; it is the contribution of the intersubjective view that may give these elements a more hopeful cast, showing destruction to be the "other" of recognition. (p. 199)

Parent-child relations are the training ground for learning to be aggressive; too often in the past only exclusive aggression has been brought to the fore, which is another reason why war and violence are so readily accepted.

On Being the Object of Aggression

When a person is the recipient of aggression coming from another, that person experiences the aggression quite differently if the aggression is of the inclusive or exclusive character; and the recipient manages the aggression differently if that person brings a healthy or a neurotic Gestalt to the relationship. In all instances of aggression, the recipient takes in what is happening to herself or to himself; the person introjects the aggression. What happens inside the person after this internalizing, and how the person acts subsequently in the relationship, depends upon how the recipient processes what has been taken in from the aggressive other.

The simplest case exists when the aggression is an inclusive one on the part of the aggressor, and the object of that aggression responds from a healthy Gestalt. Both parties to the relationship are promoting the autonomy of the other as well as their own agency, and the meeting or homonomy is made most probable. That is the ideal situation, and everyone comes away from the encounter feeling enhanced as part of a unit larger than self, as a member of a new community.

Matters become more complicated if the recipient brings a neurotic Gestalt to what is intended as an inclusive aggression. In this situation, the recipient tends to act as if the aggression is of an exclusive rather than an inclusive nature. The aggressor must now increase efforts at reassuring the other that a meeting of equals is intended rather than any domination in the relationship. In effect, the aggressor needs to assist the recipient in processing the aggression.

When the aggression is exclusive, the best that the recipient can do is to bring his or her healthy Gestalt into the relationship; that is, the person who is an object of an exclusive aggression will internalize both the intensity of the aggression meant for dominating that person and also the unacknowledged and unaccepted vulnerability on the part of the aggressor that is projected to avoid the direct experience of that felt weakness by the aggressor. Exclusive aggression tends to produce vulnerability in the object of the aggression, which must be managed as well as the aggression itself. I have described this process in a chapter detailing how a therapist best meets a client who is being oppressive in the therapy (Lichtenberg, 2004). The challenge is to experience fully the impact of the aggressor's actions, to discriminate what is one's own contribution to the felt aggression and helplessness and what is being projected by the aggressor. Then the therapist introduces vulnerability and assertion into the relation without ceding power to the client. The therapist is being vulnerable and aggressive in the context of a search for a meeting with the client.

The most complex and disruptive transaction unfolds when the recipient of exclusive aggressive actions processes the aggression and acts in the relation from a neurotic Gestalt. This may entail identification with the aggressor (self-conquest) as the recipient submits to the aggressor; or it may involve a counter-aggression that is ineffective because it contains the recipient's own unaccepted but active vulnerability. Herein is the basis for collusion of oppressor and oppressed (Lichtenberg, 1990/1994/2002). Managing one's felt vulnerability as well as the internalized aggression is the challenge for a person who is the object of an exclusive aggression.

Aggression Against the Self

In Gestalt therapy we have tended to call aggression directed inwardly against the self "Self-Conquest" (Perls et al. 1951, pp. 353 ff.) This approach limits such aggression to being only exclusive aggression and omits the possibility of inclusive aggression, that self-directed aggression which has been delineated earlier as productive self-criticism. We must remember that all energetic effort is relational as well as self-organizing, which guides us to look at how the other in the relationship experiences this self-directed aggression. Unless we do this, we fall into an individualistic rather than a relational psychology.

With recent attention to mirror neurons, we have access to the impact on others when one is directing aggression against the self. On the one hand, being self-critical socially, while communicating personal acceptance of oneself and confidence in the presence of that criticism, promotes contacting on the way to communion. It represents bringing one's fullness and complexity into the relationship. It presumes equality in the relationship. With the openness of self-criticism, others are not led to projecting upon the person when they see more of him or of her. One can be self-critical while fostering increased contact with another in the relationship.

On the other hand, self-conquest as internally-directed exclusive aggression may support inequality in a social relation, and it may do so importantly if the inequality already exists in that relationship; that is, if one party is superior and the other subordinate. In the most well-known version seen in identification with the aggressor (Lichtenberg, 1990, pp. 9 ff.), the self-directed exclusive aggression aims to separate and protect the subordinate from the aggressive superior. This self-conquest causes the person to hide his or her reactive aggression from the superior and to manage it privately. This strategy of hidden triumph over the self by the subordinate allows the aggressor to project upon the subordinate according to his or her own predisposition and colors the relationship in accord with the tendencies of the superior. In this way, the subordinate contributes to his or her inferiority in the relationship. Sooner or later, the subordinate can no longer contain the projection, and his or her own aggression surfaces.

Alternately, the superior in the relationship may develop or increase superiority by self-control of his or her exclusive aggression. When my father clenched his teeth to contain his anger with me, I became frightened and I shrank. When the president of our college displayed her displeasure by self-control, we faculty members felt intimidated. Some were later outspokenly exclusively aggressive when they were leaving the college or were retiring.

In short, aggression against the self has complex ramifications when seen in a relational frame; it is not innocent in respect of how others are affected in its presence.

Conclusion

This study in aggression is, at the same time, an exploration of vulnerability in the presence of aggression. As we change the commonsense view of aggression so that we see it in its inclusive as well as its exclusive form, we must also change the everyday meaning of being open about one's vulnerability. Here, again, Angyal's (1965) notion of universal ambiguity is relevant. To be vulnerable when acting within a neurotic Gestalt is to be indirect, self-abasing, manipulative, and essentially pathetic – hoping to be taken care of – or to dominate the other in reaction as we often see in fighting couples. Alternatively, to be vulnerable within a healthy Gestalt is to acknowledge one's weakness while also accepting one's strength and influence in the situation of dealing with an aggressive other. Being vulnerable when acting within a healthy Gestalt means a person retains his or her sense of being an agent in the relationship.

War and violence are obvious instances of exclusive aggression. They are efforts to dominate an enemy, to make the enemy vulnerable. Wars in the last one hundred years have shown us that such efforts at domination invariably fail in the long run. Sooner or later, the enemy recovers its sense of being an influence in the relationship and gives up absorbing projections. Nazi Germany learned this lesson, and the wars in Korea, Vietnam, Iraq and Afghanistan have been teaching the same lesson to the United States of America, as Afghanistan taught the Russians and the British before them. There is no end to the "war on terror."

We must reframe war so that in our moments of vulnerability – political, economic and social – we can find inclusive aggression rather than the urge to dominate assigned others. The failures of the "war on drugs," being tough on crime, putting the mentally ill in prisons rather than in therapeutic communities should have taught us the inadequacies of exclusive aggression. As capitalism continues its historical decline, leaving masses of people poor and uncared for, we will need to learn the lessons of productive and unproductive aggression if humankind is to survive.

References

Angyal, A. (1965). *Neurosis and treatment: A holistic theory* (E. Hanfmann & R. M. Jones, Eds.). New York: John Wiley.

Benjamin, J. (1999). Recognition and destruction: An outline of intersubjectivity. In S. A. Mitchell & L. Aron (Eds.), *Relational psychoanalysis: The emergence of a tradition* (pp. 181-210). New York: The Analytic Press.

Lichtenberg, P. (1988). *Getting even: The equalizing law of relationship.* Lanham, Maryland: University Press of America.

Lichtenberg, P. (1990). *Undoing the clinch of oppression.* New York: Peter Lang. Revised as *Community and confluence: Undoing the clinch of oppression* (2nd ed.). With a new preface by the author and an introduction by Gordon Wheeler. Cleveland: Gestalt Institute of Cleveland Press, 1994. Also: Cambridge, Massachusetts: GestaltPress, 2002.

Lichtenberg, P. (2000). Creating a distinct "I" and a distinct "You" in contacting. *The Gestalt Journal, 23*(2), 41-50.

Lichtenberg, P. (2004). On treating agents of oppression. In R. G. Lee (Ed.) *The values of connection: A relational approach to ethics* (pp. 222-50). Cambridge, Massachusetts, GestaltPress.

Lichtenberg, P., Kohrman, R., & Macgregor, H. (1960). *Motivation for child psychiatry treatment.* New York: Russell & Russell.

Lichtenberg, P., & Pollock, J. (1967). Clients and the sense of responsibility. *Public Welfare, 25*(4), 255-261.

Mao, T-T. (1966). *Quotations from Chairman Mao Tse-Tung.* Peking: Foreign Languages Press.

Perls, F., Hefferline, R., & Goodman, P. (1951). *Gestalt therapy: Excitement and growth in the human personality.* New York: Julian Books.

Staemmler, F-M. (2009). *Aggression, time and understanding: Contributions to the evolution of Gestalt therapy.* New York: GestaltPress/Routledge, Taylor & Francis Group.

Chapter 22. Gestalt Therapy and the Dawn of Postmodernism: A Creative Zeitgeist

Jack Aylward

Chapter Introduction

The past is something that can be changed, altered by your discretion.
William Burroughs

Historically, my focused interest on gestalt therapy theory arose out of the wider passion ignited by the American Revolution of the 1960s and 70s – an existential cracking of the frozen 50s mindset. The Free Speech Movement, integration, campus unrest, the sexual, feminist, and literary rebellions combined to ignite the retroflected fires in the bellies of a younger generation recently witness to a worldwide conflagration that provided a level of traumatic novelty incapable of being successfully assimilated. The anticipation of total annihilation remained a constant foreground with conformity and obedience to oppressive mandates touted as the true and sole effective defense methodology. Yet, as noted by Irish freedom fighter Bobby Sands: "it is repression that creates the revolutionary spirit of freedom," and yes, America exploded into what became an unprecedented era of spontaneous, creative self-expression.

Consistent with the dynamics of dialecticism, a conditioned acceptance of the inevitability of war polarized into vigorous protest against such. New and more homegrown forms of art, music, literature, dance, and theater emerged reflecting these new concerns. The Beat generation became an American standard of poetic and literary effort, giving birth to a hedonistic drive towards personal growth and self-fulfillment through ego-syntonic pleasure seeking activity. Various psychological schools broke with their predecessors' emphasis on adaptation and conditioning in favor of experimentation sans restriction or interpretation. New forms of politics confronted the more established "Old School" mentality by demanding radical changes in the here-and-now arena of social concerns. And, it was the illegally declared war on Viet Nam that brought things to an emotionally political point of conflagration that divided the nation in half, often to points of violence and death.

It was during these years that Paul Goodman emerged into his brief period of public significance based on the popularity of *Growing Up Absurd,* his critical analysis on American public education. Being a novelist, playwright, poet, political activist, and through his connection with Fritz and Laura Perls, psychotherapist, he possessed that curious and rare type of Renaissance mindfulness capable of forming creative wholes from seemingly disparate parts. He served as a human common denominator for all of what was going on then, a political, psychological, and social mosaic that he infused into gestalt therapy theory in his contributions to the 1951 tome *"Gestalt Therapy: Excitement and Growth in the Human Personality."* I WAS SOLD! Here it was – a psychological manifesto depicting the therapist not only as a healer of emotional wounding, but also as social and political activist. Goodman's contributions were revolutionary in bringing the consultation room into the streets.

While the original ideas in the 1951 PHG effort remain true today, much has changed socially over the last few decades in ways that have brought about some degree of dilution to such efforts. Part of the problem is that we have become "respectable," a situation (somewhat similar to the 1950s) requiring us to conform to certain standards of performance. After all, we are listed in texts as a legitimate "school of therapy" (read "accepted"). We have training facilities that require coursework and papers in order to get "diplomas" that in some cases allow us to be certified or licensed by state boards; we go to conferences to obtain continuing education credit; we have wandered somewhat indiscriminately into the amorphous practice of organizational consultation without checking for theoretical inconsistencies; and we have merged our approach with other therapeutic schools while often disregarding compatibility matters. While such professional change is to some extent understandable, we can do that without losing our soul.

The purpose of the following article was to address these matters; to reintroduce some readers to the influence that Paul Goodman had on the creation of the multi-dimensional psycho-social-political approach known as gestalt therapy. Very infrequently do we hear his name or attend workshops devoted to his thinking at gestalt conferences. How many of us have read his novel *Empire City*, or read his poetry or plays? From a political perspective, the gestalt principle of "organismic self-regulation" morphs quite comfortably into his anarchistic orientation since self-sufficiency inherently requires little in the way of external control of any sort. PHG is now considered by some "dated" or "quaint" or better yet "hard to read" (as if the complexity of our way of conceptualizing and working is in any way simple"). Talking politics or encouraging social action in therapy has gone the way of the empty chair or the "battacas." Reading Fritz's biography *In and Out of the Garbage Pail"* evokes somewhat embarrassing nostalgic "chuckles," and if read in the original edition, may require a more neutral book cover. The "growth" of some of the more modern growth centers revolves around financial rather than personal concerns in a manner similar to private practices that focus on full fee service ("zip code" therapy) without regards as to how one's patient load reflects one's immediate grass roots community (sliding scales, pro-bono work, reduced fees, etc.).

Before Goodman's and gestalt therapy's influence, I described myself politically as being "to the left of a libertarian and to the right of an anarchist." Since then I have felt more comfortable with Goodman's self-label as a "Neolithic conservative," someone who looks back at what works and resurrects such. And, that is what I try to do in this article. It is there and it does work and similar to

Goodman's statement: "I come as an old fashioned patriot, neither supine nor more revolutionary than is necessary for my modest goals."

Gestalt Therapy and the Dawn of Postmodernism: A Creative Zeitgeist[103]

Abstract: Beginning as a modification of Freudian psychology, gestalt therapy immigrated to the United States of America by way of Germany and South Africa. Post-World War II America was witness to a radical shift in terms of the arts, politics, and social thought. Often referred to as the "culture of spontaneity" it was a time of social protest, antiauthoritarian rhetoric, and experimental approaches to the visual, literary, musical, and plastic arts. For the first time in America's history a large segment of artistic output was being done by second generation immigrants and less classically trained artists creating a unique blend of European connection and the use of vernacular English. There was a cross-cultural emphasis on spontaneous production, risk-taking, and present-centered action. Spanning the time frame from the mid-50's to the late 60's, much of what was going on in the creative art communities provided a fertile ground for the eventual growth of gestalt therapy from a school of psychological thought to a major social phenomenon. Equally as important was the natural confluence between the political and social theories inherent in some of these artistic movements and those well woven into the fabric of gestalt therapy theory through the contributions of Paul Goodman. As such the social and psychological importance of such issues broadened the potential impact of the gestalt way of working.

The way we work as gestalt therapists is supported by rich philosophical, artistic, and political influences that emerged within the context of a creative zeitgeist — one that gave birth to social movements emphasizing human freedom and expression, antiauthoritarian social dynamics, and the creative adjustment potential of the human being. Born on the cutting edge of the cusp between the modern and the post-modern age, literature, art, and music began experimenting with spontaneous creations without the need of reference or validation through standards of "goodness" set down by the traditional "experts" in their respective fields. Rather, the focus was on the phenomenological and the co-creative efforts of the artist and the particular medium through which such creativity was being expressed. By extension, the essence of the aesthetic experience was found in the interactive connections between the viewer, reader, or listener, and the artistic effort at the moment of encounter. The experiential was valued over intellectual appreciation thus placing the essential artistic effect at the points of contact between the organism and the creative expression itself.

---

[103] Originally published as Aylward, J.(2006). Gestalt Therapy and the Dawn of Postmodernism. *International Gestalt Journal* 29/2, 121-145.

To a large extent, these artistic movements were part of a revolutionary reaction to a variety of social and political structures developed mostly in the middle part of 20th century America that valued repression of the human spirit and emphasized instead the adherence to external standards of conduct and behaviors viewed as essential for maintaining social control. "Authorities" of various kinds held the standards of value against which all art forms were to be judged, thereby filtering and, to a large extent, diluting the experiential nature of artistic contact. The gradual evolution of postmodernism witnessed a shift in the core experience of artistic connection from external definitions to internal experiences formed through co-creative contact. Meaning and truth were not viewed as being absolute or timeless, and the often hidden assumptions discovered through continued deconstructive efforts indicated that indeed there could be no "pure" meaning or knowledge outside of society, culture, or language. Meaning can never be unified given the disruption caused by differences thereby demanding that artistic endeavor of any type be constantly reinventing itself in the face of continually changing circumstances and the "what" of what that all means.

This orientation was in direct contrast to the more formal tenets of structuralism where the emphasis was on "why" meaning matters. The writings of the postmodern philosopher, Michel Foucault, were instrumental in exemplifying how definitions of self were intimately tied to social and cultural institutions. In his elaborate histories of sexuality, penal systems, social science, and psychiatry, modern definitions of self were inseparable from the workings of such social structures and institutions and their political impact on the person. From a political perspective, it was necessary to examine these complex operations of power and how they regulated the lives of the populace through surveillance and other forms of regulative monitoring. In the most postmodern fashion, Foucault saw man as a "modern and recent invention" that may be approaching its end (Rabinow, 1984).

In psychology Jacques Lacan, the French psychoanalyst, formulated the theory of the deconstructed self as a challenge to Freud's contentions with respect to the universal and more or less permanent drives that create human pathology. In contrast, Lacan (1981; MacCabe, 1981) believed that there can be no artificial disconnection or resolution between the psyche and any level of emotional discord since such discord is the psyche. Therefore he believed that the psychoanalytic approach would be better served by looking at cultural and language factors rather than the so-called "natural causes" of human distress.

The Emerging Zeitgeist

Gestalt therapy grew from similar suppositions of self, coming of age in the late fifties and, like all radical movements of that time, influenced and formed from other movements of similar philosophical concerns. Most of these perspectives were embedded in social environments that formed both the round and the experiential methodology for interdisciplinary experimentation. In ways similar to other emerging challenges to classical Freudian theory, gestalt therapists did not place primary importance on the need to "socialize" the organism's basic energies into acceptable forms. Allan Watts once described the Freudian view of human development as a system of "psychohydraulics" in which the raging currents of organismic energy is diverted and dammed up in the service of social conformity rather than being allowed to flow in self-regulative ways. Later on, Barry Stevens (1970) championed this philosophy in her book *Don't Push the River* using the metaphor of a river to symbolize the natural, free-flowing nature of organism/environment contact —a view quite consistent with the gestalt perspective.

In looking at the unique nature of gestalt therapy's evolution through such an interdisciplinary lens, we will consider surrealism, avant-garde jazz, and beat literature as important creative artistic processes that helped shape the "gestalt" of gestalt therapy. Understandably, many of these movements developed following the ravages of two world wars. Both post-war periods were marked by powerful levels of disillusionment among young intellectuals giving rise to existential concerns of life's meaning and the relevance of political and social structures in relation to human freedom and well-being. In both cases, it was hard if not impossible to find rational reasons for the loss of millions of lives based on the political or geographical realities of the conflicts. Upon reflection it is not surprising that artistic movements espousing the liberation of the human spirit surfaced spontaneously following two such cataclysmic events.

The scope of destruction and human sacrifice under these conditions presented levels of novelty that were for the most part unable to be assimilated by some individuals — a condition we now label as "post-traumatic stress disorder." In some instances this results in a closing off of any additional information or input from the environment predisposing the organism to "shut down" as a creative adjustment to both intellectual and emotional overload. Often the resultant struggle for stability triggers a mass regressive movement towards reactionary and conservative forms of patriotic expression in the hope that a more desperate form of clinging to the "tried and true" can stave off the overwhelming angst of such trauma. This in turn spawns a sense of national conformity that leads to further intellectual and emotional rigidity, political manipulation, and its associated degrees of prejudice and social narrowing.

Yet at the same historical moments we find artistic and intellectual movements that acknowledge the resultant meaninglessness and chaos and throw themselves into the vortex of uncertainty in the hope that some new type of consciousness will emerge that can provide alternatives to mass annihilation as a way of dealing with human conflict.

To do so required the courage of plumbing the depths of what it is to be human and what that is all about when it comes to relating to others. It was in this spirit that post-World War I France launched the Dada and shortly later the surrealistic artistic movements that encouraged a return to the more natural innate forms of human artistic production. This included, among other things, automatic writing, unique and radical juxtapositions of images and words in the plastic arts and in literature, and the exploration of hidden creativities believed to be found in trance and dream-like states of consciousness. Surrealism quickly announced itself as a libertarian movement in which artists and intellectuals were encouraged to struggle for the complete liberation of humankind in the absence of any influence other than the human spirit. Psychopathology intrigued the surrealists as they played with the boundaries of sanity and madness in both their art and literature. They fully appreciated the precariousness of the human spirit in its social and interpersonal encounters in the search for meaning.

To Rosemont surrealism was " . . .irrevocably on the side of the integral human personality against all retrograde forces of atomization and alienation kneeling at the cross of commodity fetishism" (in Breton, 1978, p. 4). As a philosophy, surrealism was better lived than written about. Like the beat movement that followed, the surrealists encouraged the questioning of all authority, proposing instead that the human condition is best served by breaking with the conventional and the familiar -- thus freeing the human spirit to explore the spontaneous nature of its essence through art, poetry, writing, and political expression.

Surrealism challenged Freud's theory of the unconscious, seeing it not as a dark pool of destructive instinctual libidinous energy in need of social modification, but rather as a rich resource of images and energies available for spontaneous creation. However, to do so required throwing all caution to the wind. In a short essay, the surrealist Andre Breton encouraged young artists to "Drop everything . . . Drop your wife, drop your girlfriend . . Park your children in the woods . . . Drop your comfortable life . . . Take to the road . . ." (1978, p. 93 — an encouragement subsequently made popular in the 1950's in Kerouac's (1957) *On the Road.*

The Artistic Revolution

The years immediately following World War II saw a resurgence of artistic movements that emphasized spontaneous improvisation and social rebellion. In music it was avant-garde classical and jazz that called for an emphasis on pure sound over structure, a nomadic lifestyle of freedom from social and cultural restrictions, a dedication towards living in the moment, and an artistic devotion to novelty. In literature it was the "Beat Generation" that took the place of "The Lost Generation" of writers following World War I. In seeking a synergy between the improvisational styles of beat poetics and free jazz expressionism, beat writer and poet Jack Kerouac developed the technique of "jazz writing" that entailed using a tape recorder to create "on-the-spot" creations of spontaneous environmental sounds from one's immediate surroundings and, as clearly as possible, transcribing them into writing so as to capture the heart of the human condition (Maher, 2004).

In 1954 Kerouac published a short prose piece "Jazz of the Beat Generation" in the journal New Directions describing this improvisational writing style that involved a conversational approach to vernacular prose. This approach is similar to the phenomenological here-and-now therapeutic verbal exchange encouraged by early gestalt therapists in an attempt to support a more personal therapeutic dialogue. To a large extent this process-oriented perspective provided for an important point of demarcation between the gestalt therapy technique and the more traditional interpretive interactions found in many of the therapeutic schools that came before it. In his epic poem Paterson, William Carlos Williams likens the impact of the present moment to the roaring powers of a waterfall:

> The past above, the future below
> and the present pouring down: the roar,
> the roar of the present, a speech --
> is, of necessity, my sole concern. (Williams, 1992, p. 144)

The Beat Generation also began toying with various literary experiments such as the "cut and paste" and spontaneous writing methods of William Burroughs and the poetry and prose of Paul Goodman. For instance the scene in Goodman's (1959) novel *The Empire City* in which the animals in a zoo were freed from their cages and mingled both aggressively and lovingly with the patrons mirrors the rich sense of symbolism reflective in the human condition stripped of social interference reminiscent of Burrough's emotionally primitive stream of consciousness productions. The creative pulse of bebop and the musical avant-garde blended in with beat poetry in the cadence and rhythms that incorporated both its musical and verbal expressions. Jack Kerouac described most of his poetry as "jazz blues choruses" marked by spontaneous phrasing and harmony. Allen Ginsberg's classic poem "Howl" was said to mirror the cadence of jazz saxophonist Lester Young's improvisational efforts on his classic Lester Leaps In. The creative confluence found between beat writing, jazz improvisational style, and the gestalt therapy approach is epitomized in Schumacher's analysis of Ginsberg's evolving poetic style through the realization that "eternity was found in the here and now" (Schumacher, 1992, p. 122).

Given the anti-authoritarian nature of these common efforts, it is not surprising that they had a rippling effect in various sociopolitical arenas. FBI Chief J. Edgar Hoover proclaimed the beats to be one of the three most dangerous threats to the American way of life -- the other two being "eggheads" and communists (Schumacher, 1992). There was no doubt that similar to the fine line of respectability that the early gestalt therapists walked in their respective professional communities, the beats walked a similar precarious line between their art and their asocial behavior patterns in their literature and their personal lives in ways that challenged accepted social standards of the day. Living and playing on the edge of the beat community, the writer Norman Mailer described a beat "hipster" as one who was predisposed,

> . . . to encourage the psychopath in oneself, to explore that domain of experience where security is boredom and therefore sickness, and one exists in the present, in that enormous present which is without past or future, memory or planned intention, the life where a man must go until he is beat. (Mailer, 1959, p. 339)

More recently, Michael Vincent Miller (2002) cites the musical life of jazz trumpeter Miles Davis in a similar vein as an example of an aesthetic commitment that leads to a deeper awareness of one's creative production against all social pressure likening the process to the co-creative kinds of experiences so familiar to gestalt therapy. The artistic gestalten formed by such unique combinations of literary, visual, musical, and psychological rebellions from the status quo began to form a creative quilt of mutual social concerns — ones that were dedicated to the creation of dynamics and structures aimed at providing the ultimate support for the full range of human creative expression with minimal social restriction.

An erratically published journal known as Neurotica saw only nine issues in its brief existence from 1948-1951. It was an early forum for beat writers, radical psychologists, and musicians exploring the causes of mental distress that lie outside of the individual, and instead embedded in the social and political influences that form self. In an anthology of all nine issues compiled by Landesman (1981), an editorial statement in the fifth issue defined the publication as "the first lay-psychiatric magazine" and called for contributions from mental health specialists who saw neurosis as,

> . . . the defensive activities of normal individuals against abnormal environments.
> We assume that human beings are born non-neurotic, and are neuroticized later.
> We do not agree that it is the measure of social intelligence and psychiatric health to adapt to, and rationalize for, every evil. We do not subscribe to the psychosomatic fashion of throwing the gun on the corpse and placing the blame on the victim.
> (Landesman, 1981, p. 3)

Most gestalt therapists would feel quite comfortable contributing to such a philosophical model.

In addition to sharing similar philosophies and outlooks, there were frequent personal interfaces between some of the early gestalt therapists and surrealists, members of the free jazz movement, and artists of the beat generation. In fact, at some points the boundaries between these movements appeared seamless. Beat poets often dedicated poems to artists and musicians and were often found reciting in front of a jazz combo. In turn, many jazz vocalists of that era put beat poems into musical form as part of their standard repertoire. The term "prosody" was often used by artists primarily interested in the spontaneous nature of their particular art form. In ways very similar to the kinds of encounters found in gestalt therapy work, prosody referred to the types of meaning that could be gathered not only through the spoken word, but through such nonverbal channels as body movement, tempo, inflection, and timbre found in these new art forms. As surrealism began to attain greater levels of acceptance in the art world, radical artists, writers, and social critics found increased opportunities for artistic assimilation and popularity. In music, the surrealists took on the rural blues of black America's art form as both a musical and political expression of the oppressive pain and suffering associated with slavery as manifested in the spontaneous creations of the songs' lyrics and symbolism. Looking for a creative synergy between art, music, and politics, Paul Garon found such surrealistic roots in that,

> The blues is primarily sung and, like jazz, involves the entire component, thoroughly rooted in the violent exigencies of the black proletariat throughout the post-slavery epoch, and sufficient to place it well beyond the categories of anymere 'aesthetics' of music. (1979, p. 24)

And in gestalt therapy, it was the genius and interest of Paul Goodman that allowed for a similar cross-pollination of artistic energies. He was actively associated with avant-garde theater through both his writing and in his therapy with many of its writers and actors. He was introduced to the world of jazz and beat literature through his own poetry and his literary affinity with early beat writer and playwright Leroi Jones (now Amira Baraka) and others. On January 26, 1959, Goodman shared an evening of poetry readings with Alan Ginsberg at the Living Theater. Later, in 1964, Columbia University decided against allowing a proposed poetry reading on their campus by some of the more well known beat poets. Given the strong influence of American pragmatism on Goodman while completing his doctorate at the University of Chicago, it is no small point of irony that it was the John Dewey Society at Columbia University that successfully boycotted the college's English department eventually forcing them to sponsor a poetry reading that included Peter Orlovsky, Gregory Corso, and Columbia University dropout Allen Ginsberg!

While Goodman was quite actively involved in the earlier stages of the beat scene, enchanted primarily by their reflexive style of writing and artistic expression, he eventually became disappointed in their lack of interest in developing a more solid political base, and left for more social activist interests. Goodman's subsequent contributions across several artistic modalities were formidable. In addition to his unique contribution to gestalt therapy theory and practice, he was a novelist, playwright, social critic, philosopher, libertarian, and penned hundreds of poems and ballads. While his poetry was far more intellectual in nature than what was typical of that of the beat poets, the themes of life, death, meaning, creative spontaneity, and anti-authoritarianism were his literary currency.

His banner effort, *Growing up Absurd*, gained Goodman (1960) a rare moment of popularity and in many ways connected him to similar emerging artistic efforts in the fifties and sixties. In this as in all of his writings and social commentaries, Goodman held to an underlying dedication towards human freedom through the ability of the organism to self-regulate based on its innate potential for creative adjustment. In turn, it was the responsibility of the visual artist, musician, poet, therapist, and writer working in the context of community to provide for and to encourage the maximum level of personal, political, and social degrees of freedom as a creative ground for the realization of one's potential. As noted by Belgrad,

> according to Goodman, the unconscious mind was not located only in inaccessible reaches of the brain, but was manifest in the 'attitude' of the body's muscular structure. The body, as the site of cognition, linked the individual to the world beyond, both physically and psychologically. Thus it provided a focal point for artistic intervention in the social system. (1998, p. 11)

Perhaps the most common element holding these newly emerging art forms together was spontaneity in the service of a formative artistic experience. In abstract expressionistic art, it was Pollock's "gesture painting" that integrated the body movements of artists with their talents that allowed for deeper levels of artist/object/viewer contact that in turn set the stage for the later "happenings" developed by Kaprow that encouraged full audience participation and co-creation. The jazz musicians of that era formed instinctive confluences of sound, as beat poets transformed the written word into verbal interactions between the audience and the writer, and modern dance techniques evolved from the immediate sensations of the dancers in response to the reactions of other dancers. And all of these spontaneous efforts were in the spirit of creating a sense of community — a phenomenon of experience slowly eroding in American society as the result of two catastrophic World Wars occurring within the brief time period of one half of a century.

Even after the passage of fifty years or so since gestalt therapy theory's beginnings and its current recognition as a viable therapeutic approach, the radical uniqueness of its perspective on human functioning has endured the test of time. Even by today's postmodern standards, many people within and outside the mental health profession perceive gestalt therapy as a tough, no-holds-barred, individualistic form of therapeutic intervention that stresses autonomy, independence, and self-sufficiency of the individual with minimal concern for much in the way of external structure or authority. Historically, this level of insight is understandable given that as a therapy gestalt, like surrealism, beat literature, and modern American jazz, evolved as a maverick. In the case of gestalt therapy, we grew up outside of traditional psychological academic circles and supported lifestyles and orientations that in more "respected" forms of therapeutic schools were considered pathological.

And, it was the fifties — a time of conformity with well-prescribed standards that were valued as absolute truths for guiding human behavior and social discourse. Throwing aside licensing requirements, academic transcripts, and professional identification standards, the small and radical cadre of early gestaltists valued a grass roots community approach to emotional healing. Therapists, like other artists, were seen as resources within the organic dynamics of the community serving the mental health needs of its members similar to ways in which other craft people served the common needs of their neighbors. Diagnostic attention was shifted towards the field rather than the person. Functions of contact were emphasized over individual pathology with issues of dysfunction focusing as much on the environment as on the organism. We were asking others in the health professional communities to look into society's moral expectations and politics as much as they looked into their diagnostic manuals for the origins of human distress and constriction.

Sociopolitical Implications

Thus, it is understandable that gestalt therapists embraced political and social positions that were intimately connected to and supportive of creative human functioning with respect to the individual's relationship to the environment (Aylward, 1999). Viewing the social transitions taking place in the mid to late fifties through a wider lens, gestalt therapy formed a positive confluence with other movements that emphasized the need for an optimum level of freedom of movement and expression. A common thread shared between and within these movements was the rebellion against the constrictions on free speech and expression posed by McCarthyism and the House on Un-American Activity and the resultant social paranoia that choked off a large percentage of artistic expression, encouraged a pathological approach in diagnosing certain sexual orientations and expressions, and later, provided the incoherence of a patriotic logic that set the stage for the carnage of the Vietnam war, one that Goodman actively protested both through his writings and social disobedience.

These political developments created a need in individuals within these various antiauthoritarian movements to identify with a political philosophy that would serve as a holding environment for their creative identities and to provide avenues for organized social protest. For the surrealists, Andre Breton and his followers found communism a compatible soul mate although this identification alienated others in the movement. Given the more liberal tone of European politics of the time, many of the new jazz artists, while not developing a specific political format of their own, and given the racial discrimination in America against blacks in general, emigrated in large numbers.

For Goodman, anarchy served as the dominant political support for his creative efforts in his therapeutic, social, and political viewpoints. Withstanding popular distortion of this political concept, Goodman's take on anarchy referred to an absence of authority, not order -- a definition similar to Ginsberg's assertion that "authoritarianism is an usurpation of human consciousness — open manipulation, brutalization, and arbitrary manhandling of bodies and consciousness" (2001, p. 186). As anthropological support for his theories, Goodman embraced the ideas of Kropotkin in stressing the innate harmony and cooperation between and within species over the more "survival of the fittest" outlook of Charles Darwin, again emphasizing the sense of a natural and mutually supportive community as a basic support system for optimal human functioning. As noted by Belgrad:

In his book *Gestalt Therapy*, Goodman used the paradigm of gestalt psychology to reassert the link between avant-garde art and politics. He advocated an awareness of mutual plasticity and verbal prosody as the basis for constructive social change. (1998, p. 143) Goodman's hope was to "wrest the expressive body out from the net of habit" (ibid., p. 162) through the recovery of emotion, something Goodman saw as serving for the basis of the type of judgment needed for political discrimination and revolutionary social change.

In a broader sociological sense, gestalt therapy along with the artistic movements mentioned above shared a common ground in that they embraced a similar philosophical outlook with respect to human functioning. Being on the cusp of the postmodern movement, each began to move away from the more external, predefined standards of rational thought and universal dictates of artistic, literary, and philosophical endeavors. They turned instead to more eclectic, non-authoritarian ones that embraced novelty, eclecticism, playfulness, and spontaneity. As gestalt therapists we supported the intuitive insight over the clinically precise interpretation; the creative adjustment over the corrective experience; and the idea of value-free "differentness" over judged differences.

We also share with these other art forms a core belief in the value of human experience coming from the inside out rather than the other way around — the familiar move from environmental to self-support unencumbered by diagnostic, developmental, or philosophical speculation. We share the belief that people as they are have the innate ability to find meaning and purpose through their negotiations of contact against the figure/ground fluctuations within an organism/environmental field. This interactive process, familiar to us in our clinical work, when extended to higher levels of complexity and interaction, influences artistic cultural production as well. The emphasis is in support of the co-creative energy between the artist and the environment that serves as the ultimate aesthetic standard that in turn provides ongoing nurturing social and political field supports for optimal individual growth.

Gestalt therapy's concern is more with process than content. Rather than making interpretive statements on history or the historical connections of experiences, gestalt therapy is more at home with the idea of "how" something is said has more importance than "what" is said. The emphasis is less on "the signifier" (the word, art object, etc.), and more on the "signified," the personal meaning of the experience, symbol, or action. Nowhere is this more elegantly expressed than in gestalt therapy dream work wherein the meaning of images evolves from a subjective source of knowledge in the here and now rather than from a "cookbook" of dream symbols. For gestalt therapists, personal impact is the point at which meaning is determined, gained mainly through an awareness of the flow of experience with tolerance for chaos in the face of the continuing reorganization of ongoing experiencing with issues of "past" and "future" relegated to the phenomenology of the present moment.

Like much of postmodern schools of thought, gestalt therapy disregards the concept of "pure knowledge" (the meaning of meaning) separate from society, culture, or language. Our focus on awareness, formed at the contact boundary and figure/ground fluctuations in the field, belies any belief in "pure" truth, awareness, or interpretation, other than that which evolves in the treatment process itself. Rather than "put things together" we embrace fragmentation, polarization, conflict, impasse, and discontinuity in the therapeutic process in the belief that meaning outside of such context is impossible.

The mutual emphasis on the value of ultimate freedom of the human spirit shared by gestalt therapy and its artistic counterparts can provide for strong support for the essential transitional point in the therapeutic process between awareness and action. The use of "the experiment" in gestalt therapy often serves as a testing ground for such action, completing a social gesture that may contain personal, interpersonal, artistic, and/or political revolutionary potential. In many ways the experiment is the "glue" bonding the creative therapeutic interventions of Frederick Perls to the social activism of Paul Goodman -- an essential element in shifting matters of mental health from professionalism to communitarianism.

Nowhere is the similarity between gestalt therapy theory and postmodern thinking more profound than in the conceptualization of self. Both approaches take an anti-essentialist viewpoint in locating self process in the social field in ongoing and continuous fluctuations and as such multiple in nature. There is a word "ubuntu" used by a particular tribe in South Africa, the meaning of which is that a person is a person only in the context of other people. Rather than conceptualizing self as having some type of essential, universal core base through which all actions can be explained, both perspectives take interest in how the given and the free versions of self-functioning interact in the process of creative adjustment in reaction to the changing social situations of the field. In similar fashion, the unconscious is not a buried, deep, impervious pit of unawares desires, but a process that is constantly formed and reformed by the political and social dynamics of the present. To Foucault, the definition of self lies exclusively in those social relations that in turn connect to and create systems of politics and power (Rabinow, 1984).

Unfortunately, many (if not most) gestalt therapists have undervalued these political supports in their clinical work viewing them instead as somehow different and apart from Goodman's and Perls's contributions to psychotherapy per se. What needs to be appreciated more is that this valuable and, in a sense, essential connection between the theory and practice of gestalt therapy as we know it and the political realities that support it can substantially influence our ability to be effective in what we do. Indeed we are as much a political as a therapeutic art. And yet politics, like religion, has traditionally been viewed as falling outside the realm of psychotherapy.

There has been general agreement within and across differing therapeutic schools that political discussion in the clinical hour can represent resistance, inappropriate therapist self-disclosure, deflection, a breech of transference dynamics, or coercion — in other words, poor therapeutic methodology. Even in cases where a client's trauma is the result of specific political action or consequence, therapists are encouraged to make a conscious effort to deal with the diagnostic specifics involved in the most apolitical manner possible, lest the client be unduly influenced by the therapist's political feelings or reactions. In other words, the slate upon which the client projects must be kept as clean as possible. Emotional reactivity to the political realties of either the client or the therapist is rarely mentioned or merged within the boundaries of the therapeutic encounter.

Goodman's genius in creating his unique brand of therapeutic/political confluence can be more fully appreciated through an understanding of how he extended gestalt therapy theory beyond the consulting room. In his time, Goodman shared with surrealism, progressive jazz, and anarchistic libertarian politics, a common and essential theme — the quest for the nature of self before ego. Each art in its unique way developed approaches and techniques within its particular form that shared common goals with the others: spontaneity as the basis of artistic expression; creative processes that were free of authoritarian structures; and the mutual support of like-minded artistic community members.

Being both poet and playwright, Goodman mixed his therapeutic skills with such radical literary movements as the Living Theater founded by Judith Malina and Julian Beck. In the process, he crossed boundaries in a manner that today would be deemed unprofessional if not unethical. While Malina's therapist, Goodman's plays were being presented at the Living Theater and earlier on he was instrumental in springing her from a court mandated observation at Belleview hospital after she, along with Catholic Worker editor Dorothy Day, Jackson MacLow, Ammon Hennacy, and twenty other peace activists, refused to participate in a Civil Defense exercise specifying official tactics that would be used in a simulated hydrogen bomb attack on New York City. He consistently encouraged artists to draw the line between their art and mainstream culture as a way of confronting America with radical bohemian values (MacAdams, 2001). This emphasis is consistent with the theoretical underpinnings.

In all his intellectual endeavors into psychology, education, politics, and social criticism and planning, Goodman's aim remained clear -- a dedication to the growth of the human being into culture without losing nature. He agreed with the social libertarian, Murray Bookshin who observed that:

> Life is active, interactive, procreative, relational, and contextual. It is not a 'passive lump of stuff,' a form of metabolic matter that awaits the action of forces external to it and shaped by them . . . Life is self-directive in its own evolutionary development. (1997, p. 41)

It was Goodman's belief that psychology was on the wrong track in trying to help the person adjust to given social expectations. His belief was that basic and essential changes in society would free larger numbers of people from their neuroses than was possible through individual therapy alone. Of particular concern to Goodman and his colleagues was the negative impact that organizational structures had in influencing the free choice options of the individual.

To Goodman, the boundary between therapy and community was seamless. It made little sense to him, for instance, that there was any sound clinical justification for seeing a patient for an hour a week, dust the client off therapeutically, send him or her back into a toxic social or work environment, and hope for the best until the next session. Rather, to be maximally effective, therapy needed to be holistic from a social as well as a clinical perspective. This viewpoint was clearly articulated in Communitas, a book cowritten with his architect brother Percival, published in 1947 in which the Goodmans outlined the relationship between architecture, engineering, and workplace considerations serving as a ground for optimally nurturing human behavior and contact functions. In their view it was: "Against this ground we do our work and strive towards our ideal, or just live out our habits; yet because it is background, it tends to be taken for granted and to be unnoticed" (Goodman & Goodman, 1960, p.3).

> Hence, it was the split that developed between the otherwise organic nature of the contact between the organism and the environment that produced formidable levels of pathology seen in the plain evidence that we spend our money for follies, that our leisure does not revive us, that our conditions of work are unmanly, and our beautiful American classlessness is degenerating into a static bureaucracy; our mass arts are beneath contempt; our prosperity breeds insecurity; our system of distribution has become huckstering; and our system of production discouragesenterprise and sabotages invention. (ibid., p. 5)

Goodman saw this observation in a manner that was "not an indictment of the American way of life, but rather an attempt to clarify it and find what its possibilities are" (ibid., p. 5).

While more of a libertarian than a Marxist, Goodman viewed the role of work and labor similar to that as articulated by Karl Marx in his voluminous writings on the sociology of economics. Marx emphasized the importance of the level of identification a worker experienced with the means of production, the product itself, and the significance and impact of manufacturing on the functions of the community. In his 1844 work, Economic and Philosophic Manuscripts, Marx (1844/1959) put forth the idea that the essence of what it was to be human could in fact be found in the active and creative relationship of the organism to nature through labor — a confluence best reflected in the resultant vibrancy of community structure and functioning. Any rift or rupture in this relationship was tantamount to the organism being severed from its "inorganic" body. Like Goodman, the visionary capabilities of Marx can be seen in statements he made in 1859 concerning the problems that would face America's brand of capitalism. He warned that the conditions for success included a capacity to tolerate upward and downward swings in the marketplace; an evolving dependency on technology; and an eventual need to be global to accomplish end goals (Wheen, 2000).

The essence of Marx's historical materialism as it applied to labor centered on the contact and the meaning that existed between the worker and his/her product, and the balance in the exchange ratio between labor and wage. In this conceptualization, there were specific difficulties implied with consumer-based economic systems. One of these problems was that in such economic systems economics would have a major influence on all aspects of culture. As such, there would be an imbalance in the ratio between pay and the amount of work hours based on an increased need to produce more goods and encourage the "need" for consumption thereby creating a consumer-driven marketplace that would invade all aspects of community and culture. In order to maintain a more effective sense of socioeconomic perspective, Marx believed in a balance of emphasis on goods and products between "use value" (social relevance, community, functionality, etc.) and "exchange value" (monetary worth, potential for profit on resale, etc.).

Unfortunately, over time capitalism tips the scales in favor of exchange value and as such away from worker satisfaction and on to shareholder satisfaction since it is the latter that is primarily invested financially in the product independent of its use value. Today we see the effects of this imbalance in the way corporations are held responsible to Wall Street approval through quarterly profit reports designed to inform shareholders of expected gains. To meet these quantitative realities, jobs are outsourced, workforce reduced, and benefits compromised to insure profit. The degree of alienation between worker and product increases, the disconnection between product and use value increases, and the population polarizes into class distinctions based on wealth. As we will see below, such forces have a dramatic impact on value formation and social outlook.

In a spirit similar to both Marx and Goodman, Angela Davis noted that "unless and until all work is creative and unrestrained, human beings will have to seek their self-realization, in large part, outside the realm of social production" (1998, p. 167), since, in the ideal sense of the word, labor functions as a natural mediator between external nature and the human community. And, it was this very "human community" that Paul and Percival Goodman envisioned as the essential background against which the figure of human satisfaction could be formed through the joyful connections between work and community. These possibilities as put forth in the visions of Paul Goodman and other like-minded thinkers, continue to form a mandate that impacts on our work as gestalt therapists in dealing with individuals, couples, families, groups, and organizations. The above is not an attempt to place "politically correct" value judgments on specific economic theories or organizational dynamics. As gestalt therapists, our emphasis is on process not content. As such it is useless to debate over labels such as capitalism, socialism, or communism, given their overlapping similarities. For instance, in modern business culture many international corporations mirror the monopoly position, bureaucratic rigidities, and class structures that would rival the most cumbersome, centralized, state-owned agency.

One challenge we currently face in contemporary society is the disconnection that has occurred in the relationship between the worker and the communal nature of production, especially over the last fifty years. As would be predicted, this disconnection has also been mirrored in family structures and other functions of community. The family, in many instances, has become in Angel Davis' opinion, a "windowless monad of illusionary satisfaction" (James, 1998, p. 181) wherein children introject personal and work values through the influences of the media and the educational systems. In terms of community, we are more isolated than ever as reflected in the growth of gated and "adult" communities, a lack of adequate public transportation, superficial and inane cultural opportunities, gender-based role functions, and lessened opportunities for the free and spontaneous play of children.

In terms of field theory dynamics, the alienation of self from work is mirrored in lifestyle functioning and vice versa. In the past, communities were built to accommodate production and manufacturing efficiency with respect to geographic location resulting in them becoming dependent on corporate profit for their very existence, creating feelings of unwanted dependency and discontent. In today's marketplace, fear of arbitrary job loss without adequate representative support from trade unions, triggers catastrophic fantasies of not being able to retire, send children to college, or afford adequate family healthcare. In fact, such issues are becoming more familiar in our referral populations. By failing to embrace a holistic and field-oriented perspective, we as gestalt therapists are at best restricting ourselves to a type of symptom substitution work, or at worst, joining with the very forces of continuing alienation.

As is true of most all revolutionary ideas and movements, time tends to temper the fire in one's belly and yesterday's rebellion evolves into today's mainstream. As gestalt grew in its numbers of adherents, it widened its scope of clinical practice to include couples work, family therapy, and most recently, organizational development. We now have institutes, journals, regional and worldwide organizations and conferences, and every once in a while get mentioned in textbooks that define the various "schools of psychotherapy." In the professional sense of the word, we have more or less arrived and, as is true of such status, we have become somewhat complacent especially with respect to our historic ideas. Despite this fairly natural evolutionary process of absorbing the novel into the familiar, it would serve us well as gestalt therapists to re-familiarize ourselves with our theory as a way of understanding the tactical advantages we have in this regard given the rich and clearly articulated socio-political psychotherapeutic model from which we can draw.

As Peter Schulthess has noted:

> The second and third generation of Gestalt therapists may have a different focus — one of professionalizing Gestalt therapy. They might have forgotten the side of Gestalt therapy that was critical of systems, organizational hierarchies, and political control — a priority that meant so much to the founders. (2003, p. 62)

Or as the 60's yippie Abbie Hoffman advises: "One of the worst mistakes any revolution can make is to become boring. It leads to rituals as opposed to games, cults as opposed to community, and denial of human rights as opposed to freedom" (1980, p. 106). We have a very important and radical psychological theory formed from and alongside of similarly attuned political philosophies and art forms. As a theoretical base, gestalt therapy is in and of itself a unique gestalt that fits into some contexts and not into others and we need to know those differences as a way of avoiding conflicting or contradictory purposes and aims.

It is important to keep in mind that gestalt therapy theory is as much of a political and social philosophy as it is a psychological theory and a methodology of clinical intervention, and that ultimately it favors and works towards the development of creative community. As clinicians we simultaneously and dramatically affect both the organism and the encompassing environmental field. In the fore-contact phase of engagement, vigorous discriminative focus needs to be given to field dynamics and factors that either inform or undermine support for our way of working. Without such understanding, the contact phase of engagement is vulnerable to confusion, inconsistencies, and distortions, thereby compromising both our work and our theory and what that all means for our social, political, and artistic future.

Conclusion

As can be seen through this brief retrospective, gestalt therapy theory is rich in both the depth and the breadth of its philosophy and its practice. As such it offers those who seek out our way of working maximum opportunities for growth in many related directions. However, in order to give support to the full extent of our possibilities, we as gestalt therapists would do best to absorb and reflect on our historical roots — ones that were immersed in the importance of human freedom and spontaneity supported best in environments that allowed for the maximum degrees of personal freedom. The devastation of two World Wars altered our consciousness forever and opened opportunities for artists, writers, musicians, poets, educators, and philosophers to find ways and methods of freeing the human spirit from arbitrary bonds and from subservience to repressive institutional structures so as to enable an individual's innate spontaneity to surface in ways that maximize the potential for optimal personal, artistic, social, and political functioning. As gestalt therapists we are an integral part of that culture of spontaneity and it would enhance us in the practice of our therapeutic art form to continue to immerse ourselves in our roots and our purposes. As the surrealist writer, poet, and philosopher Andre Breton reminds us, "human emancipation remains the only cause worth saving" (1978, p. 5).

References

Aylward, J. (1999). The contributions of Paul Goodman to the clinical, social and political implications of boundary disturbances. *The Gestalt Review 3/2,* 101-118.

Belgrad, D. (1998). *The culture of spontaneity.* Chicago: The University of Chicago Press.

Bookshin, M. (1997). *The Murray Bookshin reader* (J. Biehl, Ed.). London: Cassell Wellington House.

Breton, A. (1978). *What is surrealism? Selected writings of Andre Breton* (F. Rosemont, Ed.). New York: Monad Press.

Garon, P. (1979). *Blues and the abstract spirit.* New York: DaCapo Press.

Ginsberg, A. (2001). *Spontaneous mind.* New York: Perenial Press.

Goodman, P. (1959). *The empire city.* Indianapolis: Bobbs-Merrill.

Goodman, P. (1960). *Growing up absurd: Problems of youth in the organized system.* New York: Random House.

Goodman, P., & Goodman, P. (1960). *Communitas: Means of livelihood and ways of life.* New York: Vantage Books.

Hoffman, A. (1980). *Soon to be a major motion picture.* New York: Putnam.

Davis, A. (1998). *The Angela Davis reader* (J. James, Ed.). London: Blackwell.

Kerouac, J. (1957). *On the road.* New York: Viking Press.

Lacan, J. (1981). *The language of the self: The function of language in psychoanalysis.* Baltimore: Johns Hopkins University Press.

Landesman, J. (Ed.), (1981). *Neurotica: The authentic voice of the beat generation.* London: Jay Landesman.

MacAdams, L. (2001). *Birth of the cool: Beat, bebop, and the American avant-garde.* New York: Free Press.

MacCabe, C. (Ed.), (1981). The talking cure: Essays in psychoanalysis and language. Basingstoke: MacMillan.

Maher, P. (2004). Kerouac: *The definitive biography.* Lanham: Taylor Trade.

Mailer, N. (1959). *Advertisements for myself.* New York: Putnam.

Marx, C. (1844/1959). *Economic and philosophic manuscripts of 1844.* Moscow: Foreign Languages Publishing House.

Miller, M. V. (2002). The aesthetics of commitment: What gestalt therapists can learn from Cezanne and Miles Davis. *International Gestalt Journal 25/1,* 109-122.

Perls, F. S., Hefferline, R. F., & Goodman, P. (1951). *Gestalt therapy: Excitement and growth in the human personality.* New York: The Julian Press.

Rabinow, P. (Ed.), (1984). *The Foucault reader.* New York: Pantheon Books.

Schulthess, P. (2003). Gestalt therapy and politics. *British Gestalt Journal 12/1,* 62-66.

Schumacher, M. (1992). *Dharma lion: A critical biography of Allen Ginsberg.* New York: St. Martin's Press.

Stevens, B. (1970). *Don't push the river (it flows by itself)*. Moab, UT: Real People Press.

Wheen, F. (2000). *Karl Marx: A life*. New York: Norton.

Williams, W. C. (1992). *Paterson*. New York: New Directions.

Chapter 23. Creative Processes in Gestalt Group Therapy
Carl Hodges

Chapter introduction

This article was pivotal in developing, exploring, and articulating a specifically gestalt approach to group. Based in field theory of Wertheimer, Köhler, and Koffka, the founders of Gestalt psychology, this is not systems theory, not psychoanalytic group theory, not the interactionist nor the "Hot Seat Model." This was and still is a new and different way of understanding being in groups based in gestalt field theory.

Gestalt theory takes seriously the group as figure/grounds, wholes/parts, process/events, and gestalt formation/destructions.

Our client is the group/field. "Leaders," "members," "women," "men," "old-timers," "new-comers," are parts of the field: transient "figures" against the ground of evolving group. This is gestalt formation/destruction, process and events.

Every voice — including the "silent," the "deviant," the "un-named" voice — is essential, and in its here-and-now vulnerability is a part of the whole, a voice for a part of the field. The work is the progressive stating of the present actuality. This voicing is articulating, differentiating, discovering and creating the field and one's emerging, shared place-part-in it.

Our approach is radical, embracing a different style of contacting in the field–here-and-now, a new definition of "work" as exploring one's "part" of the "whole/group," guided by our autonomous criterion of contact (bright, lively, fluid, graceful, etc.).

Our goal is to articulate a shared experience, verbal and non-verbal, of the field "here-and-now." This is the process of self emergence –self-ing,

This theory/practice emerges out of our work, our experiences and experiments and our learning in group and community at the New York Institute for Gestalt Therapy. This paper grew out of an on-going dialogue and various presentations I had done at the Institute over 25 years.

Creative Processes in Gestalt Group Therapy
Carl Hodges[104]

Creare: (Latin) To make, to bring into existence.

All contact is creative and dynamic. It cannot be routine, stereotyped or merely conservative because it must cope with the novel, for only the novel is nourishing... All contact is creative adjustment of the organism and environment. (Perls et al., 1994, p 6)

Contact is awareness of the field or motor response in the field.
(Perls et al., 1994, p 5)

Gestalt Therapy is creativity. Awareness is the creation of figures and grounds. Our contacting (re)organizes our experience, creating new possibilities. Experiencing is gestalt formation/destruction.

The achievement of a strong gestalt is itself the cure, for the figure of contact is not a sign of, but is itself the creative integration of experience. (Perls et al., 1994, p 8)

A group is a gestalt!

At the New York Institute for Gestalt Therapy, through the re-examination of our foundations initiated by our senior Fellow Richard Kitzler and others, and through attending to our process as a learning community, this notion has emerged and profoundly shaped our direction. A group can be conceived, not as a "system," not as a collection of "interactions" between individuals, not as a portable "hot-seat," but as a gestalt with figure and ground, wholes and parts, processes and events, forces and constraints, gestalt formation and destruction. These concepts come from Gestalt Field Theory.

Gestalt Field Theory

Our foundations are in field theory, which revolutionized 20th century thought, perspective and existence: in physics (Faraday, Mack, Einstein, Heisenberg), in art (Picasso, Braque, Leger), in psychology (Wertheimer, Köhler, Koffka, Goldstein, then later Lewin, Bion, etc.) in biology (Von Bertalanffy,

---

[104] Originally published in Spagnuolo Lobb, Amendt –Lyon, Eds) (2003) *Creative License, the art of gestalt therapy*, Springer: New York, pp 249 – 60,

Ecology, Osama), in music (Stravinsky, Berg, Parker, etc.), in literature (Joyce, Musil). As the art critic John Berger (Dyer, 2002) has written, in a brilliant essay called "The Moment of Cubism," we became aware for the first time in history of a global whole of which we are all a part, created by it and creating it, changing our vision of time and space, rhythm and tempo, connection and relation. Picasso invites us to see a whole that shows many sides at once, challenges our previous sense of reality, involves awareness and memory; that is not complete without us making figures and grounds, traveling in and out and over, bringing our experience and history into this here and now event.

We come from a rich heritage! Wertheimer and Einstein were friends and musicians together, Kohler studied with Max Planck, and Lore Perls studied with Wertheimer and Goldstein, while Fritz worked with Goldstein and Gelb.

There are many field theories: I use the field theory of the Gestalt Psychologists Wertheimer, Koffka and particularly Kohler.

> ...we are inevitably led to the concepts of field physics. In this part of science the consideration of what might be called "processes-in-extension" is regarded as a matter of course. The term which I have just used is simply another name for the self-distributed processes to which I referred in Chapter IV. ["Dynamics As Opposed to Machine Theory"] In such processes, it will be remembered, local events occur, as they occur, only within the distribution as a whole." (Köhler, 1975, p 124)

(This is different than the later Field Theory of Kurt Lewin that tends more toward systems: structure and space, boundary between, and goals.)

The field theory of the Gestalt Psychologists is concerned with:
- figure and ground
- wholes and parts
- process and events
- forces and constraints
- gestalt formation and destruction

A field is the dynamic interplay of forces and constraints. When these forces interact without constraint, a *dynamic equilibrium* is reached. This equilibrium has form, shape, structure, and organization. This organization, this creation of a figure against a ground we call a gestalt.

A gestalt may be strong — clear, bright, energetic, flowing — or weak, less of each of the above. A gestalt can only be as strong as the field conditions (interaction of forces and constraints) allow. The forces in a field may be organized around the field's constraints: i.e. a locomotive or other machine, a T.V. picture, organic psychosis, etc.

417

A field is a process not a thing —"processes in extension" Kohler says. Field theory substitutes events for things-having-fixed properties. Part-processes are themselves determined by the intrinsic nature of the whole. (Kohler, 1975)

The familiar example is the "rock." In this place, at this time, this temperature, at this atmospheric pressure, at this gravity, we have an event which we call a rock. If we were to change this equilibrium, say the temperature a few hundred degrees up or down, or change the atmospheric pressure, etc., then we may no longer have the same event, the same "rock." Notice that the "observer" is part of this event, this figure making.

The Gestalt Group

What if we take seriously these concepts from Gestalt Field Theory - figure/ground, wholes/parts, process/events, forces/constraints, and gestalt formation/destruct — and apply them to a group? What are the implications for "treatment," learning, leadership, authority, experiment, creativity and our Gestalt Theory itself? What does such a group look like?

Some Examples

Any example, two dimensional, verbal, abstracted must seem stilted. Three come to mind anyway, from different kinds of groups.

I. This was a practicum. I was asked to "demonstrate" a Gestalt Therapy session. A young woman and myself, "the Leader," sat in the middle of a group that had been meeting for about six months, and which was at that time in or near a configuration that could be called "Intimacy." The power struggles and competition had waned, there was a feeling of working together, of sharing support, even of "family."

We sat down on the carpeted floor about two feet from each other. I felt the pressure to "do" something, to make something happen, but let it pass and noticed her eyes, her face, her body. The room disappeared, and I saw a father, a mother, siblings in and out, a childhood, difficult relationships, having to be strong, abusive hurt, tears, profound sadness, acceptance yearning: feelings evoked in me, and our seeing her seeing me seeing her - figure into figure, and like shifting sand, ground forming, shaping, re-shaping, shared in us. I felt tears and could see hers. The "session" lasted eight minutes. I said five words: she smiled and I knew she knew they were five words too many. We paused (there is no "end" to what was touched and built). We paused, breathed and sat back inviting the rest of the group, deeply moved, in. They too were participants in what had happened with their resonance, harmonies, emotions, the succession of figures and grounds evoked in them, not through our words but through our/their visions, connections, touching. Later, as a practicum again, we could talk about figure/ground, about the importance of the non-verbal communication, about awareness of what your body is sensing, experiencing without words. On a cognitive level we could talk about body position, breathing, eyes, facial expression, energy level. And yet what happened was more than all these, because field is more than stimulus-response, more than cycles, more than linear: it is apprehensive, total; it is presence in the "wholes of experience."

II. A therapy group that had gone on for some months and was in what could be called a Power and Control configuration - competitiveness and unexpressed fears of being vulnerable. A woman client, D, who had early abuse issues, was finding me, despite any best efforts, to be unsupportive: when I tried to "explain" myself she felt even more unsupported, not understood, not heard, and "abused." I was feeling misunderstood, and was beginning to feel "helpless," as our attempts to communicate with each other seemed to be driving us further apart, and making each of us feel more alienated and isolated. I felt on the spot, vulnerable, and stuffed with something that seemed to make it hard to think, or even breathe. I wondered if D and I were in the same subgroup, and if we were "holding" something for the whole group. I did breathe and noticed that all the interaction in the group was now between D and myself, and that the other group members were sitting back quietly. D and I had become figure against the ground of the group. I made a "field statement" to that effect: I said what I was experiencing in my part of the field, and described what I was noticing in the field as a whole. An experiment then occurred to me and I proposed it to D and the group: that we invert the figure/ground relationship and that we, the pair, keep silent and become ground for the rest of the group as figure. D and I would observe our own experiencing in our bodies and notice if or when we began to feel "un-stuffed." We sat as other group members talked eventually about their own vulnerability, their frustration in finding their own voice and being heard, and their irritation with the Leader, who was going too fast and demanding too much. D and I began to smile at each other as we noticed the 'stuffed' feelings begin to drain, and as the group began to take up their own aggression, vulnerability and needs, as figure.

III. In a conjoint therapy session with a husband and wife: the wife was depressed and had what the husband called "addictive behaviors," namely an obsession with telephone (sex) chat lines. Her obsession enabled her to "avoid" her husband, her children, and household chores. The husband, feeling abandoned chose to be in rage, rather than in vulnerability and hurt, and ultimately felt helpless since his ranting carried with it no consequences (he threatened many times to leave). The wife had a history of depression since pre-adolescence, and was overweight with body image issues: she appeared washed out, defeated, limp. He appeared angry, demanding, constantly defining her in his terms, speaking for her. Conversation between them in the session was remarkably one sided and she retreated more and more into the woodwork, looking more and more beaten-down. She seemed powerless with no options and grew quieter. "Where are you?," the other therapist asked gently. Eventually the patient says she wants to "get away." Her husband derides her more. "Where would you like to go?" I ask, "Can you imagine where you'd like to go?" Eventually she says she can imagine someplace by the sea, "Can you describe it?" It is a rough, powerful sea, smashing against huge rough rocks and boulders, and behind that there is a quiet, off-season deserted village. "Can you be the sea?" Eventually, at last she is able to feel her own power, energy, and excitement. "I'm a changing sea!" she says. I asked her husband if he could join her fantasy - as the rocks and boulders. "I am strong and hard and tall. I meet your strength with my strength, I feel my energy with you." In my mind a tune appears: Perry Como singing "...it's just impossible, like the shore line and the sea, it's just impossible." We talk about "paradigms," and the shoreline as a paradigm: it is the place where the sea and the land meet, the product not of one or the other but of both, a very alive, changing, active boundary where the two meet in their differences. We talk about making room for that difference in each other and being able to allow it, at time in its strength and at times in its gentleness.

Creativity In The Gestalt Group

In the Gestalt Group we are working with the organism/environment field, and we are looking for *figures* and the *grounds* from which they emerge, wholes and parts, process and events, forces and constraints, gestalt formation and destruction.

The Gestalt Group can be 3 members or 3 hundred. The prototype is not the family, with parent and child (or Teacher/student, Doctor/patient, Leader/follower). The prototype for the Gestalt Group is the Polis, as members take up their "citizenship" (de Mare et al., 1991), their flexible transient roles in a community of equals, and take up their creativity as well.

"[The self] is the artist of life." (Perls et al., 1994, p 11)

The group members are engaged in an ongoing forming, discovering, creating and re-creating of that artwork we call "group" (or "couple," or "family," or "community," or "organization"). In that forming, discovering, creating, we are looking for what is figure, and also for where the energy is - or is not! Is the interaction bright, lively, energetic, graceful, fluid in contacting?

Contact, the work that results in assimilation and growth, is the forming of a figure of interest against a ground or context of the organism/environment field... The figure (gestalt) in awareness is a clear, vivid perception, image, or insight: in motor behavior, it is the graceful energetic movement that has rhythm, follows through etc. (Perls et al., 1994, p 7)

The process of figure/background formation is a dynamic one in which the urgencies and resources of the field progressively lend their powers to the interest, brightness   and force of the dominant figure...[which is specifically psychological and] has specific observable properties of brightness, clarity, unity, fascination, grace, vigor, release (Perls et al., 1994, pp. 7-8)

This is our *Autonomous Criterion* and it is vital here, for it gives indication of "the depth and reality" of the experience and whether,

The need and energy of the organism, and the likely possibilities of the environment are incorporated and unified in the figure. (Perls et al., 1994, p 7)

Where are the forces (needs, excitements, feelings, fears) and where are the constraints (the holding back) that affect the clarity and brightness of the figure (*Prägnanz*)? What is the whole and its parts (as in Example II)?

In the organism/environment/field we may speak of whole-processes and part-processes. Everything that occurs in the group/field —thoughts, feelings, interactions, behavior, musings, day-dreams, songs, images, metaphors — emerges from the ground of the group and tells everything about what is going on — or not going on! — in the group. Every behavior emerges from the ground of the group, is event in the group's process: every part has to do with the whole.

The implications of this are many.

First, there are no "individual" issues, there are *only* group issues: there is no individual or "identified" patient; there is no pathologizing. Introjection, confluence, projection, retroflection, egotism are all seen as *group* issues, that interrupt and affect the group's flow, energy, aliveness. (They act as constraints.)

Second, whatever comes up as figure for a group member "internally or externally," in their bodies, in their emotions, or as issues or concerns is now seen as figure emerging out of the ground of the group. Whatever you're feeling in a group, given the shared ground, chances are that at least one other person is feeling or experiencing something similar. If you "voice" your feeling, issue, difficulty, you may be a voice for a part of the whole. If others *join* you in stating similar feelings and experience and together you all begin to voice, share *and explore* your experience, that is what Yvonne Agazarian, in a brilliant conceptualization, calls *"subgrouping."* (Agazarian, 1997) These mini groupings emerge as figure out of the process of the whole group: they explore their part of the field, bring into contact and context, then dissolve back into the process of the whole, their work becoming ground for the next figure.

This exploring and sharing together of your experience here and now is the definition of work in the Gestalt Group. The subgroups allow the exploration of conflicting parts and splits and enable us to see "many sides at once." Splits can then be explored not in the individual in isolation, but in the group as a whole which holds and contains all sides of the splits, in diverse subgroupings: compliance and defiance, yearning to be closer and wanting to maintain distance, wanting to aggress and the fear of aggressing , the desire to compete openly and the fear of it. The subgrouping is ongoing experiment: there is opportunity for experiencing "flexibly various" standpoints, "travelling in and out and over," exploring the diverse parts of oneself and of the field, and the opportunity to go "to the thing itself," to explore "feelings," "impulses," and "concerns" *as processes* here and now, finding words, voice, meaning. One's grounds and possibilities become larger and livelier. Members can explore in subgroups all parts of themselves, including the unfamiliar, the uncomfortable, the fearful. Distinction is made between impulse and action. Feelings, impulses, issues, concerns are experienced and explored rather than acted out or discharged, or even necessarily "expressed" to their object.

This is a slightly different style of contacting--more middle mode, more "id" oriented, being open to voicing the experience. Voicing makes more of the background foreground, which creates a different figure and a different dialogue. A member may be angry (at X). It is the *experience* of her anger here and now that is explored, and she may be joined by others who are also experiencing *anger*, though not necessarily at X. If X is experiencing anger also, he is in the *same* subgroup--one which is together exploring, digesting, and integrating anger and its meanings in this context, at this time, for this (whole) group.

This voicing together and exploring of experience in the group here and now transforms the experience as it is happening and builds a new context, re-configuring old issues and giving them new and deeply shared meanings. *This is the essence and definition of creativity in the Gestalt Group.*

Leadership

In this model leadership is seen not as a role, but as a process which any can enter. Your vulnerability expressed is your leadership. Your vulnerability is your statement of where you are in the field. If expressed it is also a statement about the field and your relation to it, and in the expression the field is *changed*; more of the background becomes foreground, more of the structure of the actual situation becomes known. The identification, articulation and expression of your vulnerability is an act of leadership in the Gestalt Group.

The "designated Leader" or "worker" is an imposed structure, a role which, like all roles, with contact and gestalt destruction/formation, over time dissolves into the fluidity of the group.

The role of the designated Leader changes according to what is required and what configuration the group seems to be in. A two-way process, the group also leads the Leader. At various times the Leader may be: a holding environment,

"Authority," a target, a steady course, a conductor, an interpreter, a model, a guide, a clarifier, an advisor, a vital member, the repository of the group's energy, faith, playfulness, history.

Words, Words, Words!

A vast amount of what goes on in a field is non-verbal, pre-verbal, a-verbal. We are creating a new shared space — a "transitional space" in Winnicott's sense: a space of projection and discovery, of play and exploration, which is transforming.

Our tools in this creating are ourselves, particularly our bodies, our images, sensations, feelings, our style of contacting and experiencing ourselves and our "other" - our ability to make a kind of poetry and dance in, with, and of our contacting.

Our language must be the language of apprehension and delight, symbol and metaphor, poetry and description. Pedestrian language cannot catch the field.

> Canst thou draw out Leviathan with a hook?
> Will he speak soft words unto thee?
> Lay Thine hand upon him,
> Remember the battle
> Do no more"
>
> Job 41:1, 3, 8

Kurt Goldstein, writing about applying Gestalt theory to the organism/environment field, spoke of the need for "symbols" and "images" in thinking about field (Goldstein, 1975), that the old constructs don't give us adequate knowledge. Metaphor and poetry evoke a "contemplative, prelogical mode of knowing, exhibited so forcefully in art, the knowing that terminates in recognitions and not 'conclusions'." (Cox and Theilgard, 1987, ix)

"The image has touched the depths before it stirs the surface." (Cox and Theilgard, 1987, p. 1950

In the Gestalt Group we take time to breathe, to pause to find our metaphors for the present actuality (as in Example III), and to let them lead us: we, too: "Attend. Witness. Wait." (Cox and Theilgard, 1987, xxix) The metaphors shared, apprehend the field and connect, rather than the usual analyzing, dissecting, distancing.

In the Gestalt Group, as the Frame of Reference or the context changes, so do the meaning of words and "existing categorizations." (Cox and Theilgard, 1987, p 196) We begin to create new shared language and new shared meanings.

Group Gestalten

A group is a gestalt. With contacting, over time, the group's gestalt or configuration changes. It may organize into millions of configurations, but heuristically I like five. The five-stage model (Garland et al., 1973) I use is not normative, not a blueprint but a map. It does not tell you where you must go or how you must go, but it does orient you as to where you might be. These group gestalten or configurations are: I Orientation; II Power and Control; III Intimacy; IV Differentiation; V Termination.

I. Orientation

When members begin a group, they first "check it out." They are orienting themselves before making any commitment and their behavior is approach/avoidance. Their Frame of Reference and their norms (about "man," "woman," "good," "bad") are from society, their culture and previous groups they have been in. The designated Leader's task is to clarify and support the approaching and avoiding, normalizing it, helping members to put it into words and into subgroups, rather than acting it out. It is no longer an individual issue if members are able to subgroup and explore together the impulse to invest more in the group, or the impulse to flee or be skeptical. The Leader helps the members to experiment and connect in a new way.

II. Power and Control (Authority)

When members do invest in the group, there is then concern about where one "fits in" with the other members and with the Leader. What behavior is valued--openness? intelligence? emotionality? defiance? Who does the Leader seem to like? Much behavior is Leader-centered, and there are competitive feelings between the members.

There is tremendous demand for creativity from the designated Leader in this configuration. Anger and frustration, fight and flight, fears about being vulnerable come up in various disguises in this configuration and must be recognized, named, experienced, explored and understood in the context of this group here and now. Feelings and the fear of feelings have to be recognized and expressed clearly and cleanly, and part of this is their being explored in subgroups. Most groups, even therapy groups, stop in this configuration of Authority/Dependence, and the relationship to authority is never examined as a group issue. In this model if the members are to go on and to create their own space, this Authority/Dependence must be explored and worked also, exploring both the compliance and defiance as *group issues* (and as ways of avoiding going deeper).

If the Leader is good, there will be a Rebellion, what Bennis and Shepard call a "barometric event," (Bennis and Shepard, 1957) a challenging and unpredictable time for the Leader-as-Authority who may feel as if

"...the storm is up, and all is in the hazard." *Julius Caesar* Act V. - W. Shakespeare

Yet, this "storm" is vital and essential for the group's growth and further development. The Leader has to steer a steady course, not deflecting or defending or explaining away, but listening. He must also support the expression of the anger, disappointment, hurt, betrayal aimed at himself and help clarify what the issues are. He has to be fully present and let the members know they have affected him. One writer calls this "Sitting in the Fire" (Mindell, 1995). The Leader acknowledges their issues and, with them, sees what needs to be changed. Was there a misunderstanding? Is there something they want to change in the group, some change in behavior, structure, time or method?

At the other end of this process, there will be a new norm, a change in structure, the Leader will do something differently, and the members will have taken on more responsibility for how the group is organized and develops. The group is no longer so Leader-centered: the member's empowerment has begun. The Frame of Reference is no longer society, but is this group at this time, what we can co-create and who we can be within it.

III. Intimacy

The group, after the Rebellion against the authority of the Leader, now turns to issues of authority and intimacy with each other, the group begins to feel more like a "family," and members "remind me of my mother, brother, sister," etc. The Leader's task is to clarify what belongs to the family "then," and what to the group now; what is similar and what is novel here and now.

"...for only the novel is nourishing. "(Perls et al., 1994, p 6)

The Leader supports the deeper levels of exploration, intimacy and sharing now possible in the subgroups. Shame issues and early trauma can now be explored in a different way, in a different context. The Frame of Reference is family, but in this group, and who we can be for one another.

IV. Differentiation

Having created a deeper level of trust, cohesion, clarity and empowerment, members are ready to bring in parts of themselves not yet explored, perhaps the unaccepted parts that make them feel existentially "different." This group is seen as a space we have created, where we can more fully be ourselves in all aspects, where we can explore ourselves with others "in the same boat," where we can connect on all levels. Where my selfing is an integral part of our "grouping," and where we can experiment with new behaviors. The Leader's task is to support this, but more and more as a resource, a consultant, as she encourages members to take on more Leadership, and supports the group in running itself.

V. Termination

"Parting is such sweet sorrow…" *Romeo and Juliet* - W. Shakespeare

"Do not go gentle into that good night…
Rage, rage against the dying of the light."
Dylan Thomas

Termination is the final configuration. Members know that the group will be ending; there may be sadness, hurt, anger, feelings of abandonment. These must be named and worked in our subgroups together. There may be a "return" to earlier forms of behavior — avoidance, defiance — or denial that the group "was that important." There may be: "I'll leave the group before the group leaves me." The Leader's task is to help the group make the feelings clear, to help reaffirm the skills that have been learned, to hold the history and the ground of what has been created and to aid the creative integration of experience, including the letting go, in this new context. She makes room for members' taking back projections and group roles, for appreciations and recognitions…and for goodbyes. Her Frame of Reference is this group and what has been gained in this special creation, now as a ground for the next steps in the journey.

"What we call the beginning is often the end and to make an end is
To make a beginning. The end is where we start from."
"Little Giddings," T.S. Eliot

Notice the enormous possibilities for new creative adjustments for selfing and exploring our issues in each configuration — dependency, authority, intimacy, shame, loss--and the tremendous support given by the subgrouping together, to "hold" those issues as they are explored. Notice also that the stereotypical social scripts, "woman," "man," "black," "white," "old," "young," will have different "meanings," will be different processes in each configuration. As the Frame of Reference changes, these scripts will dissolve, and reappear as increasingly "novel" events.

"The self is not the figure that is created but the creating of the figure."
(Perls et al., 1994, p 191)

"Anxiety as an emotion is the dread of one's own daring."
(Perls et al., 1994, p 192)

Bibliography

Agazarian, Yvonne (1997) *Systems-centered therapy for groups.* The Guilford Press, New York pp. 41-62.

Bennis WG, and Shepard HA (1957) "A theory of group development." *Human Relations* 9:4 pp. 415-437

Cox, Murray, and Theilgard, A. (1987) *Mutative metaphors in psychotherapy.* Tavistock Publications, London

De Mare, Patrick, Piper, R, Thompson, S (1991) *Koinonia: from hate, through dialogue, to culture in the large group.* Karnap Books, London, pp. 1- 74

Dyer, Geoff, ed. (2002) *John Berger selected essays.* Pantheon Books, New York, pp. 71-92

Garland, Jones and Kolodny (1973) "A five stage model for social work groups." In Bernstein, Saul, ed. *Explorations in social group work.* Milford House, New York, pp. 17-47

Goldstein, Kurt (1975) *Human nature in the light of psychopathology.* New American Library, New York, pp. 3-33

Köhler, Wolfgang (1975) *Gestalt psychology.* New American Library, New York pp. 60-79

Mindell, Arnold (1995) *Sitting in the fire: large group transformation using conflict and diversity.* Lao Tse Press, Portland, Oregon, pp. 17-47

Perls, Hefferline, and Goodman (1994) *Gestalt therapy: excitement and growth in the human personality.* The Gestalt Journal Press, Highland, New York

Chapter 24. Dual Relationships: A Gestalt Therapy Perspective

Bud Feder

Chapter Introduction

During the 1990's and first decade of this century, there was much debate over the issue of "boundary crossing"... otherwise more properly known as "dual relationships." Along with several other psychologists (most prominently Ofer Zur and Arnold Lazarus), I worked, not specifically as a gestalt therapist but as a member of the American Psychological Association, to affect changes in its Code of Ethics. During that time changes were made, loosening the rigidity that had developed probably as a result of some of the theoretical stances (though often not the actual behavior) of classical Freudian psychoanalysts. In the present article I look at these issues from a specifically gestalt therapy point of view. The article provoked very strong reactions, both positive and negative and did, I believe, help many gestalt therapists think through and come to clearer positions on these often difficult issues.

---it is very representative of the way I work with regard to this aspect

---it stirred up a lot of very strong positive and negative reactions when it came out in 2004

---I think it is well-organized and well-written

Dual Relationships: A Gestalt Therapy Perspective[105]

Session 30: Is there a way to fire N. as a painter while keeping him on as a patient? I find the conflicts he exhibits between his true and false selves fascinating and treatable. His painting skills, however are crude bordering on hopeless. Today, he painted over one of my most accessible outlets. But maybe my disappointment with N's paint job is the result of some internal conflict in myself. Will consult Ledbetter regarding countertransference in these instances.

Session 33: N. calls. He's ceasing treatment. I'm gravely disappointed; we've made some significant leaps in the past few months. X. has been doing touch-ups during his Monday sessions and now I can see an end to this journey. Although I disagree with N.'s decision, I take his certainty as an encouraging sign. Later I meet Ledbetter for a Martini. N. has been seeing him for three weeks, he says, and although he's been unable to penetrate N.'s false self, N. has been doing some first-rate plumbing. "You remember that toilet in the waiting room, how it used to run. Four sessions and it's fixed!"

The New Yorker, Sept. 10,200l – excerpts from "Shouts and Murmurs" [a humor page]

Overview

Dual relationships*have been practiced extensively in Gestalt Therapy since its inception. Initially this was done indiscriminately and promiscuously. In recent years a more responsible ethical approach to this issue, grounded in the philosophy and principles of Gestalt Therapy, has emerged. The present article reviews this, discusses the author's practice and presents – from a Gestalt therapy point of view - a case for judicious use of dual relationships as a legitimate therapeutic endeavor.

This article first appeared in *The Gestalt Review*, 2004, Vol 8, #2, pp. 135 - 145. Although, as stated above, dual relationships have been a part of Gestalt Therapy since its inception, it is also now recognized as a legitimate endeavor at times by others, too. For example, the American Psychological Association now states in its code of ethics that dual relationships are acceptable when engaged in

---

[105] Originally published in the *Gestalt Review*, 2004, 8(2), pp. 135-145.
* The term "'dual relationship used here also denotes 'multiple relationships' and is sometimes referred to in the literature as "boundary-crossing."

judiciously (Bersoff, 1999, p.12). Many examples of dual relationships exist in the literature [see for instance Lazarus, 1994; Zur, 2000; and Hays,1999.]

Dual relationships defined: Traditionally there is a contract, explicit or implicit, between therapist and client regarding when, where, for what fee and in what general way the therapeutic interaction will take place. Any instance which varies from this contract is likely to constitute a dual relationship. Some examples: playing tennis with a client, attending a client's wedding (I suppose a client's funeral is not germane), inviting a client to one's party, attending a performance by a client, attending a performance or event with a client, picking a client up at the airport (illustrated later), providing therapy to a friend, relative, acquaintance, one's hairdresser,etc. and bartering. Many more might be added to this list, depending on the creativity of the therapist – or sometimes the client.

A good perspective on the essential nature of a dual [or multiple]relationship is offered by Sonne (1994). A relationship between therapist and client can be considered dual, he writes, when the therapist "functions in a professional role and another definitive and intended role within the realms of personal, social or business relationships" (op.cit,p.337). He goes on to discuss the risks of such involvements adversely affecting the dynamics of trust, emotional vulnerability and power differential in the therapist-client relationship (ibid). I agree – there is risk -- as well as potential for therapeutic benefit.

Historical background: Gestalt Therapy came into general awareness in 195l with the publication of *Gestalt Therapy: Excitement and Growth in the Human Personality*. Although this book was written in collaboration by Frederick (a/k/a Fritz) Perls, Paul Goodman and Ralph Hefferline, only Perls remained committed to the movement. It is he who is most popularly associated with it and to a lesser extent his wife Laura Perls. Fritz Perls was a brilliant yet also flamboyant person. In the sixties he took his show on the road , demonstrating Gestalt Therapy in public places before large audiences (Shepard,1981), most prominently at Esalen in California, but also in many other parts of the country. He created the famous Gestalt Therapy 'prayer' which begins "I do my thing and you do yours" which became a rallying cry for the hippie movement. He later founded a therapeutic community at Lake Cowichan in Canada, based on the Gestalt Therapy and New Age principles of contact, self-support and openness. All this fit in very nicely with the sexual revolution and the flower child movement, and for a while Gestalt Therapy was enormously popular. Part of its popularity was due to its flagrant espousal of dual relationships, promulgated by both Perls and Goodman {Stoehr, 1994]; therapist and client were also friends, lovers, playmates, comrades and whatever came to mind, including supervisee and trainee. If the client got hurt by this, then it was her job to take care of herself (or "wipe your own ass" Perls was wont to say). I don't mean that all of this activity was unfortunate. Stoehr, in his book about Goodman's brief career as a Gestalt therapist, recounts one involvement of Goodman's with a client which I consider interesting and to me acceptable (op. cit., pp.143-145). Quoting from an unpublished book of Goodman's notes , he tells the story of Goodman's visiting a client named George in his new loft in Hoboken . George had recently separated from his wife and rented this open space. George felt lost and scared. He "felt resourceless." Goodman visited and spent a good part of the day helping George decide how to decorate the space and helping him shop for the necessary lumber and other materials needed.

"Then we went into an old restaurant and had steamed clams & their broth, which for him was a new taste" (op. cit., p. 145). My mentor, Laura Perls, often said, "Give as much support as necessary and as little as possible." In this incident I see Goodman doing that.

My own first exposure to Gestalt Therapy in 1971 was in a group run by a fellow who earned his living as an auto mechanic in upstate New York. He came to New York City every other week and led a group in someone's apartment. At my second meeting a blatantly schizophrenic woman showed up – invited by one of the participants – and monopolized the session in a meaningless way.

When I complained to the leader that this was no way to manage a group, he said "You're a psychologist; you treat her if you don't like it." I opted to drop out. Unfortunately he was all too common a phenomenon - someone who had a couple of weekends at Esalen and then became a Gestalt group leader, with an impulsive reaction to dualities, e.g. inviting me to be both fellow group member to this woman and also to "treat" her. Believe me I was in no condition at that time to take care of anyone else.

By around 1980, as the hippie movement quieted down, other voices emerged, calling for a more responsible and ethical position (Feder, 1980; Melnick, Nevis and Nevis, 1994). Today Gestalt Therapy is much more aware of the need to place the client's needs first and dual relationships are viewed in a much more balanced way, and with a clear understanding that it is not only the therapist's first obligation to do no harm, but also to take responsibility for enhancing the therapeutic experience and to avoid diluting it.

Boundary violations

An important distinction to mention is that between boundary-crossing and boundary-violating. The former has already been described. A boundary violation, on the other hand, is an entering into a dual relationship for the primary purpose of serving the therapist rather than the client. Examples are sexual overtures, the kind of barter mentioned in the New Yorker piece quoted at the outset of this article, etc. Obviously these are not the kind of contacts being discussed here as they are patently unacceptable and irresponsible. A related aspect is highlighted in a recent article by Melnick [in press] in which he presents his view of the Gestalt approach to countertransference and the ways in which it can dilute the possibilities for growth. This is equally true in the event of a dual relationship. For instance I once became aware, when playing tennis at a marathon resort with a client who reminded me of my brother whom I regularly beat up when we were kids, that I was being unprovokedly nasty and sarcastic to this client/tennis doubles partner. When she asked me why I was doing this, I was able to stop and realize the countertransferential nature of my behavior. Just as an incident of this type could occur during a therapy session, so might it take place in a dual relationship event - and as in a therapy session needs to be owned and processed.

Dual relationships and Gestalt Therapy Principles

This is not the venue for a lengthy explication of the nature of Gestalt Therapy. Nevertheless some basic principles and aspects need to be mentioned in support of dual relationships. In one of her few published pieces (this one deriving from a talk she gave in Austria in 1977), Laura Perls in her usual concise and precise way stated "The basic concepts of Gestalt therapy are philosophical and aesthetic rather than technical. Gestalt therapy is an existential-phenomenological approach and as such it is experiential and experimental" (1992, p149). She goes on to discuss the influences of Wertheimer, Lewin, Goldstein and Reich and the gradual shift from a psychoanalytical orientation to a Gestalt one with the resulting emphases on promoting awareness, contact and self-support – all essential ingredients in the ability "to live with uncertainty without anxiety" (op.cit., p. 154-5) – that is, to creatively adjust to the human predicament.

As is well known, Gestalt therapy grew out of psychoanalysis and was a reaction to it. A good deal of the basic Gestalt therapy text by Perls, Hefferline and Goodman already mentioned (1951) was devoted to discussions of, differences with and modifications of classical psychoanalytic principles and concepts (both of the Perls were analysts before developing Gestalt therapy). An oversimplification of the result would be to say that Gestalt therapy ended up emphasizing the obvious in contrast to psychoanalysis emphasizing the hidden; from another viewpoint, Gestalt therapy focuses more on direct human-to-human contact in contrast to classical psychoanalysis which focuses more on projections onto the analyst. Within this framework, the Gestalt therapist, as I see it (although all Gestalt therapists may not agree), has the option of judiciously engaging in contact with the client which fall into one or more of the categories described by Sonne (op.cit) as personal, social or business. During such contacts the therapist is, in varying degrees, still in the therapist role and also in one or more of the other roles. The event is an experiential and experimental interaction, which may or may not have therapeutic usefulness and benefits – and risks [as does any therapeutic interaction] harm to the therapist-client relationship. It is the therapist's job to creatively, responsibly, judiciously and artfully minimize the risk and maximize the benefit. Attention must be paid for instance, as in the therapy room, to avoid narcissistic involvements, engaged in to make the therapist feel good or superior. Examples of dual relationships: First I will clear up the mystery surrounding the example mentioned above of picking up a client at an airport.

Sometimes I lead training workshops in distant places. A few years ago I did so in Chicago [identifying data changed in this section] and developed a small following there of therapists interested in my work here. Recently a therapist from Chicago enrolled in a workshop I was running in New York City. Shortly before it occurred he called, asking if I would provide him with a therapy session the day before. He advised me that he was flying in to Newark Airport at such and such a time and requested a session that afternoon. As it happened I had plans to be in Newark that day and it was convenient for me to pop over to the airport, pick him up, drive home with him and see him for a session. After that he was on his own to get a bus to NYC where he would be staying with a relative. It felt like a natural thing to do. Certainly if a friend or relative told me of arriving at Newark Airport on a day and at a time when it was convenient for me to pick that person up, I wouldn't hesitate. Nor did I with Sam. In this instance there is nothing dramatic to report. The contact was uneventful and did nothing, I believe, to damage our relationship (We explored this during the   ensuing session). If anything, I think it strengthened and humanized it. Of course, anything might have happened that might have led to bad feelings. In that case, they would be grist to the therapeutic mill.

Since I am often open with clients about my life, many are aware that I am passionate about tennis. As a result I have played tennis with a number of clients and supervisees. On workshops at resorts this has usually been spontaneous, such as the incident described above. However, I do recall other specific instances of tennis encounters with clients that have resulted in significant events, leading to useful work. One time a client quite a bit younger and stronger than I asked to play. We arranged to do so and it soon became apparent that he had a better game than I and he took a large lead. However his game deteriorated and ultimately I won. Afterwards in reviewing the event, he got in touch with the kind of self-defeating thoughts which often result in his messing up his life, such as "If I beat him, he won't like me." We were able to connect this with an early decision he had made around his hot-tempered father, which led to further work and homework assignments.

Another instance was with an older man who nagged me to play with him. I was somewhat reluctant to do so, since he was not in good shape and was something of a klutz. I didn't think it would be a good match. Finally I agreed and, as I had suspected, I was much better than he and it was very one-sided. What emerged as most interesting though was an observation I made that he kept repeating the same unsuccessful tactic – a drops hot, which I was all over and easily put away for the point. Despite my success at overwhelming this tactic, he kept on doing it right until the end. At our next session I brought this up and it proved to be very valuable as we explored his rigidity and stubbornness. I could give other examples, too. Tennis mirrors life.

Like most of us, I have been asked from time to time to provide therapy to a friend or relative. Recently I have had three such requests. I tactfully [I hope] steered two of them to other therapists, explaining that it was not in anybody's best interests for me be to be in the role of both therapist and friend, especially since I was also quite friendly with the spouse of each, and there were bound to be marital issues arising in the work. However I did come up with a proposal, which was accepted, in the third instance. In this case another therapist with whom I was quite friendly asked if I would help him. He and his wife were having very disruptive problems with his son and daughter-in-law -- disruptive within each marriage and disruptive to the relationship between the two couples. They insisted that I could be of unique help to them and to some degree I thought this was true, not because I am the world's only good therapist but because it was doubtful the wife would agree to work with anyone else. So I offered the following: one session at my friend's house on a Saturday afternoon with the understanding that there was absolutely to be no fee and with no commitment on my part to go any further. I also stipulated that the length of the session would be determined by me as events unfolded. Since this is not a case history suffice it to say that it was one of the most intense, involving, satisfying and productive sessions I've ever conducted. At the end of two full hours, I proposed some specific homework for them and suggested we meet once more in about a month, this time at the son's home. We did so. The second session was much shorter and much less intense, since they had done their homework and achieved a great start on reconciliation and resolution. When they brought up fee again, I said they could take me out for a snack since this time the meeting took place during midday and we none of us had eaten lunch. We had a pleasant meal together. The follow-up information I have received over three years has been very positive, and our relationship is fine.

A natural question at this time is why did I reject two requests and accept – with conditions – the third. Here I refer to my use of the words judicious and responsible above. Based on what I knew of all the people involved and my relationship with them, it was my belief that acceding to the first two requests would have been unwise and irresponsible with a high probability of failure and/or harm — harm to them individually and harm to my close relationships with some or all of them. I was protecting both them and myself. In the third instance I came to believe after initial unwillingness — that I could be of unique help to this group and that the chance for a successful outcome was reasonably good. As it proved I was correct (whether I was correct in the other two instance I will, of course, never know). Obviously I wasn't positive of the outcome in the third instance, yet I was willing to go ahead in line with the principles of responsible judicious experimentation. This is a good point to mention that any intervention in therapy is based on the same principle.

As indicated previously there are many other possibilities for dual relationships, such as bartering, attending an event involving a client (e.g., a performance, a wedding, an anniversary party or other special party, etc.) In each instance it is the therapist's responsibility to judiciously decide if this act is, first of all likely to do no harm and secondarily to see how it can be used therapeutically, if at all. I will give one more instance of this approach, among the many options. Several years ago I began a course of treatment with Jennifer, a young mother whose initial concern was her violent outbursts at her only child Ryen. This included things like shaking the child, which — though they caused no physical damage — certainly caused emotional damage. Moreover she was afraid she might some day do him serious physical harm. After a while treatment broadened and we did some couples work, too. I very much liked these two bright creative people and I was also intrigued by their stories of their child's brilliance. One day I mused that I wished I could meet Ryen. A few months later, after they had ended a very successful treatment, Jennifer called to invite me to have dinner with the family. Although I suspected I might be seeing them again in the office sometime, having become the family's therapist, I accepted. I had a most pleasant and interesting evening (and incidentally found Ryen to be as brilliant and charming as they had stated). Later Jennifer called again, concerned about extreme fearfulness and clinginess on Ryen's part. Although the details of this are very interesting, the point is that I worked again with the family and experienced no handicap resulting from my social visit. If anything I felt more equipped to help them, based on my better feel for how they live and the rapport I had already established with Ryen. My understanding and connection with them had deepened and become more vivid, enhancing my confidence in working with them.

A poor outcome resulted from a mistake I made early in my career. I agreed to provide counseling to a relative of mine who was confused in her marriage. Although nothing very bad happened, we both became aware early on that we were uncomfortable talking about her family of origin, who of course were also my relatives. We ended the experiment pretty quickly. A legitimate question might be asked here whether I can offer guidelines about what "kinds" or "types" of clients with whom it is sensible to interact dually, and conversely what kinds or types for whom it is contraindicated. One caution is to consider carefully involvement with overly dependent or confluent persons.

This can result in demands that can lead to therapist discomfort; again though, all this can be usefully employed as Philippson so clearly explicates in his recent article on transference in gestalt therapy [2002]. In such instances the therapist must be aware of her own limits, especially in regard to her willingness to confront and be confronted. Additionally, of course, great care must be exercised with regard to borderline and psychotic clients. Essentially, each situation needs to be evaluated on its own merits and its own risks, depending on the matrix of this relationship, the phase of therapy, etc. And of course, each therapist will have her own level of comfort regarding this kind of interaction which is a good guideline [I happen to be relatively comfortable with it; when I'm ill, for instance, I often disclose it and accept recommendations for health such interactions flow organically from the contact rather than being forced or preplanned. Generally they are more the exception rather than the rule or routine. Certainly all care must be taken to avoid using any hierarchical power inherent in the therapist-client relationship, which could lead to misusing the contact for purely personal gain. Examples are picking the brain of a stockbroker accepting exorbitant gifts, or, most of all, sexual involvement Some special cases: Gestalt therapy, perhaps more than any other major approach, often employs training groups or programs over extended periods – e.g. over a weekend or even a month – and at distant venues, such as conference centers, resorts, etc. Inevitably there is social contact between leaders and participants. This is a widely accepted form of dual relationships, and brings with it all of the responsibilities, opportunities and risks already noted. The same is true of marathon groups, and both have the advantage of providing the immediate opportunity to process any significant social incidents. And related to this are the evolving dualities very familiar in gestalt therapy. Often clients 'graduate' into supervisees, supervisees mature into colleagues and colleagues sometimes become good friends. There are of course many subtleties and intricacies in these evolutions requiring careful attention. In the supervisor-supervisee relationship, for example, if there is also a career-affecting evaluation involved, it is probably best that the supervisor postpone collegiality or friendship until later.

A note about sex

For powerful reasons I have barely mentioned sexual involvement with a client, something that was common in the early days of gestalt therapy. By now it has been clearly recognized that such a duality is fraught with great danger, often leading to a rupture in the therapeutic relationship. It is likely to be essentially, or at least far too much, in the interests of the therapist rather than the client and can be disastrous for either or both. It is a consummation devoutly to be squished.

Summary

Dual relationships (also known as multiple relationships and as boundary-crossing) have now been officially termed conditionally acceptable, e.g. by the American Psychological Association, with the caveat that every care must be taken to do no harm to the therapeutic relationship. In gestalt therapy, dual relationships were initially practiced indiscriminately and no doubt often harmfully. Since then efforts have been made to instill a sense of responsibility into these kinds of contacts, emphasizing that that they need be judiciously entered into consistent with the philosophical, aesthetic and ethical principles of our elegant approach. When done so they may provide an additional dimension and richness to the therapeutic process.

References

Bersoff, D. [Ed] [1999]. *Ethical Conflicts in Psychology*. Washington, D.C.: American Psychological Assn.

Feder, B [1980]. Responsibility in gestalt therapy. *The Gestalt Journal*, 1, 46- 50.

Hayes, K. F. [1999]. *Working it Out: Using Exercise in Psychotherapy*. Washington, D.C. American Psychological Assn.

Lazarus, A. [1999]. How certain boundaries and ethics diminish therapeutic effectiveness, in Bersoff above

Melnick, J, Nevis, S. and Melnick, G. [1994] Therapeutic Ethics: A Gestalt Perspective. *The British Gestalt Journal*, 3, 105-113.

Perls, F., Hefferline, R., and Goodman, P [1951]. *Gestalt Therapy: Excitement and Growth in the Human Personality*. NY: Julian Press.

Perls, L. [1992]. *Living at the Boundary*. Highland, NY: Gestalt Journal Press.

Shepard, M. [1980]. Fritz. Moab, UT: Franklin Watts.

Sonne, J. *Multiple Relationships: Does the Ethics Code Answer the Right Questions*, in Berson cited above.

Stoehr. T. [1994]. *Ilere, Now Next*. San Francisco: Jossey-Bass

Stur, O. In Celebration of Dual Relationshiops. *The Independent Practioner*, American Psychological Assn, 20, 97-100.

Chapter 24: That Which Enables: Support as Complex and Contextually Emergent
Lynne Jacobs

Chapter Introduction

I have always loved the simplicity of Laura Perls' adage that there is no contact without support. But what we mean by support has begged further elaboration. Enamored of her adage, moved by Malcolm Parlett's simple statement, "support is that which enables," and aware of my own impoverished understanding of what we mean by 'supports,' I wrote this paper as a journey of discovery.

It seems only fitting, then, that an article on support be my submission for the NYIGT anthology. As a visitor from afar, I have sometimes envied NYIGT its strong connection to our roots. I have also felt intimidated at times, as I am less rooted. I am encouraged by those at NYIGT who remind me, through their writings, of the crisp vitality of gestalt therapy. I am also encouraged that NYIGT has room for the evolution of ideas, including critiques of our original ideas. Evolution and critique are necessary to keep gestalt therapy alive, and the lively discussions at meetings and on the listserve testify to plurality (not without its tensions, of course!) and commitment to the further development of gestalt therapy.

Pluralistic sensibility matters greatly to me, since I live in two worlds (psychoanalysis and gestalt therapy). I continue to explore and try to understand how the therapeutic relationship matters in gestalt therapy, and that sometimes leads me in directions that are controversial. And yet, I consider gestalt therapy my true home, and I am grateful to those at NYIGT and the larger gestalt world who make room for me with my differences.

That Which Enables: Support as Complex and Contextually Emergent[106]

Abstract: This paper undertakes to elaborate various understandings of "support," including its complexity, its emergent quality, its intimate intertwining with creative adjustment, and its bi-directionality

Key words: support, context, creative adjustment, emergent, bi-directional

"C'mon Lynne! Don't look away. Look the ball into your glove!" These were the admonitions of my softball coach, shouted loudly and violently. He was throwing balls so that they would bounce at my feet and if I did not catch them they would either bounce once again onto my badly bruised shins or they would bounce up and hit me in the chin again. "Turn your glove a bit more to the outside!" I was tired. I was frightened as the balls bounced wildly towards my body. "No. No. Softer hands! Yes, better. Again." He was tough. It meant to me that he thought I was worth the effort. I wanted to prove myself to him. I wanted to improve my skills. I wanted to develop the courage to keep my eye on the ball without moving my head away even as the bouncing ball menaced me. I improved, became more confident, which supported an increase in courage and tenacity.

Not all support is gentle or even kind. But importantly, every life event, every interaction, supports, and is supported by, *something* and at the same time does *not* support something else, just as awareness is always of something and not of something else, and contacting is always with something and not with something else. If I hand someone a gun, I am supporting shooting.

The Nearer Present: My Journey Begins

In 2004, Malcolm Parlett and I were soaking up some sun, sitting on a rustic porch, taking a break during a weekend study group at Esalen, California. We were talking about one of his favorite subjects, "support." At one point he mentioned that he thinks of support as "that which enables." His parsimonious phrase sparked my interest. It was expansive in its reach while simple in its presentation. Meanwhile, a colleague Mark Fairfield had just written about support as a fluidly complex constellation of self and environmental resources for self-regulation. Among other ideas, he pointed to his homeless teen clients' drug usage as a resource for regulating emotions in an otherwise impoverished field (Fairfield, 2004).

---

[106] This article first appeared as Jacobs, L. (2006). "That Which Enables: Support as Complex and Contextually Emergent." *British Gestalt Journal*, 15(2): 10.

I realized that my own thinking about support was woefully impoverished, despite the fact that I, like many other gestalt clinicians, have an implicit understanding of the notion. I sometimes use writing as a support for my further exploration and learning, hence this article. I have here undertaken a study of support that I hope respects its unending complexity. To this end, I will expand upon Parlett's statement and enumerate some propositions about support. I hope my ideas stimulate — support — further thought for all of us.

That which enables

In gestalt therapy, support refers particularly to the contacting process. We speak of support for contacting. We certainly owe a debt of gratitude to Laura Perls, who emphasized support as a necessary precondition for contacting, and therefore support was an important therapeutic starting point. "Laura's most famous contribution to Gestalt therapy theory was her insistence on support as the implicit condition for contact" (Bloom, 2005, p. 83). There is no such thing as unsupported contacting.

While I have no argument with this statement, it bears expansion as well as refinement because the notion of contact is very broad and encompassing. I seek to expand my grasp of the ubiquity and significance of support, and also refine my creative use of support in the therapy process.

Complexifying Support: Emergence and Context

One of the complexities of support is that, whether or not a specific interaction—be it speech or other action—supports contacting depends on the immediate context of the moment. And yet supports seem to me to operate both in the most immediate context and also at a meta-level. That is, support for contacting in a specific moment also may be a step along the way toward the development of an enduring capacity or reorganization of experience.

1. Supports are contextually emergent phenomena, meaning that whatever skills, capacities and resources exist as potentially, they can only „e-merge," for use in a specific place, at a specific time, in a specific context. And the context shapes both what can emerge and what is most relevant as a support. Staemmler, (personal communication, 2006) has suggested a parsing of Parlett's phrase, which I have altered (and therefore may no longer represent a position with which Staemmler will agree) that directly addresses context:

A. Support is that which enables *a person to do (or experience) something*.

B. Support *in therapy* is that which enables a *client* to do (or experience) something.

C. Support in therapy is that which
   a. *makes it possible* for a client *to acquire an until-now lacking ability and/or to put an existing ability into practice, the practical use of which has been blocked by fears, avoidances, etc.*
   b. *Makes it possible for a client to have a new experience or organizationof experience, the accessibility of which has been been blocked by fears, avoidances, etc.*
D. Support in therapy is that which makes it possible for a client *to take the respective next step that is necessary in order*
   a. to acquire an until-now lacking ability and/or to put an existing ability into practice, the practical use of which has been blocked by fears, avoidances, etc.
   b. Acquire a new organization of experience, the development of which has been blocked by fears, avoidances, etc.

For instance, a patient—a therapist himself-- who was phobic of blood and medical procedures was preparing to undergo surgery. He said that discussions with his surgeon left him feeling faint, and he dreaded fainting during the pre-surgical preparations. At one point he began to well with tears as he spoke. I was mostly quietly receptive, saying little.

The next session he told me he became desperately distressed after our session. He said that he sensed my participation in my few emotionally charged, soft-spoken words, but he hungered for me to „make an interpretation!" We had spoken previously about how his mother used the intensity of her emotional reactions to him to usurp his emotional life, leaving him feeling bereft, adrift, in danger of drowning. He had felt dropped and abandoned by me. He said that an interpretation would reassure him that I understood his misery and was still able to think about him rather than be consumed by my own emotional responses.

I had failed him in this way more than once in our work, so I thought it best to try to sort out what was happening between us. At one point I said that he and I seemed to need very different responses when we are upset. I said that I had wanted my therapist to let my misery move him, and that an interpretation meant to me that my therapist was distant, and quite likely telling me that I needn't feel this way if only I saw things the way he did! My patient laughed heartily and said he now understood the disrupted reactions some of his patients had to him when he made interpretations. I laughed and said he was helping me to understand patients who, like him, felt abandoned by my more immediate emotional responses. We both became intrgued and had a robust conversation about our respective personal and clinical experiences.

I had a pretty clear sense at the time that our conversation was supporting him to have a vivid conversational experience in which his anger, dread and fascination could all be fully experienced. I could not have predicted how this experience supported something less immediate and less visible. He told me at his next session that he had been just fine in his discussion with the surgeon and in the pre-surgical preparations. He said that the atmosphere of intimate collegiality and the robustness of our conversation had fortified him, given him a sense that he was a capable and resourceful adult, a sensibility that changed his attitude and experience regarding his surgery.

Our conversation helped him to contact his emotional life more vividly, in a way that supported rather than disrupted, his on-going self-regulation in the moment, and that experience supported the expansion of his confidence. Our supports for vivifying his contacting emerged between us from such things as; our shared history, the match of our listening and speaking, and our commitment to our task and our respective roles in relation to that task. And the session also—by his report—allowed him to experience himself differently in the world. In essence, points C and D, above came to fruition.

Ordinarily it is important for us to remember that our patients may not be supported by offerings we intend as supports. It behooves us to explore together what *would* support the next step in an their therapeutic exploration, and perhaps to understand together why the support that I intend to offer is *not* a support. This involves looking to our phenomenal fields to discern how our differently organized fields lend differing meanings to our current shared figure of interest.

2. This story also illustrates that there is no such thing as a singular support, isolated from any other support. Support also involves contextualization in terms of our complexly organized aspirations. Support is one of those mind-bending concepts that is infinitely recursive and complex. By that I mean that there is no final resting point where we might say, "ah, and this is the support for that, and we have hit bedrock." For every support for contacting that we may point to, we find that the necessary precondition for the existence of that support is another support. For instance, without my commitment to the task of therapy, our conversation might well have taken a different direction. And my commitment to the task is facilitated—or supported—by my prior successes with dialogue in the service of the task. Each success and each failure is also rife with a collection of creative adjustments that contribute to the clinical wisdom that came into play in this session. My patient's straightforward articulate statments support my ability to understand how my ground was different from his. Add to the interaction of

creative adjustments and support is that I aspire to serve the task to the best of my ability most of the time.

We used to speak of growth and development as the movement from environmental support to self-support, but we know better now. Nothing happens without an interaction between those supports conceived of as self-supports, and supports conceived of as environmental supports, not ever. As Wheeler so eloquently describes, any contact, any change, results from a reconfiguration of self and environmental supports (2000). And Wheeler also reminds us that when we think of supports as field phenomena, then the range of available supports is always in the eye of the beholder. That is, if I do not experience something as a support that you do experience as a support, then it is useable for you, not for me. Actually, later in this paper I will point to supports that operate outside of awareness, but these are technically not "field" (organism/environment) supports, rather they are contextual supports that shape our fields.

3. Every life event, every interaction, can be understood as a point along the way in an intertwined flow of supports and creative adjustments, as we move into our coming solutions. This is an explanatory, as opposed to phenomenological, statement. And this is one of the other complexities of the concept of support. There are certain times when an interaction may not be *experienced* as a support, and yet can, in retrospect be acknowledged as an event that facilitated contact with an aspect of experience which then facilitated further contact, in a process that ultimately satisfied an important aspiration. A clinical example I use below will address this point.

4. Support always involves an interaction between the individual's resources and the resources of the environment.

The use of any support—so-called self support, or so-called environmental support--requires the participation of the user. Support involves as well contextualization in terms of our complexly organized aspirations. And yet the ability to participate is built on other supports, (e.g. having been supported to develop a sense of agency). Finding relevant supports calls for recognizing one's aims and needs, which requires other supports, *ad infinitum*.

For instance, we can take a rather absurd example, one that I sometimes use with patients who are pessimistic about the value of engaging more fully in their lives, and wish instead to be utterly passive and allow their environment to take total care of them. We can go to great lengths to draw on environmental supports to keep us breathing in such a way that we need not participate. We could use an iron lung or a respirator belt (although we would certainly have to participate enough to arrange for such services!). The question becomes one of whether arranging such caretaking interferes with other aims a patient may have, such as the desire to ride a bike, go to a movie or walk on the beach.

Note that this understanding of the complex interplay of systems of support removes the therapist from the position of taking a moral stance that the patient ought to move from environmental support to self-support (an impossibility), or even that their use of support systems ought to become more sophisticated. By helping patients to know their aspirations — small and large — we can help them to assess what supports best serve those aims and which do not. If patients desperately want the symbolic experience of being well cared for by having their breathing done for them, we need merely engage in an exploration of how they might obtain that, and bear witness to the limitations posed by that or any other choice. My "thought experiment" about an iron lung is comically extreme, but Fairfield (2004) makes a compelling case for adopting this same attitude when working with dually diagnosed teens.

I think it is also important to note, in both these propositions, that there is a danger inherent in the explanatory, as opposed to phenomenological perspective on support. The danger is that of forgetting that the assignment of the terms "self" and "environmental" to our understanding of the location of supports are both somewhat arbitrary and contingent on the perspective of the speaker. What the therapist may think of as a self-support may well be experienced by the patient as an environmental support. At a process level, we might consider that what is important here is not the reputed location of any particular support, but rather that our patients come to appreciate that so-called self and environmental supports—that is, supports that they experience some agency with, and supports that they experience as beyond their agency—are always intimately intertwined.

Creative Adjustment and Support

5. Support and creative adjustment are intimately intertwined.

6. What is occurring in the present moment is what is being supported in the present moment. This includes current diminutions and interruptions in the flow of excitement and interest.

a. Current interruptions are creative adjustments being supported by the therapeutic pair.

b. And the interruption supports something else (is a creative adjustment).

c. Support for something means something else is not supported.

To add further complexity to the mix, while we often look at what supports are needed for this-or-that kind of contacting, I think it also behooves us to ask what kinds of contacting are being supported by the present constellation of supports. This turns our usual question on its head, but helps us to examine just how the current contacting process is a creative adjustment to current resources. Such a deconstruction is especially useful when trying to understand how a particular therapeutic knot is being reinforced in our current therapeutic dialogue. In essence, this begs two questions in our therapeutic work: what is being supported now between us, and how? What would the patient and I like to support together?

Creative adjustment and support are supports for the each other, and we are engaged in creative adjustments at every moment of living. Creative adjustments are assembled from the available supports, and each adjustment becomes a support for another creative adjustment. So when we therapists find ourselves thinking that patients are interrupting the flow of their experiencing, or deflecting, we might explore together what about our situation supports that quality of engagement. The answer to such a question likely reveals how the patient and I together are supporting the interruption — I might notice that I am holding my breath and clenching my jaw — and that this interruption supports another aim, such as a sense of safety for each of us in varying degrees, which a free flow of experiencing might jeopardize.

For example, let us trace the flow of adjustments and supports that can be discerned in the following clinical vignette:

> I had returned from a ten day trip, and the patient had recounted some signs of his sense of being "untethered" while I was gone. He was a bit flustered by this "confession," because he does not feel particularly invested in our relationship, and prefers to keep his distance. Then, speaking quickly, with little breath support, he went on, referring to his experience of reconvening our sessions,

> P: Well now that I am tethered ... [thrown out as a transition, with no apparent connection to the words. Felt empty to me]

> T: [after a few other sentences that seemed empty and lifeless to me] May I go back a step? I wonder, you said, "now that you feel tethered ..." Do you?

> P: Well, I don't know what I feel. [said with interest and a bit of surprise]

> T: Yeah ... What made you say that [the tethered comment], do you think?

> P: [long pause, puzzled look, consternation]

> T: [I thought that perhaps my question might have aroused some shame. He seemed interested in my question, but also perhaps afraid of being

criticized. I wanted to find a way to support his interest, given that interest in his moment-to-moment experiencing is a relatively new experience for him.] I can tell you why I am asking. It seemed as if that sentence did not actually convey your experience. So I was wondering, if you were not speaking at that moment to say something of your experience, I wonder what function that sentence was meant to serve.

P: Oh . . . [appeared relieved and increasingly interested] It was some kind of transition . . . [pause]

T: So if you were to say, "I want to change the subject now," would that fit better?

P: Well, no, I think it is something else. [browed furrowed reflecting apparently greater concentration and focus] My sentence held a kernel of truth in it, but I cannot get at it . . .

T: Try this on, "I am glad to be back . . ."

P: [quick guilty embarrassed smile of recognition] Yes, but even *closer* is, "I am glad to be back here with *you!*" [broad smile, both of us chuckle]

In this exchange we flowed through a *mélange* of supports and adjustments, only a few of which can be described. My inquiry about his experience of saying he was tethered moved us into a process that Erv Polster (1999) calls tight "therapeutic sequences." Tight sequences are often used as a support for closer contact with one's immediate experience. But the ostensible support of my attention to immediate experience only becomes useable if my patient contributes with his own interest.

Recently in our work, tight sequencing has engaged his interest more strongly, rather than merely evoking his fear (which it had often done in the past). His interest was the creative adjustment, and it drew on the supports of the tight sequence, his recent history of expansive discoveries from such work, and his growing faith in our dialogic process. Also, note that the flowering of his interest was almost derailed until it could be supported by my contextualizing my question. My first efforts to tighten the sequence were not experienced by my patient as a support. His interest then became a support that, along with my explanation of my purpose, became supports for further sharpening his figure. The gradually sharpening figure, along with my feeding him a sentence, were supports for taking a risk with me that was another creative adjustment.

7. Supports for therapeutic contacting are bi-directional (we do our best work when we get supports from our clients).

The, emergent quality of supports can be seen when the patient's interest *became available* in our dialogue. This — fluid, subject to re-configuration, context-dependent — phenomenon is true for the therapist as well as the patient. For instance, initially I felt some disappointed annoyance that the patient wanted me to engage with him in apparently meaningless conversation. We had travelled that unsatisfying road together too many times for my taste. But I used the supports of my faith in inclusion (empathy) and my recent satisfying history with this patient to adjust my focus. I shifted from focusing on my annoyance to focusing on his strivings — what did he hope to achieve by speaking in this manner? His responsiveness to my creative adjustment was one of the supports for the *emergence* of a more compassionate sensitivity to the effects of my inquiry, which was a support for both of us to refine his figure in an atmosphere of acceptance and shared interest.

One can see in what I have described above, another important dimension of support in therapy. Supports are bi-directional. We tend to do our best work when our patients support our talents, creativity, self-esteem and compassion by their responsiveness. For this reason I have often said that the mark of good therapists is not their art as therapists, but rather their willingness to hang in when the work is messy, clumsy, and deflating. Our determination and emotional courage when our environment (our patient) can give so little in return is a crucial self-support for the difficult practice of psychotherapy.

Supporting Supports: A Partially Invisible, Unending Ball of Twine

8. Most supports are ground phenomena, having a taken-for-granted granted quality. An example is that of white skin privilege. They become figural only in their absence (e.g., oxygen), that is, when they are no longer available as supports, but exist in our awareness as a *potential support;* something we need but do not have. We can never know the full range of supports we are engaging.

9. Many supports are communal or cultural, leading to individual talent and yet not possible without community support.

There are supports that my patient and I may be drawing on that derive from our cultural location. These may or may not become figural, depending in part on how much cultural similarity we share. The more we share, the less likely it will become figural.

Our culture itself is a support. Without culture we have no organized experience, no map for being-in-the-world, and no language. Language is a necessary support for the possibility of understanding each other. Socio-cultural supports operate largely invisibly, because our culture is largely invisible to us. As Wheeler has pointed out, in an eloquent exposition on selfhood and culture,

"culture ... is everything we assume about the way the world 'just is.' Paradoxically the most basic level of acculturation is that which does not strike us a cultural, but universal" (2005, p. 50).

I suspect that the cultural supports that are most invisible are those that emerge from and support privilege. Similarly, the experience of autonomy and agency is not a product of independence, but is an emergent phenomenon that is utterly dependent on smoothly functioning interdependency.

Different cultures and cultural experiences differentially support and inhibit different styles of living. Of course, as Wheeler stresses (2005), we all inhabit multiple cultures, so at times resources from one of our cultures might be used as supports in dealing with problems in one of our other cultures. A sociological researcher Srole came to this same conclusion when he studied a large minority (a sub-culture) of people who had survived extreme urban poverty in the United States of America, and yet remained psychologically intact. His data analysis suggested that "...three socio-cultural resources were instrumental in 'eugenically fortifying and immunizing against the potentially shattering impact of extreme, exogenous adversity,': a stoic fortitude, 'be grown up' ethos; strong kinship alignments; and a sense of special group identity" (in Antonovsky, 1987, p. 56)

Other largely invisible supports are drawn from our bodies and the gravity that supports our movement through space. I need not expand here. The healthier are our bodies, the less we attend to their supportive functions. As our health becomes problematic, we become more aware of the necessity for support from our bodies in order to pursue various life aims.

What about the invisible supports that operate interpersonally? Here is where some interesting early ideas from Laura Perls come into play. In early discussions on contacting, Laura Perls initially distinguished between the background flow of being-in-contact, which is roughly equivalent to "going-on-being," or "being-in-the-world," and the more episodic moments she labelled "contact-making." Bloom made reference to

> "...her more nuanced yet earlier use of contacting: being-in-contact is the background for the foreground activity of *contact-making*. *Contacting is a function*, which is to say, *it is an integrative organising of the organism/environment field — integrative of its contingencies and its biological, social, cultural, and historical complexities. Being-in-contact with one's background — history, education, style, posture, breath, for example — is the ground, the support, for making-contact with novelty. (*2005, p. 83 — italics in original*)*

Laura Perls herself said it this way:

> Support starts with primary physiology like breathing, circulation, and digestion, and continues with the development of the cortex, the growing of teeth, upright posture, coordination, sensitivity and mobility, language and its uses, habits and customs, even and particularly the hang-ups which were formed as support at the time of their formation. All the experience and learning that has been *fully assimilated and integrated* builds up a person's background, which gives meaning to the emerging gestalten and thus supports a certain way of living *on* the boundary *with* excitement. (1992, pp. 153f. — italics in original)

> "And note: support is the underpinning of function, the platform for action. "Support is not some soft pillow of a hug, not a consoling anodyne, but rather the very foundation for contacting itself: *support is the being that enables the making, the ground that empowers the acting*" (Bloom 2005, p. 84 — italics in original).

This "being-in-contact" operates largely outside of awareness. As Bloom is emphasizing, our entire past experiencing, and how it has been integrated is the ground of support for the emerging moment.

By the way, our integrated history is a good example of the interplay of creative adjustments and support in the reconfiguration of experience. Most of us have had the experience that our "history" changes over time. The facts probably do not change, but the meanings do. Some facts become less interesting, some more so. Some facts take on different meanings. For instance, at this point in my life I find — with grateful thanks to various therapists in my life — I am less in the thrall of the severe emotional neglect that characterized my childhood, and am more pleased with the memories of the easy-going manner and humane values that also permeated my family home. Each reconfiguration of my history has drawn on new or newly reconfigured supports, and each reconfiguration also becomes a support that can be used in a variety of life situations.

Contextualizing Support: Back to "Go"

As useful as I find Laura Perls' statement above, I must argue with her assertion that *starts* with primary physiology. Support cannot begin in such a linear fashion as Perls described. Primary physiology is supported by environmental supports such as gravity, temperature, and our relational surround. These bodily and environmental supports work together at all times. Not only does linearity fall by the wayside with a more contextualist sensibility, but describing support in the way she does leans more toward an individualist, rather than a more contextualist or field-oriented model of support (I suspect were she to speak today, her descriptions would be different).

By the same token, I also take issue with one of Laura Perls's oft-quoted gems, "I give as much support as needed, and as little as possible (in Bloom, pg. 6)." Such a statement makes a few non-contextualist assumptions. It assumes that we know what we do that supports, and that we know what we are supporting. It assumes that we are able to see clearly what is "needed" (and need and experience of need are highly complex, contextually-emergent phenomena themselves!). It assumes also that offering something that may be desired but not logically necessary is always a bad idea. I can well remember times in my life when my therapists supported me in ways that I did not need — as far as I could tell — but the meaning of the support enhanced my trust in their care, which supported me to risk closer contact with my most vulnerable and ashamed states of mind. I am mindful that there are many moments when her adage suits the moment quite well, but warn against hardening it into a rule.

You Can't Tell a Support by its Cover

10. You can't tell by looking outside the person's frame of reference whether something is a support or not.

Often we discover by subsequent experiences that something that happened in the therapeutic process was a support for a desired next step. I once said to a very distraught patient that we did not understand yet what a particular event meant to him. The next session he told me that the word "yet" had given him hope that there was a tomorrow, that emotional understanding could evolve over time, that his distress did not mean that his world had been crushed forever. Throughout his therapy he occasionally referred to the power of "yet." I had barely noticed my use of the word!

At other times, something we may intend as a support may not be experienced as such. Fortified by my prior experience with the word "yet," described above, I found myself saying it again with another patient. He experienced my use of the word very differently. He thought I was saying to him either that he was deficient and inadequate, or that I thought he was "making a mountain out of a molehill." Perhaps I emphasized the word — being more conscious of it — in a provocative way. Or perhaps it was the word itself. Perhaps something in our history together primed him to expect me to judge him. Exploring all of these possibilities proved fruitful for illuminating his developmental history, and also supported his dawning sense of empowerment to speak his mind.

Patients' developmental and cultural histories also provide supports in surprising ways. One cannot tell by the look of a stressor, for instance, what it supports (Antonovsky, 1987). Adversity supports not only such things as pessimism, rigidity, emotional constriction and isolation. It can also be a support for developing such talents as perseverance, perceptiveness, courage, and gratitude for what one has (obviously, my list here is incomplete).

Finally, we have all had experiences in therapy where we have been confronted or have confronted our patients. Such difficult exchanges are often quite useful spurs for development. I have a patient to whom I sometimes say, "don't bullshit me, now." He is proud of the times he is able to bullshit me successfully, but also somewhat sad about it. When I "catch" him he is usually temporarily flustered but he is also pleased at the invitation to "get closer" to himself.

Case Example

In the case that follows one can find the issue of supports becoming figural at times, and at other times being enacted without being directly addressed. Throughout the session (and many sessions with this man) there was a question from him: Can I trust you to engage with me in a way that supports *my* aims, even if they go against *your* agenda?

Greg's initial consultation with me centred on his urgent suicidal thoughts, depression and despair. He said he thought of his (highly successful, both personally and professionally) life as a beautifully appointed, perfectly maintained Porsche. But he could not enjoy it, and thought he should give his life away to someone who would be able to derive pleasure form driving that magnificent car.

For several months he told me stories laced with bitter despair. He went on angry tirades about the selfishness of women. He also challenged me often about the usefulness of therapy. He was extremely mistrustful of the therapeutic profession, and loath to admit that I or anyone else could offer meaningful help to him. It was important to him that I did not try to defend my profession, and that I remained humble about whether or not I might be able to help him myself.

He was bright and intellectually curious, and together we mused about many of life's mysteries. I also tried to track his emotions as closely as I could, and he became increasingly aware of, and articulate about their rich variability. We sometimes also ventured into stories about his appallingly neglectful and abusive developmental history. He also made it clear to me that he wanted to hear my ideas about what he presented, and he wanted room to disagree with me.

Within a few months of working together, he was more confident, increasingly optimistic about life, more resilient in the face of disappointments, except for the fact that his image of suicide popped into his mind on an almost daily basis. At first we understood this as an expression of his dread of retraumatization; the image occurred in response to minor disappointments as if to say, "don't be fooled. This disappointment is a harbinger of things to come. Be ready to admit there is no point to life!"

Ultimately, however, I offered two other formulations of the meanings of the suicidal imagery. Both formulations pointed to the suicidal imagery as a support for important aims in Greg's life. The first was that since choice and autonomy are so important to Greg, a reminder that he could *choose* to live or die was an important building block for his sense of vitality and authenticity. Secondly, I thought he needed the imagery as a point of comparison and contrast. It helped him have perspective on the ups and downs in his life when he measured them against his image of suicide. Greg was very appreciative of my ability to understand his "bizarre" experience in a way which affirmed his striving for a vital existence.

We had been meeting for four months. We were meeting three times weekly. As I attempted to arrange a fourth meeting per week, he told of some childhood fears, including one where the bathtub might fill with water and drown him. We discussed that fear as representative of impersonal forces which would annihilate him and he could not influence the force to stop, because it had no ears with which to hear his pleas. I wondered aloud if he experienced my efforts to find a fourth session as a drowning force. He replied that the water was up to his neck already. I suggested our pacing needed to more accurately reflect *his* wisdom, and that I had been momentarily blinded by my own wishes. Such "blind" action was a repetition of the insensitive environment of his youth.

I remember wondering whether he would now decide to quit therapy, or cut down to just once weekly, as his commitment to the therapy itself has always been tenuous. At the next session he averred that three meetings per week seemed to be a good rhythm for him, and he would consider increasing the frequency only if I thought it would enable him to complete his therapeutic project more quickly. Obviously, I could not make such a statement. Also, by now I had learned that any exploration of his wish to finish quickly only exacerbated his defensiveness. Instead, I tended to look for ways to understand his wish in ways that he could hear as my supporting his striving for a vital life. Such an interpretation was possible only days later, in the session I wish to describe.

The night before our session, I found out that the Grateful Dead rock group would be singing the national anthem at a televised sporting event. Greg is a sports fan, and an ardent "Dead Head." He had spoken at length about the transporting experience of attending Dead rock concerts. I debated mentioning the upcoming anthem event to Greg. I finally decided I would mention it, although I could not articulate to myself a good reason to do so. The session began by my mention of the announcement I had heard. He grinned, and as he moved to sit on the floor, said he wanted to change his normal routine (sitting on couch) to "change the scene, maybe get into what I need to do here,...so I can get out of here." Something in his wry seriousness led me to want to play. I responded by saying, "I like you too!" We both laughed deeply.

Greg went on to say he was feeling much better, and of course he wanted to finish up as fast as he could. He mentioned that childhood memories were beginning to pop up (he claims poor memory for childhood events), that he might want to explore them, but he was not sure how that would be helpful to him, and he did not know what it meant to "explore" them, anyway. His attitude was slightly defensive, as if he was preparing for me to argue with him and point out the defensive nature of his ambivalence about remaining in therapy, and about exploring childhood memories.

I said that my sense was that for him, finishing would be when his predominant mood was no longer despairing and bleak and when he believed he was worthy of being on this planet. I thought maybe exploring his memories would be a pathway to those goals, but then again, maybe not.

What follows is a dialogue I reconstructed based on notes made on the day of the session:

Greg: [after a brief silence] I know you know I have ideas about your profession. I should give a treatise at a convention some day.

Me: Or at least tell *me*? Here? Now? [the invitation for a tight sequence]

Greg: [angry, determined tone of voice] You all are not accountable. And you cannot explain why I need to "work through." What is that? What happens in one's brain? [turning to me and speaking with less anger] At least you don't pretend the field is more advanced than it is. But advice can be given with no accountability for where it goes, no concern [he continues in this vein for a few minutes].

I ended up giving my view of how talking of his memories might work. I suggested that when certain events had occurred, they left him with a belief that he deserved bad treatment, hence he is unworthy of kindness (he had talked of his parents' random kindnesses as confusing). I thought that maybe retelling his stories with me, over time might lead to an erosion of his prior belief, as new perspective gained by my emotional reactions and our emotionally based explorations takes hold (a "talking about" that respected his wish to have his intellectual interests taken seriously, and also a pretty good description of how our participation together in building a narrative might work. I had never put it into words before, and he could sense that we were exploring together in that moment.)

He asked why the explorations had to be emotionally tinged. I said emotionally based beliefs appear to need emotionally based counter-reactions, like a backfire. I said that was not a technical explanation, but was a useful metaphor for me. I said it was based on my experience, and I was staying close to my phenomenology because I could not speak with any authority on brain functioning and brain research.

Greg and I both talked of his needing different emotional experiences that can attract him to life. He spoke of the importance of music to him. I said I was reminded of his story of his first experience of listening to a radio.

Eventually Greg told of a memory of an experiment with a coke bottle and balloon. He had put some baking soda in the coke bottle, placed the balloon over the mouth of the bottle, and delighted as the balloon inflated. He repeated the experiment the next day. When his mother came upon him doing it again, she was angry and disapproving because he was being so impractical. Greg focused his thoughts on his mother's pressures on him to be practical and functional. There was no room for aimlessness and play.

Me: This might be a bit arrogant, but my association is to our relationship. You *enjoyed* that experiment. Then your mother says, "get over it as fast as you can, with as few repetitions as possible." I think you really *enjoy* spending time with me, and your enjoyment is not reason enough to allow you to stay and be with me for the pleasure of it.

Greg sobbed deeply with relief and recognition. He talked more of his parents begrudging him his pleasures. I reiterated that play in childhood is experience with an emotional state that we then create in different ways in adulthood that gives us a reason to wake up everyday. And his parents begrudging his play meant they could not support that in him.

Greg: [wistfully] I just wish that once I could have looked up from my play and found my mother . . .

Me: . . . beaming at you? Because the beaming is part of the building block of being able to seek such experiences. [to me, this ending was ironic because

I had started the session with a reference to play (Dead performance), and I had played with him at the beginning ("I like you too!")]

Greg left pretty excited and shy.

What's a Therapist to Do?

In the face of all of this complexity, understanding that the arena of supports has no boundaries and can only be partially known, what is the therapist's participation in supporting a patient's recovery from trauma and a patient's further development (not that these two ideas can be neatly separated)? I do think that there are some supports that therapy is beautifully situated to offer. After all, to the degree that we can support our patients to develop and refine their skill with contacting, we contribute to establishing and refining meaningfulness, the development of emotional skills, and the evocation of faith in one's coming solutions and a sense of belonging-in-the-world.

Antonovsky (1987), an Israeli sociologist, has studied many groups of people, including holocaust survivors, war veterans and disparaged poor people. He and fellow researchers find repeatedly that people who respond to stressors in ways that are health-enhancing (or, at the very least, illness-resisting), have been able to develop a meaningful narrative about their lives and the events therein. I recently spoke with a woman whose son died fighting in Iraq. She has found purpose and meaning by protesting the war. She said it lifted her profound depression.

As therapists we participate with patients' stories. Our participation, which is a combination of bearing witness, call-and-response, helping to refine, amplify, grasp the essence of the story lines, changing our stories as they change theirs, helps our patients to gain flexibility and resilience, to loosen their stories and complexify them. The more complex the stories become, the more emotional richness ensues.

Emotional skills develop in a context where one's emotional process is respectfully and compassionately met. Our dialogical stance is one that welcomes, even embraces, a patient's experiential world. It is also one in which we are especially attuned to the emergence and ramifications of shame, since shame is a statement of radical non-belonging. In fact shame is one of the most common, persistent, and intractable constricting influences upon one's ability to recognize and use environmental resources. So the restoration of dignity that ensues from attention to and resolution of shame as it appears in the therapeutic dialogue is a crucial support for broadening access to other supports for contact (Jacobs, 1995).

At certain times tight sequencing supports more vivid moment-to-moment emotional awareness. At other times, looser sequences allow a taste of flow, cresting and surrender to dialogical process. When we are attuned to a patient's emotional process, and we receive and respond in the spirit of dialogue, we are embodying the paradoxical theory of change (Beisser, 1970) while at the same time we are walking alongside our patients through their suffering. By so doing, no experience remains unbearable, or alienated, however profound the suffering. When a patient does not need to constrict his emotional experience, he will become skilled at living with himself and others with his fullest range of emotions.

Existential Story Lines Have no Endings

I can aver that emotional skill is the crux of the ability to recognize and act in concert with one's coming solutions. And I can suggest that a therapist's attunement, sensitivity to shame, the paradoxical theory of change, commitment to dialogue, all are supports for the kind of contacting that embraces our patients' emotional lives. But in truth, I have no graceful way to bring an end to an exploration of supports. This exploration has only been a beginning, and it has no end. There are so many aspects of our therapeutic dialogue that support the dialogue, support our patients' next steps in their development, and we will only be able to identify a few of them. This work calls on us to surrender to a process that we can never nail down. Our theories and our personal and therapeutic experiences are supports for that surrender.

This paper is one more support for my surrender to the complex, awesome process we call gestalt therapy, and I am grateful to Malcolm for awakening my interest with his gem of a statement that support is "that which enables."

References

Antonosvky, A. (1987). *Unraveling the mystery of health: How people manage stress and stay well.* San Francisco: Jossey-Bass.

Beisser, A. R. (1970). The paradoxical theory of change. In J. Fagan & I. L. Shepherd (Eds.), *Gestalt therapy now* (pp. 77-80). New York: Harper Colophon.

Bloom, D. (2005). The aesthetic of commitment — Lecture delivered at the Munich gestalt therapy conference on the occasion of Laura Perls' 100th birthday, June 3, 2005. *British Gestalt Journal 14/2*, 81-90.

Fairfield, M. (2004). Gestalt therapy: A harm reduction approach. *British Gestalt Journal 13/2*, 100-110.

Jacobs, L. (1995). Shame in the therapeutic dialogue. *British Gestalt Journal 4/2*, 86-90.

Perls, L. (1992). *Living at the boundary: Collected works of Laura Perls* (J. Wysong, Ed.). Highland, NY: Gestalt Journal Press.

Polster, E., & Polster, M. (1999). *From the radical center: The heart of gestalt therapy* (A. Roberts, Ed.). Hillsdale, NJ: The Analytic Press (GICPress).

Wheeler, G. (2000). *Beyond Individualism: Toward a new understanding of self, relationship and experience.* Hillsdale, NJ: The Analytic Press (Gestalt Press).

Wheeler, G. (2005). Culture, self, and field. In T. L. Bar-Yoseph (Ed.), *The bridge: Dialogues across cultures* (pp. 27-50). New Orleans, LA: Gestalt Institute Press.

Authors

Jack Aylward is the Director of the Plainfield Consultation Center in Watchung, NJ, U. S. A. He has been a trainer and supervisor of gestalt therapists for several years. He serves as an editorial consultant to several journals and has written on the impact of Paul Goodman on the social and political aspects of gestalt therapy theory. Address for correspondence:Plainfield Consultation Center, 32 Johnston Drive, Watchung, New Jersey, 07069, U. S. A.
jackatpcc@aol.com

Dan Bloom JD, LCSW (www.nydowntowntherapist.com) is a psychotherapist in private practice in New York City. He is a Fellow and past president of New York Institute for Gestalt Therapy and past president of the Association for the Advancement of Gestalt Therapy. He is also a member of the European Association for the Advancement of Gestalt Therapy. He is the former Editor-in-Chief of *Studies in Gestalt Therapy: Dialogical Bridges*, an associate editor of the *Gestalt Review,* and book review editor of *Quaderni di Gestalt* and a member of the Scientific Board of the Gestalt Therapy Book Series published by Franco Angeli. Dan teaches and is adjunct faculty at gestalt therapy institutes around the world. Dan has presented workshops at many international conferences. He independently trains and supervises gestalt therapists. Dan has published articles and chapters and edited books on gestalt theory and practice. He can be contacted at dan@djbloom.com.

Frank Bosco, MA, LCAT, MT-BC, LMT, RPP, SEP, has maintained a full-time private practice since 1980 as a gestalt trained Certified Music Therapist and a Licensed Massage Therapist. Over the years he has integrated a wide range of somatic and psycho-therapy practices including shiatsu, NMT, Polarity, NLP, hypnosis and gestalt therapy. Using the energy principles (primarily from Ayurveda) of Polarity Therapy as a basis, his work combines bodywork and psychotherapy with theoretical and technical understandings from the field of music therapy. This has resulted in the creation of an approach he calls "Elemental Music Alignment" for which he offers sessions and training. He is the founder/director of Sound Health Studio, a center in New York City that offers studies and services including a variety of music therapy approaches, psychotherapy, bodywork and acupuncture. Professional affiliations include: NYU, the American Polarity Therapy Association, the American Music Therapy Association, and full membership status in the New York Institute for Gestalt Therapy.

Philip Brownell, MDiv, PsyD, is a clinical psychologist licensed in the USA and registered in Bermuda. He is certified as a gestalt therapist by the European Association for Gestalt Therapy (EAGT), a member of the New York Institute for

Gestalt Therapy, the Association for the Advancement of Gestalt Therapy (AAGT), and Divisions 12 (Society for Clinical Psychology) and 29 (Psychotherapy) of the American Psychological Association. He is a member of the Scientific Board of the Research Committee and Editor at Gestalt Research Press for the EAGT, a member of the AAGT's Research Committee, and English-Speaking Coordinator for the international research project using Single Case Timed Series Design. He has a private practice in Bermuda and can be reached through his web site (www.drphilipbrownell.com).

Sylvia Fleming Crocker, Ph.D., M.S., M.A., trained with Erving and Miriam Polster and at the Gestalt Therapy Institute of Los Angeles. She is a full member of the New York Institute for Gestalt Therapy. She is an international trainer, and the author of a number of Gestalt journal articles, book chapters. Her book, *A Well-Lived Life: Essays in Gestalt Therapy,* is now in its third printing.

Bud Feder, who earned a doctorate in clinical psychology from Columbia University in 1961, has been a member of the NYIGT since 1971 until the present. During this time he has served the institute as treasurer as president and as conference convener. He is very grateful to the institute: for being a second family, for helping him reshape his life and for the many colleagues over the years to whom he became closely connected. One of them, Ruth Ronall (1925-2003) was particularly important as a friend, a co-trainer and a co-editor. With her he co-edited the seminal *Beyond the Hot Seat: Gestalt Approaches to Group* (1980), which launched his career as a trainer, particularly of interactive gestalt group therapy, in New York, Berkeley and many countries in Europe, as well as Australia. Since that 1980 publication he was co-edited two other books, written one and published many journal articles. He is also a founding member of AAGT, a past president of it and current co-chairperson of its Scholarship Fund.

Gianni Francesetti is a Gestalt therapist, psychiatrist and international trainer. He is also the program coordinator of the two year International Training Program on Gestalt Approach to Psychopathology and Contemporary Disturbances organized by the Istituto di Gestalt H.C.C. Italy. He is the President of the EAGT (European Association for Gestalt Therapy), Former President of the Italian NOGT (SIPG, Italian Gestalt Psychotherapy Association), President of the Italian NAO (FIAP, Italian Federation of Psychotherapy Associations), and an associate member of the New York Institute for Gestalt Therapy. He has authored articles, chapters, and books in the field of psychiatry and psychotherapy. He lives and works in Turin as a psychiatrist, psychotherapist and supervisor. Via Cibrario, 2910143 – Torino (Italy) gianni.francesetti@gestalt.it

Ruella Frank, Ph.D., has been exploring early infant movements and their relationship to the adult since the mid-1970s. She brings many years of experience to her work as a gestalt psychotherapist — as a professional dancer, yoga practitioner/teacher, student of various movement theories and therapies, and student of Laura Perls, co-founder of gestalt therapy. Ruella is founder and director of the Center for Somatic Studies, faculty at Gestalt Associates for Psychotherapy and the New York Institute for Gestalt therapy, and also teaches throughout the United States, Europe and Mexico. She is author of articles and chapters in various publications, as well as the book *Body of Awareness: A Somatic and Developmental Approach to Psychotherapy*, (available in four languages) and she is co-author of *The First Year and the Rest of Your Life: Movement, Development and Psychotherapeutic Change*, (available in three languages). Her new video, *Introduction to Developmental Somatic Psychotherapy*, is now available on her website www.somaticstudies.com

Zelda Friedman is a full member emeritus of the New York Institute for Gestalt Therapy and a member of the Association for the Advancement of Gestalt Therapy-an International Community. She has written and presented on gestalt theory with special attention to its political/philosophical aspects as well as its relevance to feminist issues. Retired from over thirty-five years of gestalt therapy practice, she remains ardently interested in the lively activities of the gestalt community.

Elinor Greenberg, PhD, CGP, is a licensed psychologist and Gestalt therapy trainer in private practice in New York City, who has been studying, teaching, and writing about personality disorders for over thirty years. She is a member of the New York Institute for Gestalt Therapy, adjunct faculty for the Gestalt Center (NYC), and a former faculty member of The Masterson Institute, an Object Relations training institute that specializes in the diagnosis and treatment of Borderline, Narcissistic and Schizoid Disorders of the Self. She is on the editorial board of the *Gestalt Review*. In her spare time, she studies pre-psychoanalytic systems of personal growth.

Susan Gregory is a Gestalt therapist in private practice in New York City, where she also teaches the Gindler approach to breath and body work. She is a full member of the New York Institute for Gestalt Therapy, and is co-chair of the somatics interest group of the Association for the Advancement of Gestalt Therapy. Her article on Elsa Gindler was first presented at the EAGT conference in Stockholm, September 2001. Ms. Gregory is also a recital artist and former opera singer. Her article "A Gestalt Therapist Teaches Singing" appeared in the *Australian Gestalt Journal*, Winter 2000.

Carl Hodges has an abiding interest in Gestalt psychology and Gestalt field theory, and the application of Gestalt field theory concepts to the varieties of social organizations – self, groups associations, community. He has taught at Hunter College in New York and is a trainer at the New York Institute for Gestalt Therapy, a visiting trainer at the Gestalt Centre London and the Istituto di Gestalt –HCC, Italy He was the second president of the New York Institute for Gestalt Therapy and the third president of the Association for the Advancement of Gestalt therapy. He is a Fellow of the New York Institute for Gestalt Therapy.

Karen Humphrey has been a member of the New York Institute for Gestalt Therapy since 1962 and is a Fellow of the Institute. She had the good fortune to work at different times with Lore Perls, Paul Goodman, Isadore From, Patrick Kelley, and Richard Kitzler. Currently she makes her home in a Co-Housing Community in Saugerties, New York, where she also performs in an improvisational theater group.

Lynne Jacobs, Ph.D.,Psy.D. lives in two psychotherapy worlds. She is co-founder of the Pacific Gestalt Institute and also a training and supervising analyst at the Institute of Contemporary Psychoanalysis. She is co-author (with Rich Hycner), of The Healing Relationship in Gestalt Therapy: A Dialogic / Self Psychology Approach (1995). She and Hycner co-edited Relational Perspectives in Gestalt Therapy (2010). She has also written numerous articles for gestalt and for psychoanalytic publications. She has an abiding interest in furthering our understanding of relational factors in the therapy process. *Address for correspondence:* 1626 Westwood Bl., Los Angeles, CA 90024, U. S. A. Lynnejacobs@gestalttherapy.org

Perry Klepner, MBA, LCSW, is a full member, Fellow and president, 1993-95, of the New York Institute for Gestalt Therapy, where he studied with Laura Perls, Isadore From and Richard Kitzler. He has been on the faculty of several institutes and is in private practice in New York City and Kingston, NY, where he provides training, supervision and individual, couples and group therapy. He has instructed, authored articles and papers, and conducted workshops in Gestalt Therapy theory/practice, intimacy, sexual addiction, and process groups in the United States, Canada and Europe.
Email: perry302@aol.com.sychotherapy.

Philip Lichtenberg is Mary Hale Chase Professor Emeritus in Social Science, Social Work and Social Research at Bryn Mawr College (Pennsylvania) where he taught for over 35 years. Among the doctoral and master's level courses he taught were: Gestalt Therapy; Freud's Psychoanalytic Theory; Psychoanalysis after Freud; Personality Theory; and Change and Resistance to Change. He was a founding member of The Gestalt Therapy Institute of Philadelphia, where he continues to teach. He is the author of 6 books and numerous articles and chapters in books. He received his Ph.D. at Case Western Reserve University in 1952. He has been married for 64 years, is the father of 4 sons, and has 8 grandchildren.

Kenneth Meyer, PH.D. is a co-founder and former Director Training of the Gestalt Center of Long Island and has served as the Academic Director of the Gestalt Center in New York City. He currently teaches at several Gestalt programs, provides advanced training workshops and supervision for graduates and maintains a therapy practice in Greenwich Village and Monroe, NY. He is a Full Member of the New York Institute for Gestalt Therapy and is a regular presenter at local, regional and international conferences.

Brian O'Neill, B.A. (Hons), MAPS is co-director of the Illawarra Gestalt Centre, past president of AAGT and on the editorial boards of the *Gestalt Review* and *Studies in Gestalt Therapy: Dialogical Bridges*. He has published on field theory, relationship therapy and edited the text *Community Psychotherapy and Life Focus: A Gestalt Anthology of the History, Theory and Practice of Living in Community* (Ravenwood Press). He collaborates with his wife Jenny in writing on gestalt couples therapy and the use of group in training and they have been training and supervising therapists for many years both in Australia and internationally. Brian is currently a senior fellow in mental health at the University of Wollongong, Clinical Director for *Lives Lived Well*, a state-wide service working with substance misuse and also youth mental health across Queensland. As well as bringing gestalt therapy to the relationship field, he has worked extensively in Drug and Alcohol (was Head of the NSW State Drug Treatment Unit), and Mental Health (awarded the Australia and New Zealand Gold Medal for mental health achievement by the Governor General, Sir William Deane). He is an Associate member of the New York Institute of Gestalt Therapy.
email: boneill@uow.edu.au and brian.oneill@liveslivedwell.org.au

Jean-Marie Robine, Psy. Dipl., Gestalt-therapist, supervisor and international trainer, Founder of Institut Français de Gestalt-thérapie. Full member of New York Institute for Gestalt Therapy and of the European Association for Gestalt Therapy (and past president). Author of many articles and of 7 books about Gestalt Therapy translated into several languages. The last but one *On the Occasion of an Other"* =is translated into English (Gestalt Journal Press). The last one *Social Change begins With Two* is in process. Founder of 2 French Gestalt Journals and currently editor and publisher of *L'exprimerie,* a publishing company for Gestalt Therapy in French, with already about 30 books available. He lives in the countryside near Bordeaux.
contact : jm.robine@me.com

Margherita Spagnuolo Lobb, Director (since 1979) of the Istituto di Gestalt HCC Italy (Siracuse, Palermo, Milan), post-graduate School of Gestalt Therapy approved by the Minister for Universities. International trainer, Full Member of the *New York Institute for Gestalt Therapy*, past-president of the *Italian Federation of the Associations of Psychotherapy* (FIAP), past-president and first Honorary Member of the *European Association for Gestalt Therapy* (EAGT), past- and Honorary President of the *Italian Association of Gestalt Psychotherapy* (SIPG). Editor (since 1985) of the Italian journal *Quaderni di Gestalt,* co-editor of the International Journal *Studies in Gestalt Therapy. Dialogical Bridges,* has written many articles and chapters published in various languages, edited 5 volumes and written 2 books, the most recent being *The Now-for-Next in Psychotherapy. Gestalt Therapy Recounted in Post-Modern Society* (2011). She is Scientific Director of the International Training in Gestalt Psychopathology and co-editor of the Gestalt Therapy book series published by Franco Angeli.

Anne Teachworth was founder and director of the Gestalt Institute of New Orleans/New York and Gestalt Institute Press, an active publishing company . Anne was a Fellow of the American Psychotherapy Assn., a long time Associate Member of the NYIGT, and author of *Why We Pick The Mates We Do.* She has just finished her second book, *History Repeats Itself* and is busy on her third, If You Could Change Your Parents. She is in private practice in New Orleans for the last 30 years specializing in couple, parenting and family counseling. (This bio appeared in the original publication of Anne's paper.)

Gary Yontef, Ph.D., ABPP, Diplomate in Clinical Psychology, American Board of Professional Psychology and Fellow of the Academy of Clinical Psychology has been a gestalt therapist since training with Frederick Perls and James Simkin in 1965 and a supervisor and trainer since 1971. Formerly on the UCLA Psychology Department Faculty and Chairman of the Professional Conduct Committee of the L.A. County Psychological Association, Gary has a private practice in Los Angeles, California. He is a past president of the Gestalt Therapy Institute of Los Angeles (GTILA) and for 18 years was Chairman of the Faculty. He is has been on the editorial board of the International Gestalt Journal (formerly The Gestalt Journal), an Associate Editor of the Gestalt Review, and is editorial advisor of the British Gestalt Journal. He was the first Chairman of the International Gestalt Therapy Association and a faculty member of the Gestalt Therapy International Network (GTIN). He is a co-founder of the Pacific Gestalt Institute (PGI) and teaches and consults internationally. . Gary has written one book *Awareness, Dialogue and Process: Essays on Gestalt Therapy* (published in 6 languages and now available in Kindle) and numerous articles and chapters on gestalt therapy theory, practice, and supervision.

Lee Zevy, CSW, received her MSW from Fordham School of Social Welfare and is a past President, a graduate, and current faculty member of New York Institute for Gestalt Therapy. She is a founder, trainer, supervisor and past Clinical Director of Identity House and the Past President, New York City Coalition for Women's Mental Health. She is a Fellow of the New York Institute for Gestalt Therapy. Address correspondence to: Lee Zevy, 171 West 23rd St. #2e, New York, NY 10011 (E-mail: lzevy@verizon.com).

Made in the USA
San Bernardino, CA
15 April 2014